Postcolonial Transitional Justice

Transitional justice processes are now considered to be crucial steps in facilitating the move from conflict or repression to a secure democratic future.

This book contributes to a deeper understanding of transitional justice by examining the complexities of transition in postcolonial societies. It focuses particularly on Zimbabwe but draws on relevant comparative material from other postcolonial polities. Examples include but are not limited to African countries such as South Africa, Rwanda and Mozambique. European societies such as Northern Ireland, as well as other nations such as Guatemala, are also considered. While amplifying the breadth of the subject of transitional justice, the book addresses the claim that transitional justice mechanisms in postcolonial countries are necessary if the rule of law and the credibility of the country's legal institutions are to be restored. Drawing on postcolonial legal theory, and especially on analyses of the relationship between international law and imperialism, the book challenges the assumption that a domestic rule of law 'deficit' may be remedied with recourse to international law. Taking up the paradigmatic perception that international law is neutral and has fixed rules, it demonstrates how complex issues which arise during postcolonial transitions require a more critical adoption of transitional justice mechanisms.

Khanyisela Moyo is based at the School of Law/Transitional Justice Institute, University of Ulster, Northern Ireland.

Part of the Transitional Justice series
Series editor
Kieran McEvoy, *Queen's University Belfast, UK*

for information about the series and details of previous and forthcoming titles, see www.routledge.com/Transitional-Justice/book-series/TRANJ

A GlassHouse book

Postcolonial Transitional Justice

Zimbabwe and Beyond

Khanyisela Moyo

Routledge
Taylor & Francis Group
LONDON AND NEW YORK

First published 2019 by Routledge

2 Park Square, Milton Park, Abingdon, Oxon, OX14 4RN
605 Third Avenue, New York, NY 10017

Routledge is an imprint of the Taylor & Francis Group, an informa business

First issued in paperback 2020

A GlassHouse book

British Library Cataloguing-in-Publication Data
A catalogue record for this book is available from the British Library

Library of Congress Cataloging-in-Publication Data
Names: Moyo, Khanyisela, author.
Title: Postcolonial transitional justice: Zimbabwe and beyond / Khanyisela Moyo.
Description: Abingdon, Oxon; New York, NY: Routledge, 2019. | Series: Transitional justice | Based on author's thesis (doctoral—University of Ulster, 2009) issued under title: The multitudinous complexities of transitional justice in post-colonial societies: a Zimbabwean case study.
Identifiers: LCCN 2019009304 (print) | LCCN 2019009889 (ebook) | ISBN 9781351048200 (ebk) | ISBN 9781138485747 (hbk)
Subjects: LCSH: Justice, Administration of—Zimbabwe. | Transitional justice—Zimbabwe.
Classification: LCC KTZ46.8 (ebook) | LCC KTZ46.8 .M69 2019 (print) | DDC 340/.115096891—dc23
LC record available at https://lccn.loc.gov/2019009304

ISBN: 978-1-138-48574-7 (hbk)
ISBN: 978-0-367-72843-4 (pbk)

Typeset in Galliard
by Apex CoVantage, LLC

Contents

Acknowledgements

Several people contributed to the success of the project. I would like to thank Professor Colm Campbell for encouraging me to write the book and Niel Gordon for reading draft chapters. I also thank my mother, Siyabonga, Kelly and Lindokuhle for their prayers and support during the writing process.

The project also benefitted from the facilities offered by the School of Law and Transitional Justice Institute at the University of Ulster. I wish to thank Professor Rory O'Connell and Professor Eugene McNamee for their leadership.

1 Introduction

Transitional justice is that which seeks to re-establish order, the rule of law and justice in the wake of armed conflict, authoritarianism or repression. Clearly, this is a huge topic, and so it is not surprising that different pundits differ about the definition and scope of the subject.[1] Historically, theorists have debated issues concerning peace versus justice, the legality of amnesties and whether transitional justice is the victor's justice. These types of inquiries are still part of transitional justice discourses today, but they have now been supplemented by what Dustin Sharp calls peripheral fourth generation issues.[2] As Sharp aptly put it:

> [T]he need to account for the underlying politics of transitional justice work, the need to balance local and international agency and the need for greater economic justice now sit alongside concerns from previous eras such as debates over victor's justice and the role of amnesties.[3]

At the heart of these contemporary issues is the need for transitional justice to deal with the root causes of the conflict and abuses of all rights.[4] Arguably, the history of modern conflicts, which are the focus of contemporary transitional justice discourses, are rooted in those polities' colonial past. Fletcher et al. have noted that the legacy of a colonialism is found mainly in three areas.[5] First, the power is concentrated within a few elites. Second, there is a mixed legal system

1 Some of the definitions are discussed in Rosemary Nagy, 'Transitional Justice as a Global Project: Critical Reflections' (2008) 29(2) *Third World Quarterly* 275 at 276–278.
2 Dustin N. Sharp, 'Interrogating the Peripheries: The Preoccupations of Fourth Generation Transitional Justice' (2013) 26 *Harvard Human Rights Journal* 149.
3 Ibid at 157.
4 Summary and Principle 9, United Nations Secretary-General, 'Guidance Note on the United Nations Approach to Transitional Justice' (2010) <www.un.org/ruleoflaw/files/TJ_Guidance_Note_March_2010FINAL.pdf>.
Paul Gready and Simon Robins, 'From Transitional to Transformative Justice: A New Agenda for Practice' (2014) 8 *International Journal of Transitional Justice* 339.
5 Laurel E. Fletcher, Harvey M. Weinstein and Jamie Rowen, 'Context, Timing and the Dynamics of Transitional Justice: A Historical Perspective' (2009) 31(1) *Human Rights Quarterly* 163.

where Western (civil) judicial structures are combined with customary law. The effect of this hybrid legal system is the use of Western standards in urban areas and the administration of customary law by chiefs in rural areas, 'with no set standards, marked variation in punishments, gender bias, nepotism and crony influence'.[6] Third, there is mistrust of Western interventions.

Postcolonial contexts present both policy makers and pundits with difficult questions on the 'transition' element of transitional justice. In particular, the question is asked as to whether transitional justice should focus on the immediate past or encompass historical injustices, including the colonial legacy. This book contributes towards a deeper understanding of transitional justice and links to the ongoing debates in the discourse about the field's boundaries, localized justice and the role of international law.[7] A deeper, more accurate understanding, particularly of the limitations and potential of international law when it comes to the concerns of postcolonial subjects, is crucial for the effective implementation of transitional justice mechanisms.[8]

1.1 Postcolonial transitional justice

> [W]hile colonialism by definition is a relationship of domination and subordination; it does not entail unidirectional determinism. As Subaltern studies have brought into sharp relief, the colonized are never passive mimics of the colonial script; their strategies of resistance give rise to innovative vocabularies and relationships.[9]

Postcolonial legal theory is an offshoot of critical studies, which (amongst their other aspects) draw on the unequal relationships of states caused by the colonial legacy, to explore the often-sidetracked questions of the law's consanguinity with that heritage.[10] Six particular untold issues are exposed in this work. The first one is the hegemonic bias of international law.[11] The second is the law's inability

6 Ibid at 195.

7 See, for example, Chris Dolan, Nokukhanya Mncwabe and Chrispus Okello (eds), *Where Law Meets Reality: Forging African Transitional Justice* (Pambazuka Press 2012). See also Nagy (n.1).

8 Khanyisela Moyo, 'Feminism, Postcolonial Legal Theory and Transitional Justice: A Critique of Current Trends' (2012) 2 *International Human Rights Law Review* 237, George M. Carew, *Democratic Transition in Postcolonial Africa: A Deliberative Approach* (Edwin Mellen Press 2006).

9 Tayyab Mahmud, 'Citizen and Citizenship within and beyond the Nation' (2005) 52 *Cleveland State University Law Review* 51.

10 See Vidya S.A. Kumar, 'A Proleptic Approach to Post-Colonial Legal Studies? A Brief Look at the Relationship between Legal Theory and Intellectual History' (2003) 2 *Law, Social Justice and Global Development Journal* <www2.warwick.ac.uk>.

11 Chapter 2.

to address the colonial legacy's creation of unequal economies.[12] Third, there is a realization that international law is blind to the fact that not all states, West or North or postcolonial, have completed the nation-building project, thereby excluding voices of the disgruntled ethnic groups within postcolonial societies.[13]

Fourth, international law does not attend to the decolonization process's complicity in creating a legacy of legally sanctioned amnesia, thereby creating a culture of impunity.[14] Fifth, there is a Western bias in international law in that it privileges civil and political rights over economic, social and cultural rights. Finally, international law is steeped in liberalism's public versus private dichotomy, which has the effect of excluding harms that are peculiar to women and other persons who occupy a subordinate position.

A number of approaches to transitional justice can be drawn out from postcolonial legal studies' analysis of how international law relates to imperialism. The first view is the neo-colonialist notion that the doctrines and institutions of international law have always been circumscribed, by and for the use of the powerful states in order to serve their interests.[15] Consequently, transitional justice is rejected as it is seen as a tool by which the '*Self*' flexes its power over the '*Other*'. The fact that the West funds most transitional justice projects in postcolonial societies seems to support this viewpoint.[16]

The second perception is that international law stands for universal and sovereign equality, although it is open to different cultural interpretations.[17] It is unfortunate that universal values are often appropriated by former colonial powers and used for purposes of oppressing the developing world. For this school of thought, the problem with transitional justice is its potential for distorted use by imperialists in their hegemonic projects. The last viewpoint is that even though international law can be complicit as a principal facilitator of exploitation and discrimination, it also has the potential to play a transformative role.[18] Adopting this approach, this work sees law, during transitional periods, as a ground for struggle.[19]

12 Chapter 4.

13 Chapter 5.

14 Chapter 6.

15 See the line of thinking in Berta E. Hernandez-Truyol, 'The LatIndia and Mestizajes: Of Cultures, Conquests, and LatCritical Feminism' (1999) 3 *Journal of Gender, Race and Justice* 6 and Makau wa Mutua, 'Savages, Victims, and Saviors: The Metaphor of Human Rights' (2001) 42 *Harvard International Law Journal* 201.

16 For examples of transitional justice projects funded by the US government, see Neil J. Kritz, *Transitional Justice: How Emerging Democracies Reckon with Former Regimes, Vol 1* (United States Institute of Peace Press 1995), page xxix.

17 This is the cultural relativist argument. See wa Mutua (n.15).

18 It is in some way influenced by the writings in Issa G. Shivji, *The Concept of Human Rights in Africa* (Codesria Book Series 1999), and Issa G. Shivji, 'Law's Empire and Empire's Lawlessness: Beyond Anglo–American Law' (2003) *Law, Social Justice and Global Development Journal (LGD)* <www2.warwick.ac.uk>.

19 Ibid.

In reaching this thesis, the study is guided by key non-legal expositions of postcolonialism evinced by the studies of Michel Foucault, Robert Young, Edward Said, Homi Bhabha and Gatayri Spivak, among others.[20] The work of Foucault, for example, is the source of this study's distinction between transitional justice as a field whose contours are still to be bounded, and the discourse of transitional justice.[21] Thus, in this work, the discourse of transitional justice refers to a restricted ambit of knowledge, and this is the case because those with power control the dissemination of this information.[22]

The study then builds on Edward Said's celebrated work *Orientalism*, which through the notion of discourse makes a link between culture and imperialism to show how this creates binary divisions of the *Self* and the *Other*.[23] Thus, in the context of transitional justice, power and knowledge are important in the interaction between Western states and postcolonial states, and an exclusive focus on accountability and punishment is used to depict Western governments as liberators and the postcolonial leaders as criminals.[24]

However, Homi Bhabha's exposition of the ambivalent relationship which exists between the *Self* and the *Other* disproves this simplistic notion of a direct one-way diffusion of norms from developed countries to less developed ones.[25] This ambivalence is seen in that, while Western governments do want to modernize their former colonies, they do not want to make those states similar to theirs, for doing so would destroy the binary division of *Self* and *Other* which is necessary for the maintenance of the Western hegemonic power.[26]

In the case of Zimbabwe, this explains why developed countries would rather give the country aid than commit the United Kingdom to fund the land reform programme as such a move might stir rebellion in other former colonies.[27] Therefore, former colonial masters are forced to engage with the local laws, and 'hybridity' occurs.[28] This disrupts the bipolar relationship and creates a more complex transfer of norms than an otherwise immutable exchange. This occurrence, which is common to most postcolonial transitions, is demonstrated in

20 For a comprehensive bibliography of postcolonial theory and its criticism, see *Postcolonial Web* <www.postcolonialweb.org/>. See also Bill Ashcroft, Gareth Griffiths and Helen Tiffin (eds), *The Post-colonial Studies Reader* (Routledge 1995) and Bart J. Moore-Gilbert, *Postcolonial Theory: Contexts, Practices, Politics* (Verso 1997).
21 See Chapter 2 for a definition of transitional justice as a field. On the issue of discourse, see Michel Foucault, *The Archaeology of Knowledge, and the Discourse on Language* (Pantheon Books 1972).
22 Foucault, ibid.
23 Edward W. Said, *Orientalism* (Pantheon Books 1978).
24 See Chapter 2 for this analysis.
25 Homi Bhabha, 'Of Mimicry and Man: The Ambivalence of Colonial Discourse' in Homi Bhabha (ed) *The Location of Culture* (Routledge 1994).
26 Ibid. See also Chapter 2.
27 See Chapter 4.
28 Ibid.

Chapters 3 to 6, which develop this main argument by way of an evaluation of Zimbabwe's challenges and prescriptions drawn from comparative materials of other postcolonial societies, which have faced similar challenges.

Further, from Bhabha the study borrows the notion that hybridity creates opportunities for agency or resistance which takes place at a 'third space of enunciation'.[29] The ambivalence at the origination of fixed discourses of power facilitates a form of uproar located in the inconstancy that changes paradoxical positions of power into a justification for action.[30]

This form of *agency* is already evident in Zimbabwe. It is fair to assume that Western support for the country's non-governmental organizations' advocacy work was largely driven by the desire to protect property rights and highlight the criminality of the Robert Mugabe regime. However, this intervention has been appropriated by a number of domestic groups not only to align themselves with either the West or the domestic authoritarian regime, but to attract a debate on a wide range of issues, which include, *inter alia*, women's rights, minority rights and redress for atrocities committed during the colonial era. It is axiomatic that when Western governments funded non-governmental organizations, their original aim was to promote a certain ideology and not these side-tracked issues.

It is also fair to state that part of the reason why *agency* is possible is because motives of Western actors are not one-dimensional. For within the West, there are some idealists who may not support government policies that are driven by aggrandizing interests.[31] Similarly, postcolonial resistance to the Western discourse is not always productive, since different actors within these societies can also be influenced by various motives and perceptions. Indeed, it is possible for imperialism and cultural relativism to be used by groups to either subjugate women and minorities or to deflect attention from domestic human rights violations.

Nonetheless, another key lesson which this work borrowed from the work of Bhabha is that *agency* is a form of 'negotiation' which is possible only within the contours of the Western discourse.[32] Thus it sees the state-led radical land reform programme of Zimbabwe which was carried out after 2000 as a direct confrontation or an attempt to dismantle the master's discourse and thus an exercise in futility. Therefore, the study is of the view that a form of connivance between the *Self* and the *Other* is necessary in transitional contexts.

29 Homi Bhabha, 'Cultural Diversity and Cultural Differences' in Bill Ashcroft, Gareth Griffiths and Helen Tiffin (eds) *The Post-Colonial Studies Reader* (Routledge 1995).

30 Ibid.

31 For example, even though Saddam Hussein's ouster was in furtherance of a Western regime change agenda, Western idealists insisted on the observance of due process standards. See Miranda Sissons and Ari S. Bassin, 'Was the Dujail Trial Fair?' (2007) 5(2) *Journal of International Criminal Justice* 272.

32 Chapter 2.

1.2 Zimbabwe

In this work, Zimbabwe's challenges are presented as depicting a microcosm of the multitudinous complexities of transitional justice in postcolonial societies. When Zimbabwe attracted international attention during its violent land reform programme in 2000, external reaction varied and in fact rekindled the ideological debates of the Cold War.[33] The contemporary variance pitted postcolonial Africa, with the support of Russia and China, against Western governments led by the United Kingdom (UK) and the United States of America (USA). The former insisted that narratives of the Zimbabwean crisis should take into account the indelible mark left by colonialism. They also proposed African solutions to African problems and respect for the principle of equal sovereignty. On the other hand, Western governments focused on governance and called for tougher international action against what they perceived to be a rogue administration which does not respect property rights and the rule of law. This strain in international relations reawakened the Cold War notion that opposition parties and human rights advocates are vicarious operatives of foreign ideologies.[34]

The country is yet to make a clear break with the past, but a window of opportunity has now been presented by the replacement of the country's executive president with Emerson Mnangagwa in November 2017. Unlike his predecessor Robert Mugabe, whose language had the effect of isolating Zimbabwe, Mnangagwa seems keen to liberalize the economy and end the country's isolation. Quite significantly, the new president signed the National Peace and Reconciliation Commission (NPRC) Act into law on 5 January 2018.[35] The NPRC is an independent commission tasked with ensuring post-conflict justice, healing and reconciliation.[36] However, human rights violations are ongoing. For example, the security forces are said to have killed at least 12 people and injured dozens following the protests against increased fuel prices which started on 14 January 2019.[37] At least 700 people were also detained on trumped-up charges.[38]

Notwithstanding the politicians' irresoluteness, transitional justice questions have been anticipated amongst Zimbabwean political parties, academics and civic society since the country's independence from colonial rule in 1980.[39] The

33 See Sue Onslow, 'Rhodesia and the Cold War' Paper presented at the *First European Conference of African Studies, SOAS*, University of London, 30 June 2005.

34 See David Moore, 'Unmasking ZANU-PF Hypocrisy about NGOs' *Zimbabwe Independent* (Centre for Civil Society 2003) <www.theindependent.co.zw/2003/05/23/unmasking-zanu-pf-hypocrisy-about-ngos-2/>.

35 National Peace and Reconciliation Act [Chapter 10:32].

36 S252 Constitution of Zimbabwe Amendment (No. 20) Act, 2013.

37 Amnesty International UK, 'Zimbabwe: Brutal Crackdown Continues as Protesters Killed, Raped and Tortured by Security Forces' 25 January 2019 <www.amnesty.org.uk>.

38 Ibid.

39 Staffan Darnolf and Liisa Laako (eds), *Twenty Years of Independence in Zimbabwe: From Liberation to Authoritarianism* (Palgrave Macmillan 2003). If we are to include human rights documentation as being within the ambit of transitional justice, then Zimbabwe civic society has been handling transitional justice issues even before the country's independence.

focus in the period after independence was on restorative justice, compensation for human rights abuses, reconciliation, amnesties and the need for institutional reform.[40] Even though these pundits did point out that the 'forgive and forget' strategy which was adopted at independence was likely to breed a culture of impunity, there was no examination of the issue as to whether the amnesties granted to those who were individually responsible for colonial era atrocities were consistent with international law.

This issue of individual responsibility received attention only in contemporary transitional justice proposals of academics and civic society.[41] These can be traced to 2001, when the country could hardly be described as a transitional society since prospects of political talks or a negotiated settlement between Zimbabwe's opposition parties were still conjectural.[42] Indeed, possibilities for puissant change seemed remote, especially in the wake of the split and the weakening of the main opposition party, the Movement for Democratic Change (MDC), in 2005.[43]

Nevertheless, the existing literature on transitional justice in Zimbabwe can be roughly split into two camps. Firstly, there are the reports of human rights organizations, proceedings of civic society symposiums and statements from legal commentators and political parties.[44] The primary focus of these renditions is accountability for human rights abuses and the potential role for civic society in this regard.

40 See Michael Garcia Bochenek, 'Compensation for Human Rights Abuses in Zimbabwe' (1995) 26(2) *Columbia Human Rights Law Review* 483, Victor de Waal, *The Politics of Reconciliation: Zimbabwe's First Decade* (Hurst & Co 1990), Richard Carver, *Zimbabwe: A Break with the Past? Human Rights and Political Unity* (Africa Watch 1989), Richard Carver, 'Zimbabwe: Drawing a Line through the Past' (1993) 37(1) *Journal of African Law* 69, and Richard Carver, 'Zimbabwe: Drawing a Line through the Past' in N Roht-Arriaza (ed) *Impunity and Human Rights in International Law and Practice* (Oxford University Press 1995) pages 7–50. Restorative justice projects carried out were in the form of memorialization and exhumations; see Centre for the Study of Violence and Reconciliation (CSVR), 'Memorialisation and Reconciliation in Transitional Southern African Societies' (2005) <www.csvr.org.za>.

41 For a discussion of most of these initiatives, see Zimbabwe Human Rights NGO Forum, 'Exploring Transitional Justice Options in Contemporary Zimbabwe' *Special Report* (January 2006) <www.hrforumzim.com/>, and Max du Plessis and Jolyon Ford 'Justice and Peace in a New Zimbabwe; Transitional Justice Options' (2008) *ISS Occasional Paper 164.*

42 See Financial Gazette (Harare), 'Zimbabwe: UN Hopes for Negotiated Settlement' 6 July 2006 <http://allafrica.com/>.

43 For details on the split of these two main opposition parties see Movement for Democratic Change (UK) <www.mdcuk.com/>.

44 See Zimbabwe Human Rights NGO Forum (n.41), The Redress Trust, 'Zimbabwe: From Impunity to Accountability, Are Reparations Possible for Victims of Gross and Systematic Human Violation' (2004) <www.redress.org>, The Redress Trust, 'Torture in Zimbabwe, Past and Present: Prevention, Punishment, and Reparation? Survey of Law and Practice' (2005) <www.redress.org>, Penny Morrel and Piers Pigou, *Civil Society and Justice in Zimbabwe: Proceedings of a Symposium Held in Johannesburg 11–13 August 2003* (Themba Lesizwe 2003).

A key example of this approach is the 'Civil Society and Justice in Zimbabwe' symposium convened in Johannesburg in August 2003.[45] This event brought together 70 civic society organizations in Zimbabwe and South Africa, as well as transitional justice experts from other jurisdictions. Whilst this symposium made some reference to the issues of land, the rule of law and other matters, its final conclusion focused on the choice of a Truth, Justice and Reconciliation Commission (TJRC) as a mechanism for dealing with the legacy of human rights abuses. To pre-empt the criticism that the participants were conduits of imperialist ideologies, it was agreed that this TJRC would look into the abuses of both the colonial era and the postcolonial state.

In addition to securing redress for human rights violations, civic society lawyers have put considerable attention into legal and constitutional issues surrounding the transition.[46] There are also efforts to train domestic lawyers in transitional justice.[47] What has been absent in this debate is a comprehensive discussion on the judiciary, which is the key institution for interpreting the law both during ordinary times and in times of crisis.[48]

The second group of writings is that of academics and a number of students who have chosen to write theses on the area.[49] In this category, the focus of legal writings has been on the issue of how to address the legacy of human rights abuses.[50] Other transitional justice issues which do not necessarily relate to dealing with the legacy of past human rights violations have been considered mainly by non-legal scholars in disciplines such as land studies, political economy, developmental studies, history, peace and conflict studies and some other social sciences.[51]

The analysis of transitional justice in this work falls into the second tent of writings on the subject. It differs from most legal writings on Zimbabwe's transitional justice issues in its starting premise that the law is not always a tool for justice.[52] It also notes that conventional transitional justice discourses do not necessarily respond to local priorities. Further, its focus is not only on traditional

45 Morrel and Pigou, ibid.

46 See 'Constitutional and Legal Issues: Presentation and Group Discussion' <www.sarpn.org.za/documents/>.

47 See 'The Zimbabwe Lawyers for Human Rights; Transitional Justice Project' <www.zlhr.org.zw/>.

48 This issue is the subject matter of Chapter 3.

49 See, for example, Andrew R Illiff, 'Arresting Impunity: Toward a Transitional Justice Paradigm for Zimbabwe' *Dissertation Prepared in Partial Fulfillment for a Degree with Honors – Bachelor of Arts* (Harvard College 2004) and Tendai Chabvuta, 'Exploring Transitional Justice for Past Human Rights Violations: The Case of Zimbabwe' *Unpublished LL.M Dissertation* (Transitional Justice Institute, University of Ulster 2006).

50 See, for example, Illiff, ibid.

51 See, for example, the range of essays in Brian Raftopoulos and Tyrone Savage, *Zimbabwe: Injustice and Reconciliation* (Institute for Justice and Reconciliation 2005).

52 See Chapter 2.

transitional justice issues of criminal justice, histories and reparations. Rather, this work adopts a holistic approach which also addresses issues at the periphery of paradigmatic transitional justice discourses, including land issues and minority rights.

In particular, the study's analytical breadth encompasses four issues.[53] These are: (1) rule of law and judicial independence, (2) land reform in transition, (3) minorities in societies in transition and (4) combating the legacy of human rights abuses.[54] Overall, the gender dimension is embraced in the spirit of the Fourth World Conference on Women in Beijing in 1995, which asserted that when attending to conflict, a progressive and ascertainable policy of mainstreaming a gender dimension into the agenda ought to be advanced, so that prior to making policy choices, it is established how such choices would impact respectively on both men and women.[55]

It has to be pointed out that these critical areas of the research are entwined. Pundits who have proposed a number of transitional justice mechanisms for Zimbabwe have stated that these are necessary if the rule of law and the credibility of the country's legal institutions are to be restored. Their simplistic assumptions are that the domestic rule of law deficit may be remedied by recourse to international law. In this vein, judicial independence is measured by the application of universal international legal standards. International law does contain some minimum standards which are of universal application, but its provisions are abstract, and its enforcement as well as its interpretation is often based on contemporary politics and interests rather than on shared values.[56] This fact is demonstrated in this work, which attends to both the complex and the context.

It may be difficult to comprehend the role which the law ought to play in dealing with Zimbabwe's past without appreciating the country's rule of law challenges as exemplified by the issue of judiciary independence which arose during the controversial land reform question. Also, while Western attention to the fairness of Zimbabwean elections, governance and human rights abuses largely followed the invasions of white-owned commercial farms in 2000, in reality widespread and systematic abuses, which claimed approximately 20,000 lives from one black minority group, occurred between 1983 and 1987.[57] Thus, any

53 Chapters 3–6 deal with these matters in detail.

54 Ibid.

55 Beijing Declaration and Platform for Action, Fourth World Conference on Women, A/CONF.177/20 (1995) and A/CONF.177/20/Add.1 adopted 15 September 1995 (see also the United Nations Security Council resolution 1325 (2000) on Women and peace and security S/Res/1325 (2000).

56 For critical insights on international law, see Anthony Anghie, *Imperialism, Sovereignty and the Making of International Law* (Cambridge University Press 2005).

57 Carver (1995) 9 (n.40) has it that in 1985 a BBC television crew was shown a mass grave in Nkayi (Matebeleland) containing bodies of people alleged to have disappeared. Allegations of six other graves in the vicinity were made.

interrogation of the country's legacy of impunity inevitably touches on the subject of minority rights.

1.3 Outline of the book

This chapter has set the scene for the discussion of international law and postcolonial comparative material in the chapters that follow. Chapter 2 functions as a conceptual and theoretical framework. It starts by drawing on scholarly legal treatises and political science authorities in its contribution to the debate on the definition of transitional justice. This discussion also explains how the critical areas of the research fit within the field. It takes into consideration the goals of transitional justice, grey areas in the discipline and some new developments and controversies. This is followed by a postcolonial critique of transitional justice. In this regard the chapter draws on the writings of highly qualified postcolonial theorists who challenge key assumptions in conventional thinking.[58] The chapter then presents the book's main argument, which is that even though the transitional justice discourse is largely controlled by those with power, it is open to seizure by less powerful states.[59]

Chapters 3–6 develop the main idea through engaging with context and by way of exposing the complex in discussions of international law and comparative material as they relate to the four areas of the study. For background information, and at the domestic level, these chapters take into account national constitutions, applicable legislation, domestic cases/reports of truth commission/findings of commissions of inquiry and peace agreements. Where applicable, and for comparative purposes, further reliance is placed on the basic documents, activity reports, decisions or communications, resolutions and the jurisprudence of regional human rights mechanisms, with a special attention on the work of the African Commission on Human and People's Rights. Useful insights are also taken from other social science disciplines, which include developmental studies, history, economic history, political science and land studies.

The chapters further draw from reports and conference proceedings of credible domestic and international human rights organizations that have closely monitored the Zimbabwean situation.[60] Concluding observations on the Zimbabwean

58 Indicative studies are those of Walter Mignolo, *Local Histories/Global Designs: Coloniality, Subaltern Knowledges, and Border Thinking* (Princeton University Press 2012), Homi Bhabha, 'Of Mimicry and Man: The Ambivalence of Colonial Discourse' in Homi Bhabha (ed) *The Location of Culture* (Routledge 1994) and Anthony Anghie, *Imperialism, Sovereignty and the Making of International Law* (Cambridge University Press 2005).

59 Moyo (n.8).

60 These include, *inter alia*, the Zimbabwe Human Rights NGO Forum's monthly and special reports, publications of the International Bar Association, Amnesty International country specific reports, relevant reports produced by Human Rights Watch, publications of the Redress Trust and those of the Institute for Justice and Reconciliation.

government's reports to the United Nations' treaty-monitoring bodies are also taken into account.[61]

In developing the four chapters' normative framework, the study is largely guided by the relevant provisions and *travaux praparatories* of the core international human rights instruments. Where appropriate, the chapters also draw from the jurisprudence of these treaty-monitoring bodies. These incorporate General Comments, concluding observations on state parties' reports and cases decided by these bodies. The United Nations Security Council's resolutions and press releases on the essentials of post-conflict reconstruction, which arguably influence the evolution of international law, are also considered.[62] These include the resolution on women and armed conflict and the press release on restoring the rule of law in post-conflict dispensations.[63]

Chapter 7, the concluding chapter, sums up the main arguments and elaborates on the study's main contribution to transitional justice research. It is alive to the fact that focused research cannot cover all the issues which are identified in the process of analysis or those research questions which are products of the study. Thus, it also identifies areas which may require further exploration.[64]

61 See the Office of the High Commissioner for Human Rights <www.ohchr.org>.

62 Examples are UN Security Council resolution 1325 (2000) on Women, Peace and Security S/RES/1325 (2000) and UN (2003), 'Restoring Rule of Law Absolutely Essential for Resolving Conflict, Rebuilding Secure, Humane Societies' *United Nations Press Release*, SC/7884, 30 September 2003 <www.un.org>.

63 Ibid.

64 Ibid.

2 Basic concepts of the study and a postcolonial critique

2.1 Introduction

Contemporary transitional justice has come to presage an array of legal and political processes that are employed to undo a past and build a better future in the passage from war to peace or from authoritarian rule to democracy. Typically, this involves four kinds of approaches, namely, criminal prosecutions, truth recovery, reparations and legal and institutional reforms to restore confidence and avert recurrence of abuses.[1] Of these approaches, this study concerns itself with the complexities of those processes that are geared towards restoring the rule of law and judicial independence, dealing with past land injustices, minority rights and the legacy of impunity in Zimbabwe, as an example of a postcolonial dispensation.

In order to identify the complexities of addressing these questions in Zimbabwe and other postcolonial societies, a broad overview of the field of transitional justice and its areas of oversight is necessary. With regard to limitations in the discourse, it is axiomatic that an exploration of all of the related research questions which emerge as a consequence of any such analysis is impossible, particularly in a focused study. Therefore, this chapter restricts itself to postcolonial concerns. The chapter is in three parts. The first part defines transitional justice. The second part locates the four critical areas of the study within the transitional justice discourse. The third part presents a postcolonial critique which is followed by concluding observations.

2.2 The field of transitional justice

2.2.1 Transition

A widely cited definition of transitional justice is that of Ruti Teitel, who stated that it is the:

> [C]onception of justice associated with periods of political change, characterized by legal responses to confront the wrongdoings of repressive predecessor regimes.[2]

1 Par 23 Report of the Special Rapporteur on the promotion of truth, justice, reparation and guarantees of non-recurrence, Pablo de Greiff, U.N. Doc. A/HRC/30/42 (2015).

2 Ruti Teitel, 'Transitional Justice Genealogy' (2003) 16 *Harvard Human Rights Journal* 69.

Thus, the difference between ordinary justice and transitional justice is the use of law to effect regime change when a society is moving from conflict to peace. In view of this outlined complicity of the law in periods of repression, legal undertakings in transitional times are complex.[3] This issue has been traditionally explored from realist, idealist, critical and liberal theoretical perspectives which largely focus on the relationship between law and politics.[4] Teitel, however, has adopted a pragmatic approach, which points out that there is a dialectical relationship between law and politics in transitional times.[5] Law in times of transition is not just a product of political change; it actually provides a framework for the transition.[6] As Teitel notes:

> [L]aw is caught between the past and the future, between backward looking and forward looking, between retrospective and prospective. Transitions imply paradigm shifts in the conception of justice; thus law's function is inherently paradoxical. In its ordinary social function, law provides order and stability, but in extraordinary periods of political upheaval, law maintains order, even as it enables transformation. Ordinary predicates about law simply do not apply. In dynamic periods of political flux, legal responses generate a *sui generis* paradigm of transformative law.[7]

While heralding and sticking to the new liberal regime's undertaking to abide by principles of democracy and rule of law, law in transitional contexts authenticates a demarcation between the outgoing regime and the new dispensation.[8] Since domestic law is often politicized, international law, by virtue of its externality to the conflict, plays a significant role in the broader issues of national sovereignty.[9] It preserves the ordinary meaning of the rule of law, which entails notions of continuity and certainty that have often been absent from the outgoing regime.[10]

Indeed, law structures transitions in three different ways. First, it provides the normative basis for political transformation.[11] Second, legal norms and institutions

3 Ruti Teitel, *Transitional Justice* (Oxford University Press 2000). See also the discussion in Christine Bell, Colm Campbell and Fionnuala Ní Aoláin, 'Justice Discourses in Transition' (2004) 13 *Social and Legal Studies* 306.

4 Ruti Teitel, 'Transitional Jurisprudence: The Role of Law in Political Transformation' (1996–1997) 106 *Yale Law Journal* 2009.

5 Ibid.

6 Ibid. See also the foreword by Lord Wright of Richmond in Michael Byers (ed), *The Role of Law in International Politics: Essays in Law and International Relations* (Oxford University Press 2000).

7 Teitel (n.4).

8 See Neil J. Kritz, *Transitional Justice: How Emerging Democracies Reckon with Former Regimes* (United States Institute of Peace Press 1995) Volume 1, page xxi.

9 See Teitel (n.3) and Teitel (n.4). See also Colm Campbell and Fionnuala Ní Aoláin, 'The Paradox of Transition in Conflicted Democracies' (2005) 27 *Human Rights Quarterly* 173.

10 See Teitel (n.4).

11 The authorities are just too many to be fully referenced here see among others: Ruti Teitel, 'How Are the New Democracies of the Southern Cone Dealing with the Legacy of Past

underscore the illegitimacy of the prior regime.[12] Third, law is instrumental in advancing the political transition.[13] Put simply, different mechanisms employed in the aftermath of repression are based on international human rights convictions. Consequently, in challenging states to stop, delve into, penalize, mend and forestall human rights abuses, scholars and practitioners rely on international humanitarian law and international human rights.[14]

Nonetheless, another widely cited definition of transitional justice is that of the United Nations Secretary General (UNSG), which states that transitional justice

> [C]omprises a full range of processes and mechanisms associated with a society's attempts to come to terms with a legacy of large-scale past abuses, in order to ensure accountability serve justice and achieve reconciliation. These may include both judicial and non-judicial mechanisms, with differing levels of international involvement (or none at all) and individual prosecutions, reparations, truth-seeking, institutional reform, vetting and dismissals, or a combination thereof.[15]

Thus, transitional societies *transition to* a reconciled and just society. The definition also states that transitional societies are those with a legacy of large-scale past human rights abuses. It is unclear whether those abuses need to be widespread or state-orchestrated and whether transitional justice concerns itself with abuses, which occurred in the immediate past. Knowledge of where transitional societies *transition from* is necessary, as it would put restrictions on when transitional justice can legitimately be applied.

2.2.2 Transition from what?

Transitional justice mechanisms are adopted after 'virtually every period of repression or civil violence'.[16] A pre-transition regime's illegitimacy is evident in

---

Human Rights Abuses' in Neil J. Kritz (ed) *Transitional Justice: How Emerging Democracies Reckon with Former Regimes, Vol 1* (United States Institute of Peace Press 1995), Naomi Roht-Arriaza (ed), *Impunity and Human Rights in International Law and Practice* (Oxford University Press 1997), Juan E. Mendez, 'In Defense of Human Rights' in James A. McAdams (ed) *Transitional Justice and the Rule of Law in New Democracies* (University of Notre Dame Press 1997) page 5, Diane F. Orentlicher, 'Settling Accounts: The Duty to Prosecute Human Rights Violations of a Prior Regime' (1991) 100 *Yale Law Journal* 25 and Christine Bell, 'Dealing with the Past in Northern Ireland' (2003) 26 *Fordham International Law Journal* 1095.

12 Ruti Teitel, 'Paradoxes in the Revolution of the Rule of Law' (2004) 19 *Yale Journal International Law* 239.

13 Bell, Campbell and Ní Aoláin (n.3).

14 Ibid. See also Teitel (n.3) page 5.

15 Par 8, UN Security Council, 'Report of the Secretary-General – The Rule of Law and Transitional Justice in Conflict and Post-Conflict Societies' S/2004/616*.

16 Tricia D. Olsen et al., *Transitional Justice in the Balance: Comparing Processes, Weighing Efficacy* (United States Institute of Peace Press 2010) page 38.

the general discontent within the population, with its laws and institutions. It is usually characterized by widespread and largely state-orchestrated human rights abuses. Often, the state does not acknowledge the existence of these human rights abuses. Instead of respecting the rule of law, it 'rules by law', seeing the law as imposing obligations on the citizens and not on the regime itself. Clear-cut examples of transitional societies would include post-Pinochet Chile and post-apartheid South Africa.[17] Unclear cases include those countries which Joanna Quinn has labelled as being non-transitional states and pre-transition countries.[18]

Non-transitional countries which have adopted what looks like transitional justice mechanisms include Canada, Australia and the USA.[19] In the cases of Australia and Canada, the issue relates to the national policy put in place to deal with the forcible removal of aboriginal children in Australia and the Canadian truth and reconciliation commission on residential schools. With respect to the USA, consideration is given to the Greensboro Truth and Reconciliation Commission which was established in 2004.[20] This commission was intended to deal with the killing of five protestors and wounding of ten others by the Ku Klux Klan and the American Nazi Party in November 1979.

All three countries are firmly established democracies that are largely peaceful. Joanna Quinn has explained that whereas Australia, Canada and the USA may have been peaceful, firmly established democracies, the aboriginals and the Greensboro community were not afforded the same equality as non-aboriginals and the rest of the American population.[21] Thus, aboriginals and the Greensboro community were not living in the same peaceful democratic state as the rest of the population, hence the relevance of transitional justice. The raises the question whether transitional justice has to deal with atrocities which occurred in the immediate past, or whether it can also attend to historic injustices.

Quinn describes pre-transition countries as those in 'which there has not been a definite transition from one regime to the next, nor a clear move from conflict to peace'.[22] An example of a pre-transition country is Uganda, which has been

17 Cath Collins, 'Human Rights Trials in Chile during and after the "Pinochet Years"' (2009) 4(1) *International Journal of Transitional Justice* 67. See also François du Bois and Antje du Bois-Pedain (eds), *Justice and Reconciliation in Post-Apartheid South Africa* (Cambridge University Press 2009).

18 Rosemary L. Nagy, 'The Scope and Bounds of Transitional Justice and the Canadian Truth and Reconciliation Commission' (2013) 7(1) *International Journal of Transitional Justice* 52. See also Jeff Corntassel et al., 'Who's Sorry Now? Government Apologies, Truth Commissions, and Indigenous Self-determination in Australia, Canada, Guatemala, and Peru' (2008) 9(4) *Human Rights Review* 465.

19 Joanna R. Quinn, 'Whither the Transition of Transitional Justice' (2014–2015) 8(1) *Interdisciplinary Journal of Human Rights Law* 63. See also Nicola Henry, 'From Reconciliation to Transitional Justice: The Contours of Redress Politics in Established Democracies' (2015) 9(2) *International Journal of Transitional Justice* 199.

20 Greensboro Truth and Reconciliation Commission, 'Greensboro Truth and Reconciliation Commission Report: Executive Summary' (2006).

21 Quinn (n 19) 68

22 Ibid at 72.

wracked by conflict since independence. There has never been a transition in Uganda, but Yoweri Museveni, who came to power in 1986 by means of military force, has implemented transitional justice mechanisms.[23] For example, two truth commissions have been convoked to deal with abuses committed between 1962 and 1986 as well as disappearances committed under Idi Amin. The International Criminal Court is also currently dealing with the crimes alleged to have been committed by the Lord's Resistance Army.

Uganda is not an exception in this regard. This seems to be a feature of most postcolonial polities. For example, as will be demonstrated in Chapter 6 of this book, Zimbabwe has been wracked by conflict since the colonial era and has adopted transitional justice mechanisms in different epochs. The country has yet to make a clean break with its past. With the exception of the period 2008–2013 when the country had an inclusive government made up of ZANU PF and the two MDC formations, Zimbabwe has been ruled by one political party (ZANU PF) in its almost 39 years of existence.[24]

Nonetheless, the International Centre for Transitional Justice (ICTY) has stated that the question of whether a country is in a period of transition is not complex.[25] The issue is whether 'an opportunity has emerged to address massive violations, even if it is a limited opportunity'.[26] Opportunities have been presented by peace negotiations which have seen the incorporation of transitional justice as part of the conditions for ending conflict. Also, transitional justice mechanisms have been adopted by new governments replacing repressive regimes.

2.3 The 'justice' part of 'transitional justice'

To take Aristotle's distinction between corrective and distributive justice from which most discussions derive,[27] is transitional justice based on corrective justice or distributive justice? Does it provide for the rectification of wrongs when one person causes harm to another, or does it also require the sharing of various goods according to some relevant formula, for example, desert, need or equality? On this note the 2017 report of the former Special Rapporteur on the promotion of truth, justice, reparation and guarantees of non-recurrence states that:

> [T]ransitional justice is a *corrective and preventive justice* tool that stands in a complex set of relations with other kinds of justice measures, including distributive justice initiatives, but that cannot replace them (emphasis added).[28]

23 Ibid at 74.

24 Between 2008 and 2013, there was an inclusive government made up of ZANU PF and the two factions of MDC (MDC-T lead by Morgan Tsvangirai and MDC-M lead Arthur Mutambara).

25 See International Centre for Transitional Justice (ICTJ), 'What Is Transitional Justice?' <www.ictj.org/about/transitional-justice>.

26 Ibid.

27 Aristotle, *Nicomachean Ethics*, V, 2–5.

28 Par 86, Report of the Special Rapporteur on the promotion of truth, justice, reparation and guarantees of non-recurrence on his global study on transitional justice (7 August 2017) A/HRC/36/50/Add.1.

However, other studies perceive transitional justice as including both corrective and distributive justice. For example, according to Jeremy Weber, transitional justice consists of three forms of justice, namely:

> [t]he retrospective (backward-looking), the prospective (forward-looking), and the adjustment of contending legal and political orders.[29]

Of these three forms, Weber argues that the retrospective is corrective and the prospective is distributive.[30] Similarly, Nancy Fraser argued that one of the major dilemmas of justice projects is in striking a balance between commitments to redistribution and recognition.[31] Within the context of transitional justice, 'justice' as recognition may involve prosecutions, the creation of truth commissions or commissions of inquiry whose role is to recognize and acknowledge the atrocities of the past regime.[32] By contrast, justice as 'redistribution' seeks to re-order property or land rights and can symbolically redistribute shame, from the victim to the perpetrator.[33]

Another scholar, Rama Mani, identified rectificatory, legal and distributive justice as the three dimensions of justice that must all be pursued during transitions.[34] Rectificatory justice concerns redress for the explicit human outcomes of conflict structured in gross human rights abuses, war crimes, crimes against humanity and other injustices inflicted upon human beings.[35] Legal justice addresses the notion of the establishment of the rule of law that often loses its legitimacy, deteriorates or is destroyed both during and after a conflict.[36] Distributive justice focuses on economic and political inequalities, which are seen as the root causes of most conflicts.[37]

Also noteworthy is Ruti Teitel's expansive approach to the discourse, which delineates criminal justice, historic justice, reparatory justice, transitional constitutionalism and legislative and administrative responses as various legal approaches to injustices in the passage from repression to a liberal democracy.[38] She stated that

> [a]djudications of the rule of law construct understandings of what is fair and just. Criminal, administrative, and historical investigations establish past wrongdoing. Reparatory projects vindicate rights generated by past wrongs

29 Jeremy Webber, 'Forms of Transitional Justice' (2012) 51 *Nomos* 98.
30 Ibid at 102–103.
31 Nancy Fraser, *Justice Interruptus: Critical Reflections on the 'Postsocialist'* (Routledge 1997).
32 See Katherine M. Franke, 'Gendered Subjects of Transitional Justice' (2006) 15(3) *Columbia Journal of Gender and Law* 813.
33 Ibid.
34 Rama Mani, 'Beyond Retribution: Seeking Justice in the Shadows of War' (Polity 2002) page 5.
35 Ibid.
36 Ibid.
37 Ibid.
38 Teitel (n.3) 7.

> to victims as well as to the broader society. Transitional constitutionalism and administrative justice reconstruct the parameters of the changing political order in a liberalization direction.[39]

Nonetheless, the view articulated by all these studies is that 'justice' in a transitional context incorporates a totality of reform strategies that deal with the previous regime's injustices. It is now widely accepted that 'justice' in transitional justice is comprised of four elements, namely, truth, justice, reparation and guarantees of non-recurrence. As the first Special Rapporteur on the promotion of truth, justice, reparation and guarantees of non-recurrence aptly put it:

> [T]he most important contribution of transitional justice has been, quite simply, its unpacking of the concept of justice into constituent and mutually reinforcing elements: truth, justice, reparation and guarantees of non-recurrence.[40]

However, this is not a template to be used in every situation as the type of justice adopted is linked to the appropriate definitive political context.[41] On this note, cognisance ought to be made of Fletcher and Weistern's arguments that justice needs to be both cemented on and focused on the communities, cultures and contexts of the regime in transition.[42] Put simply, 'justice' in transitional justice is largely dependent on context of the past injustices of the transitioning regime.[43] Therefore, in the context of Zimbabwe, arguably, 'justice' incorporates *inter alia* those mechanisms that address issues of the rule of law and judicial independence, land reform, minority rights as well as mechanisms for dealing with the legacy of impunity.

2.4 Locating the critical areas of the research within the transitional justice field

2.4.1 Rule of law and judicial reform

It is now widely accepted that the 'rule of law' is a notion that is at the heart of the shift from repression, authoritarianism or war to a liberal democracy.[44] In its

39 Ibid.
40 Par 25, Report of the Special Rapporteur on the promotion of truth, justice, reparation and guarantees of non-recurrence (n.28).
41 Ibid. See also Ruti Teitel, 'Transitional Justice in the New Era' (2003) 26 *Fordham International Law Journal* 893, Ruti Teitel, 'The Law and Politics of Contemporary Transitional Justice' (2005) 38 *Cornell International Law Journal* 837, Ruti Teitel, 'Transitional Justice: Post-War Legacies' (2005–2006) 27(4) *Cardozo Law Review* 1615.
42 Laurel E. Fletcher and Harvey M. Weinstein, 'Violence and Social Repair: Rethinking the Contribution of Justice to Reconciliation' (2002) 24 *Human Rights Quarterly* 573. See also Paul Gready, 'Reconceptualising Transitional Justice: Embedded and Distanced Justice' (2005) 5(1) *Conflict Security & Development* 3.
43 Ibid.
44 See Report of the Secretary-General on the Rule of Law and Transitional Justice in Conflict and Post-conflict Societies. S/2004/616, 23 August 2004 (hereinafter Report of the Secretary General S/2004/616). Teitel (n.3) 7 and chapter 1, Bell, Campbell and Ní Aoláin (n.3),

less developed form, the concept connotes that governmental authority may be enforced only in conformity to prescribed norms, which were adopted following proper procedures. Arbitrary rulings are therefore not permissible. In its complete form, it guarantees equal and moral justice in the application of the law. Basically, the rule of law is a very broad concept, with several strands marked by aims and characteristics that are often at variance. These include the notion that political power should be legally restrained, the quest for an egalitarian society, maintenance of law and order, the expectations of certain and effective justice as well as the obligation to abide by human rights norms.[45] For the United Nations, the rule of law is:

> [A] principle of governance in which all persons, institutions and entities, public and private, including the State itself, are accountable to laws that are publicly promulgated, equally enforced and independently adjudicated, and which are consistent with international human rights norms and standards. It requires, as well, measures to ensure adherence to the principles of supremacy of law, equality before the law, accountability to the law, fairness in the application of the law, separation of powers, participation in decision-making, legal certainty, avoidance of arbitrariness and procedural and legal transparency.[46]

A broader discussion of these issues is beyond the scope of this book. It suffices to point out that these ideals can be ensued only in the presence of an independent judiciary since this is the state arm which is the custodian of the rule of law.[47] Furthermore, international and regional human rights bodies have acknowledged that judicial independence is essential in the promotion, protection and fulfilment of human rights.[48]

Neil J. Kritz, 'The Rule of Law in the Post-Conflict Phase: Building a Stable Peace' in C.A. Crocker, F.O. Hampson and P. Aall (eds) *Managing Global Chaos: Sources of and Responses to International Conflict* (United States Institute of Peace Press 1996).

45 Thomas Carothers, 'Rebuilding Developmental States: From Theory to Practice Judicial Reform and the Rule of Law' (2006) *Oversees Development Agency, Meeting Series. January–April 2006.*

46 United Nations Security Council (2004) Report of the Secretary General, 'The Rule of Law and Transitional Justice in Conflict and Post-Conflict Societies' S/2004/616.

47 Ayoub M. Al-Jarbou, 'Judicial Independence: Case Study of Saudi Arabia' (2004) 19(1) *Arab Law Quarterly* 5. For a definition of judicial independence, see Daniel Brinks, 'Judicial Reform and Independence in Brazil and Argentina: The Beginning of a New Millennium' (2004–2005) 40 *Texas International Law Journal* 595.

48 The United Nations treaties that stipulate this are: Article 10 *UDHR*, and Article 14 *ICCPR*, as read with the Basic Principles on the Independence of the Judiciary, adopted by Seventh United Nations Congress on the Prevention of Crime and the Treatment of Offenders, Milan 1985, endorsed by General Assembly Resolution 40/32 of 29 November 1985 and Resolution 40/146 of 13 December 1985. See G.A. Res. 40/32, U.N. GAOR, 40th Sess., Supp. No. 53, at 204, U.N. Doc. A/40/53 (1985); Res. 40/146, U.N. GAOR, 40th Sess., Supp. No. 53, at 254, U.N. Doc. A/40/53 (1985) and *Gonzalez del Rio v Peru*/263/1987, 28 October 1992, Report of the Human Rights Committee, vol. II (A/48/40), 1993, 20. In the African region, this provision is found in Article 7 of the African [Banjul] Charter on

A politicized or weakened judiciary often characterizes human rights abusing regimes.[49] Often this state of affairs may be a product of three distinct causes. First, there could be governmental attacks on the independence of the judiciary, including pressure or outright intimidation.[50] Second, judges and prosecutors can be unequivocally biased towards the political establishment.[51] Third, the judiciary may lack both resources and capacity.[52] The judiciary's lack of capacity or credibility indicates an absence of the rule of law. Against that backdrop, the adverse circumstances presented by a dysfunctional justice system are core transitional justice challenges.

Vetting, training and judiciary reform are elements of guarantees of no-recurrence.[53] According to Pablo de Greiff, the former Special Rapporteur on the promotion of truth, justice, reparation and guarantees of non-recurrence, there is a conceptual difference between:

> guarantees of non-recurrence and the remaining three core elements of a comprehensive transitional justice approach, namely, truth, justice and reparation. While those three elements refer to measures, guarantees of non-recurrence is a function that can be satisfied by a broad variety of measures. The foundational texts already demonstrate this variety, pointing to, inter alia . . . vetting the security forces and the judiciary.[54]

2.4.2 Land reform in transitional contexts

Illiberal rule and war frequently result in the attrition of property rights.[55] Thus, most transitional societies often enact legislation which addresses competing rights claims to property.[56] These claims range from refugees' rights to return to their country of origin, to land claims based on the inequity or loss of livelihoods caused by the state's unjust distribution of land, to restitution or compensation

---

Human and Peoples' Rights, adopted 27 June 1981, OAU Doc. CAB/LEG/67/3 rev. 5, 21 I.L.M. 58 (1982), entered into force 21 October 1986 (hereinafter African Charter).

49 For an illustration of this see Albert P. Melone, 'The Struggle for Judicial Independence and the Transition Toward Democracy in Bulgaria' (1996) 29(2) *Communist and Post-Communist Studies* 231.

50 See Report of the Special Rapporteur of the Commission on Human Rights on the Independence of Judges and Lawyers 2005 61st session CHR E/CN.4/2005/60. (Report of the Special Rapporteur: situations in specific countries or territories).

51 Melone (n.49).

52 International Crisis Group (2003) 'Afghanistan: Judicial Reform and Transitional Justice' *Asia Report No. 45* <www.crisisgroup.org/home/i> (Accessed 4 September 2018).

53 Par 52–61 Report of the Special Rapporteur on the promotion of truth, justice, reparation and guarantees of non-recurrence, Pablo de Greiff, A/HRC/30/42 (7 September 2015). See also paragraphs 107–109.

54 Par 23 ibid.

55 Jon D. Unruh, 'Land and Property Rights in the Peace Process' in Guy Burgess and Heidi Burgess (eds) *Beyond Intractability* (Conflict Research Consortium, University of Colorado 2004) <www.beyondintractability.org> (Accessed 3 November 2006).

56 Ibid.

claims by those whose land was expropriated by the outgoing regime.[57] As a detailed discussion of all three scenarios is impracticable, it is sufficient to point out that this work's focus is on the latter two possibilities.[58]

Dealing with postcolonial land injustices is a cross-cutting issue which can be relevant to all four pillars of transitional justice. First, truth commissions can investigate complaints of the dispossession of land and build a national consensus around the history of land claims.[59] Second, criminal prosecutions can deal with perpetrators of land violations such as displacement[60] Third, reparation initiatives have focused on either restitution orders requiring that land be returned to the dispossessed, or compensation orders where a compensation payment is made to the dispossessed.[61] Finally, land tenure reform can be undertaken in part as a non-recurrence initiative.[62]

2.4.3 Minority rights in transition

The notion that the promotion and protection of the rights of persons belonging to minority groupings is a fundamental aspect of a democratic regime based on the rule of law is gaining wide acceptance.[63] Outgoing regimes that make the

57 Article 12(4) of the ICCPR has it that, 'No one shall be arbitrarily deprived of the right to enter his own country'. See the discussions in Christine Bell, *Negotiating Justice: Human Rights and Peace Agreements* (International Committee on Human Rights Policy 2006) pages 60–62, and Lewis Saideman, 'Do Palestinian Refugees Have a Right of Return to Israel: An Examination of the Scope of and Limitations on the Right of Return' (2003–2004) 44 *Virginia Journal of International Law* 829.

58 Historic significant transitions that addressed issues of state expropriations, compensation and restitution are the demise of the Eastern European communist dispensations. These transitions will not be considered in this chapter. The issue that is explored here is the changing property rights regimes of postcolonial governments.

59 See United States Institute for Peace, 'Truth Commission: Mauritius' <www.usip.org/publications/2012/02/truth-commission-mauritius>. Other truth commissions which attended to land issues include those in countries such as Liberia, Sierra Leone, Timor Leste, Guatemala and Kenya.

60 Roger Duthie and Paul Seils, *The Case for Action on Transitional Justice and Displacement Strategies during and after Conflict* (International Centre for Transitional Justice 2016) <www.ictj.org/sites/default/files/ICTJ_Briefing_Displacement_2016.pdf>.

61 For the link between repairing the past and land, see Bell (n.57) 55, and James A. McAdams, *Judging the Past in Unified Germany* (Cambridge University Press 2001). For an understanding of reparations, see Siri Gloppen, 'Reparatory Justice, a Road to Reconciliation? On the Role of Reparations in Transitional Justice Theory' in George Ulrich and Louise Krabbe Boserup (eds) *Human Rights in Development Yearbook 2001: Reparations: Redressing Past Wrongs* (Kluwer Law International 2003).

62 For the link between transitional justice and land tenure reform see Chris Huggins, *Linking Broad Constellations of Ideas: Transitional Justice, Land Tenure Reform, and Development* (International Centre for Transitional Justice 2009) <www.ictj.org/sites/default/files/ICTJ-Development-LandTenureReform-ResearchBrief-2009-English.pdf>.

63 'Report of the Secretary-General on the Effective Promotion of the Declaration on the Rights of Persons Belonging to National or Ethnic, Religious and Linguistic Minorities', U.N. Doc. A/60/333 (6 September 2005). For a discussion on self-determination generally,

transition to a liberal democracy or peace often harbor ethnic, cultural or religious communities that cannot peacefully co-exist.[64] Differences between the majority and minority groupings normally arise when the latter are of the viewpoint that the state is not respecting, protecting or fulfilling their rights.[65] This is more so given that their numerical inferiority might preclude them from securing their interests through democratic processes.[66] In some cases this tension could be the root cause of the authoritarianism or war.[67] Against this backdrop, regimes in transition to a liberal democracy apply international human rights norms on minority rights and the right to self-determination in their transitional framework.[68]

In the context of transitional justice, legislation on group rights and political accommodation is a subset of what Ruti Teitel has labelled as constitutional justice.[69] Citing case studies of post-Nazi Germany, Italy after Fascism and post-Stalin Russia, Professor Mauro Capelleti defines constitutional justice as a major legal justice-related solution to governmental subjugation.[70] It denotes the creation of new constitutional provisions, institutions and processes for restraining and regulating the exercise of political power.[71] Similarly, Teitel argues that transitional constitutionalism differs from ordinary constitutionalism in that its purpose is not just to create mechanisms for limiting governmental power; it also constructs the transition.[72] It is both backward and forward looking; that is, while constituting the new political order, it also responds to previous injustices.[73] Further, she explains

---

see Antonio Cassese, *Self-Determination of Peoples: A Legal Reappraisal* (Lauterpacht Memorial Lectures 1995). See also the discussion in Daniele Archibugi, 'A Critical Analysis of the Self-determination of Peoples: A Cosmopolitan Perspective' (2003) 10(4) *Constellations* 488.

64 Examples in this regard include Northern Ireland and Afghanistan. Northern Ireland is discussed in this regard in Colin Warbrick, Dominic McGoldrick and Geoff Gilbert, 'The Northern Ireland Peace Agreement, Minority Rights and Self-Determination (1998) 47 *International and Comparative Law Quarterly* 943, Bell, Campbell and Ní Aoláin (n.3) and Christine Bell and Kathleen Cavanaugh, 'Constructive Ambiguity or Internal Self-Determination? Self-Determination, Group Accommodation and the Belfast Agreement' (1998–1999) 22 *Fordham International Law Journal* 1345. For Afghanistan, see Peter Marsden, *Afghanistan: Minorities, Conflict, and the Search for Peace* (Minority Rights Group International 2001).

65 Deon Geldenhuys and Johann Rossouw, *The International Protection of Minority Rights* (F W de Klerk Foundation 2001).

66 Ibid. See also Stephen Wheatley, 'Deliberative Democracy and Minorities' (2003) 14(3) *European Journal of International Law* 507.

67 Geldenhuys and Rossouw (n.65). See also Jon Abbink, 'Ethnicity and Constitutionalism in Contemporary Ethiopia' (1997) 41 *Journal of African Law* 159.

68 See Bell et al. (n.3) 317.

69 This issue is discussed in Teitel (n.3) chapter 6 and Teitel (n.4). See also the Ethiopian example in Abbink (n.67).

70 Mauro Cappelletti, 'Repudiating Montesquieu? The Expansion and Legitimacy of Constitutional Justice' (1985) 35(1) *Catholic University Law Review* 1.

71 Ibid. See also the discussion in Christopher L. Eisgruber, 'The Living Hand of the Past: History and Constitutional Justice' (1997) 65(4) *Fordham Law Review* 1611.

72 Teitel (n.3) 191–192.

73 Ibid.

that transitional constitutions are not as fixed and sustained as ordinary constitutions; they are pro tempore, and they include both interim provisions and some features which could be firmly established with time.[74] As Vivien Hart aptly puts it:

> [R]ecent experience of constitutional making amid conflict and division suggest a middle position, that the 'old constitutionalism' is augmented rather than displaced by the 'new'. . . . The purpose . . . however, is not just to create strong, just or efficient government. It is also to recognise, include, give voice to, equalize, or advantage, and to exclude, silence, or stigmatize people and peoples.[75]

Pablo de Greiff, the former Special Rapporteur on the promotion of truth, justice, reparation and guarantees of non-recurrence, included transitional constitutional reforms which removes discriminatory provisions and introduces mechanisms of inclusion in his examples of elements of guarantees on non-recurrence.[76] Constitutional provisions dealing with group rights and political accommodation serve two purposes in a transitional context. First, these provisions assist in including threatened minorities in the political process in tandem with assuring the same that in future they will be no governmental encroachment on their rights.[77] Second, noting that disgruntled minorities can easily be mobilized for opposing change, these entrenchments can help in fostering peace and restoring or creating democracy depending on the transitional circumstances.[78] These issues will be covered in Chapter 5.

2.4.4 Combating impunity

Transitional justice discourses are often dominated by discussions on the tension between the need to hold perpetrators of gross human rights violations accountable for their actions and the pragmatic demands of conflict resolution.[79] Juan Mendez noted that there are moral, political and legal justifications for the

74 Ibid at 196.
75 Vivien Hart, 'Constitutional Making and the Transformation of Conflict' (2001) 26(2) *Peace and Change* 153.
76 Par 63 and 64 23 Report of the Special Rapporteur on the promotion of truth, justice, reparation and guarantees of non-recurrence, 2015 (n.1).
77 Rumyana Kolarova, 'Tacit Agreements in the Bulgarian Transition to Democracy: Minority Rights and Constitutionalism' (1993) *The University of Chicago Law School Roundtable* 23 at 24.
78 Ibid.
79 See Neil J. Kritz (ed), *Transitional Justice: How Emerging Democracies Reckon with Former Regimes, Vols 1–3* (United States Institute of Peace Press 1995), Christine Bell, *Negotiating Justice: Human Rights and Peace Agreements* (International Committee on Human Rights Policy 2006) page 19 and Juan E. Mendez, 'Accountability for Past Abuses' (1997) 19 *Human Rights Quarterly* 255.

pursuit of retrospective justice in the democratization process.[80] These include, *inter alia*, providing legitimacy to new political and legal institutions, giving victims the truth to which they are entitled and promoting national reconciliation.[81] Accountability also deters the new regime from complacently violating human rights norms.[82] Further, through the adoption of a number of international human rights law and humanitarian law standards, the international community has affirmed that transitional societies have an obligation to investigate, prosecute and punish serious violations of international law.[83]

In spite of these international legal developments, some transitional societies elect not to punish or even interrogate their human rights–violating past.[84] Furthermore, even in those regimes where there are national and international efforts at fulfilling international obligations to investigate, prosecute and punish, in practice full accountability is never accomplished.[85] Indeed, in most societies where the outgoing regimes still retain considerable power, punishment is avoided out of fear that insistence on the same would destroy any chance of reconciling the society and achieving stability.[86] In some transitional societies, lack of financial and other resources have hindered the attainment of full accountability, more so in those societies where there are large numbers of human rights violators and

80 Mendez, ibid. Juan E. Mendez, 'In Defence of Human Rights' in James A. McAdams (ed) *Transitional Justice and the Rule of Law in New Democracies* (University of Notre Dame Press 1997) page 5.

81 Bell (n.79).

82 Diane F. Orentlicher, 'Settling Accounts: The Duty to Prosecute Human Rights Violations of a Prior Regime' (1991) 100 *Yale Law Journal* 2357.

83 These include the Convention on the Prevention and Punishment of the Crime of Genocide (1948), G.A Rees 260 A (111), U.N.T.S. 277 (hereinafter Genocide Convention 1948), United Nations Convention against Torture and Other Cruel, Inhuman or Degrading Treatment or Punishment, G.A. Res. 39/46, annex, 39 U.N. GAOR Supp. (No. 51) at 197, U.N. Doc. A/39/51 (1984), *entered into force* 26 June 1987 (hereinafter Torture Convention), Protocol Additional to the Geneva Conventions of 12 August 1949, and Relating to the Protection of Victims of Non-International Armed Conflicts (Protocol II), 1125 U.N.T.S. 609, *entered into force* 7 December 1978. A list of the relevant international standards can be found in Naomi Roht-Arriaza, 'Sources in International Treaties of an Obligation to Investigate, Prosecute and Provide Redress' in Naomi Roht-Arriaza (ed) *Impunity and Human Rights in International Law and Practice* (Oxford University Press 1995) pages 24–56, and Asbjørn Eide, 'Preventing Impunity for the Violator and Ensuring Remedies for the Victim' (2000) 69 *Nordic Journal of International Law*. Note also the regional case, 32 Velasquez-Rodriguez Case, Inter-Am. Ct. H.R. (ser. C) No. 4 Para 166.

84 An example would be Zimbabwe's transition from colonial rule discussed in Richard Carver, 'Zimbabwe: Drawing a Line through the Past' in Naomi Roht-Arriaza (ed) *Impunity and Human Rights in International Law and Practice* (Oxford University Press 1995) pages 7–50.

85 Madeline H. Morris, 'International Guidelines against Impunity: Facilitating Accountability' (1996) 59 *Law and Contemporary Problems* 29.

86 Ibid. Examples of such societies include South Africa and Argentina. For the discussion on the Argentina example, see Carlos S. Nino, 'The Duty to Punish Past Abuses of Human Rights Put into Context: The Case of Argentina' (1991) *100 Yale Law Journal* 2619.

victims.[87] Also, in cases where there is no regime change, there might be a lack of political will to account for past human rights atrocities.[88]

Consequently, perpetrators of severe human rights atrocities have been spared prosecution or full accountability through the adoption of blanket amnesties or compromise approaches to accountability depending on the transitional circumstances.[89] The wrongfulness or otherwise of these approaches is a complex issue given the fact that international law seems to permit and even call for a certain degree of post-conflict amnesty.[90] Nevertheless, human rights practitioners, activists and academics have demonstrated that failure to punish perpetrators of human rights norms creates a culture of impunity and amnesia.[91] Thus, recently there have been considerable attempts at ensuring that victims of gross and systematic human rights abuses enjoy their right to effective remedy.[92] The contemporary practice and thinking is that there should be a holistic approach which yokes together truth, justice and reparations.[93]

These issues will be explored more broadly in Chapter 6.

2.5 Critique, transitional justice and postcolonial theory[94]

2.5.1 A vignette of postcolonial legal theory

In the context of globalization and the post–September 11 recrudescent neo-colonialism, the appellation 'postcolonial' (or 'post-colonial') has been subject

87 An example would be Rwanda; see Erin Daly, 'Between Punitive and Reconstructive Justice: The Gacaca Courts in Rwanda' (2002) 34 *New York Law School Journal of International Law and Politics* 355.

88 Morris (n.85).

89 Eide (n.83). An example of a blanket amnesty is the Chilean Law of 18 April 1878; Chile Law of Amnesty, No. 2.191 (18 April 1978), reprinted from *Diario Oficial, No. 30.042.* For a blanket amnesty example, see Carver (n.84). Morris (n.85) discusses compromise approaches.

90 Article 6 (5) of Protocol 11 of the Geneva Convention. See the discussion in Bell (n.79) 8.

91 The term impunity is derived from the Latin term '*impunis*' which means unpunished. In law it has come to presage a regime where some people manage to commit egregious crimes without any fear of punishment, investigation or justice. See the definition adopted in; Louis Joinet, 'Report of the Special Rapporteur on the Question of Impunity of Perpetrators of Human Rights Violators' U.N. Doc. E/CN.4/Sub.2/1997/20/Rev.1 (2 October 1997). The term 'amnesia' is used to show that by drawing a line through the past, such transitional societies choose to lose their memories or engage in selective amnesia. See the discussion in Heinz Klug, 'Amnesty, Amnesia, and Remembrance: International Obligations and the Need to Prevent the Repetition of Gross Violations of Human Rights' (1998) 92 *American Societies of International Law Proceedings* 316.

92 Eide (n.83).

93 Cath Collins, 'Truth-Justice-Reparations Interaction Effects in Transitional Justice Practice: The Case of the "Valech Commission"' (2016) 49(1) *Journal of Latin American Studies* 55.

94 This section is reproduced from Khanyisela Moyo, 'Feminism, Postcolonial Legal Theory and Transitional Justice: A Critique of Current Trends' (2012) 1(2) *International Human Rights Law Review* 237. The pages reproduced are from 257–276.

to serious rancour. The major objection to the use of the moniker has been the assertion that alleged former colonies are still colonies. Proponents of this view include Ngugi wa Thiong'o and Miyoshi Masao.[95] Such views can be very compelling, and it is noteworthy that they acknowledge that nowadays imperialism is disguised. However, this work's view is that notwithstanding the evidence of resurgent neo-imperialism, former colonies are no longer really colonies since:

> [T]hey have their own governments, which in most cases appear vastly different from the colonial regime. These new governments may represent improvements, new hope, or terrible disappointments, but they are not the same. The newly liberated nations may be ravaged by corruption, violence, and disease, and those horrors may be the direct or indirect result of having been colonized – and that is the subject for investigation by postcolonial studies, not a denial of their value'.[96]

Nonetheless, according to Fitzpatrick and Darien-Smith, postcolonial legal theory is an examination by legal scholars of the side-tracked theme of 'law's consanguinity to the postcolonial'.[97] The history of colonialism and the current experiences of neo-colonialism have made postcolonial legal scholars overtly conscious of interstate power relations and the manner in which any intended international norm will in reality impact on the administration of power.[98] In evaluating power relations and their effect on the implementation of international law, postcolonial legal thinking has derived inspiration from non-legal major intimations of postcolonialism, reflected in the works of Michel Foucault,

95 Masao Miyoshi, 'A Borderless World? From Colonialism to Transnationalism and the Decline of the Nation-State' (1993) 19 *Critical Inquiry* 750, and Robert Spencer, 'Optimism of the Intellect and Optimism of the Will: The Unseasonable Art of Ngugi wa Thiong'o' (2003) 2 *Electronic Law Journals – LGD* <www2.warwick.ac.uk/fac/soc/law/elj/lgd/2003>. See also Sundhya Pahuja, 'The Postcoloniality of International Law' (2005) 45 *Harvard International Law Journal* 459.

96 George P. Landow, 'Why I Use the Term 'Postcolonial' or Some Words from Your Webmaster' *Postcolonial Web* <www.postcolonialweb.org/poldiscourse/themes/gplpoco.html>.

97 Peter Fitzpatrick and Eve Darian-Smith, 'The Laws of the Post-Colonial: An Insistent Introduction' in Eve Darian-Smith and Peter Fitzpatrick (eds) *Laws of the Postcolonial* (University of Michigan Press 1999).

98 Anthony Anghie and Bhupinder S. Chimni, 'Third World Approaches to International Law and Individual Responsibility in Internal Conflicts' (2003) 2 *Chinese Journal of International Law* 78. Whilst an ubiquitous postcolonial theory can outline encyclopedic lessons that may be of use in addressing problems confronting former colonies, specific cases demonstrate that the experiences of (for example) non-settler, settler and partially settled colonies are divergent. Examples of settler colonies are Australia and Canada. An example of a non-settler colony would be Nigeria and a partially settled colony is Zimbabwe. Noteworthy also in the context of Africa are the differences in the effects of colonialization on Francophone, Lusophone and Anglophone colonies. It would be overly ambitious, in such a focused study, to delve into the polemics of postcolonialism, so this work will extract from the discourse only the notion that while law is largely at the service of the empire, it is also open to seizure by the colonized.

Robert Young, Edward Said, Homi Bhabha, Gatayri Spivak and Frantz Fanon, among others.[99]

Indeed, as a result of the thinking of these groundbreaking postcolonial theorists, some concepts have become associated with and perceived in a certain way in postcolonialism.[100] For example, whereas 'discourse' in linguistics simply refers to any segment of dialogue which is more than a sentence, in postcolonial studies the term is associated with Foucault's enunciations.[101] Foucault saw discourse as a firmly circumscribed scope of knowledge, a philosophy with which the world can be recognized.[102] Those with power control this knowledge, how it is imparted, and exercise authority over those who have no say in what is known.[103]

This nexus between power and knowledge is essential in interactions between former colonies and their colonial masters and was seized by first-generation postcolonial legal theorists who explained how traditional understanding of international human rights law (in common with other facets of international law) imbricate with colonial needs.[104] They specifically blamed international law for rendering legitimacy to the imperialists' objectives of subjugating the colonized and systematically pillaging their resources.[105] From this theoretical angle, a deceitful positivist myth of sovereign equality which assumes that all states are the principal actors of international law who are bound by international human rights norms that they have freely and voluntarily consented to was rejected.[106]

99 See, for example, the style adopted in Balakrishnan Rajagopal, 'International Law and Social Movements: Challenges of Theorizing Resistance' (2003) 41 *Columbia Journal of Transnational Law* 397, Beth Lyon, 'Discourse in Development: A Post-Colonial Theory "Agenda" for the UN Committee on Economic, Social and Cultural Rights' (2002) 10 *Journal of Gender, Social Policy & the Law* 3, Anghie and Chimni (n.98) and Roshan de Silva Wijeyeratne and John Strawson, 'Tracks and Traces of the Law' (2003) 12(2) *Griffith Law Review* 157.

100 Bill Ashcroft, Gareth Griffiths and Helen Tiffin, *Post-Colonial Studies: The Key Concepts* (Routledge 2007).

101 See Michel Foucault, *The Archaeology of Knowledge and the Discourse on Language* (Tavistock 1972).

102 Ibid.

103 Ibid.

104 See Ram P. Anand, *Confrontation or Cooperation? International Law and the Developing Countries* (Kluwer Law International 1987). Anghie and Chimni have also pointed out that Northern international legal scholars set standards on what is considered suitable knowledge of international law. Consequently, issues which are relevant to postcolonial peoples, for example race and colonialism, are either disregarded or given little prominence. Anghie and Chimni (n.98).

105 Justification for this thinking can be found in the doctrinal genealogy from Wheaton's 'Elements of International Law' see Henry Wheaton, *Elements of International Law* (Little Brown 1855). Wheaton has it that 'the law of nations or international law, as understood among civilized, Christian nations, may be defined of consisting of those rules of conduct which reason deduces, as consonant to justice, from the nature of the society existing among independent nations; with such definitions and modifications as may be established by general consent' (at page 47).

106 Anthony Anghie, 'Finding the Peripheries: Sovereignty and Colonialism in Nineteenth Century International Law' (1999) 40 *Harvard International Law Journal* 1.

In his expostulation of Orientalism, Edward Said builds on Foucault's understanding of discourse to connect culture and imperialism.[107] He points out that during the enlightenment period, the Western discourse assisted the Occident in constructing, embodying and prevailing over the Orient.[108] In postcolonial studies, *Orientalism* has come to be understood as a way in which Western culture and stereotypes reinforce global depictions of non-Western cultures.[109] The effect is felt not only in political and economic structures and institutions but in the creation of a binary fashion of seeing the colonialists as the *Self* and the colonized as the *Other* who need civilization.[110]

Drawing on Said's theory, Antony Anghie stated that most of international law's core doctrines are a product of efforts by European jurists to legally account for the imperial distinctions between the civilized European world and the non-civilized non-European world.[111] Similarly, Siba N'Zatioula Grovogui demonstrated that European viewpoints of the *Self* and their philosophical depictions have been essential in the formation of international law.[112] As James Thuo Gathii puts it:

> [T]hese representations of the European *self*, and the contrasting non-European *other*, form the basis of simultaneous exclusion and inclusion and are grounded on differences or similarities of religion, culture or race.[113]

In a global order that classifies nations as developing and developed, modern and pre-modern and as inhabiting different worlds, human rights norms are seen to be the new yardstick that have ousted civilization as the postcolonial test for separating the *Self* from the *Other*.[114] Commenting on the realization that the majority of cases that are being addressed by human rights bodies are from postcolonial countries, Makau Mutua had this to say;

> [I]t is in this sense that the 'other culture', that which is non-European, is the savage in the human rights corpus and discourse. . . . Many are women

107 Edward Said, *Orientalism* (Pantheon Books 1978).

108 The Occident refers to France, Britain and the United States. The Orient was a term coined by Edward Said for the Far East and the Middle East.

109 See the analysis in Shahnaz Khan, 'Race, Gender and Orientalism: Muta and the Canadian Legal System' (1995) 8 *Canadian Journal of Women Law* 249.

110 Ibid.

111 Anthony Anghie, 'The Heart of My Home: Colonialism, Environmental Damage, and the Nauru Case' (1993) 34 *Harvard International Law Journal* 445.

112 Siba N. Grovogui, *Sovereigns, Quasi Sovereigns, and Africans: Race and Self-Determination in International Law* (University of Minnesota Press 1996) page 21.

113 James T. Gathii, 'International Law and Eurocentricity' (1998) 9 *European Journal of International Law* 184.

114 Makau wa Mutua, 'Savages, Victims, and Saviors: The Metaphor of Human Rights' (2001) 42 *Harvard International Law Journal* 201. See also Gerrit W. Gong, The *Standards of 'Civilisation' in International Society* (Clarendon Press 1984), for an elaborate consideration of the distinction between civilized and uncivilized nations in international law in the nineteenth century.

> and children twice victimised because of their gender and age, and sometimes the victim of the savage culture is the female gender itself.[115]

Indeed, in relying on an overly generalized victim subject mostly representative of Western privileged women's concerns, the women's human rights movement has been critiqued for its hegemonic bias.[116] According to this viewpoint, postcolonial women are largely depicted as victims of their societally bad cultural practices.[117] This approach bolsters stereotyped and racist images of that culture, favouring Western culture.

Notwithstanding its compelling articulation of discursive colonialism, *Orientalism* represents an exceedingly general and fixed Western cultural imperialist notion.[118] In particular, it tends to relegate the *Other* to a mere end result of the colonizer's discourse. This tendency is manifested, for example, in Said's assertions that the:

> [O]rient was not (and is not) a free subject of thought and action.[119]

In view of this difficulty, Homi Bhabha seized upon Orientalism to point out the ambivalent relationship that exists between the *Self* and the *Other*.[120] His philosophy basically unsettles the definitive power of colonial superiority since it disrupts the uncomplicated relationship between the colonizer and the colonized.[121]

First coined in psychoanalysis, the term 'ambivalence' illustrates a constant alteration between desiring something and desiring its antithesis.[122] Applied to postcolonial discourse theory by Bhabha, the term depicts the love–hate relationship that exists between the colonizer and the colonized.[123] For example, while some colonial subjects struggled against colonialism, others collaborated with the colonizer, and yet the actions of other colonized subjects alternate between

115 Ibid. Similarly, Raimundo Pannikar noted that 'human rights are universal from the vantage point of modern Western culture, but not universal from the outside looking in'. Raimundo Pannikar, 'Is the Notion of Human Rights a Western Concept?' (1982) 120 *Diogenes* 76 at 94.

116 See Chandra T. Mohanty, 'Under Western Eyes: Feminist Scholarship and Colonial Discourses' in C.T. Mohanty, A. Russo and L. Torres (eds) *Third World Women and the Politics of Feminism* (Indiana University Press 1991).

117 Ratna Kapur, 'The Tragedy of Victimisation Rhetoric: Resurrecting the "Native" Subject in International/Post-Colonial Feminist Legal Politics' (2002) 15 *Harvard Human Rights Journal* 1. See also Annie Bunting, 'Theorizing Women's Cultural Diversity in Feminist International Human Rights Strategies' (1993) 20(1) *Journal of Law and Society* 6.

118 Ilan Kapoor, 'Acting in a Tight Spot: Homi Bhabha's Postcolonial Politics' (2003) 25(4) *New Political Science* 561.

119 Said (n.107) quoted by Kapoor, ibid.

120 Homi Bhabha, 'Of Mimicry and Man: The Ambivalence of Colonial Discourse' in Homi Bhabha (ed) *The Location of Culture* (Routledge 1994).

121 Ashcroft, Griffiths and Tiffin (n.100).

122 Robert J.C. Young, *Colonial Desire: Hybridity in Theory, Culture and Race* (Routledge 1995) page 161.

123 Bhabha (n.120).

complicity and resistance.[124] On the same note, while the colonizer's objective is to create deferential subjects who 'mimic' the colonizer, it creates fluctuating subjects whose replication of the colonizer's expectations, attitudes and ideals is far removed from mockery.[125]

According to Bhabha, the execution of colonial power is weakened by the process's perpetual ambivalence.[126] This is evident in that even though the colonizer sets out to impose its own values on the colonized, the colonizer does not really intend to produce precise mimics.[127] Reproducing exact clones is scary since it would disrupt the notion of alterity–the distinction between the *Self* and the *Other* which is necessary for the colonizer to be identified as master.[128] To explain this ambivalent process in the exercise of colonial power, Bhabha formulated the term 'hybrid'. He gives a classic example in Charles Hunt's bid to covert Indians to Christianity in 1792.[129] Hunt wanted Indians to adopt Christian beliefs but feared that this could stir a liberation rebellion; thus, he mixed Christian tenets with factious caste practices.[130] 'Hybridity', or the engagement by the colonizer with the culture of the colonized, thus disrupts the exceedingly general and fixed Western cultural imperialist notion.[131]

A significant part of Bhabha's theory is dedicated to explaining how hybridity can generate opportunities for agency.[132] Agency, in postcolonial theory, denotes the ability of the colonized to engage with or resist colonialism.[133] According to Bhabha, the ambivalence at the origination of established discourses on power facilitates a form of turbulence based on the fluctuation that modifies paradoxical situations of authority into a justification for action.[134] His famous illustration of this resistance is an incident whereby a group of villagers in India rebelled against an attempt to convert them to Christianity.[135] The villagers are said to have declined the sacrament on the basis that the teachings of God emanated from a meat-eater and not a vegetarian.[136]

It needs to be pointed out that Bhabha does not restrict the use of the powers of hybridity to resist colonial authority to colonial times.[137] He also gives a

124 Ibid.
125 Ibid.
126 Ibid.
127 Ibid. See also Kapoor (n.118).
128 For an explanation of alterity see Ashcroft, Griffiths and Tiffin (n.100).
129 Bhabha (n.120).
130 Ibid.
131 Ibid.
132 Kapoor (n.118). See also Ilan Kapoor, 'Capitalism, Culture, Agency: Dependency versus Postcolonial Theory' (2002) 23(4) *Third World Quarterly* 647.
133 See the discussion in Ashcroft, Griffiths and Tiffin (n.100).
134 In asserting this, Bhabha seems to be responding to Foucault's notion that 'there are no relations of power without resistance'. Homi Bhabha, *The Location of Culture* (Routledge 1994) page 112. See also Michel Foucault, 'Power/Knowledge' Selected Interviews and Other Writings 1972–1977 in C Gordon (ed) (Oxford University Press 1980) page 142.
135 Bhabha, ibid at 121.
136 Ibid.
137 Ibid at 229.

postcolonial example of agency; that is, the way in which a British group, Women Against Fundamentalism, appropriated the news of the condemnation to death of Salman Rushdie in 1989.[138] Women Against Fundamentalism used the Rushdie affair not to align themselves with either Christianity or conservative Islam, but to attract a debate on issues that affect women.[139]

Further, Bhabha stresses that agency emanates only from the contours of the master's discourse.[140] Therefore, a form of connivance and abetment between the colonizer and the colonized is inevitable.[141] This explains Bhabha's reference to agency as a form of 'negotiation'.[142] To him this 'negotiation', or playing out of 'hybridity', takes place at a 'third space – a middle, disparate site where supplementary discourses move in to maintain their distinctiveness'.[143]

It should be pointed out that Bhabha is emphatic that colonialism is said to have pronounced the distinction between the former colonial powers and their former colonies; thus it is hopeless to attempt to recover the pre-colonial identity.[144] For this reason, he is wary of any attempts at directly confronting the dominant discourse as the product is likely to be reverse Orientalism and racism, or a replacement of one authority with another. Concurring with this line of reasoning, Bart Moore-Gilbert argues for a form of agency which disrupts the master's discourse from within.[145]

Parallels can be drawn between Bhabha's understanding of the relationship between the colonizer and the colonized and some legal scholars' attitudes to international law.[146] First, there is postcolonial scholarship which seeks to prove that the encounter between the European and the non-European world contributed to the creation of the core principles of international law, thereby unsettling the notion that international law is a sole product of European culture.[147]

Second, it could be said that the Bhabhanian philosophy is best demonstrated by the ambivalent attitudes of these pundits to international law.[148] From one viewpoint, these scholars criticized international law for adding legitimacy to

138 Ibid. For an understanding of Salman Rushdie's *Satanic Verses*, see Sten P. Moslund, 'Literature as Discourse: An Analysis of the Discursive Strategies in Salman Rushdie's *The Satanic Verses*' (2006) 61(4) *Orbis Litterarum* 291–309.

139 Bhabha (n.134) 229.

140 Gayatri C. Spivak, 'Poststructuralism, Marginality, Postcoloniality and Value' in P. Collier and H. Geyer-Ryan (eds) *Literary Theory Today* (Polity Press 1990) page 228. See also the criticism by Robert Young, *White Mythologies: Writing History and the West* (Routledge 1990) page 152.

141 Kapoor (n.132) 652.

142 Ibid.

143 Bhabha (n.134) 37.

144 See the discussion in Kapoor (n.132) 652 and an analogous argument in Gayatri C. Spivak, 'Can the Subaltern Speak?' in N. Cary and L. Grossberg (eds) *Marxism and the Interpretation of Culture* (University of Illinois Press 1988) pages 271–313 at 291.

145 Bart Moore-Gilbert, *Postcolonial Theory* (Verso 1997) page 85.

146 See Gathii (n.113).

147 Ibid.

148 Ibid at 193.

colonialism.[149] Yet, from another angle, these scholars accepted international law and even devoted research in proving that non-European states were not new-comers to the concept of international law.[150] According to Makau wa Mutua, the suggestion that Africans did not have ideas of human rights is Eurocentric.[151] Authentic universality of the human rights regime can occur only if analogous doctrines from postcolonial legal systems and cultures were also included in the paradigmatic human rights discourse.

Third, postcolonial scholars sought opportunities of *agency* within the international legal machinery. Believing that concerns of the newly liberated states could be addressed through the United Nations (UN) system, they contended that General Assembly resolutions imposed legal obligations on member states.[152] This strategy was employed in attempts to address several issues, including the end of colonialism, racial discrimination, sovereign equality of state and non-intervention by powerful states in the affairs of the new states.[153] Having succeeded in spearheading the decolonization process, they noted that political independence without economic liberation was insufficient.[154] Therefore, they wishfully sought to re-order the uneven economic relations between the North and the South through the inauguration of a New International Economic Order (NIEO).[155]

149 Grovogui (n.112), and Anthony Anghie, *Imperialism, Sovereignty and the Making of International Law* (Cambridge University Press 2005).

150 Anghie and Chimni (n.98).

151 Makau wa Mutua, 'The Ideology of Human Rights' (1996) 36 *Virginia Journal of International Law* 589.

152 See Obed Asamoah, 'The Legal Effect of Resolutions of the General Assembly' (1963–1964) 3 *Columbia Journal of Transnational Law* 210, and Christopher C. Joyner, 'U.N. General Assembly Resolutions and International Law: Rethinking the Contemporary Dynamics of Norm-Creation' (1981) 3 *California Western International Law Journal* 445.

153 See Declaration on the Granting of Independence to Colonial Countries and Peoples, G.A. Res. 1514, U.N. GAOR, 15th Sess., Supp. No. 16, at 66, U.N. Doc. A/4684 (14 December 1960) (hereinafter cited as Declaration on the Granting of Independence to Colonial Countries and Peoples), Declaration on the Inadmissibility of Intervention in the Domestic Affairs of States and the Protection of Their Independence and Sovereignty, GA Res. 2131 (XX), U.N. GAOR 20th Sess, Supp. No 14, at 11, U.N. Doc. A/6014 (21 December 1965) and Declaration on Principles of International Law Concerning Friendly Relations and Co-operation among States in Accordance with the Charter of the United Nations, G.A. Res. 2625 (XXV), U.N. GAOR 25th Sess., U.N. GAOR 25th Sess., U.N. Doc. A/8028 (24 October 1970).

154 Mark E. Ellis, 'The New International Economic Order and General Assembly Resolutions: The Debate Over the Legal Effects of General Assembly Resolutions Revisited' (1985) 15 *California Western International Law Journal* 647.

155 Two resolutions adopted in pursuance of this goal are the *Declaration on the Establishment of a New International Economic Order* G.A. Res. 3201 (S-V1, 29 U.N. GAOR Supp. (No.1) at 3, U.N. Doc. A/9559 (1 May 1974) and the *Programme of Action on the Establishment of a New International Economic Order*, G.A. Res. 3202 (S-VI), 29 U.N. GAOR Supp (No.1) at 5, U.N. Doc. A/9559 (12 December 1974) (hereinafter cited as Programme of Action). The ideas represented in the two documents were refined and codified in the Charter of Economic Rights and Duties of States likewise adopted as a General Assembly

In spite of this ambitious attempt, the gap between the rich and the poor widened, and the NIEO vision collapsed with the end of the Cold War in 1989.[156] It can be argued that the failure of the NIEO illustrates Bhabha's notion that agency and subjectivity are closely connected. Indeed, several underpinnings of the NIEO ideology qualify the ideas of agency and subjectivity.

First, the NIEO was an attempt by the '*Other*' to radically force transformation of international law on the '*Self*' who play a significant role in the market economy.[157] This differs from the quest for decolonization and national self-determination, which was steeped in Western liberal thought and was achieved with the tacit support of the *Self*.[158] Former colonial masters were not wary of political independence since they had already arranged the structures of the market economy in such a way that territorial strength and economic strength were divorced.[159] As the then-spokesman of the developing nations, President Boumedienne of Algeria, aptly put it:

> [I]n fact the colonialist and imperialist powers accepted the principle of the right of the peoples to self-determination only when they had already succeeded in setting up the institutions and machinery that would perpetuate that system of pillage established in the colonial era.[160]

Consequently, the binary divisions of the '*Self*' and the '*Other*' produced by the colonial encounter were preserved, since after political liberation, former colonial masters still controlled the international economic and trading systems.[161]

Resolution. *Charter of Economic Rights and Duties of States*, G.A. Res. 3281, 29 U.N. GAOR Supp. (No. 30), at 50, U.N. Doc. A/9631 (1974) (hereinafter cited as the Charter of Economic Rights).

156 Eric A. Engle, 'The Failure of the Nation State and the New International Economic Order: Multiple Converging Crises Present Opportunity to Elaborate a New Jus Gentium' (2003) 16 *St. Thomas Law Review* 187.

157 This can be assumed from the voting patterns at the adoption of the General Assembly resolutions which proclaimed the New International Economic Order. The NIEO declaration and the Program of Action were adopted without a vote. The Charter of Economic Rights and Duties of States was passed by a recorded vote of 120 affirmative votes, 6 opposing (Belgium, Denmark, West Germany, Luxembourg, the United Kingdom and the United States) and 10 abstentions (Austria, Canada, France, Ireland, Israel, Italy, Japan, the Netherlands, Norway and Spain). See the discussion in Edward McWhinney, 'The International Law-Making Process and the New International Economic Order' (1977) 14 *Canadian Yearbook of International Law* 57.

158 No colonial power voted against the Declaration on the Granting of Independence to Colonial Countries and Peoples. It was passed with 89 affirmative votes and 9 abstentions (Australia, Belgium, the Dominican Republic, France, Portugal, South Africa, Spain, the United Kingdom and the United States).

159 Ellis (n.154).

160 These remarks were made in his opening speech at the 6th Special Session of the UN General Assembly which passed the NIEO declaration and Programme of Action (U.N. GAOR, 28th Sess., A/PV. 2208 (10 April 1974) page 2).

161 Ellis (n.154).

Developing nations which continued to be the source of cheap raw materials were still dependent on the industrialized West for capital, finished products and technology.[162]

Second, this NIEO strategy was founded on the notion that socially generated resources and knowledge ought to be socially distributed.[163] This highlights a suspicious attitude towards international law by developing countries and a refusal to accept capitalist ideas of trade by the same.[164] Inherent in such a viewpoint was a recognition of the hypocritical nature of colonialism.[165] This was tantamount to outright rejection of the Western discourse as a philosophical basis, a move that Bhabha warns against.[166] Against this backdrop, Eric A. Engle argues that any transformation of the current economic arrangements will be effected progressively within the Bretton Woods institutions.[167]

It is axiomatic from the discussion above that in the era of the NIEO, postcolonial legal scholars backed the postcolonial state in furtherance of its nation-building responsibility.[168] To them, sovereignty was negative, inhered in the newly liberated state, and it gave the state a right to be liberated from foreign interference.[169] The state was seen as a unitary, ideal body unaffected by class, race, tribal or gender-related disagreements.[170] As a result of this viewpoint, there was no focus on the postcolonial state' authoritarianism, nor was there any interrogation of its failure to provide governance.[171]

The post-NIEO era saw an end to postcolonial wars that had been previously exacerbated by the superpowers' Cold War.[172] It also saw a rise in pro-democracy movements that either were engaged in constitutional re-engineering in the passage from war or to peace or were calling upon the postcolonial state to respect its citizenry's wider human rights.[173] In the contemporary era of globalization, such struggles have become an acceptable model for the rule of law.[174]

162 Ibid.

163 Engle (n.156).

164 Ibid.

165 Ibid.

166 Ibid.

167 Ibid at 196.

168 Anghie and Chimni (n.98) 82.

169 Ibid. For an understanding of sovereignty see Chapter 4. See also Martti Koskenniemi, *From Apology to Utopia: The Structure of the International Legal Argument* (Finnish Lawyers' Publishing Company 1989).

170 Engle (n.156) 196.

171 Ibid.

172 Ali A. Mazrui, 'Planned Governance and the Liberal Revival in Africa: The Paradox of Anticipation' (1992) 25(3) *Cornell International Law Journal* 541.

173 Ibid. There are other viewpoints to the effect that a focus on the domestic violence of the postcolonial state in the post-NEO era was inspired by the Eastern European regimes' transitions from repression to liberal democracies – a period that Ruti G. Teitel refers to as Phase 11 of transitional justice. Teitel (n.2).

174 Teitel (n.2).

For postcolonial legal philosophers, these developments necessitated a shift from absolutist notions of state sovereignty to a revised idea of sovereignty which emanate from the will of the people and is related to people's rights, even though their elected representatives might exercise it.[175] Understood in this way, sovereignty allows for intervention in a state's domestic affairs for grave human rights atrocities.[176] It affirms the view that the state has rights as well as obligations and that these responsibilities may be enforced both by its citizens' struggles for civil liberties and by the international community's techniques for humanitarian intervention.[177] International law can therefore be invoked in the event of a state's failure to provide good governance so as to ensure that the people's right to democratic entitlement is protected, respected and fulfilled.[178] This tendency to resort to human rights and humanitarian law in the aftermath of war or authoritarianism homogenizes a broad study of humanitarian justice, establishing a legal corpus related to prevalent conflict – the transitional justice discourse.[179]

2.5.2 Postcolonial theory and transitional justice

Efforts to construct a postcolonial understanding of the role of international law in a transitional context inevitably lead to an exploration of the extent to which the transitional justice discourse is bedeviled with the umbra of international law's complicity in facilitating imperialism. This is more so in the current context of globalization and the war on terrorism, where power and fundamental relationships which are entrenched and depicted in international law are undergoing much scrutiny.[180] It is distinctly regrettable that these budding critiques of transitional justice unpretentiously mimeo the precepts of colonialism. Indeed,

175 Anghie and Chimni (n.98) 82. See also Richard Falk, 'Sovereignty and Human Dignity: The Search for Reconciliation' in F.M. Deng and T. Lyons (eds) *African Reckoning a Quest for Good Governance* (Brookings Institution Press 1997).

176 David Kennedy, 'International Law and the Nineteenth Century: History of an Illusion' (1996) 65 *Nordic Journal of International Law* 385.

177 Falk (n.175).

178 Ibid.

179 Ibid. See also Ruti Teitel, 'The Law and Politics of Contemporary Transitional Justice' (2005) 38 *Cornell International Law Journal* 837.

180 Anthony Anghie has it that 'one of the consequences of current U.S. policy and the war in Iraq in particular is that it has made imperialism a central and inescapable aspect of contemporary analysis'. Anthony Anghie, 'Decolonizing the Concept of "Good Governance"' in B.G. Jones (ed) *Decolonizing International Relations* (Littlefield Publishers 2006) page 110. See also Nico Krisch, 'International Law in Times of Hegemony: Unequal Power and the Shaping of the International Legal Order' (2005) 16(3) *European Journal of International Law* 369, and Christine Bell, Colm Campbell and Fionnuala Ní Aoláin, 'The Battle for Transitional Justice: Hegemony, Iraq and International Law' in K. McEvoy, J. Morrisson and G. Anthony (eds) *Judges, Transition and Human Rights Cultures: Essays in Honour of Stephen Livingstone* (Oxford University Press 2007).

axioms of imperialism are liable to be repeated in the use of international law in a transitional context.[181]

First, in as much as international law is indicted for facilitating imperialism's civilizing mission, the purpose of which was to emphasize control and power through knowledge formulation and the cultural creation of 'otherness', the same can be said of the role of law in transitional justice.[182] This can be inferred from the observation that:

> [I]n the context of the ongoing violence in the international system, it is significant that since the beginnings of international law, it is frequently the 'other' the non-European tribes, infidels, barbarians who are identified as the source of all violence. . . . However, this violence when administered by the colonial power is legitimate because it is inflicted in self-defence or because it is humanitarian in character and indeed seeks to save the non-European peoples from themselves.[183]

This 'subject-constituting project' is illustrated by the characterization of the wars in Iraq and Afghanistan.[184] Bell, Campbell and Ní Aoláin have elucidated on how, having failed to offer a credible explanation for their invasion of Iraq, the United States and its coalition partners legitimatized the war by pointing to the human rights atrocities and the democratic deficit of Saddam Hussein's regime.[185] Indeed, the ghost of the civilizing mission was revived when terms such as 'democratization' and 'human rights' were used to produce knowledge of a pre-invasion Iraq which was in turmoil and in need of the coalition's intervention for its liberation.[186]

In a similar vein, and with regard to postcolonial women, Anne Orford borrows Gatayri Spivak 's famous adage 'white women . . . saving brown women from brown men' as she notes how certain feminist legal literature sees the role of international law and 'white women' as being the liberation of third world women from their cultures.[187] According to this school of thought, international

181 For the nexus between international law and imperialism, see Anghie (n.149).

182 See Anghie and Chimni (n.98) 85–86.

183 Ibid.

184 The term 'subject-constituting project' is borrowed from Gayatri C. Spivak, *A Critique of Postcolonial Reason: Toward a History of the Vanishing Present* (Harvard University Press 1999). See also Anne Orford, 'Feminism, Imperialism and the Mission of International Law' (2002) *71 Nordic Journal of International Law* 275. Brett Bowden has made a similar critique of the war on terrorism. According to him, the war on terrorism is being represented as a war fought by the '*Self*' in defence of the interests of civilization against the savage *'Other'* who oppose and seek to destroy civilization. Brett Bowden, 'The Colonial Origins of International Law. European Expansion and the Classical Standard of Civilization' (2005) 7 *Journal of the History of International Law* 1.

185 Bell, Campbell and Ní Aoláin (n.180).

186 Ibid.

187 Orford (n.184) 276.

law must set out to reform these savage cultures so that they can mimic those of powerful countries'.[188]

Second, it could be said that almost all the key concepts associated with transitional justice – democratization, liberalization and rule of law – denote a progression from the Occident to the Orient.[189] They imply the transformation of certain values that have professedly been developed by the untainted benevolent *Self* and must now be embraced by the *Other* if it is to make a successful transition to an internationally acceptable liberal democracy.[190] They are also based on the racist stereotypes of the postcolonial people as devoid of any philosophy for reconstructing their communities.[191] These nuances can be deciphered from then British Prime Minister Tony Blair's address to the US Congress in 2003.[192] In his speech, Blair dismissed critiques that liberty, democracy and human rights are Western values and assertions that Serbian citizens, the Iraq people and the women of Afghanistan were content under the leadership of their outgoing regimes.[193] According to Blair, the United States and its coalition's values are:

> [N]ot Western values, they are the universal values of the human spirit. And anywhere . . . anytime ordinary people are given the chance to choose, the choice is the same: freedom, not tyranny; democracy, not dictatorship; the rule of law, not the rule of the secret police. . . . And just as the terrorist seeks to divide humanity in hate, so we have to unify it around an idea. And that idea is liberty. We must find the strength to fight for this idea and the compassion to make it universal.[194]

In the current context, where those initiatives are entangled in intricate issues of power, efforts at making those values 'universal' are likely to be viewed with cynicism.[195] As the case of Iraq demonstrates, while those universal values stipulate that institutions and practices which are inimical to human rights must be

188 Ibid at 276–277.

189 The terminology used here is borrowed from Said (n.107).

190 This can be implied from Blair's remarks that 'How hollow would the charges of American imperialism be when these failed countries are and are seen to be transformed from states of terror to nations of prosperity, from governments of dictatorship to examples of democracy, from sources of instability to beacons of calm'. Britain's Prime Minister Tony Blair's speech delivered at a joint meeting of the US Congress on Thursday, 17 July 2003. The transcript of his speech is at <http://edition.cnn.com/2003/US/07/17/blair.transcript/>.

191 Anghie (n.180). See also James T Gathii, 'Representations of Africa in Good Governance Discourse: Policing and Containing Dissidence to Neo-Liberalism' (1998–1999) *Third World Legal Studies* 65.

192 Ibid.

193 Ibid.

194 Blair (n.190).

195 James T. Gathii, 'Dispossession through International Law: Iraq in Historical and Comparative Context' in B.G. Jones (ed) *Decolonizing International Relations* (Rowman & Littlefield Publishers, 2006).

transformed, use of force which justifies the reconstruction of a less powerful society by definition also necessitates imposition of the victor's justice.[196]

Furthermore, given transitional justice's relation to the Western view that the individual is the principal holder of rights in tandem with its marginalization of economic, social and cultural rights, the values it transmits cannot be said to be universal.[197] Postcolonial Africa, for example, accords economic, social and cultural rights the same status as an individual's civil and political rights.[198] The Eurocentric notion cannot also adequately account for the multifariousness of group and individual rights in a postcolonial state.[199] This attitude also testifies to the masculinity of transitional justice since as a social class, women are the conventional care givers who are more directly affected by a state's failure to respect, protect and fulfil its citizens' economic, social and cultural rights.[200]

Third, international law's inattention to a historic fact that in most cases, postcolonial authoritarianism and violence was sustained and maintained by external historic and prevailing processes attracts criticism that transitional justice serves to deflect attention from and entrench impunity for human rights atrocities committed by former colonial powers' violence.[201] The Cold War is often cited as an example of a historical process which upheld authoritarianism and wars in many

196 Ibid at 147.

197 This is contrary to international human rights institutions and monitoring bodies' increasing realization that human rights are indivisibleness and inter-dependent. See also Beth Lyon, 'Discourse in Development: A Post-Colonial Theory "Agenda" for the UN Committee on Economic, Social and Cultural Rights' (2002) 10 *Journal of Gender, Social Policy & the Law* 3, and Joe Oloka-Onyango, 'Reinforcing Marginalized Rights in an Age of Globalization: International Mechanisms, Non-State Actors, and the Struggle for People's Rights in Africa' (2003) 18 *American University International Law Review* 857. The notion of the indivisibility and interdependence of rights is articulated in Article 5, Vienna Declaration and Programme of Action, A/CONF.157/23, adopted 12 July 1993. On transitional justice's marginalization of economic, social and cultural rights, see Sigrun I. Skogly, 'Crimes against Humanity Revisited: Is There a Role for Economic and Social Rights' (2001) 5 *International Journal of Human Rights* 58.

198 Oloka-Onyango, ibid. See also Articles 15, 16, 17 and 18 of the African Charter.

199 Group rights are provided for in Articles 20, 21, 22, 23, 24 and 25 of the African Charter. See also Makau Mutua, 'Why Redraw the Map of Africa: A Moral and Legal Inquiry' (1995) 16 *Michigan Journal of International Law* 1113.

200 Fionnuala Ní Aoláin, 'Political Violence and Gender during Times of Transition' (2006) 15 *Columbia Journal of Gender and Law* 829.

201 According to Henry J. Richardson, III: '[C]urrent Northern Tier political and legal theory among dominating elites aims to suppress accountability for colonialism's destructive effects by burying it under mounds of responsibility placed on the present "failed" governments for all the deficiencies among its peoples'. Henry J. Richardson, III, 'Failed States, Self-Determination, and Preventive Diplomacy: Colonialist Nostalgia and Democratic Expectation' (1996) 10 *Temple International & Comparative Law Journal* 1. Further, in his critique of the Yugoslav and Rwanda tribunals, Makau Mutua has questioned whether the motivation of their establishment could have been to sate the conscience of powerful states that rejected measures for preventing and stopping the violence. Makau Mutua, 'Never Again: Questioning the Yugoslav and Rwanda Tribunals' (1997) 11 *Temple International & Comparative Law Journal* 16. See the response in Peter Rosenblum, 'Save the

countries, while the current war on terrorism and the United States' hegemonic inclinations are contemporary illustrations.[202]

Fourth, in giving tacit approval to exploitative economic practices which often occur alongside the implementation of transitional justice mechanisms, and for both to be given legitimacy as promoters of liberal democracy by the international community, international law can be charged with advancing neo-colonial projects of economic exploitation. As Anne Orford remarked:

> [H]ow did it come to seem almost remarkable, in the aftermath of a 'war on terror', to be told in November 2001 that the government of Afghanistan was being 'freely determined' by its people in Bonn, while the World Bank, the United Nations Development Program and the Asian Development Bank co-hosted a meeting in Islamabad to decide how to transform Afghanistan into a market economy.[203]

A recent example of this phenomenon is the Western expropriation of Iraq's resources and assets after the overthrow of Saddam Hussein.[204] The occupying powers privatized Iraq in a manner which could be seen as a violation of the Iraq citizenry's international legal right to self-determination.[205] This process, which was undertaken without the consent of the Iraqi people, included giving Western investors the power to control almost all Iraqi companies without any profit repatriation terms.[206] The Iraqi oil industry was also placed under the control of an independent professional management team chaired by the former chief executive of Shell Oil Company.[207] These programmes were based on the understanding that a regime administered under a free-market democracy paradigm would not be authoritarian or compelled to purchase weapons of mass destruction.[208]

It may *prima facie* appear unproblematic that transitional justice and free market capitalism have a complementary and mutually reinforcing relationship.[209] This is because both practices purportedly set out to spread and improve human

---

Tribunals: Salvaging the Movement – A Response to Makau Mutua' (1997) 11 *Temple International & Comparative Law Journal* 190.

202 Ibid.

203 Orford (n.184) 288–289.

204 Gathii (n.113) 139–143.

205 Ibid at 143. Common article 1(1) of the ICCPR and ICESR has it that 'All peoples have the right of self-determination. By virtue of that right they freely determine their political status and freely pursue their economic, social and cultural development'. For a legal analysis on the relationship between the transformation of an economy, the right to self-determination and the manner of occupation, see Nisuke Ando, *Surrender, Occupation and Private Property in International: An Evaluation of US Practice in Japan* (Clarendon Press 1991).

206 Gathii (n.195) 142.

207 Ibid.

208 Ibid at 143.

209 It is axiomatic that the essence of transitional justice – liberal democratization – is a counterpart of free market systems. Also, focus on transitional justice ensued after the Cold War and became normalized in the current era of globalization, amidst the background of a free

rights norms.[210] According to liberals, as multinational enterprises operate globally within the system of free trade and investment, they progressively impart human rights values in transitional societies.[211] To illustrate, the rule of law which is essential for the development of both the free market and democracy is enforced to ensure certainty in legislation which relates to foreign investment and the general conduct of business.[212] In particular, primacy is given to an individual's right to property and sanctity of contract.[213] This legal certainty results in greater foreign investment, leading to domestic economic growth which will be instrumental in, or lead to an unavoidable socialization of, human rights norms and usher in a democratic regime.[214]

A close postcolonial legal scrutiny of this relationship, however, reveals that it is paradoxical that transitional justice discourses purport to move citizens from an unjust regime to a just establishment while embracing the notion of free markets.[215] This is because the argument that free market capitalism contributes towards the promotion of people's welfare has been largely disproved.[216] In fact, postcolonial legal theorists have pointed out that international financial institutions' structural adjustment and trade liberalization policies' insensitivity to budgetary actualities of postcolonial states weaken the economic, social and cultural rights of people in these societies.[217] These neo-colonial agents (multinational companies) have also been accused of failing to adhere to international legal requirements of minimum labour and environmental standards.[218]

Despite recent international legal recognition that non-state actors can be perpetrators of human rights atrocities, transitional jurisprudence has embraced this notion only in as far as it relates to civil and political rights violated by armed rebels.[219] This inattention to international economic institutions and multina-

market capitalism model of human rights. See the genealogy of transitional justice presented in Teitel (n.2). See also Gathii (n.191).

210 Democracy is a human right (Article 21 UDHR and Article 25 ICCPR). However, both the UDHR and the ICCPR do not state that member states should accept free trade policies or deregulate their markets so as to realize democracy. Authoritative texts on transitional justice, however, imply that the objective of the discourse is to create a 'liberal democracy' which suggests a correlation between transitional justice and free market capitalism. See Henry J. Steiner, 'Do Human Rights Require a Particular Form of Democracy' in E. Cotran and A.O. Sherif (eds) *Democracy: The Rule of Law and Islam* (Kluwer Law International 1999).

211 Ibid.

212 Steiner (n.210).

213 Ibid.

214 Ibid.

215 Orford (n.184).

216 Andrew Heywood, *Political Ideologies: An Introduction* (McMillan Press 1992) pages 15–52.

217 Gathii (n.191).

218 Orford (n.184).

219 Manisuli Ssenyonjo, 'Accountability of Non-State Actors in Uganda for War Crimes and Human Rights Violations' (2005) 10 *Journal of Conflict and Security Law* 405, Sigrun I. Skogly and Mark Gibney, 'Transnational Human Rights Obligations' (2002) 24(3) *Human*

tional companies' well-documented contribution to the humanitarian crisis and human rights atrocities of outgoing regimes further reinforce the argument that there is complicity between the practice of transitional justice and the neo-liberal practices of economic exploitation.[220]

However, none of these compelling postcolonial critiques of transitional justice celebrate postcolonial African leadership's mismanagement and corruption which exacerbated the colonial legacy of inequalities they failed to address as a prerequisite to independence.[221] They also do not totally dismiss transitional justice as an extension of the civilizing mission, cultural imperialism or a promotion of neo-colonial practices of economic exploitation.[222]

To re-iterate, Homi Bhabha has eloquently pronounced that civilizing projects are undermined by the ambivalent representation of colonial power.[223] A postcolonial legal understanding could, therefore, also endeavour to unsettle the contradiction between the Occident and the Orient, by interrogating the crucial connivance between the conditions in which the '*Other*' is produced in transitional jurisprudence, and the '*Self*' that is circumstantially produced.[224] In scrutinizing treatises on transitional justice, this work has already highlighted the analogy between the construction of the benevolent, valorous, masculine *Self* of the international actors and the *Other* against whom 'justice' mechanisms ought to be employed so as to diffuse 'universal values'.

Yet, authoritative texts on transitional justice are outlined in a similar manner. For example, Teitel's analysis of the genealogy of transitional justice marks the discourse's key historical epochs as the period after Second World War, the post-Cold War era and the contemporary period of globalization which is distinct for its persistent conflict.[225] It is remarkable that in the period after the Second World War, former colonial powers were involved in conflicts aimed at suppressing anti-colonial movements as well as preventing the expansion of Communism.[226] After the Cold War, these operations gained prominence in postcolonial societies as armies of the superpowers increasingly turned to global peacekeeping and policing activities.[227] It is noteworthy that in these interventionist activities, Western powers have been implicated in conduct which the field of transitional justice

Rights Quarterly 781. An example of recognition of violation of human rights by non-state actors is the indictments of Ugandan rebels by the International Criminal Court on 7 October 2005.

220 See Orford (n.184).

221 Grovogui (n.112).

222 Anghie and Chimni (n.98) 85–86.

223 Bhabha (n.120).

224 Ibid.

225 Teitel (n.2).

226 See Daniel S. Papp, 'National Liberation during Detente: The Soviet Outlook' (1977) 32 *International Journal* 82.

227 See Sandra Whitworth, 'Where Is the Politics in Peacekeeping' (1995) 50 *International Journal* 427.

associates with the inhuman acts of 'rogue' authoritarian leaders of outgoing regimes.[228] To use Anne Oxford's words;

> [T]hat with which we charge the other – that it founds a masculinity, racially exclusionary, violent and nationalist political order on the expulsion and wounding of women and children – is in fact the basis of the international community as constituted through intervention narratives. The attempts to disavow this leads to more violence.[229]

This demonstrates that the practice of transitional justice is not a one-way process in which 'rogue' leaders of 'failed' states are either sanctioned or reconstituted in the image of an untainted benevolent international community. Rather, and to borrow from Bhabha's exposition on the ambivalence of the colonial exchange, an inevitable consequence of this contradictory colonial exchange is the occurrence of hybridity which creates opportunities for the appropriation of powerful imperial knowledge for anti-colonial resistance purposes.[230] These counter-colonial projects draw upon various local and hybrid practices to challenge, undermine and occasionally supplant the authority of the colonial discourse.[231]

A classic example of this hybridity and agency is the African Charter on Human and People's Rights (Banjul Charter) which emerged as a simultaneous reaction to dictatorship in postcolonial Africa and a site for resisting all kinds of imperialism.[232] At its birth, the Banjul Charter was seen as unconventional, since it went further than embracing an individualistic universal rights notion to also incorporate collective rights as well as economic, social and cultural rights.[233] Its crucial aspiration was captured in the *Social and Economic Rights Action Centre (SERAC) and the Center for Economic and Social Rights (CESR) v Nigeria decision* (*SERAC & CESR v Nigeria*), where the Commission aptly stated thus;

> [T]he uniqueness of the African situation and the special qualities of the African Charter on Human and Peoples' Rights impose upon the African Commission an important task. International law and human rights must be responsive to African circumstances. Clearly, collective rights, environmental

228 Susan A. Notar, 'Peacekeepers as Perpetrators: Sexual Exploitation and Abuse of Women and Children in the Democratic Republic of the Congo' (2006) 14(2) *American University Journal of Gender Social Policy and the Law* 421.
229 Orford (n.184) 287.
230 Bhabha (n.120).
231 Ibid.
232 African (Banjul) Charter on Human and Peoples' Rights, adopted 27 June 1981, OAU Doc. CAB/LEG/67/3 rev. 5, 21 I.L.M. 58 (1982), entered into force 21 October 1986. This spirit of the Banjul Charter can be discerned from its preamble. See also Julia Swanson, 'The Emergence of New Rights in the African Charter' (1991) 12 *New York Law School Journal of International and Comparative Law* 307.
233 See the discussion in Oloka-Onyango (n.197) and Swanson, ibid.

rights and economic and social rights are essential elements of human rights in Africa.[234]

It can be said that by engaging with and considering that features of African traditions and the values of the continent's civilization can be its foundation, the Charter undermines the original civilizing mission of human rights.[235] These developments however, do not obliterate the critique that because of its liberal bias, the transitional justice discourse may not be an appropriate tool for dealing with the postcolonial world's injustices.[236] Underlying tenets of liberalism do not amply consider these societies' political, economic and cultural conditions.[237]

A postcolonial legal reading could, however, attempt to strike a balance between, on the one hand, the need to decolonize humanitarian legal and human rights standards which form the normative basis of transitional justice and, on the other hand, a recognition that these international legal standards can be both viperous and redeeming. Further, and against the backdrop that globalization has reconfigured, disrupted and destabilized the notion of the sovereign state, postcolonial legal scholarship can also engage with non-state actors and other locations of power so as to holistically address rights and sites that concern injustices perpetrated on postcolonial subjects and women.

2.6 Conclusion

This chapter has defined transitional justice and also presented a postcolonial critique of the same. It has been explained that transitional justice discourses concern themselves with the democratization and liberalization of regimes that have previously stifled societal growth and human development through various proportions of authoritarianism and human rights atrocities. This discourse derives its normative basis from international human rights norms, standards of humanitarian law, international criminal law, international refugee law and ordinary criminal law. These standards are not just a product of transition; they actually play a constructive role in the passage to an acceptable democracy.

The spectrum of justice pursued at the point of transition is very wide and includes truth, justice, reparations and guarantees of non-recurrence. Measures adopted to address a dysfunctional justice sector are elements of guarantees of non-recurrence. Efforts passed to deal with land injustices are relevant to all four pillars of transitional justice. Legislation on group rights and political

234 Par 68, *Social and Economic Rights Action Centre & the Centre for Economic and Social Rights v Nigeria*. Cited as: Communication No. 155/96. (African Commission on Human and People's Rights, 27 October 2001) (hereinafter *SERAC and CESR v Nigeria*).

235 Par 4 preamble of the African Charter (n.232).

236 Gathii (n.191) and Alexander Reilly, 'Can Liberalism Be PC?: Duncan Ivison's Postcolonial Liberalism' (2003) 28 *Australian Journal of Legal Philosophy* 171. For a contrary view, see Duncan Ivison, *Postcolonial Liberalism* (Cambridge University Press 2002).

237 Ibid.

accommodation in transitional contexts is a subset of constitutional justice, which is an example of guarantees of non-recurrence. Truth-telling, criminal prosecution and reparations are measures which can be used to deal with the legacy of impunity and amnesia.

Postcolonial legal theories are among some of the most dominant critiques of the transitional justice discourse. They direct their criticisms at the discourse's foundational concepts, namely rule of law, liberalism, democracy and human rights. They start from the premise that the liberal notions of democracy, rule of law and human rights were invented by an authoritarian society. For postcolonial legal theorists, this dominant group is their former colonial masters. They focus on the rights of a group and not necessarily on individual rights. Finally, the theorists want economic, social and cultural rights to be at par with civil and political rights.

3 Rule of law and judicial independence

3.1 Introduction

As demonstrated in previous chapters, transitional justice facilitates the passage from violence and authoritarianism to a democracy which is committed to fundamental human rights and the rule of law. Since the conduct of the judiciary is an important element in the protection of human rights, and this body is presumed to be the axiomatic custodian of the rule of law, transitions necessitate the building or rebuilding of a judiciary that is independent.[1] Often, this arm of the state has been either undermined by the repressive regime or complicit in the outgoing administration's abuses of human rights. There can also be a case for a judiciary that lacks the capacity to deal with the challenges presented by the transition.[2]

Societies faced with such challenges have therefore (depending on the particular circumstances), adopted constitutional safeguards for the independence of the judiciary and retrained, vetted or left the tainted judges to reform through transformative adjudication.[3] In dealing with this transitional challenge international law steps in to provide legal certainty and a continuity that is often missing in the domestic rule of law.[4]

As we saw however, from the postcolonial legal critique presented in Chapter 2, international law cannot be said to be a neutral mediator since it lacks clarity, has imperial origins and is biased towards male Eurocentric ends. It can

1 Muna B. Ndulo and Roger Duthie, 'The Role of Judicial Reform in Development and Transitional Justice' (2009) *ICTJ*.

2 See Tanja Hohe, 'Justice without a Judiciary in East Timor' (2003) 3(3) *Conflict, Security and Development*, 335. Amnesty International, *Afghanistan: Re-establishing the Rule of Law* (London: Amnesty Secretariat 2003).

3 See Office of the United Nations High Commissioner for Human Rights, *Rule of Law Tools for Post-Conflict States, Vetting: An Operational Framework* (United Nations 2006), Office of the United Nations High Commissioner for Human Rights, *Rule of Law Tools for Post-Conflict States, Mapping the Justice Sector* (United Nations 2006), Donald P. Kommers, 'Transitional Justice in Eastern Germany' (1997) 22 *Law and Social Inquiry* 830, Ruti Teitel, *Transitional Justice* (Oxford University Press 2000) at 22–25 and Eric Brahm, 'Rule of Law' in G. Burgess and H. Burgess (eds) *Beyond Intractability* (Conflict Research Consortium, University of Colorado 2005).

4 Teitel, ibid at 20–21.

also be easily appropriated for hegemonic projects. Nonetheless, this imperial discourse does contain a space within it in which postcolonial struggles can be advanced.

Essentially, Chapter 2 contended that the practice of transitional justice, which is *prima facie* an imperialist discourse, is also open to seizure by the other. This is largely attributed to the ambivalent nature of the transitional civilizing mission. It is ambivalent in the sense that while the mission of globally perceived democracies is to use the law as an instrument of moulding so-called failed states in their image, the intention is not to achieve *de facto* equality. Otherwise, the colonial binary divisions of the *Self* and the *Other* would be erased. Such ambivalence awakens the postcolonial to the rule of law deficit in international legal enforcement measures. More importantly, an unexpected result of the ambivalent colonial project is the ensuing hybridity. This occurs when the dominant international law is combined with local concerns and understandings to produce mechanisms which are context specific. Such 'agency' is desirable and has sometimes resulted in transitional justice mechanisms which are legitimate and likely to foster sustainable peace.

Tensions between local history and the paradigmatic discourse can be read from Zimbabwe's experience with the rule of law and judicial reform since the country's transition from colonial rule to the current epoch.[5] Therefore, this chapter offers a scrutiny of the rule of law and judicial reform in transition with particular exploration of Zimbabwe as a case study.[6] In so doing it embraces postcolonial legal concerns which are largely overlooked in Western writings on the subject.

At the first instance, the chapter discusses international legal standards on the rule of law and judicial independence and relates them to transitional contexts. Second, it notes the relevant special challenges of postcolonial societies. This section gives detailed accounts of Zimbabwe's experience with the notion of rule of law and judicial independence. The content covers both institutional and individual independence read from an analysis of the institutional safeguards and the ability of individual judges to impartially adjudicate on contentious policy issues.[7] The issues that this background presents for the transition are examined. Third, the chapter offers a comparative analysis of relevant legal standards which were adopted by those postcolonial societies which have faced similar challenges in the past. Finally, the chapter concludes with viewpoints which are of relevance not only to the Zimbabwean passage from a dictatorship to an acceptable democracy, but to other similar postcolonial contexts.

5 On challenges to judicial independence in Zimbabwe, see Charles Goredema, 'Whither Judicial Independence in Zimbabwe' in B. Raftopoulos and T. Savage (eds) *Zimbabwe: Injustice and Reconciliation* (Institute for Justice & Reconciliation 2004) page 115.

6 For a general understanding on the rule of law and judicial reform in transitional countries, see United Nations Development Programme, *Judicial Independence in Transitional Countries* (Oslo Governance Centre, United Nations Development Programme 2001).

7 In Par 75, Laxmi Mall Singhvi, 'The Administration of Justice and the Human Rights of Detainees: Study on the Independence and Impartiality of the Judiciary, Jurors and Assessors and the Independence of Lawyers' *Final Report* (Geneva: United Nations 1985), U.N. Doc. E/CN.4/Sub.2/1985/18 and Add. 1–6 (1985). See also Lydia B. Tiede, 'Judicial Independence: Often Cited, Rarely Understood' (2006) 15 *Journals of Contemporary Legal Issues* 129.

3.2 Normative framework[8]

The legal basis for rule of law promotion projects is the UN Charter as read with international norms and standards on human rights law, humanitarian law, criminal law and refugee law.[9] The UN Charter which came into force in 1945 reaffirms belief in human rights, in individual dignity and worth and in the equality of men and women as well as states.[10] It also contains a determination by the international community to create conditions under which justice as well as adherence to international law can be sustained.[11]

This principle can also be found in the Universal Declaration of Human Rights (UDHR), which has it that the basis for peace, freedom and justice is the guarantee of an individual's inherent dignity in tandem with the recognition of equal and inalienable rights.[12] In Articles 8, 10 and 11, the UDHR clearly provides that everyone has a right to an effective remedy by independent and impartial courts that fairly and publicly hear cases and do not discriminate.[13]

These rights are restated and explicated in the International Covenant on Civil and Political Rights (ICCPR).[14] The ICCPR stipulates that the principles of legality and the rule of law ought to be maintained even in times of a state of emergency.[15] Indeed, in General Comment No. 29, the Human Rights Committee (HRC) clearly explained that the rule of law is of paramount importance during such times.[16] In their administration of justice, member states of the ICCPR are required to ensure equality before the law, and unprejudiced and public trials, that presume that the accused are innocent, among other minimum procedural safeguards. For the purposes of this analysis, Article 14 is worth particular attention since it states that:

> [A]ll persons shall be equal before the courts and tribunals. In the determination of any criminal charge against him, or of his rights and obligations in a suit at law, everyone shall be entitled to a fair and public hearing by a competent, independent and impartial tribunal established by law.[17]

8 For a brief discussion of the legal superstructure see Par 9 Secretary-General's report on the rule of law in conflict and post-conflict societies. S/2004/616.

9 Ibid.

10 Preamble, United Nations Charter, signed at San Francisco on 26 June 1945, entry into force 24 October 1945.

11 Ibid.

12 Preamble, Universal Declaration of Human Rights (hereinafter UDHR), G.A. Res 217 A (III) of 10 December 1948.

13 Articles 8, 10 and 11 UDHR.

14 See preamble, Articles 2, 4, 6, 9, 10, 12, 13, 14, 17 and 26 International Covenant on Civil and Political Rights (hereinafter ICCPR), G.A. Res. 2200A (XXI), 21 U.N. GAOR Supp. (No. 16) at 52, U.N. Doc. A/6316 (1966), 999 U.N.T.S. 171, entered into force 23 March 1976.

15 Article 4, ICCPR, ibid.

16 Par 2 General Comment No. 29: States of Emergency (article 4): 31/08/2001. CCPR/C/21/Rev.1/Add.11, General Comment No. 29 (General Comments) (hereinafter ICCPR General Comment No. 29).

17 Article 14 ICCPR.

In ratifying both the ICCPR and the *International Covenant on Economic, Social and Cultural Rights* (*ICESCR*), member states have committed to make progress towards the gradual realization of the rule of law by all suitable means. This includes constitutional and other legal provisions on the independence and impartiality of the judiciary.[18]

By way of General Comment No. 13, the HRC has noted that the provisional guarantees for the administration of justice stipulated in Article 14 apply to both criminal and civil charges.[19] They also relate to ordinary as well as specialized courts and tribunals.[20] In their periodic reports to the HRC, member states are obliged to state how they are progressively realizing these minimum guarantees.[21] Specifically,

> [S]tate parties should specify the relevant constitutional and legislative texts which provide for the establishment of the courts and ensure that they are *independent, impartial and competent*, in particular with regard to the manner in which judges *are appointed, the qualifications for appointment, and the durations of office; the condition governing promotion, transfer and cessation of their functions and the actual independence of the judiciary from the executive branch and the legislative* (emphasis added).[22]

HRC General Comment No. 13's interpretation of the concept of judicial independence and impartiality was further built consolidated by the UN Congress in 1985 when it passed the UN Basic Principles on the Independence of the Judiciary (*Basic Principles on the Independence of the Judiciary*).[23] These spell out the essential elements of the concept, which include the constitutional enshrinement of the principle of judicial independence by states who are obliged to respect and adhere to this notion.[24] The judiciary should be able to enjoy exclusive power to decide a case they are competent to handle, in accordance

18 Common Article 2 ICCPR, and International Covenant on Economic, Social and Cultural Rights, G.A. Res. 2200A (XXI), 21 U.N. GAOR Supp. (No. 16) at 49, U.N. Doc. A/6316 (1966), 993 U.N.T.S. 3, entered into force 3 January 1976 (hereinafter ICESCR). The UN Secretary General has explained that the rule of law is important in the protection of both economic and social rights and civil and political rights. See Par 9 Report of the Secretary General S/2004/616, supra note 8.

19 Pars 1 and 2, General Comment No. 13: Equality Before the Courts and the Right to a Fair and Public Hearing by an Independent Court Established by Law (Art. 14): 13/04/84. CCPR General Comment No. 13 (General Comments) (hereinafter ICCPR General Comment No 13).

20 Par 4, ICCPR General Comment No. 13.

21 Par 3, ICCPR General Comment No. 13.

22 Ibid.

23 U.N. Basic Principles on the Independence of the Judiciary, Adopted by the Seventh United Nations Congress on the Prevention of Crime and the Treatment of Offenders held at Milan from 26 August to 6 September 1985 and endorsed by G.A. resolutions 40/32 of 29 November 1985 and 40/146 of 13 December 1985.

24 Par 1, ibid.

with the law and without any pressure from anyone or any personal bias.[25] Judges ought to have security of tenure, be adequately remunerated and given enough resources to perform their functions.[26]

The *Basic Principles on the Independence of the Judiciary* also elucidate on the judiciary's right to freedom of expression and association, qualifications, appointments and training.[27] They also offer guidance on the manner in which judges can be disciplined, suspended or removed.[28] At the international level, these principles draw on, and have been repeated and further fleshed out by numerous principles which have resulted from conferences of bar associations and international jurists.[29]

From these international conventions as read with the HRC General Comments, several principles, declarations and recommendations that are included within the internationally accepted substance of judicial independence can be discerned. These comprise an institutional framework for judicial independence (separation of powers), financial mechanisms for judicial independence, arrangements for judicial security of tenure, sufficient remuneration for the judiciary, a transparent method of selecting, disciplining and removing judges and finally, judicial accountability.[30]

It can also be seen from these international standards that there are two elements of judicial independence: the 'institutional' and the 'individual'.[31] Institutional independence, or external independence, refers to judicial autonomy

25 Pars 2, 3, 4, 5 and 6, ibid.
26 Pars 7, 11, 12, 13, 14, 15 and 16, ibid.
27 Pars 8, 9 and 10, ibid.
28 Pars 17, 18, 19 and 20, ibid.
29 These include; Syracuse Draft Principles on the Independence of the Judiciary, Prepared by a Committee of Experts, Assembled by the International Association of Penal Law, the International Commission of Jurists and the Centre for Independence of Judges and Lawyers at Syracuse, Sicily on 25–29 May 1981, Montreal Universal Declaration on the Independence of Justice, Adopted during the 1st World Conference on the Independence of Justice, 1983, The Draft Universal Declaration on the Independence of Justice ('Singhvi Declaration'), Prepared by Mr L.V. Singhvi, UN Special Rapporteur on the Study on the Independence of the Judiciary, 1989, the Universal Charter of the Judge, Adopted by the International Association of Judges, on 17 November 1999 and The Bangalore Principles of Judicial Conduct (hereinafter Bangalore Principles of Judicial Conduct), Adopted by the Judicial Group on Strengthening Judicial Integrity (Judicial Integrity Group) as revised at the Round table meeting of Chief Justices held at The Hague, Netherlands, in 2002. Note that these principles were endorsed by the U.N. Social and Security Council Resolution 2006/23. Most of these have been discussed in: The Judicial Integrity Group, 'Commentary on the Bangalore Principles of Judicial Conduct' *Outcome of Open-Ended Inter-Governmental Expert Group Meeting held in Vienna on the 1st and 2nd of March 2007.*
30 James Melton and Tom Ginsburg, 'Does De Jure Judicial Independence Really Matter?' (2014) 2 *Journal of Law and Courts* 187.
31 See Par 75, Laxmi Mall Singhvi, 'The Administration of Justice and the Human Rights of Detainees: Study on the Independence and Impartiality of the Judiciary, Jurors and Assessors and the Independence of Lawyers' *Final Report* (Geneva: United Nations 1985), U.N. Doc. E/CN.4/Sub.2/1985/18 and Add. 1–6 (1985).

from outside forces which include the executive, legislature and political parties.[32] Individual or internal independence, on the other hand, implies that in the exercise of their judicial discretion, individual judges should be autonomous from their colleagues and personal prejudices.[33] Dr L.M. Singhvi noted in 1985 that the notion of judicial impartiality differs in a way from the idea of judicial independence.[34] It indicates autonomy from:

> [B]ias, prejudice and partisanship; it means not favoring one more than another; it connotes objectivity and an absence of affection or ill-will. To be impartial as a judge is to hold the scales even and to adjudicate without fear or favor in order to do right.[35]

The circumstances under which a judge can disqualify himself/herself from hearing a case on the basis of possible 'bias, favour or prejudice' are stipulated in *value 2.5* of the *Bangalore Principles of Judicial Conduct.*[36] Judicial independence in principle does not mean lack of judicial accountability. Nonetheless, courts should have discretional power to fulfil their role as the principal custodians of legality.[37]

3.3 Rule of law and judicial independence in transitions

> [T]he relationship between transitional justice and judicial reform exists at three levels. First, judicial reform can constitute an element of transitional justice. Second, judicial reform may facilitate transitional justice, and in some instances may be a precondition of certain justice measures, particularly criminal prosecution for human rights violations. Third, transitional justice may contribute to judicial reform efforts.[38]

In his 2005 report, Leandro Despouy, the United Nations Special Rapporteur on the independence of judges and lawyers, established a link between the need to re-establish judicial independence and transitional contexts.[39] He notes that while the principal justice challenges in the passage from an undemocratic regime to democratic rule are the right to truth, punishment of the perpetrators

32 See the discussion in Luu Tien Dung, *Judicial Independence in Transitional Countries* (Oslo Governance Centre, United Nations Development Programme 2003), and Tiede (n.7).

33 Ibid.

34 Par 79, Singhvi (n.31). This distinction is also made in values 1 and 2 of the Bangalore Principles of Judicial Conduct (2002) (n.29).

35 Ibid. Luu Tien Dung has further pointed out that this 'impartiality' relates to both the individual judge's exercise of judicial discretion and the adjudication process. Dung (n.32).

36 Value 2.5 *Bangalore Principles of Judicial Conduct (2002)* (n.29).

37 See Tiede (n.7).

38 Ndulo and Duthie (n.1).

39 Leandro Despouy (United Nations Special Rapporteur on the independence of judges and lawyers), 'Civil and Political Rights, Including the Questions of Independence of the Judiciary, Administration of Justice, Impunity' *2005 Report CHR E/CN.4/2005/60.*

and reparations for victims, there is also a dilemma as to how judges who were selected by the previous rogue regime can try those criminals.[40] Thus;

> [O]ne priority of the State in transition may therefore be to clean up the judiciary in order to restore its legitimacy, independence and impartiality, and hence its public credibility.[41]

Similarly, Diane Orentlicher, the Independent Expert on Impunity, has noted that legal and judicial reform are necessary to ensure respect for the rule of law and to foster as well as sustain a culture of human rights.[42] Such reform has sometimes taken the form of vetting, which refers to the removal of those judicial officers who are found to have been complicit in the previous regime's atrocities.[43] It is a way of holding a particular judge to account for his/her past behavior and to deter the same from engaging in similar conduct in future.[44] This builds or restores public trust in the legal institutions.[45]

In accordance with the UN Secretary General's 2004 report on the rule of law, vetting processes ought to be carried out in such a way that both the needs of victims and the due process rights of those suspected of having committed human rights abuses are taken into consideration.[46] Thus, as each judge should be treated on the basis of their individual record, wholesale purges are not recommended.[47] Of cause, vetting is one of the many post-conflict institutional reform measures which include, *inter alia,* transparent judicial selection processes, training of judicial officers, personnel policies and judiciary codes of conduct.[48] Often, provisions for the adoption of such measures are included in the particular post-conflict society's peace agreement or in a separate form and largely draw from relevant international and regional standards.[49]

3.4 The postcolonial context

It is impossible in such a focused study to discuss the rule of law challenges of all postcolonial societies. Thus this section gives a brief overview of the circumstances in postcolonial Africa. The colonization of Africa saw the establishment of

40 Pars 43 and 44, ibid.
41 Par 44, ibid.
42 Principles 36, 37 and 38 D. Orentlicher (Independent Expert to Update the Set of Principles to Combat Impunity), 'Updated Set of Principles for the Protection and Promotion of Human Rights through Action to Combat Impunity' 8 February 2005, E/CN.4/2005/102/Add.1.
43 Par 2, Report of the Secretary General (n.8).
44 Ibid.
45 Par 53, ibid.
46 Ibid.
47 Par 52, ibid.
48 Office of the United Nations High Commissioner for Human Rights, *Rule of Law Tools for Post-Conflict States, Mapping the Justice Sector* (New York and Geneva: United Nations 2006).
49 Ibid.

the colonialist's legal system.[50] Earlier processes of dispute resolution were seen as fit for natives only and thus could be applied only in rural areas.[51] Nonetheless, African societies have not rejected the imposed frameworks. In fact, international standards on the rule of law and judicial independence have been reproduced in various regional instruments.[52] In the case of postcolonial Africa, Articles 7(1d) and 26 of the *African [Banjul] Charter on Human and Peoples' Rights (ACHPR)* as well as developments in this area are worth special focus.[53] Article 7(1d) of the ACHPR states that:

> [E]very individual shall have the right to have his cause heard. This comprises: . . . d) the right to be tried within a reasonable time by an impartial court or tribunal.

Article 26 pronounces that member states have a duty to guarantee the courts' independence.[54] Further, ever since the adoption of international principles on judicial independence, a number of resolutions, declarations and principles have been produced by the ACHPR member states to clarify and reaffirm the notion of the independence of the courts in postcolonial Africa.[55] These commenced with the *Resolution on the Right to Recourse and Fair Trial* adopted in Tunisia in March 1992.[56] In this resolution, ACHPR state parties undertook to elaborate on the right to fair trial by an independent, competent court and to create

50 See Sandra F. Joireman, 'Inherited Legal Systems and Effective Rule of Law: Africa and the Colonial Legacy' (2001) 39(4) *Journal of Modern African Studies* 571, David M. Bigge and Amelie von Briesen, 'Conflict in the Zimbabwean Courts: Women's Rights and Indigenous Self-Determination in Magaya v. Magaya' (2000) 13 *Harvard Human Rights Journal* 289.

51 Joireman, ibid.

52 See Article 6(1), European Convention for the Protection of Human Rights and Fundamental Freedoms 213 U.N.T.S. 222, entered into force 3 September 1953, as amended by Protocols Nos 3, 5 and 8 which entered into force on 21 September 1970, 20 December 1971 and 1 January 1990 respectively (hereinafter ECHR), Article 8(1), American Convention on Human Rights, O.A.S. Treaty Series No. 36, 1144 U.N.T.S. 123, entered into force 18 July 1978 (hereinafter ACHR) and Articles 7(1) and 26, African [Banjul] Charter on Human and Peoples' Rights, adopted 27 June 1981, OAU Doc. CAB/LEG/67/3 rev. 5, 21 I.L.M. 58 (1982), entered into force 21 October 1986 (hereinafter ACHPR). In the Asian-Pacific area, where there is no regional human rights machinery, it is significant to note that chief justices met in Beijing in 1995 and adopted the Beijing Statement of Principles of the Independence of the Judiciary in the LAWASIA Region [1995] CCJAP Res 1 (19 August 1995) (hereinafter Beijing Principles). In Latin America, there is the Caracas Declaration which was adopted during the Ibero-American Summit of Presidents of Supreme Justice Tribunals and Courts, in Caracas, Venezuela, in 1998. For the Middle East, see the Beirut Declaration and Recommendations of the First Arab Conference on Justice, Adopted in Beirut, 14–16 June 1999.

53 See Charles M. Fombad, 'A Preliminary Assessment of the Prospects for Judicial Independence in Post-1990 African Constitutions' (2007) *The Denning Law Journal* 17.

54 Ibid.

55 See ACHPR <www.achpr.org/english/>.

56 Resolution on the Right to Recourse and Fair Trial, ACHPR/Res.4 (XI) 92, <www.achpr.org/sessions/11th/resolutions/4/>.

greater awareness of this right.[57] This resolution was explicated upon by the 1996 ACHPR Resolution on the Respect and the Strengthening on the Independence of the Judiciary (hereinafter 1996 ACHPR Resolution).[58]

The 1996 ACHPR Resolution linked the notion of judicial independence to justice which it considered to be a key aspect of both human rights and democracy.[59] A credible, impartial and competent judiciary was said to be necessary for a sustainable democracy and development.[60] The resolution also pronounced that the role of the judiciary was not just the preservation of law and order, but also economic advancement.[61] It thus called upon state parties to respect the principle of judicial independence and to make their domestic legislation consistent with the notion, in particular with respect to the manner in which judges are appointed and selected.[62] Member states were also implored to meet some minimum standards for the recognition of the independence of the judiciary.[63] These include, *inter alia*, providing sufficient resources to the judiciary (subject to international assistance), improving working and living conditions for judges and the adoption of universal principles affirming judicial independence by member states in their national laws.[64]

The 1996 ACHPR Resolution was further developed by the 1999 Dakar Declaration and Recommendations on the Right to a Fair Trial in Africa (Dakar Declaration and Recommendations).[65] Apart from clarifying previous pronouncements, the Dakar Declaration and Recommendations extended the principle of judicial independence and impartiality to military courts, special tribunals and traditional courts.[66] Quite significantly, the recommendations embrace a gender perspective, noting the necessity for effective female representation in the judiciary and also that procedures for the administration of justice should not discriminate against women.[67] It also recognizes that judicial law enforcement officials need to receive training in gender awareness.[68] A similar commitment

57 Pars 4 and 5, ibid.

58 Resolution on the Respect and the Strengthening on the Independence of the Judiciary (1996), ACHPR/Res.21(XIX)96:

59 Ibid.

60 Ibid.

61 Ibid.

62 Ibid.

63 Ibid.

64 Ibid.

65 Dakar Declaration and Recommendations on the Right to Fair Trial in Africa, adopted by Resolution on the Right to Fair Trial and Legal Aid in Africa (1999): ACHPR/Res.41 (XXVI) 99. In the same year and in accordance with the Resolution on the Right to Fair Trial and Legal Aid in Africa (1999), Principles and Guidelines on the Right to a Fair Trial and Legal Assistance in Africa <www.achpr.org/instruments/principles-guidelines-right-fair-trial/>.

66 Pars 2, 3 and 4, ibid.

67 *Dakar Declaration and Recommendations on the Right to Fair Trial in Africa*, The notion of gender parity is also incorporated in the Resolution on the Establishment of an Effective African Court on Human and Peoples' Rights: ACHPR/Res. 76 (XXXVII) 05.

68 *Dakar Declaration and Recommendations on the Right to Fair Trial in Africa*, Equally, noteworthy, are the recommendations that judicial officials had a role to play in ensuring that

to gender equality was also made at Harare in 1991 by former British colonies.[69] Quite significantly, by way of the *Harare Declaration of 1991,* Commonwealth members determined that their political values were;

> [D]emocracy, democratic processes and institutions which reflect national circumstances, the rule of law and the independence of the judiciary, just and honest government; fundamental human rights, including equal rights and opportunities for all citizens regardless of race, color, creed or political belief.[70]

Commitment to these values was affirmed and elaborated on by the *Latimer House Guidelines on Parliamentary Supremacy and Judicial Independence for the Commonwealth* and by the *Commonwealth Principles on the Accountability of and the Relationship between the Three Branches of Government.*[71]

These developments are consistent with international standards and also give insights into the special concerns of African postcolonial societies. The first of these is that of limited resources.[72] This is of great significance since failure by such states to adequately remunerate the judiciary has often bred corruption in these polities. It is axiomatic that corrupt judges cannot impartially interpret the law. The second issue is that of legal illiteracy gleaned from the recognition by state parties that their judiciaries may require training in gender awareness. The third is the view that rule of law projects have to advance the goal of development. This is a very controversial issue which may contradict Thomas Carothers's liberal notions of the rule of law. This issue was examined in Chapter 2, where it was demonstrated that the co-relation between market-based notions of the rule of law and development is contentious.[73] This view will be qualified by the Zimbabwean experience to be presented here.

---

their independence was protected, including curbing practices like corruption which often undermine their independence and impartiality.

69 Par 4, Commonwealth Secretariat, 'Harare Commonwealth Declaration' (1991) <www.thecommonwealth.org/ (Last visited 10 June 2009) (hereinafter *Harare Declaration 1991*).

70 Par 9, 'The Harare Commonwealth Declaration' (1991) <http://thecommonwealth.org/>.

71 Latimer House Guidelines on Parliamentary Supremacy and Judicial Independence for the Commonwealth, Guidelines on Good Practice Governing Relations between the Executive, Parliament and the Judiciary in the Promotion of Good Governance, the Rule of Law and Human Rights to Ensure the Effective Implementation of the Harare Principles (Adopted at Latimer House in the United Kingdom, June 1998, updated March 2002) (hereinafter Latimer House Guidelines). The Latimer House Guidelines were later revised and approved by the Commonwealth Heads of Government in 2003 as the Commonwealth Principles on the Accountability of and the Relationship between the Three Branches of Government (hereinafter the Principles).

72 This explains why the provision of adequate remuneration has been subjected to international assistance.

73 Chapter 3. See also Paul T. Zeleza and Philip J. McConnaughay (eds), *Human Rights, the Rule of Law and Development in Africa* (University of Pennsylvania Press 2004).

3.5 Zimbabwe: the rule of law and judicial independence

To fully comprehend the issue of rule of law and judicial independence in Zimbabwe (formerly called Southern Rhodesia), one first has to consider the circumstances which prevailed in the country's transition from a racist colonial past to black majority rule.[74]

3.5.1 Southern Rhodesia

The British South African Company, which administered the territory, introduced on 10 June 1891 Roman–Dutch Law as it was administered in the Cape of Good Hope. Since this law already had English traces, it was inevitable that English common law also became a significant part of the legal system.[75] Thus, Southern Rhodesia had a dual legal system: Roman–Dutch common law, which governed white settlers; and customary law, which applied to natives.[76] Roman–Dutch common law was administered by the common law courts, and customary law was interpreted by tribal chiefs in African civil disputes courts and tribal courts.[77] On this note, it needs to be pointed out that African tribal courts had no jurisdiction to handle criminal matters.[78]

This does not mean that the criminal justice system was integrated.[79] There was special legislation dealing with African criminal matters which, significantly, did not include trial by jury for blacks, even though criminal matters involving whites were subject to trial by juries.[80] The rationale for this differentiation was that jurors who were mostly white would not understand the mindset of black people.[81] One could dismiss this justification on the grounds that even the white adjudicators who presided over matters relating to black people did not really understand the mentality of the accused. Africans could not even expect

74 For a scrutiny of the rule of law in Southern Rhodesia, see Christopher H. Zimmerli, 'Human Rights and the Rule of Law in Southern Rhodesia' (1971) 20 *International Law and Comparative Law Quarterly* 239.

75 For example, J.H. Jeary has noted that the Roman–Dutch criminal procedure was supplanted by the English criminal procedure when the Cape of Good Hope became a British colony. See J.H. Jeary, 'The Structure, Composition and Jurisdiction of Courts and Authorities Enforcing the Criminal Law in British African Territories' (1960) 9 *International and Comparative Law Quarterly* 396. See also *Richard Mapolisa v R* (Southern Rhodesia, Privy Council Appeal No. 19 of 1964. Judgment delivered on 10 November 1964).

76 Joireman (n.50).

77 The structure of the courts before independence has been briefly discussed by Andrew Ladley, 'Changing the Courts in Zimbabwe: The Customary Law and Primary Courts Act' (1982) 26(2) *Journal of African Law* 95.

78 Jeary (n.75).

79 Zimmerli (n.74) 286–287.

80 Ibid.

81 Ibid. See also the discussion in Emmet V. Mittlebeeler, 'Race and Jury in Rhodesia' (1968–1969) 15 *Howard Law Journal* 181. Claire Palley, 'The Judicial Process: UDI and the Southern Rhodesian Judiciary' (1967) 30(3) *Modern Law Review* 263 at 264 offers an analysis of the nexus between the race of the judges and their judgements.

an effective remedy from the chiefs who presided in their civil dispute courts and tribal courts as the office bearers were not necessarily the traditional successors to that office.[82] Even those who were legitimate heirs could be said to have been tainted since their remuneration was based on their collaboration with the establishment.[83]

Nonetheless, this section highlights not detailed accounts of the Rhodesian court structures and jurisdictional issues, but those matters related to the rule of law and judicial independence.[84] This necessitates a brief descriptive analysis of the clauses on the judicature incorporated in the territory's 1961, 1964, 1965 and 1969 Constitutions.[85]

Subsequent to the annexation by the British Crown in 1923, Rhodesia became a self-governing colony of the United Kingdom and received the 1961 Constitution from the Southern Rhodesia (Constitution), Order in Council.[86] The split-up of the Central Africa Federation necessitated the repeal and substitution of the former with the 1964 Constitution (hereinafter referred to as the 1961/1964 Constitution).[87] This Constitution incorporated a Declaration of Rights which had to be safeguarded by High Court Judges.[88] It also embraced the notion of separation of powers.[89] Justice Fieldsend had this to say on this issue;

> [T]he powers and duties of the separate organs of government are prescribed, and for any organ to act in contravention of those provisions is illegal. This puts a particular responsibility upon the judiciary, which is raised in effect to a position above that of the other elements of government, and which is the only sure guardian of the terms of the Constitution.[90]

Matters relating to the qualifications, appointment and tenure of the judges were dealt with in Chapter V, which created the High Court of Southern Rhodesia (HC), made up of an Appellate and a General Division.[91] It expressly established HC judges' security of tenure and provided strict rules for their removal.[92] Rhodesian HC judges were to be appointed by the Governor on the advice of

82 Claire Palley, *The Constitutional History and Law of Southern Rhodesia, 1888–1965* (Clarendon Press 1966).

83 Ibid.

84 There is analogous work by Zimmerli (n.74). See also Jeary (n.75).

85 Palley (n.81).

86 Ibid.

87 Constitution Amendment Act, 1964 of Southern Rhodesia.

88 Chapter VI, s57–72, 1961/1964 Constitution.

89 See assertions by A.J.A. Fieldsend in *Madzimbamuto v Larder-Burke N.O and Another, N.O, Baron v Ayre, N.O and Others, NN.O.*, 1968(2) S.A. 284 (R.A.D) (hereinafter the Constitutional Case) at 424.

90 Ibid.

91 S50, 1961/1964 Constitution.

92 S56A and S56B, 1961/1964 Constitution.

the Prime Minister' and required to take an oath of allegiance to the Queen of England before assuming duty.[93]

Thus, on the face of it, it could be said that Southern Rhodesia's institutional framework conformed to Western or international values of limited government and adherence to human rights norms. Claire Palley has, however, exposed the racial substance which was central to this seemingly enabling legal framework.[94] For example, she notes that in situations whereby the declaration of rights prevented the government from curtailing the civil liberties of its opponents, the state frequently took advantage of the shortcomings in the law to impede the application of those liberties to blacks.[95] In some cases, the extension of individual rights to blacks was done away with either through specific legislation or by judges who were biased towards the maintenance of law and order rather than the rule of law and human rights.[96]

Nevertheless, a state of emergency was declared in 1965 by Ian Smith and his supporters who, on 11 November, issued a Declaration of Independence (UDI), suggesting that Southern Rhodesia had ceased to become a British colony.[97] The conduct of Smith and his colleagues was motivated by apprehension that Britain would attempt to defend its liberal credentials by granting the territory black majority rule. In the opinion of the white settlers, the black majority could not provide civilized leadership. Nonetheless, the UDI was pronounced illegal by the Governor, who dismissed the Prime Minister and his administration.[98] The later ignored the Governor's declaration and their dismissal and indicated that they were adopting a new Constitution (the 1965 Constitution) which they substituted with the republican Constitution of 1969.[99]

Most of the provisions which dealt with the judicature before UDI were preserved by the 1965/1969 Constitution, save for the oath of loyalty to the Queen, and the provision that Rhodesian HC judges had to be appointed by the Governor.[100] The office of the Governor was in fact abolished, but the judges who served under the 1961 Constitution were retained.[101] S128(4) of the 1965

93 Sections, 1(1), 54(1), 54(3) and 55, ibid.

94 Palley (n.81).

95 Ibid.

96 Ibid. See, however, *Minister of Justice and Law and Order v Musarurwa and Others,* 1964 (3) S.A. 209(S.R).

97 Ibid. On the state of emergence, see Zimmerli (n.74).

98 See Southern Rhodesia Constitution Order, 1965 (S.I. 1965 No. 1952. United Kingdom).

99 The relevant sections of these Constitutions are discussed in *Adams v Adams* [1971] page 188.

100 Chapter VI, S56 (3), Rhodesian 1965 Constitution.

101 The 1965 Constitution did not provide for a Governor. Its chapter 11 allowed for an 'officer administering the government in and over Rhodesia'. See also S128(1) which stated: 'The High Court of Southern Rhodesia in existence immediately prior to the appointed day shall be deemed to have been duly constituted as the High Court of Rhodesia under this constitution'.

Constitution is worth special attention as it permitted the previous bench to continue in office on condition that the Prime Minister or his messenger insist that any of the judges should obey the 1965 Constitution, swear allegiance to it or leave office.[102]

Initially, most of the judges were contemptuous of this provision and were reluctant to pronounce that the UDI government was a *de jure* government.[103] Yet, they continued in office purportedly to sustain peace and good governance as well as for the maintenance of law and order.[104] In a later judgement of *R v Ndlovu*, however, the judges had changed their minds, choosing to defer to the authority of the UDI government and the 1965 Constitution.[105] From this background, it can be imputed that the judges who continued to serve under the UDI regime were either compromised or complicit in the racial realities which were fundamental to the Rhodesian legal structure.[106]

The notion that judges who served during the UDI period were tainted could be qualified by their attitude towards the state of emergency which existed throughout this period.[107] It is axiomatic that the rule of law cannot exist in a state of emergency.[108] Yet, there is ample evidence that the Rhodesian judiciary condoned the existence of a permanent state of emergency.[109] Chief Justice Beadle, for example, opined that:

> [P]roclamations made for the maintenance of public order and the preservation of peace must be regarded as matters of everyday occurrence in the conditions presently existing in Southern Rhodesia.[110]

Even without the state of emergency, it could not be said that the rule of law existed in Southern Rhodesia since legislative power was broadly delegated.[111] The executive also welded enormous powers which were largely unchecked.[112] Quite significantly, S84 of the 1969 Constitution curtailed the judicial power to deliberate on or declare that any legislation was inconsistent with the Declaration of Rights.[113]

102 S128 (4) Rhodesian 1965 Constitution. See the discussion in Claire Palley, 'The Judicial Process: UDI and the Southern Rhodesian Judiciary' (1967) 30(3) *Modern Law Review* 263.
103 Palley, ibid. See also *Madzimbamuto v Larder-Burke N.O and Another, N.O, Baron v Ayre, N.O and Others*, 1968(2) S.A. 284 (R.A.D).
104 Ibid.
105 *Ndhlovu v The Queen* (1968) (4) S.A. 515.
106 This issue has been discussed by Palley (n.109).
107 See Zimmerli (n.74).
108 Ibid.
109 Ibid.
110 In *Madzimbamuto v Larder-Burke N.O and Another, N.O, Baron v Ayre, N.O and Others* (n.103) 353.
111 Zimmerli (n.74).
112 Ibid.
113 S84, 1969 Constitution of Rhodesia. See the discussion in Zimmerli (n.74).

Without dwelling too much on the past, in colonial Rhodesia, the rule of law meant conformity to the written law which at most protected white settlers' privileges.[114] The composition of the legislature, executive and judiciary did not reflect any equity in terms of gender, physical ability and racial equity.[115] All three arms of the state were at most the preserve of a white minority.[116] Pundits writing on the subject largely describe the Rhodesian legal system as having been imperialistic and its adjudicators, including tribal chiefs, as stooges who at most relied on governmental patronage.[117]

3.5.2 *Zimbabwe: institutional framework*

> [T]he essential questions we have posed constantly to ourselves and which we insist must be understood by all seriously concerned with a solution include the following . . . 4. What type of administration and judiciary shall serve the people of our country, Zimbabwe . . .? 7. Whose laws will govern such elections?. These and similar issues are those which should be placed on the agenda of this Conference and before the world if real peace is to return to our beloved Zimbabwe.[118]

The establishment of the rule of law and the need for judicial reform was part of the agenda of the male-dominated Lancaster House elite group which deliberated on arrangements for the move from Rhodesia to Zimbabwe.[119] Thus, they produced a Constitution (hereinafter referred to as Lancaster House Constitution) which guarantees equality in the function of the law.[120] This Lancaster House Constitution was in use until 2013. It was the supreme law of Zimbabwe, meaning that any laws which were not consistent with it were of no legal force.[121]

The Lancaster House Constitution was *prima facie* compatible with international and regional instruments on the rule of law and judicial independence. This is because it incorporated provisions which *prima facie* protected both the individual and the institutional independence of the judiciary.[122] Specifically, it

114 Ibid.
115 Goredema (n.5).
116 Ibid. The profiles of some of the HC Rhodesian judges can be found in Palley (n.81).
117 See Palley (n.81) and Zimmerli (n.74).
118 Speech by Joshua Nkomo on behalf of the Patriotic Front at the Constitutional Conference held at Lancaster House in 1979, page 11. Annex A, B; Southern Rhodesia: Report of the Constitutional Conference, Lancaster House: London, September–December 1979; <https://sasspace.sas.ac.uk/5847/5/1979_Lancaster_House_Agreement.pdf>.
119 Report of the Constitutional Conference, Lancaster House: London, September–December 1979, ibid.
120 S18, Lancaster House Constitution of Zimbabwe.
121 Section 3, Lancaster House Constitution of Zimbabwe.
122 See Lovemore Madhuku, 'Constitutional Protection of the Independence of the Judiciary: The Position in Southern Africa' (2002) 46(2) *Journal of African Law* 232, and Goredema (n.5).

prescribed the powers and duties of the separate arms of the state.[123] It also focused on the manner in which judges are appointed, their security of tenure, their remuneration, restrictions on the removal of judges and the issue of their removal.[124] Quite explicitly, section 79B of the Constitution stated that;

> [I]n the exercise of his judicial authority, a member of the judiciary shall not be subject to the direction or control of any person or authority, except to the extent that a written law may place him under the direction or control of another member of the judiciary.[125]

This express pronouncement on judicial independence was, however, weakened by a constitutional provision which permitted the legislature to confer the adjudicating role on a person or authority other than the courts.[126] This stipulation, which resulted from a constitutional amendment made ten years after Zimbabwe's independence, is ironically a revival of the situation in Rhodesia.[127] It presented a challenge to the concept of judicial independence, more so in a country where the ruling party controlled parliament. It enabled government to bypass the courts in contentious issues by vesting judicial authority in compromised bodies.[128]

Another weakness of the Lancaster House Constitution was that the President had exclusive control over the appointment of High Court and Supreme Court Judges. This is because the Lancaster House Constitution provided that these judges shall be appointed by the President after consulting the Judicial Service Commission (JSC).[129] The President was not obliged to consider the recommendations of the latter as the Lancaster House Constitution took into cognisance the possibility of appointments which are inconsistent with the views of the JSC. If the President decided to disregard the choice of the JSC, he/she only had to inform parliament of this inconsistency.[130] There was no provision on what parliament should do upon receipt of that information. Further, it cannot be said that recommendations from the JSC safeguarded against the appointment of judges on the basis of their loyalty to the establishment since the JSC itself was composed of presidential appointees.[131]

These weaknesses, amongst others, were factored when a new home-grown Constitution was adopted in 2013. As in the Lancaster House Constitution, the 2013 Constitution has a clear statement for the protection of judicial

123 See in particular Chapters IV, V and VIII, Lancaster House Constitution of Zimbabwe.
124 S84, 86, 87 and 88, Lancaster House Constitution of Zimbabwe.
125 S79B, Lancaster House Constitution of Zimbabwe.
126 S79 (2), Lancaster House Constitution of Zimbabwe.
127 Zimmerli (n.74).
128 Madhuku (n.122) 233.
129 S84(1) Lancaster House Constitution.
130 S84(2) Lancaster House Constitution.
131 S90 Lancaster House Constitution.

independence.[132] However, it has a more transparent method for the appointment of judges. In S180 it states that:

> [T]he Chief Justice, the Deputy Chief Justice, the Judge President of the High Court and all other judges are appointed by the President in accordance with this section 2. Whenever it is necessary to appoint a judge, the Judicial Service Commission must – a. advertise the position; b. invite the President and the public to make nominations; c. conduct public interviews of prospective candidates; d. prepare a list of three qualified persons as nominees for the office; and e. submit the list to the President; whereupon, subject to subsection (3), the President must appoint one of the nominees to the office concerned.

Before elaborating on other provisions which strengthen or undermine the independence and impartiality of the judiciary, it needs to be pointed out that there are various levels of adjudicative tribunals in Zimbabwe.[133] The judiciary power of Zimbabwe vests in the magistrates' courts and in customary law courts which are inferior courts and act as courts of first instance in certain criminal and civil cases. The High Court, Supreme Court and Constitutional Court are superior courts. The High Court hears appeal cases from the lower courts and also has original jurisdiction on grave criminal cases and unlimited jurisdiction in civil cases.[134] The Supreme Court is the final court of appeal except in matters over which the Constitutional Court has jurisdiction.[135] The Constitutional Court deals with constitutional matters and disputes concerning the election of the President and Vice President.[136] There are other courts with specific mandates; examples are the Administrative Court and the Labour Court.[137] There is no jury system, although an allowance is made for assessors in some cases.

Minimum qualifications for persons who can sit as High Court, Supreme Court Constitutional Court, Labour Court and Administrative Court judges are stipulated in the Constitution.[138] This contributes to the independence of the judiciary, since merit-based appointments reduce the risk of having political appointees.[139] According to Dr Lovemore Madhuku, selecting judges from a restricted class reduces the risk of political appointees because there may be few individuals from that select group who are willing to become political instruments.[140] Also, ethics which bind members of the restricted group may prevent

132 S164(1), 2013 Constitution of Zimbabwe.
133 See S162, 2013 Constitution of Zimbabwe.
134 S171, 2013 Constitution of Zimbabwe.
135 S169, 2013 Constitution of Zimbabwe.
136 S167, 2013 Constitution of Zimbabwe.
137 S162(d) and (e), 2013 Constitution of Zimbabwe as read with S172 and S173, 2013 Constitution of Zimbabwe.
138 S177, S178 and S179, 2013 Constitution of Zimbabwe.
139 It is consistent with Article 14 ICCPR as read with Par 3 ICCPR General Comment No 13.
140 Madhuku (n.122) 241.

them from sacrificing the law so as to defer to political powers.[141] Similar sentiments were uttered by Gubbay CJ in the case of *Banana v Attorney General* where he opined:

> [O]nly a remote possibility exists of a judge imbued with basic impartiality, legal training and power of objective thought, being consciously and subconsciously influenced by extraneous matter.[142]

In the same case, however, the Supreme Court of Zimbabwe accepted that as part of the human race, judges have human weakness and can be influenced by adverse information which is not part of court records.[143]

Nonetheless, hope for protecting the independence of the judiciary can be gleaned from the constitutional provisions on the superior courts judges' security of tenure and remuneration.[144] The salaries of High Court and Supreme Court judges are periodically fixed by an Act of Parliament and paid out of the Consolidated Revenue Fund.[145] They cannot be reduced during the judge's tenure.[146]

The Constitution provides that Constitutional court judges are appointed for a non-renewable term of 15 years, after which they can be appointed as judges of the High Court or Supreme Court.[147] High Court and Supreme Court judges may serve until they reach the age of 70. A superior court judge can be removed only under three exceptional circumstances, namely, incapacity to discharge duties because of a mental or physical ailment, gross incompetence or gross misconduct.[148] The decision on whether or not to remove a judge on the grounds mentioned here can be arrived at only after investigation by a tribunal whose concluding observations should be obeyed by the President.[149]

3.5.3 *The record of individual judges*

Challenges to the rule of law and judicial independence in Zimbabwe are much more multifarious than the obvious issues relating to an enabling institutional framework. This can be traced back to the decolonization process. This work will thus scrutinize four significant historical periods which relate to Zimbabwe's official policies towards the rule of law and judicial independence.[150] Such a scrutiny

141 Ibid.
142 CJ Per Gubbay in *Banana v Attorney General*, 1999 (1) BCLR 27 (ZS).
143 Ibid at 36.
144 S186 and S188, 2013 Constitution of Zimbabwe.
145 S188, 2013 Constitution of Zimbabwe.
146 Ibid.
147 S186(1), 2013 Constitution of Zimbabwe.
148 S187, 2013 Constitution of Zimbabwe.
149 S187(7 and 8), 2013 Constitution of Zimbabwe.
150 Just like any discussion on the Zimbabwean crisis, there are different narratives on when exactly the rule of law collapsed in Zimbabwe, According to the Hon. Anthony Gubbay, for example, it all started with the abduction of the editor and reporter of an independent

explains how the Lancaster House umbra still affects the coming to terms with the past and paving the way forward during the state's in-system reform.[151] The four distinct epochs are: 1980–1987, 1988–1999, 2000–2008 and 2008 to date.

a. 1980–1987

In 1980, at independence, while the legislative and the executive bodies were transformed, pragmatic considerations of efficiency and capacity led to the retention of an allegedly tainted colonial judiciary that reflected white, male supremacy.[152] Justice McDonald, for example, an ardent supporter of Ian Smith's UDI racist regime, was responsible for the swearing in of Robert Mugabe, the Prime Minister elect, on the day of Independence.[153] This retention of the colonial judiciary was to be used later by the Mugabe regime at an opportune moment as a trump card.[154]

Apart from inheriting the colonial judiciary, independent Zimbabwe also retained the legal framework for nullifying the rule of law.[155] The state of emergency which Smith's UDI had used for detaining nationalists without trial was kept by the new regime for the first ten years.[156] This meant that during that period, the government could infringe on citizens' liberties without the threat of a constitutional challenge.[157] The new regime's justification for keeping the legislation which it had previously described as 'repressive' and 'fascist' was that those laws were now necessary for the prevention of neighboring apartheid South Africa's destabilization efforts.[158] Equally noteworthy is the fact that even the security personnel who were involved in the violation of human rights during the Rhodesian era remained in their offices.

---

newspaper (Mark Chavunduka and Ray Choto) in 1999. The Hon. Anthony Gubbay, Address delivered for the John Foster Charitable Trust Annual. Lecture, 5 November 2001, pages 4–8.

151 This point was made in Chapter 1.

152 Goredema (n.5).

153 See O.N. Musamirapamwe, 'The Evian Agreements on Algeria and the Lancaster Agreements on Zimbabwe: A Comparative Analysis' (1982) 12 *Georgia Journal of International and Comparative Law* 153, and Xan Smiley 'Zimbabwe, Southern Africa and the Rise of Robert Mugabe' (1979–1980) 58 *Foreign Affairs* 1061.

154 In the post-2000 era this fact was used to justify a radical land reform exercise. For direct quotes of statements by government officials, see Goredema (n.5).

155 See Derek Matyszak, 'Democratic Space and State Security: Zimbabwe's Public Order and Security Act' (2005) <http://archive.kubatana.net/>, and John Hatchard, 'Detention without Trial and Constitutional Safeguards in Zimbabwe' (1985) 29 *Journal of African Law* 39.

156 S68(1) of the Lancaster House Constitution of Zimbabwe stated that the state of emergency which existed in Rhodesia was considered to continue to be effective on and after independence as if it were declared under this provision. See S14 Zimbabwe Constitution (Transitional, Supplementary and Consequential Provisions) order 1980.

157 Matyszak (n.155).

158 Ibid. See also Peter Costea, 'The Legal System and the Judiciary in the Marxist Leninist Regimes of the Third World' (1990) 16 *Review of Socialist Law* 225 at 239.

The new government, however, did change some aspects of the colonial legal system.[159] These changes included the replacement of the colonial tribal court system with the 'people's courts'.[160] The antecedent of these courts were the 'people's revolutionary tribunals' which had been created by the ruling party nationalists during the liberation war.[161] It is significant to note that political morality, rather than customary law, was prioritized by these tribunals.[162]

Therefore, in the new Zimbabwe, the view was contrary to conventional legal expectation that in exercising their judicial review mandate, the judiciary acts as checks and balances against governmental excesses.[163] The conception became that since the legislature and the executive branch were composed mostly of nationalists who had fought during the liberation struggle and were elected by the people, they represented popular ideological, political and diplomatic interests.[164] The judiciary, on the other hand, was largely perceived to be a preservation of the oppressive past.[165]

The first clash between the executive and the judiciary took place in 1982, during the state of emergency in the case of *York v Minister of Home Affairs and Ors*, where two white farmers were arraigned for possessing weapons.[166] The state wanted to detain the two suspects continuously without trial on the basis that since they were being held under 'investigative' and not preventive detention, the rights enshrined in the constitution were not available to them.[167] The court opposed this reasoning and held that any form of detention without trial was unconstitutional.[168] Robert Mugabe, then Prime Minister, reacted by stating that the courts could operate in a manner with which they were comfortable, and the government would act as it pleased.[169]

Subsequent significant differences between the executive and the judiciary also arose in the 1985 case of *PF ZAPU v Minister of Justice* and the 1987 case of *Rushwaya v Minister of Local Government 1987 (1) ZLR 5*, when the Supreme Court held that it had the mandate to intervene in executive actions.[170] In disdain, the

159 See by Andrew Ladley, 'Changing the Courts in Zimbabwe: The Customary Law and Primary Courts Act' (1982) 95 *Journal of African Law* 26.
160 Costea (n.158) 239.
161 Ibid.
162 Ibid.
163 Goredema (n.5).
164 Ibid.
165 Ibid.
166 *York v The Minister of Home Affairs and Others, HC-H-264-82/* and *Minister of Home Affairs v York & Another 1982 2 ZLR 48(SC)*.
167 Ibid.
168 See also Anthony R. Gubbay, 'The Protection of Fundamental Human Rights: The Zimbabwean Experience' (1997) 19 *Human Rights Quarterly* 228 and Adrian de Bourbon, 'Human Rights Litigation in Zimbabwe: Past, Present and Future' (2003) 3 *African Human Rights Law Journal* 195.
169 Goredema (n.5). See also Tendai Biti, 'A Predatory State and the Rule of Law in Zimbabwe' (1999), 1 *Zimbabwe Human Rights Bulletin* 97.
170 *Pf-ZAPU v Minister of Justice 1985 (1) ZLR 305, Rushwaya v Minister of Local Government 1987 (1) ZLR (5).*

executive reacted by asking parliament to pass Constitutional Amendment No. 7, which stipulated, amongst other issues, that the courts could not interfere with executive prerogatives.[171]

The biggest problem in Zimbabwe, then, was the executive's undermining of the judiciary, whereby then President Mugabe and his ministers verbally attacked judiciary members who made adverse judgements.[172] The latter also refused to carry out those court orders they perceived to be inimical to the interests of the state. Thus, while the inherited colonial judiciary did make progressive pronouncements on human rights–related issues, it was easy for the ruling party to undermine the same without inviting any public backlash.[173]

b. 1989–1999

The period between 1988 and 1999 saw marked economic, political and legal developments in the history of Zimbabwe.[174] These accounts had an acute impact on the relations between the three arms of the state and the masses.[175] They are also of much relevance to the issue of the rule of law and judicial independence.[176]

Economically, pressure from the Bretton Woods institutions and the conditionalities tied to foreign aid forced the government to withdraw its control of the domestic economy in 1990.[177] Thus, the era saw the introduction of economic structural adjustment programmes (ESAP), trade liberalization and the privatization of some parastatals.[178] As is typical of such reforms, standards of living declined.[179] The impoverishment of the masses was further exacerbated by recurring droughts and famines.[180] This led to increased calls for redress of

171 Constitution of Zimbabwe Amendment (No. 7) Act, 1987.

172 Goredema (n.5), Richard Carver, 'Zimbabwe: Drawing a Line through the Past' in Naomi Roht-Arriaza (ed) *Impunity and Human Rights in International Law and Practice* (Oxford University Press 1995) and Geoff Feltoe, 'The Rule of Law in Zimbabwe – A Façade of Democracy' in P. Morrel et al. (eds) *Civil Society and Justice in Zimbabwe: Proceedings of Symposium Held in Johannesburg 11–13 August 2003* (Pretoria: Themba Lesizwe 2003).

173 Examples of such progressive reasoning are; *Pf-ZAPU v Minister of Justice* 1985 (1) ZLR 305, *Rushwaya v Minister of Local Government* 1987 (1) ZLR (5). *York v The Minister of Home Affairs and Others,* HC-H-264-82 and *Minister of Home Affairs v York & Another* 1982 2 ZLR 48(SC).

174 For an insight into some aspects of political and economic changes, see Sam Moyo, 'The Political Economy of Land Acquisition and Redistribution in Zimbabwe' (2000) 26(1) *Journal of Southern African Studies* 5.

175 See Patrick Bond and Masimba Manyanya, *Zimbabwe's Plunge: Exhausted Nationalism, Neoliberalism and the Search for Social Justice* (University of Natal Press 2002).

176 Some aspects of this issue have been discussed in Adrian de Bourbon (n.168) 202.

177 Bond and Manyanya (n.175).

178 Ibid.

179 Ibid. Professor Geoff Feltoe, however, largely blames the government for the economic mess. To him, reference to the contribution of the international institutions is delusional. Geoff Feltoe, 'The Onslaught against Democracy and the Rule of Law in Zimbabwe' (2001) 4 *Zimbabwe Human Rights Bulletin* 130 at 132.

180 Ibid.

inequitable colonial distribution of land, as only the white commercial farmers had the best land and irrigation facilities. Decline in living standards also triggered serious opposition to the regime, mostly from trade unionists, student activists, women's organizations and human rights advocates.[181] The economic crisis is possibly a contributing factor to incidents of corruption which began to surface within the magistrates' courts.[182]

Politically, there were major constitutional changes to the state's legislative and executive structures.[183] In 1980, the Lancaster House Constitution provided for a bicameral parliament consisting of a House of Assembly and a Senate (upper house).[184] The House of Assembly had 100 members, 20 elected by white voters and 80 who were elected by the non-white voters' roll.[185] The senate consisted of 40 members, of which 14 were selected by the 80 House of Assembly members from the non-white common voters' roll, 10 were chosen by the white House of Assembly members, 10 were appointees of the council of chiefs and 6 were Presidential nominees on the advice of the Prime Minister.[186] Until 1987 this racial substructure could be amended only by a unanimous vote of parliament.[187]

In August 1987, as soon as the constitutional impediment ceased to exist, the clause providing for separate white representation in parliament was voided.[188] The Prime Minister's office was also abolished, and Robert Mugabe became the first executive president in that year.[189] On 22 December 1987, a unity accord was signed resulting in the merger of the ruling party and the then biggest political opponent, namely Joshua Nkomo's PF-ZAPU.[190] This implied that Zimbabwe was then a *de facto* one-party state.[191] Constitutional amendments also resulted in the abolishment of the Senate and the creation of a unicameral parliament.[192]

181 See Patrick Bond, 'Zimbabwe, South Africa, and the Power Politics of Bourgeois Democracy' (2002) 54(1) *Monthly Review* <www.monthlyreview.org/>. Organized opposition to the ruling party followed this pattern: first the food riots of 1996–1999, then the formation of the National Working People's Convention of February 1999 and finally, the birth of a formidable political party, the Movement for Democratic Change (MDC), in 1999.

182 Angela P. Cheater, 'Human Rights in Zimbabwe July–December 1999: A Baseline Report' (1999) 2 *Zimbabwe Human Rights Bulletin* 2 at 3.

183 See Constitution of Zimbabwe Amendment (No. 9) Act, Act 31/1989.

184 E (1), Annexure C, Southern Rhodesia: Report of the Constitutional Conference (n.118).

185 E (10) a & b, ibid.

186 E (6), ibid.

187 E (29), ibid.

188 Constitution of Zimbabwe Amendment (No. 9) Act, Act 31/1989.

189 For a discussion, see Brian Kagoro, 'Constitutional Reform as Social Movement: A Critical Narrative of the Constitution-Making Debate in Zimbabwe, 1997–2000' in B. Raftopoulos and T. Savage (eds) *Zimbabwe: Injustice and Reconciliation, Institute for Justice and Reconciliation* (Institute for Justice and Reconciliation 2004).

190 See Masipula Sithole, 'Zimbabwe's Eroding Authoritarianism' (1997) 8(1) *Journal of Democracy* 127.

191 Ibid.

192 S5, Constitution of Zimbabwe Amendment (No. 9) Act, Act 31/1989.

Quite significantly, this meant that the ruling party could pass legislation without any serious opposition.[193]

In the legal arena, three relevant developments that are inextricably linked to the heightened tension between the judiciary from the mid-1980s until the forced resignation of white judges in 1999 are worth noting.[194] First, Anthony R. Gubbay (Gubbay) was appointed Chief Justice of the Supreme Court in 1990.[195] Gubbay CJ is white, was born in England and was educated in South Africa and the United Kingdom.[196] At the time of his appointment as a Chief Justice, he had practiced law in Rhodesia and had served in the High Court of Rhodesia since 1977 and the Supreme Court of Zimbabwe since 1983.[197] Much more importantly, the then Chief Justice was renowned for his ardent support of judicial activism.[198] This is confirmed by his own assertions that;

> [T]he Supreme Court has utilized the technique of liberal interpretation with an eye to the spirit as well as the letter of constitutional provisions. We have endeavored to move away from formalism and to use judicial activism as a tool for making human rights a practical reality for the people. After all, a constitution is a living piece of legislation. . . . Judges should address human rights issues with boldness, imagination, and creativity. Their primary duty is to make the constitution grow and blossom in order to meet the just demands and aspirations of an ever-developing society.[199]

Thus, during Gubbay CJ's tenure, the Zimbabwean Supreme Court adopted a bold pro-active approach when interpreting fundamental rights.[200] It often had

193 See The Redress Trust, 'Torture in Zimbabwe, Past and Present: Prevention, Punishment, and Reparation? Survey of Law and Practice' (June 2005) page 17, <www.redress.org/publications>. Parliamentary elections took place in 1990, and Mugabe was re-elected with 78.3% of the vote. The other 21.7% of the votes were taken by Edgar Tekere's new party, the Zimbabwe Unity Movement (ZUM). With regard to parliamentary seats, ZANU PF won 117; two went to ZUM, and one to ZANU-Ndonga. Subsequent elections were held in 1995; once again ZANU PF won. However, both elections were marred by state-orchestrated violence against political opponents and their supporters. Initially, the executive saw electoral victory as conferring authority on the government to create a one-party state. This notion was vigorously opposed both domestically and internationally, and even internally within the ruling party itself. This growing discontent led to increased repression, which increased the tension between the executive and the judiciary.

194 Some of these issues are raised in Feltoe (n.179).

195 Anthony R. Gubbay, 'The Protection of Fundamental Human Rights: The Zimbabwean Experience' (1997) 19 *Human Rights Quarterly* 228.

196 Ibid.

197 Ibid.

198 Andrian de Bourbon is of the view that the period during which the Supreme Court was headed by Dumbutshena and Gubbay was the golden era of human rights in Zimbabwe. See de Bourbon (n.168).

199 Gubbay (n.195).

200 de Bourbon (n.168).

recourse to international human rights treaties and international comparative material when interpreting the rights stipulated in the Constitution.[201]

Second, in addition to the UN Convention against Torture and Other Cruel, Inhuman or Degrading Treatment or Punishment (CRT) and the International Convention on the Protection of all Migrant Workers and members of their families (ICRMW), Zimbabwe ratified or acceded to the other five core international human rights treaties.[202]

Third, the Lancaster House Constitution's ten-year moratorium relating to amendment of protective provisions of the Declaration of Rights expired in 1990.[203] In spite of its international commitments to human rights norms, the government used its newly acquired power to amend clauses on the Declaration of Rights as a reaction to the judiciary's liberal interpretation of constitutionally enshrined rights.[204]

Indeed, during this period the government often reacted to unfavorable rulings of the Supreme Court with constitutional amendments, thereby undermining both the Declaration of Rights and the judiciary.[205] For example, in 1989, in the case of *State v Juvenile*, the Supreme Court held that juvenile corporal punishment violated S15 of the Zimbabwean Constitution since it was cruel, inhuman and degrading treatment or punishment of young offenders.[206] At the same time, the court was due to hear a test case on the question of whether execution by hanging was cruel, inhuman and degrading punishment.[207]

In an apparent show of disdain for the *State v Juvenile* decision, and in an axiomatic pre-emption to anticipated judicial activism in the proposed execution by hanging test case, the executive did not resort to the verbal attacks of the 1980s. It rather used its majority representation in parliament to pass a constitutional amendment which added two savings clauses to Section 15(1) of the Constitution of Zimbabwe.[208] The savings clauses provided that corporal punishment inflicted upon male juveniles and execution by hanging shall not be held to be inhuman and degrading.[209]

On 14 January 1991, on the occasion of the opening of the 1991 legal year, Chief Justice Gubbay emotively articulated concerns of the judiciary regarding

201 See, for example, *S v Ncube and Others 1987 (2) ZLR 246(S)*, where the Supreme Court relied on international human rights comparative material to make a finding that adult corporal punishment was unconstitutional as it 'strips the recipient of all dignity and self-respect'.

202 See UN Human Rights Treaty Bodies' database <http://indicators.ohchr.org/>. Zimbabwe is also a state party to the African Charter on Human and People's Rights. However, it has not acceded to the statute of the International Criminal Court.

203 Annexure C, Southern Rhodesia: Report of the Constitutional Conference (n.118).

204 Biti (n.169).

205 Ibid.

206 *State v A Juvenile 1989(2) ZLR 61.*

207 Gubbay (n.195).

208 Ibid.

209 Constitution of Zimbabwe Amendment, Act 11/1990.

these savings clauses.[210] He particularly expressed the view that a justiciable bill of rights is strengthened by the executive and the legislature's lack of interference with the interpretive role of the judiciary.[211] For the legislature to restrict the application of a right which has been either interpreted by the judiciary, or is due to be deliberated on by the same, creates a bad precedent which is not reconcilable with both the notion of separation of powers and the independence of the judiciary.[212] Four days later, the executive's response to the Chief Justice's concerns was carried by the daily state-controlled newspaper, the *Herald*.[213] It stated that the judiciary had no jurisdiction in political matters. Robert Mugabe bluntly retorted that:

> [I]f certain laws are repulsive to the conscience of a Judge, then that Judge and conscience should not sit as a judge. Pure and simple.[214]

The Attorney General also stated unequivocally through the press that judges had no legislative mandate.[215] However, governmental attacks did not deter the judiciary from its activism.[216] In the 1993 case of *Catholic Commission for Justice and Peace v Attorney General and Others*, the Supreme Court held that delay in execution amounted to inhuman and degrading treatment and was therefore unconstitutional.[217] In 1994, it also held in *Rattigan and Others v Chief Immigration Officer* that the immigration authorities' refusals to grant permanent residence to foreign husbands of Zimbabwean women violated Section 22(1) of the Zimbabwean Constitution that provides for freedom of movement.[218] As usual, the executive reacted by approaching parliament for the promulgation of amendments which added savings clauses to the Constitution and had the effect of reversing the constitutional rulings of 1993 and 1994.[219]

Writing in 1995, Richard Carver stated that Zimbabwe has:

> [A] vigorous independent judiciary and a Declaration of Rights that is enforceable by the courts. It does not lack the institutional means to enforce respect for human rights. . . . The problem is essentially political rather than institutional.[220]

210 Biti (n.169) 102.
211 Ibid.
212 Ibid.
213 Ibid.
214 Ibid.
215 Ibid.
216 Ibid.
217 *Catholic Commission for Justice and Peace v Attorney General and Others* 1993 (1) ZLR (S).
218 *Rattigan and Others v Chief Immigration Officer*, 1994 (2) ZLR 54 (S). See also *In re Munhumeso*, 1994 (1) (ZLR) 61(S) & *Salem v Chief Immigration Officer*, 1995 (4) SA 280 (Zimb. Sup. Ct).
219 Amendments (No. 13) Act of 1993 and Amendment No (14) Act of 1996.
220 Carver (n.172) 79.

This work contends that the problem was essentially that of postponed legal and judiciary transformation in the passage from Rhodesia to Zimbabwe. For whilst the majority of the judges who were involved in the fall-out between the government and the judiciary in the period between 1989 and 1999 were appointed and promoted after the birth of Zimbabwe, the composition of the superior courts did not reflect any equity in terms of race, physical ability and gender.[221] On the question of the judiciary's gender representation, a study conducted by the Women and Law in Southern Africa (WLSA), in 1999, discovered that 58 out of 197 magistrates in Zimbabwe were women.[222] Out of the country's five Supreme Court Judges, only one was a woman, and there were only three female judges out of 18 High Court Judges.[223]

In this period, other racial sectors were overlooked while the white sector of the legal fraternity was favoured with a number of appointments.[224] This racial and gender bias in composition of the superior court benches, a reflection of the colonial era, meant that the governmental notion that judiciary opposition to the government in ideological, diplomatic and political interests was a betrayal of popular interests, and this betrayal resonated with a large sector of society.[225] This became more so in the period between 2000 and 2003 during the radical land redistribution process.[226]

The case of *Davies and Others v The Minister of Land, Agriculture and Water Development* is worth noting in this regard.[227] White farmers whose land had been designated in 1995 for acquisition by the government pursuant to *The Land Acquisition Act of 1992* (the Act) instituted a legal action whereby they contended that the designation of their farms was unconstitutional.[228] They argued that the Act granted the government the power to designate land for acquisition without requesting the title holders' consent.[229] While the court correctly held that the Act was not unconstitutional, its ruling was unsatisfactory in its reliance on American constitutional jurisprudence and its inattention to Zimbabwe's colonial legacy.[230] This failure by the judiciary to engage and acknowledge the injustices of the colonial era could be one of the explanations why, in 1999, the government

221 For identities of those who served on the Zimbabwean benches in different eras, see Otto Saki and Tatenda Chiware, 'The Law in Zimbabwe' *Globalex* (2007) <www.nyulawglobal.org>.

222 Women and Law of Southern Africa (2000), *In the Shadow of the Law: Women and Justice Delivery in Zimbabwe* (WLSA Trust 2000).

223 Ibid.

224 Goredema (n.5).

225 Ibid.

226 Ibid.

227 *Davies and Others v the Minister of Land, Agriculture and Water Development* 1997 (1) SA 228 (ZSC).

228 Ibid.

229 Ibid.

230 Rahman Ford, 'Law History, and the Colonial Discourse: Davies v Commissioner and Zimbabwe as a Colonialist Case Study' (2001) 45 *Howard Law Journal* 213.

managed to garner support in its campaign to force those judges who were seen as stumbling blocks in the alleged quest for social justice to resign.[231]

In reality, the colonial legacy can never be erased from Zimbabwe's legal system since it continues to have an effect on the tension between universal rights and the rights of the indigenous people to self-determination.[232] In addition to the issue of land reform discussed previously, a similar debate has arisen in the interpretation of customary law.[233] In this regard, the case of *Magaya v Magaya* is an illustrative example.[234] This case dealt with the issues of women's rights and inheritance law.[235] It involved sibling differences over heirship to their father's intestate estate.[236] Both the Community Court and the Supreme Court opined that males are rightful heirs under customary law and that regardless of their seniority, female children cannot be heirs when there is a male heir.[237]

This judgement was passed notwithstanding the fact that any kind of discrimination against women violates a number of international and regional instruments which bind Zimbabwe.[238] The Supreme Court even dismissed the contention that such an understanding was a breach of the constitutional protection against the discrimination of females.[239] According to Justice Muchechetere, who based his judgement on his own personal understanding of customary law, the constitutional creation of a binary division between customary and civil laws precluded this issue from being subjected to constitutional examination.[240] On the face of it, Muchechetere's reasoning is consistent with the emerging norm of group self-determination articulated in the Draft Declaration on the Rights of Indigenous Peoples (DDRIP).[241] Article 33 of the DDRIP states that:

> [I]ndigenous peoples have the right to promote, develop and maintain their institutional structures and their distinctive juridical customs, traditions, procedures and practices, in accordance with internationally recognized human rights standards.[242]

231 See International Bar Association (2001), 'Report Highlighting the Critical Situation Faced by Judges and Lawyers in Zimbabwe' <www.ibanet.org>.

232 See David M. Bigge and Amelie von Briesen, 'Conflict in the Zimbabwean Courts: Women's Rights and Indigenous Self-Determination in Magaya v. Magaya' (2000) 13 *Harvard Human Rights Journal* 289.

233 Ibid.

234 *Magaya v Magaya*, SC NO. 210–98; [1999] 3 LRC 35.

235 Ibid.

236 Ibid.

237 Ibid.

238 See Preamble, Convention on the Elimination of All Forms of Discrimination against Women, G.A. Res. 34/180, 34 U.N. GAOR Supp. (No. 46) at 193, U.N. Doc. A/34/46, entered into force 3 September 1981, Articles 2(1), 3 and 26 ICCPR & Articles 2 (2) and 3 ICESCR.

239 *Magaya v Magaya* (n.234).

240 Ibid.

241 Articles 3 and 33, Draft Declaration on the Rights of Indigenous Peoples, U.N. Doc. E/CN.4/Sub.2/1994/2/Add.1 (1994).

242 Ibid.

This case, therefore, highlights the difficulties of implementing a dual legal system developed by the former colonial masters, whose purpose for creating the structure could have been to foster the binary divisions between the *Self* and the *Other*. It is of interest to note that such divisions were maintained by the postcolonial government.[243] This is seen in that while all issues affecting white Zimbabweans and the black elite were under the jurisdiction of civil courts, family law and succession law matters involving poorer black people were still being addressed by customary law.[244] Anyone, however, can approach the Supreme Court on a constitutional question.[245] Deference to customary law by the Supreme Court in the *Magaya v Magaya* case is actually ironic. It points to the inconsistencies of the Gubbay-led bench which had notoriety for its frequent recourse to international law and its liberal application of human rights norms.

Another way of looking at it is that the case exposed the contemporaneous 'maleness' of the Zimbabwean Supreme Court. Lack of female representation in this superior court might have influenced the bench's seeming legal paralysis when it came to interpretations of women's rights and customary law.[246] This is verified by the fact that the legislature, which had a sound female representation, promptly responded to the post-*Magaya v Magaya* feminists' lobby by enacting a piece of legislation which overturned the decision.[247]

Thus, this era witnessed serious clashes between the executive and a judiciary headed by an activist white Supreme Court Judge. The government often reacted to unfavorable rulings of the Supreme Court with constitutional amendments, thereby inviting criticism that it was undermining the Declaration of Rights and the judiciary.

c. 2000–2008

> [N]o sane Zimbabwean should expect the judiciary to be headed by a foreigner – especially a British – 20 years after our independence, just like it would be insane to have a foreign or British president or speaker of parliament.[248]

Tensions between the government and the judiciary reached their peak between 2000 and 2001 in the advent of the fast track land reform process. In fact, global

243 Supra note 822.

244 Bigge and von Briesen (n.232).

245 Saki and Chiware (n.221).

246 See Amy S. Tsanga, 'Judges Must Be More Sensitive to Gender Issues' *Zimbabwe Independent*, 7 May 1999, cited in Bigge and von Briesen (n.232).

247 See Administration of Estates Act, Chapter 6:01 as amended to Act 22/2001, See also Par 6, Concluding observations of the Committee on the Elimination of Racial Discrimination: Zimbabwe, CERD/C/304/Add.92, and 4 April 2000.

248 These words were uttered in 2000 by then Government spokesman Jonathan Moyo and were first printed by the *Sunday News* (Zimbabwe), reproduced in BBC, 'Zimbabwe Fear Spreads' 6 June 2000 <http://news.bbc.co.uk/1/hi/world/africa/780172.stm>.

attention to Zimbabwe's alleged lawlessness and repression started when a draft Constitution prepared by a Government Commission was rejected at the polls in February 2000 for the reason that it sought to consolidate the position of the executive. The government's viewpoint, however, was that the rejection was due to a campaign by white commercial farmers who were opposed to the proposed new Constitution since this document would have empowered its administration to compulsorily acquire land without compensation for the actual value of the property.

Soon after the rejection of the draft constitution, sporadic farm invasions began, led by war veterans of the 1970s liberation war. While verbally and publicly accepting the outcome of the referendum, the government also passed a constitutional amendment which provided a framework for the acquisition of land from commercial farmers with compensation only for the improvements effected on the property and not for the cost of the land.[249]

Noting lack of governmental police intervention in the farm invasions, the Commercial Farmers Union (CFU) on several occasions obtained High Court and Supreme Court orders with the consent of the police commissioner, compelling the police to stop the unlawful farm invasions.[250] The law enforcement agencies simply ignored these orders. The Supreme Court also had occasion to deliberate on the legality of the government's fast track resettlement programme.[251] It held that the fast track land reform programme was haphazard and unlawful.[252] It also reasoned that the exercise was a serious disregard for the rule of law as the farm workers and the farmers had been deprived of the protection of the law.[253]

Government officials, war veterans, traditional chiefs and others, including President Mugabe, verbally attacked the judiciary for its reasoning in the fast track land reform cases. Patrick Chinamasa, the then Minister of Justice, found the racial character of the Supreme Court problematic. He linked the judicial reasoning of the Supreme Court to the bench's ties with Ian Smith's racist regime. Questioning the credibility of some of the justices, he stated:

> [H]ow can personnel so high up in the pecking order of a regime grounded in a racist grundnormfaithfully serve a democratic state.[254]

249 Constitution of Zimbabwe Amendment (No. 16) Act, 2000, Act 5/2000 commenced on 20 April 2000. See also the discussion in Amnesty International, 'Zimbabwe: Power and Hunger – Violations of the Right to Food (Report)' 15 October 2004 <www.amnesty.ie/zimbabwe-power-hunger-violations-right-food/>.

250 See, for example, *Commissioner of Police v Commercial Farmers Union*, 2000(1) ZLR 503(H).

251 *Commercial Farmers Union v Minister of Lands, Agriculture and Resettlement & Ors, Const.* Application no 262/2000.

252 Ibid.

253 Ibid.

254 SW Radio Africa, 'The State of Justice in Zimbabwe' December 2004 <www.swradioafrica.com/>.

In addition to verbal attacks, war veterans invaded the Supreme Court on 24 May 2000 asking for the resignation of the judges, especially Chief Justice Gubbay. No prosecution of perpetrators ensued.[255] In fact, the legislature reacted by passing the *Rural Land Occupiers (Protection from Eviction) Act* which barred courts from issuing eviction orders against farm invaders.[256]

The dangerous precedent established by the non-prosecution of those who had government backing was highlighted by Gillespie J in the case of *S v Humbarume and Anor.*[257] This case involved an individual who sought to coerce his ex-employer to pay some benefits which were due to him.[258] In so doing, he adopted the style of the war veterans, and through banging doors and chanting political slogans he was able to extort money from his ex-employer.[259] However, since he was not politically connected, he was prosecuted.[260] Against this background, Gillespie J, the judge who presided over these review proceedings, stated that this reflected a case of selective prosecution which posed a danger to the administration of justice.[261] Selective prosecution was also a contravention of the constitutional entitlement to equal protection of the law.[262] To this High Court Judge:

> [A] person who commits an offence and is prosecuted, while others who commit the same offence have official support and encouragement extended to them, as well as immunity from prosecution, is not receiving equal treatment at the hands of the law. A judge who finds he has to administer law only against opponents of the government and not against its supporters faces the challenge to his conscience; whether he can still sit as an independent judge in an impartial court.[263]

Nonetheless, the general feeling of those who hurled attacks on the white judges was that these judicial officers were allied with big business and the commercial farmers.[264] These were sectors which were under the control of Zimbabwean whites and Western countries perceived to be opposed to the economic empowerment and advancement of blacks. For example, in rationalizing his non-compliance with court orders, the Commissioner of Police stated:

255 This non-prosecution prompted the war veterans to further position themselves as the labour courts of the land. They purported to address unresolved labour grievances by occupying business premises, threatened management and violently demanded benefits of victims of alleged unfair labour practices.

256 *Rural Land Occupiers (Protection from Eviction) Act, 2001 (Chapter 20:26).*

257 *S v Humbarame and Another* 2001(2) ZLR 234(H).

258 Ibid.

259 Ibid.

260 Ibid.

261 Ibid.

262 Ibid.

263 Ibid.

264 Goredema (n.5).

> [T]hese are not disputed but suffice to point out that the rule of law which is divorced from justice and just laws becomes a hollow concept. Enforcement of unjust and iniquitous ethically land ownership structure, through the application of brutal state power, such as demanded by the respondent, is not promotive of the rule of law.[265]

Even the judiciary did not escape politicization.[266] For example, the then Judge President, Godfrey Chidyausiku publicly made statements insinuating that Chief Justice Gubbay favoured commercial farmers and had given white farmers assurances that if they approached the court on matters relating to land reform, they would be successful.[267]

In the midst of these disturbances, major rule of law concerns were raised, by human rights activists and academics, that with the complicity of the government, law enforcement agents were not impartial.[268] This was evidenced by the fact that they flouted court orders and were often in contempt of courts.[269] These actions of law enforcement agents and the government undermined the judiciary.[270] It was highlighted that the legal practitioners, in particular those who were human rights defenders, were often incarcerated, threatened with violence, assaulted or even tortured.[271] The government had also created draconian laws which it used as weapons against independent, dissenting and critical protesting voices.[272]

Further, there were echoes to the effect that issues of appointment, security of tenure and remuneration of judges needed revisiting.[273] Against this backdrop, and following intimidation and pressure from the government, the Chief Justice, and subsequently other affected judges, took early retirement.[274] Exclusively black appointments were thereafter made.

Consequently, the white, activist Chief Justice Gubbay was succeeded by Justice Godfrey Chidyausiku, who overtly supported of the fast track land reform programme.[275] The new Chief Justice had chaired the Constitutional Commission which produced the rejected draft Constitution. Interestingly, the Chidyausiku-headed Supreme Court overturned its precursor's ruling on the legality of the

265 Cited in International Bar Association (n.231).
266 Ibid.
267 Ibid.
268 Geoff Feltoe, 'The Rule of Law in Zimbabwe: A Façade of Democracy' in P. Morrel et al. (eds) *Civil Society and Justice in Zimbabwe: Proceedings of Symposium Held in Johannesburg 11–13 August 2003* (Pretoria: Themba Lesizwe).
269 Ibid.
270 Ibid.
271 Ibid.
272 Legislation which was criticized for being draconian included the Public Order and Security Act (Chapter 11:17) (POSA) and the Access to Information and Protection of Privacy Act (Chapter 10:27) (AIPPA).
273 Feltoe (n.268) and Goredema (n.5) 106.
274 Ibid.
275 Ibid.

land reform process.[276] It held that the land reform programme was 'not strictly speaking a legal issue', but a matter of 'social justice'.[277] The new judges also held that by legalizing the allegedly illegal occupations, the *Rural Land Occupiers (Protection from Eviction) Act* had re-established the rule of law.[278]

This raises a question of the appropriateness of the appointment of the new black judges, the purpose of whose nomination seems to have been to reverse the liberalizing tendencies of the Gubbay CJ Supreme Court, especially considering that in 2001 the issue of seniority was overlooked in the promotion of both the Judge President and the Chief Justice.[279]

Concerns particularly arose relating to the conception by civic society that the judiciary was now compromised.[280] These were magnified amidst revelations that the new appointees, including the Judge President and the Chief Justice, had acquired farms under the new fast track land reform process.[281] Although some of the post-2001 appointments could be said to be progressive in the sense that they involved the elevation of women into the superior courts bench, unease was caused by the information that most of these new judges had been previously connected to the ruling party.[282] Despite these pressures, the qualifications and competences of the judges appointed after the resignation of Anthony Gubbay have not been questioned.[283] In fact, they have been said to discharge their duties both impartially and professionally.[284] Actually, in the 2006 constitutional application of *Claudious Marimo & Movement for Democratic Change v the Minister of Justice Legal and Parliamentary Affairs & Ors*, the new appointees pronounced that the judicial appointment process must guarantee judicial autonomy from other state organs.[285] In making this decision, the bench expressly stressed the doctrine of separation of powers and judicial independence.[286] As Ziyambi JA aptly stated;

> [J]udges in Zimbabwe are appointed and hold office in terms of the Constitution of Zimbabwe. Their security and tenure of office is guaranteed by the

276 *Minister of Lands, Resettlement v Commercial Farmers Union* S-111-01 (2001).
277 Ibid.
278 Ibid. See also *Igudu Farm (Pvt) Ltd v Commissioner of Police & Ors*, HH-143-2001; *Trustees of Roper Trust v District Administrator, Hurungwe* (1) HH-192-2001; *Trustees of Roper Trust v District Administrator, Hurungwe* (2) HH-200-2001.
279 Note that the post of the Judge President is the highest position in the High Court and the Chief Justice is the head of the Supreme Court in Zimbabwe.
280 Goredema (n.5).
281 Further details of the beneficiaries, including the details of the farms they acquired are highlighted by Saki and Chiware (n.221).
282 For example, the then Judge President Rita Makarau is a former ZANU PF non-constituency member of parliament who served on the controversial year 2000 government Constitutional Commission.
283 Zimbabwean lawyers and academics who have written on the subject have not raised this issue. See Goredema (n.5) 106.
284 Feltoe (n.268).
285 *Claudious Marimo & Movement for Democratic Change v the Minister of Justice Legal and Parliamentary Affairs & Ors*, SC 25/06, Constitutional Application No. 160/05.
286 Ibid.

> Constitution. Thus the terms and conditions of their appointment cannot without their consent, be altered during their tenure of office. These provisions make for the independence of the judiciary from the other arms of the State being the executive and the legislature.[287]

It has to be noted that in respect to the contentious issue of land, the jurisdiction of the courts was effectively ousted by the Constitutional Amendment (No. 17) Act.[288] This amendment confirmed the fast track land reform process which commenced in 2000. It also permitted the retrospective application of the law as it concerns the acquisition and vesting of full title of the acquired land to the state. The jurisdiction of the Zimbabwean Courts to decide on the merits or any other issue relating to the acquisition of that land was also ousted. The Government of Zimbabwe perceived this ouster clause to be a reconstruction of the rule of law.[289]

Such an amendment, however, can be interpreted as a legislative abrogation of the rule of law since it had the effect of denying concerned citizens the right to effective remedy.[290] Actually, the African Commission on Human and People's Rights (African Commission) has held that such clauses violate Article 7 of the ACHPR on the right to remedy and Article 26 on the independence of the judiciary.[291]

Notwithstanding the fact that the need for the restoration of the rule of law is included in the GPA of 2008, the position of the government of Zimbabwe (goZ) has consistently been that theirs is a democratic state which adheres to the rule of law and human rights.[292] As far as the government was concerned, there is separation of powers; the three main state organs complement each other, and the judiciary is independent.[293]

d. 2008–2018

Between 2008 and 2018, there were three notable political changes in Zimbabwe. The first was the formation of a government of national unity (GNU)

287 Ibid.

288 Constitution of Zimbabwe Amendment (No. 17) Act, 2005, commenced 16 September 2005.

289 See Government of Zimbabwe Report to the 41st Ordinary Session of the African Commission on Human and People's Rights, ACCRA: Ghana, May 2007 <www.achpr.org/english/communiques>.

290 The right was enshrined in Article 18 of the Lancaster House Constitution of Zimbabwe. The right to effective remedy is also guaranteed in a plethora of international and regional instruments which are binding on Zimbabwe. These include Article 2 (3), ICCPR, and Article 7, ACHPR.

291 *Civil Liberties Organization v Nigeria*, African Commission on Human and Peoples' Rights, Comm. No. 129/94 (1995) & *Dawda Jawara v The Gambia, African Commission on Human and Peoples' Rights*, Comm. Nos. 147/95 and 149/96 (2000).

292 See, for example, the combined 7th, 8th, 9th and 10th periodic report submitted by the Government of Zimbabwe to the African Commission in terms of Article 62 of the ACHPR in October 2006.

293 Ibid.

made up of the Zimbabwe African National Union Patriotic Front (ZANU PF), the Movement for Democratic Change (MDC) led by Morgan Tsvangirai and the MDC led by Arthur Mutambara in February 2009.[294] The second change occurred in 2013 when the coalition government ended following ZANU PF's electoral victory. The third change was brought about by the bloodless coup of 2017, which saw the appointment of Emmerson Mnangagwa as the new president. This was followed by an election in 2018, which saw Mnangagwa's controversial election as the president.

The GNU's key transitional justice measure was the Constitution of 2013. The Constitution included guarantees for the independence of the judiciary[295] and established the National Peace and Reconciliation Commission (NPRC).[296] The NPRC's duties are to 'ensure post-conflict justice, healing and reconciliation'.[297] Although the NPRC was established in 2013, it became operational only after the adoption of the NPRC Act in 2018.[298]

Nonetheless, in 2013 a controversy surrounding judicial independence arose when High Court judge Justice Hungwe, was harassed in the state media and accused of professional misconduct.[299] He was alleged to have delayed to sentence a convicted murderer for ten years. Those who saw this as an attack on judicial independence suspected that he was being persecuted for granting a search warrant for the Zimbabwe Anti-Corruption Commission (ZACC) to search the offices of senior ZANU PF officials and the National Indigenization Economic Empowerment Board (NIEEB).[300] Hungwe's crime also appears to have been his issuing of a court order for the release of human rights lawyer Beatrice Mtetwa.[301] However, it may be simplistic to characterize Justice Hungwe as a persecuted anti-government judge since he is a war veteran who chaired the Zimbabwe National Liberation War Veterans Association when it was formed in 1990. War veterans were key supporters of the ruling party.

Therefore, it is difficult to use one particular incident to assess a judge's independence. For example, Justice Priscilla Chigumba was seen as independent when she struck down a statutory instrument used to ban street demonstrations in 2016.[302] Yet, in 2018 she was accused of being pro-government when she chaired the Zimbabwe Electoral Commission (ZEC).[303]

294 See Treda Mukuhlani, 'Zimbabwe's Government of National Unity: Successes and Challenges in Restoring Peace and Order' (2014) 2(2) *Journal of Power, Politics & Governance* 169–180.

295 Chapter 8, Constitution of Zimbabwe.

296 S251–253, Constitution of Zimbabwe.

297 S252, Constitution of Zimbabwe.

298 National Peace and Reconciliation Commission Act [Chapter 10:32]

299 See Jacob W. Chikuwa, *Zimbabwe, The End of a First Republic* (AuthorHouse UK 2013).

300 Ibid.

301 Ibid.

302 The Legal Monitor, 'Resisting Capture, Lawyers Judge Defend Independence of the Judiciary' 12 September 2016 <www.zlhr.org.zw/wp-content/uploads/2017/01/LM-Edition-353.pdf>.

303 See *Daily News*, 'Knives Out for Chigumba' 24 June 2018 <www.dailynews.co.zw/articles/2018/06/24/knives-out-for-chigumba>.

3.6 How to read Zimbabwe's experience with rule of law and judicial independence

As stated in the normative section, transitional judicial reform covers both the institutional frameworks and the individual record of judges in times of crisis. These two questions arise from Zimbabwe's experience with the rule of law and judicial independence.

3.6.1 *Institutional frameworks*

This chapter has demonstrated that both the Lancaster House Constitution and the new Constitution of Zimbabwe subscribe to the idea of rule of law and judicial independence. The two Constitutions embrace those aspects, which international and regional instruments have prescribed as measurements for the degree of judicial independence. Nonetheless, there were concerns with the Lancaster House Constitution. Some of these are the Constitution's lack of domestic legitimacy, existence of repressive legislation, possibility that adjudicating functions can be vested on compromised bodies and the presidential upper hand in the process of judicial appointment.

Thus, the adoption of the new Constitution in 2013 involved citizens in its construction so as to give the public a sense of ownership of the new legal framework of Zimbabwe. Zimbabwe is not the only postcolonial society whose independence Constitution resulted from an agreement entered into by a few elites.[304] Most postcolonial states have found it difficult to use imposed legal frameworks which do not take into account the needs and aspirations of their citizens.[305] This is more so given that dictatorial postcolonial rulers had during their tenure amended the Constitution to fit their goals.[306]

It logically followed, therefore, that a transitional agenda which does not include the revision of unjust laws and sanitization of the judiciary would lead to the wraith of Robert Mugabe's repressive regime haunting the new democratic dispensation a few years later. Legal and judicial reform would rebuild the independence and impartiality of this institution, thereupon contributing to the public tenability of both the judiciary and the laws. It would also establish a basis for an effective and efficient passage to peace and the rule of law. This explains regional and international organizations' emphasis on, for example, the repeal of repressive legislation as one of the preconditions to be met before a society can even negotiate terms for its transition to democracy.[307]

304 See Heinz Klug, 'Postcolonial Collages: Distribution of Power and Constitutional Models – With Special Reference to South Africa' (2003) 18 *International Sociology* 114, and Charles M. Fombad, 'Challenges to Constitutionalism and Constitutional Rights in Africa And the Enabling Role of Political Parties: Lessons and Perspectives from Southern Africa' (2007) 55 *American Journal of Comparative Law* 1.

305 Klug, ibid.

306 Ibid, and Fombad (n.304).

307 An illustrative example would be ¶6 (d), Declaration on Apartheid and its Destructive Consequences in Southern Africa, G.A. Res. S-16/24, secs. 5, 6(a), U.N.Doc. A/RES/S-16/1 (1990).

These concerns are actually reflected in Articles VI and XI of the 2008 Zimbabwean GPA which the work considers to be a peace agreement for facilitating Zimbabwe's transition from the regime which existed before the GNU.[308] This provision is not peculiar to the case of Zimbabwe, as similar concerns have been included in a number of recent postcolonial peace initiatives.[309] The clauses have addressed both the legal framework for establishing the rule of law and judicial independence and extra-legal measures for fostering and sustaining these imperatives.

3.6.2 The record of individual judges

The fate of white judges in Zimbabwe is evidence of how the ghost of Rhodesia continued to haunt Zimbabwe approximately 20 years after the country gained independence. This is because, despite these judges' progressive interpretation of constitutionally enshrined rights, Robert Mugabe's government was able to undermine them and their like-minded colleagues without inviting any marked domestic public outcry.[310] It may be that the lack of support for the judges was prompted by public acquiescence in the government's suspicion that the judiciary was perpetuating a continuation of an unequal racist past.[311] It could also have been a case of mere ignorance of the effect of the government's actions, since both the law and legal institutions in Zimbabwe are largely elitist. In fact, even human rights activism in Zimbabwe has historically been a preserve of white activists and a few black lawyers mostly employed in law firms associated with whites.[312]

308 Articles VI and XI Global Political Agreement <www.pindula.co.zw/Global_Political_Agreement>.

309 These include, *inter alia*, Article 24, Peace Agreement between the Government of the Republic of Sierra Leone and the Revolutionary United Front of Sierra Leone (RUF) (The Abidjan Agreement), Article 5, Accord between the National Government, the Political Parties, the M-19 and the Catholic Church in the capacity of a moral and spiritual guide for the process (March 1990, Columbia), Agreement between the Government of the Republic of Angola (GRA) and the Union for the Total Independence of Angola (UNITA) (Lusaka Protocol, 15 November 1994). Annexure B: Belfast Agreement (April 1998, Northern Ireland) which focused on the review of the criminal justice system, including the issue of arrangements for making appointments to the judiciary and magistracy, and safeguards for protecting their independence, agreement on the strengthening of civilian power and the role of the armed forced in a democratic society (September 1996, Guatemala) and Peace Agreement between the Government of the Republic of Rwanda and the Rwandese Patriotic Front (1993), see <www.incore.ulst.ac.uk/services/cds/agreements>.

310 Critiques of the government's conduct came only from Western-based international non-governmental organizations and the domestic elite.

311 It would have been possible for a lay person to conclude that the Supreme Court which had a 60% white composition and ruled against land reform was inclined towards preserving the status quo.

312 As of 2002, both the Zimbabwe Human Rights NGO Forum and the Zimbabwe Lawyers for Human Rights were headed by a white person with a foreign law degree (Beverly Hargreaves). Until late 2008, the Zimbabwe Human Rights NGO Forum was headed by a white

No legally sound evidence links sitting judges to the incumbent regime's human rights abuses. From the narrative in this chapter, it has been established that as far as the judges are concerned, they are willing to dispense impartial justice but are let down by inadequate funding.[313] They have expressly emphasized the principle of separation of powers and judicial independence.[314]

The legal qualifications of sitting judges is not an issue in Zimbabwe, as concerns of those who have contended that the post-Gubbay judiciary was compromised have been threefold. First, some of the new appointees had fought during the liberation war and had been formerly associated with the ruling party.[315] Second, it was asserted that promotions were not based on seniority and that under the Lancaster House Constitution, the President had unfettered power over their selection since he was empowered by the Constitution to act after consulting a JSC made up of his own appointees.[316] The President was not even required to take the views of the JSC into consideration.[317] Third, evidence that some of the new judges benefitted from the controversial land reform process has led to insinuations that the regime had bought their patronage, hence their judgement in favour of the land reform exercise.[318]

None of these allegations offers concrete evidence as to the incumbent benches' complicity in the state's repressive conduct. Surely, mere support for and active participation during the liberation war cannot correlate to a person's complicity in the nationalist government's post-independence atrocities. Such insinuations would logically question international attitudes of some of the judges who served in Gubbay's bench, including the Chief Justice himself, who had served in the courts of racist Rhodesia. To re-iterate, the Gubbay-led bench was hailed by both the International Bar Association and academics for being independent and progressive when it came to the interpretation of constitutionally enshrined rights.[319]

The President's enormous power over the appointment of the judges has now been rectified by the 2013 Constitution. Nonetheless, power over the appointment of judges does not necessary correlate to the judiciary's lack of independence. Judicial activist and Chief Justice Antony Gubbay, for example, was promoted by President Robert Mugabe, yet he clashed with the government on several occasions. There is also evidence that some of the judges appointed

---

person (Eileen Sawyer) and the chairperson of both the Zimbabwe Lawyers for Human Rights and Legal Resources Foundation (Nokuthula Moyo) was an employee of a white law firm.

313 Ibid.

314 *Claudious Marimo & Movement for Democratic Change v the Minister of Justice Legal and Parliamentary Affairs & Ors*, SC 25/06, supra notes 1050–52.

315 Saki and Chiware (n.221).

316 Goredema (n.5).

317 Ibid. But note the 2006 Supreme Court decision of *Claudious Marimo & Movement for Democratic Change v the Minister of Justice Legal and Parliamentary Affairs & Ors*, supra note 1197.

318 Saki and Chiware (n.221).

319 See Carver (n.172) as read with International Bar Association (n.231).

by Mugabe after 2000 have ruled against the government in certain politically charged matters. Quite significantly, an Afro barometer survey carried out by the University of Cape Town in 2006 found that public trust in the courts of both South Africa (an internationally hailed democracy) and Zimbabwe (a classified failed state) was at 43%, well ahead of peaceful Lesotho.[320] With regard to Zimbabwe, this study concluded that;

> [D]espite immense pressure and severe resource constraints, an underlying professionalism remains noticeable in many judgments, especially from the High Court.[321]

Judges' acceptance of farms during the land reform process cannot be said to be conclusive proof that the establishment bought their allegiance. This is because the general consensus in Zimbabwe accepts that the land reform process was desirable. Non-governmental organizations and the opposition parties have merely criticized the manner in which the process was carried out.[322] In fact, benefitting from land reform by judges cannot be said to be a case of illicit gain, since access to land was supposed to be open to every Zimbabwean who applied for it, and the official position was that names of all the beneficiaries were to be publicized in the public media.[323] Interestingly, even some opposition party parliamentarians were allocated farms.[324] It can also be contended that in the Zimbabwean context, where no public sector employee can survive on a salary, judges should be allowed to engage in other income-generating projects, as are other public service employees.[325]

Further, in a country like Zimbabwe where judges and magistrates are not required to disclose their incomes, assets or even liabilities, there is no evidence that in ruling against land reform, the Gubbay-led bench was truly defending property rights of every Zimbabwean.[326] It is most likely that either these judges

320 This is even more that the percentage of public trust in courts in peaceful Lesotho which is 40%. See Linda van de Vijver (ed), *The Judicial Institution, in Southern Africa, a Comparative Study of Common Law Jurisdictions* (Democratic Governance and Rights Unit, University of Cape Town 2006).

321 Ibid.

322 See Human Rights Watch, 'Zimbabwe: Fast Track Land Reform Program' 2002 <www.hrw.org/reports/2002/zimbabwe/ZimLand0302-02.htm>.

323 Government of Zimbabwe Online, 'Land Reform Program' <www.lands.gov.zw/landreform>. For a contrary view, see Goodhope Ruswa, 'A Study on the Impact of Governance on Land Reform in Zimbabwe' *Minithesis Submitted in Partial Fulfilments for the Degree of Master of Economics in the Institute for Social Development* (University of Western Cape, 2004) <http://etd.uwc.ac.za/>.

324 Professor Welshman Ncube, the Movement for Democratic Change Secretary General, is the most cited beneficiary of the land reform process. See Willmore Kanyongo, 'Powell Ignorant of Zimbabwean Situation' *Race & History*, 2 July 2003 <www.raceandhistory.com>.

325 The financial plight of judges was highlighted in Goredema (n.5).

326 *Commercial Farmers Union v Minister of Lands, Agriculture and Resettlement & Ors, Const.* Application, supra note 1006.

were protecting their own privileges, or the government was correct in its assertions that they were protecting big business. This is particularly since international law does not provide clarity on the issue of the right to property. This raises the question as to what core values should be protected by the Zimbabwean courts. Is it corrective or distributive justice? Was it not the duty of these courts to strike a balance between the rule of law and social justice concerns? In the era of globalization where non-state actors have more power over the government, should the concern over the independence of judges be on their independence from governmental pressure or big business as well?

3.7 Insights from other postcolonial polities

From the discussion in the last section, it can be said that while the strengthening of institutional provisions on the rule of law and judicial independence will obviously take some time and require a lot of funding, such programmes are feasible. However, this is not the case with the issue of personnel reform which is likely to be faced with practical and legal difficulties. Practically, and in view of Zimbabwe's small legal fraternity, wholesale purges based on suspicions of political affiliation may be tantamount to an illegitimate exercise which may deplete the much-depleted institutional capacity.

Also, notwithstanding this work's submission that judges' participation in the land reform process is not necessarily an indication of compromise, it recognizes the necessity for curtailing judges' participation in income-generating activities or business that may reduce public faith in their independence. This has an added significance in the passage from repression where the concern is not only with regaining public confidence in the judiciary, but also with re-building trust and positive perceptions among international actors. During Rwanda's transition to peace and democracy, this realization led to the inclusion in the Code of Ethics of a provision which stated that;

> [T]he functions of a career judge shall be incompatible with political mandate, any management and any other public or personal service, whether directly or by employing people.[327]

A similar spirit existed in the in-house reform processes of many other African countries such as Ghana and Tanzania, where legislation which provides that all public officials (including judges) are expected to disclose their income, assets and liabilities was adopted.[328] These pieces of legislation are part of the stratagem

327 Article 18, Law Relating to the Code of Ethics for the Judiciary, cited in Sam Rugege, *Paper presented at the Judicial Independence and Legal Infrastructure: Essential Partners for Economic Development Conference*, University of the Pacific, McGeorge School of Law' Sacramento, CA, 28 October 2005. <www.mcgeorge.edu/documents/Conferences/JUDIND_RUGEGE_MASTER.pdf>.

328 S286, Constitution of the Republic of Ghana (1992) as read with Public Office Holders (Declaration of Assets and Disqualification) Act 550/1998 & Part 111, Tanzania's Public

for curbing corruption, in tandem with establishing integrity and transparency in the public sector.[329]

In Ghana, the requirements for disclosure of assets was part of the Constitution which introduced democracy in 1992. This was preceded by the Public Office Holders (Declaration of Assets and Disqualification) Act 1998 (Act 550), which expanded the category of public officers expected to declare their assets and liabilities. In the judiciary those who were required to disclose their assets are the Chief Justice, judges of superior courts, regional tribunal chairman, Commissioner for Human Rights and Administrative Justice, his deputies and all judicial officers.[330] Quite significantly, in contrast to Rwanda, the legal framework of Ghana leaves open the possibilities for judges to have other sources of income.

In Tanzania, assets have to be declared by the Chief Justice, judges, magistrates and the Attorney General.[331] Uganda, on the other hand, prescribes that the Chief Justice and other judges down to the Chief Magistrate ought to disclose their assets.[332] It is of interest that assets which need to be disclosed include land, and in Tanzania, disclosure of farms is limited to those which are used for commercial purposes.[333]

Lessons can also be learnt from reforms introduced in Tanzania during the tenure of Chief Justice Francis Nyalali.[334] The Nyalali-led bench adopted a Code of Ethics for the judiciary which outlawed corruption.[335] This code was reinforced by a constitutional amendment which made its violation a basis for removal from the bench.[336]

A similar Code of Ethics was adopted in Rwanda during the 2003–2004 judicial reform process.[337] This Code requires that judges should be impartial, be diligent and have integrity. Corruption is specifically addressed in Article 7, with a provision to the effect that judges should fight against the practice and other similar criminal conduct in an exemplary manner. However, this Code of Eth-

---

Leadership Code of Ethics (No. 13) of 1995. See also Kenya's Prevention of Corruption Act 1965, Uganda's Leadership Code (Act No. 8) of 1991 and Mozambique's Ethics Law 1998.

329 See Alhaji B.M. Marong, 'Toward a Normative Consensus against Corruption: Legal Effects of the Principles to Combat Corruption in Africa' (2001–2002) 30 *Denver Journal of International Law and Policy* 99.

330 S286 (5) (e), Constitution of the Republic of Ghana 292.

331 Part I, Tanzania's Public Leadership Code of Ethics.

332 George A. Larbi, 'Between Spin and Reality: Examining Disclosure Practices in Three African Countries' (2007) 27 *Public Administrations and Development* 205 at 208.

333 S11 (2) (f), Tanzania's Public Leadership Code of Ethics (n.331).

334 Nyalali served as a Chief Justice of Tanzania from 1976 to 1999. See Jennifer A. Widner, *Building the Rule of Law: Francis Nyalali and the Road to Judicial Independence in Africa* (W. W. Norton & Company 2001).

335 Code of Conduct for Judicial Officers of Tanzania, adopted by the Judges and Magistrates Conference, 1984.

336 Widner (n.334) 279.

337 See Law relating to the Code of Ethics for the Judiciary, No 09/2004 of 29/04/2004.

ics complemented the vetting operation, which was the first step in the reform process. This entailed the termination of sitting judges' contracts and the making of fresh recruitments based on the legal qualifications and integrity of judges. Candidates who had a history of misconduct and corruption were not admitted to the bench. Quite significantly, due process rights of suspected judges were respected; that is, before the dismissal or exclusion of a candidate on the basis of corruption or misconduct, such allegations were first investigated by the Supreme Council of the Judiciary, and the accused judicial officer was given the chance to defend himself/herself.

George L. Larbi has demonstrated, however, that in Ghana, Uganda and Tanzania, such institutional measures did not necessarily translate into lack of corruption in public service.[338] Some enforcement challenges still exist.[339] In Ghana, for example, the Auditor General has no authority to take any action against those officials who provide false information or who do not comply with the law on declaration of assets.[340]

Thus, institutional arrangements for judicial independence and integrity should not be seen as isolated measures but as an aspect of a combination of mechanisms for rebuilding the rule of law and judicial independence. In Rwanda, some of these mechanisms included sensitizing the judiciary on the importance of judicial independence and integrity. This can be complemented by programmes which are aimed at improving the quality of justice, such as training court support staff on case-flow management methods so as to clear civil and criminal dockets.[341] To achieve these ends, in Tanzania, during the Nyalali era, an institute for training registrars and court clerks was established.[342]

Judges can also earn public confidence in their impartiality through transformative adjudication.[343] In particular, they can demonstrate their adherence to liberal democratic principles through the progressive interpretation of the rights incorporated in the Constitution.[344] Such a move was adopted by the South African Constitutional Court during the country's transition from apartheid.[345] The issue, which will be examined in greater depth in the next two chapters, is that international law does not provide clarity on controversial questions which reoccur in postcolonial contexts.[346] Examples of such legal questions which lack clarity are the right to property and the right to self-determination.[347] Nonetheless, judges in other postcolonial contexts, including Tanzania, have also promoted public understanding

338 Larbi (n.332).
339 Ibid.
340 Ibid.
341 Widner (n.334) 390.
342 Ibid.
343 Teitel (n.3) 22–25.
344 Ibid.
345 See, for example, *Government of the Republic of South Africa v Irene Grootboom and Others* (CCT11/00) [2000] ZACC 19; 2001 (1) SA 46; 2000 (11) BCLR 1169 (4 October 2000).
346 To be explored in Chapters 4 and 5.
347 Ibid.

and trust in the courts through participation in legal literacy programmes.[348] This involved regular contributions to newspapers as well as participation in law-related educational enterprises on television and radio.[349]

Judges can also protect their institution from legislative and executive interference through setting up partnerships with bilateral and international donors so as to attract funding for court reform programmes.[350] In Tanzania's transition to democracy, the Nyalali-led bench clearly recognized international donors as interim sources of financial assistance.[351] Similarly, Peter Vondoep has it that in 2001, such alliances assisted Malawian judges in preventing the legislature from impeaching their colleagues who had passed adverse judgements against the government.[352]

In view of the often weak economies of postcolonial transitional societies, the judiciary's partnership with foreign donors might be seen as commendable and pragmatic. Nevertheless, such alliances can be problematic in a postcolonial context. Indeed, in Zimbabwe, the perception that donor funding may result in the promotion of foreign interests over local needs, thereby undermining national sovereignty, can create cynicism. Indeed, the attachment of such suspicions to a pivotal state organ like the judiciary can be harmful to efforts at establishing sustainable peace.[353] It has been suggested that in Tanzania, such fears were laid to rest when judges had ensued that donor funding was open, targeted and effective.[354]

Experience, however, has shown that donors usually put their money in projects which advance their interests. These programmes usually benefit those who are already empowered, that is, foreign investors and the local elite. Concerns of the women and the poor are often sidelined. For instance, the World Bank has been traditionally renowned for its concentration on programmes aimed at strengthening the market. This has included improving debt-recovery methods, training judges in commercial law, arbitration and prompt dispensation of commercial disputes. Celestine Nyamu-Musembi has highlighted that less donor interest is shown in informal justice institutions where women and the poor predominate.[355] Such informal mechanisms are relevant in Zimbabwe, as they resolve disputes relating to family matters and most cases in rural areas where most Zimbabweans living in poverty reside.

348 Widner (n.334) 322.

349 Ibid.

350 Ibid at 394–395.

351 Ibid.

352 Peter Vondoepp, 'The Problem of Judicial Control in Africa's Neo-Patrimonial Democracies: Malawi and Zambia' (2005) 120 *Political Science Quarterly* 275 at 288 239 and Widner (n.334) 394–395.

353 These connotations actually contributed to the lawlessness in contemporary Zimbabwe.

354 H. Kwasi Prempeh, 'African Judges, in Their Own Cause: Reconstituting Independent Courts in Contemporary Africa' (2006) 4 *International Journal of Constitutional Law* 592.

355 Celestine Nyamu-Musembi, 'Ruling Out Gender Equality? The Post-Cold War Rule of Law Agenda in Sub-Saharan Africa' (2006) 27(7) *Third World Quarterly* 1193.

It is therefore preferable that Zimbabwe's anticipated rule of law programmes would also target informal judicial institutions. The South African model provides best lessons in this regard.[356] For instance, in addition to recognizing the juridical power of traditional courts, S211 of the South African Constitution subjects these informal institutions to the Constitution.[357] Also, the South African Law Commission (Commission) which consulted widely on the function of these institutions came up with some minimum standards for the function of these courts.[358]

In particular, the Commission recommended, *inter alia*, that there should be reasonable participation of women, that parties who were unsatisfied with the decisions of these adjudicating mechanisms should be free to pursue the matter in a tribunal of their choice and that individuals should not be compelled to participate in informal mechanisms.[359]

Finally, another innovation which is also contentious and can be borrowed from the Nyalali era is that of a temporary judicial collaboration with the politicians during the transitional phase.[360] In Tanzania, this involved judges' active participation in a presidential Commission whose recommendations facilitated Tanzania's passage from a one-party state to a multiparty democracy in the 1990s.[361] To re-iterate, such a move could be viewed with suspicion in Zimbabwe since the chairmanship of the former Chief Justice (Chidyausiku) in the 2000 Constitutional Commission is often cited as part of reasons advanced by those who are of the opinion that he was impartial.[362]

One could contend, however, that the transitional Commission will not be associated with the tainted regime; thus any judge's input into the process would not be contentious. However, judges' interactions with politicians might clash with the widely held view that the judiciary should be separated from the other two arms of state. A caveat to this could be that transitional periods are for nation-building and thus require the co-operation of all major stakeholders.

3.8 Conclusion

This chapter has highlighted those international norms which demonstrate that rebuilding the rule of law, including an independent judiciary, is essential in a country's passage from repression to democratic rule. In the case of Zimbabwe, it started from an understanding that Zimbabwe's racist colonial past affected the postcolonial government perception of its relationship to the judiciary. It demonstrated

356 Nyamu-Musembi (2006), supra note 597.

357 Section 211(3) of the Constitution of South Africa (1996) states that; 'The courts must apply customary law when that law is applicable, subject to the Constitution and any legislation that specifically deals with customary law'.

358 Nyamu-Musembi (n.355).

359 Ibid.

360 See Prempeh (n.354).

361 Ibid.

362 Supra notes 852–1172.

how in contrast to traditional legal understandings of the roles of the three state organs, the nationalist government saw itself as the true custodian of the people's rights.

This was in contrast to a judiciary which was not transformed in the country's passage from the white-minority regime of Rhodesia to black-majority rule and largely seen as a preservation of the repressive past. Thus, in common with other African postcolonial societies which gained their independence in the 1960s, Zimbabwe saw the judiciary as a stumbling block in its nation-building project. This was despite the sitting judges' public declarations that they were committed to the progressive interpretation of constitutionally enshrined rights.

The question of whether the Zimbabwean current judiciary is compromised was also explored. This work is not convinced by allegations put forward by those who have alleged that the bench is tainted. It sees the question as hinging on broader issues of the ideology which should inform the interpretation of constitutionally enshrined rights. Nonetheless, it recognizes that while vetting might not be a desirable option since it would be based on political opinion and might deplete the country's much-needed institutional capacity, public confidence in the judiciary has to be restored in the country's transition. There is also a realization that judges should desist from taking part in activities which might create public perceptions that they are not impartial in delivering their judgements. Thus, it recommended that the Zimbabwean judiciary has to disclose its assets and be sensitized on the concept of judicial independence as well as its value. This training can also be extended to the court support staff. Judges can also work towards earning public trust in their impartiality, integrity and independence, through legal literacy programmes, transformative adjudication and the creation of democratic space through the formation of alliances with donors.

The chapter further noted that the intervention of international actors can lead to the promotion of masculine Eurocentric ends. Nonetheless, it has recognized that some postcolonial societies have created a third space within the dominant discourse in which the needs of women and minorities have been included in the targeted donor projects. This demonstrates that whereas international law has acted as a reference point in postcolonial transitions, the imperial script has been modified to suit the local context.

Finally, it is unclear whether Zimbabwean judges who were appointed after 2000 may be compromised because of their judgement in favour of land reform. This is because international law does not provide clarity on the right to property. This theme will be developed in the ensuing chapter.

4 Land reform and transitional justice

4.1 Introduction

Using Zimbabwe as a case study, Chapter 3 addressed the issue of the rule of law and judicial reform in transition. In the discussion it emerged that the issue of land reform is a major issue of controversy which might have influenced public perceptions on the partiality or otherwise of the country's judiciary. This is a complex matter since international law does not provide legal clarity on how a postcolonial state can expropriate land within its territory without abandoning its adherence to Western notions of the rule of law. This chapter qualifies these assertions.

War and authoritarian rule often cause disruption to property rights.[1] Thus most countries in transition have to address conflicting property rights entitlements which range from facilitating refugees right to return to challenges that arise from the outgoing regime's expropriations.[2] Of these, this work confines itself to land issues which stem from prior expropriations. As stated in Chapter 2, this is a cross-cutting issue which touches on all the four pillars of transitional justice.

Dealing with land injustices in postcolonial transitions is in particular an extremely delicate matter, largely because of the mixed layers of expropriations which have occurred since the construction of most of these states.[3] These

1 Jon D. Unruh, 'Land and Property Rights in the Peace Process' in G. Burgess and H. Burgess (eds) *Beyond Intractability* (Conflict Research Consortium, University of Colorado 2004) <www.beyondintractability.org>.

2 The references on these issues are too many to be fully cited here. Nonetheless, see Rhodri C. Williams, *The Contemporary Right to Property Restitution in the Context of Transitional Justice* (International Center for Transitional Justice 2007), Jon D. Unruh, 'Postwar Land Dispute Resolution: Land Tenure and the Peace Process in Mozambique' (2001) 18 *International Journal of World Peace* 3, Jon D. Unruh, 'Local Land Tenure in the Peace Process' (2002) 1 *Peace Review* 337, John D. Unruh, 'Land Tenure and Legal Pluralism in the Peace Process' (2003) 28 *Peace and Change: A Journal of Peace Research* 352, and Jon D. Unruh, 'Property Restitution Laws in a Post-War Context: The Case of Mozambique' (2005) 1 *African Journal of Legal Studies* 147.

3 See Ndiva Kofele-Kale, 'Asserting Permanent Sovereignty over Ancestral Lands: The Bakweri Land Litigation against Cameroon' (2007) 13 *Annual Survey of International and Comparative Law* 103.

complexities can be recognized in postcolonial Zimbabwe's struggle with land reform since the country's independence and up to the present time.[4] Against this background, this chapter offers a scrutiny of land reform in transition with particular application to Zimbabwe. In no way is Zimbabwe entirely representative of all postcolonial societies, but it does depict a microcosm of a bigger picture.

The rest of this chapter consists of five parts. Section 4.2 provides the theoretical framework which establishes a nexus between land reform and transitional justice. Section 4.3 then explores the reality of land reform in postcolonial transitions. Obviously, it would be impossible to go in depth into all experiences of former colonies, thus the section considers the case of Zimbabwe. This is because Zimbabwe is the most recent former colony to embark on a land reform exercise which was dramatic in scale. Section 4.4 demonstrates the challenges which the Zimbabwean experience poses to the paradigmatic discourse. It substantiates its analysis by drawing on the experiences of other postcolonial societies. Section 4.5 follows on by using the relevant comparative material from postcolonial jurisdictions to illustrate the point that notwithstanding the limitations of international law, transitional contexts create an opportunity for *agency*. The outcome of such *agency* is not legal transplantation but mimicry of the dominant discourse. The chapter concludes with viewpoints which are useful when looking at how postcolonial post-conflict land experiences have contributed to transitional justice.

4.2 Land reform and transitional justice

There is a paucity of scholarship on land and transitional justice.[5] Paradigmatic transitional justice discourses are largely steeped in Western philosophies, thus there is a focus on violations of civil and political rights.[6] Key transitional justice pundits and practitioners tend to relegate efforts to address land rights and other socioeconomic rights to the forward-looking fields of development and the general protection of human rights.[7] Matthew Evans has suggested that transitional justice has no capacity to deal with land and other structural injustices; he has instead proposed the use of the tools of transformative justice.[8] Seemingly, transitional

4 See Alison van Horn, 'Redefining "Property": The Constitutional Battle over Land Redistribution in Zimbabwe' (1994) 38(2) *Journal of African Law* 144.

5 Bernadette Atuahene, 'Property and Transitional Justice' (2010) 58 *UCLA Law Review Discourse* (2010) 65.

6 Khanyisela Moyo, 'Feminism, Postcolonial Legal Theory and Transitional Justice: A Critique of Current Trends' (2012) 1(2) *International Human Rights Law Review* 237–275.

7 See essays in Pablo de Greiff and Roger Duthie (eds), *Transitional Justice and Development: Making Connections* (The Social Science Research Council 2009).

8 Matthew Evans, *Transformative Justice: Remedying Human Rights Violations beyond Transition*. Transitional Justice Series (Routledge 2018). See also Lars Waldorf, 'Anticipating the Past: Transitional Justice and Socio-Economic Wrongs' (2012) 21(2) *Social and Legal Studies* 171.

justice scholarship has not caught up with developments in human rights law on the indivisibility, interrelatedness, interdependence and equal hierarchy of rights.[9]

Nonetheless, land reform policies include 'restitution, land redistribution, tenure reform and compensation'.[10] And, as previously stated, transitional justice typically involves four kinds of approaches, namely, criminal prosecutions, truth recovery, reparations and legal and institutional reforms to restore confidence and avert recurrence of abuses. Of these transitional justice approaches, the vast literature has explicitly linked reparations to the land policies of restitution and compensation.

> [R]estitution concerns the reconstitution of property rights which preceded the outgoing regime's appropriations. In situations where restitution is not possible, victims are restored through compensation to the position they would have been in had no land expropriation taken place.[11]

Restitution and transitional justice have a shared genealogy and a common goal of returning victims to their pre-abuse status.[12] The United Nations Basic Principles and Guidelines on the Right to Remedy and Reparation for Victims of Gross Violations of International Human Rights Law and Serious Violations of International Humanitarian Law (UN Reparations principles) lists restitution and compensation as two of the four forms of reparations.[13] The subject matter of restitution includes a return to property, and this has now been extended beyond protecting legally held property to include unregistered rights in housing and land. This nexus with the right to housing provides stronger human rights protections as compared to rights to land and property which occupy an uneasy place in international human rights law. In post-conflict contexts, this has provided a legal basis for the return of displaced persons and refugees to their original homes.[14]

However, reparations in the form of restitution and compensation are not the only transitional justice mechanisms for dealing with past land injustices. Chris Huggins has linked land tenure reform to transitional justice in polities where

9 Evelyne Schmid and Aoife Nolan, '"Do No Harm"? Exploring the Scope of Economic and Social Rights in Transitional Justice' (2014) 8(3) *International Journal of Transitional Justice* 362–382.

10 Khanyisela Moyo, 'Mimicry, Transitional Justice and the Land Question in Racially Divided Former Settler Colonies' (2014) 9(1) *International Journal of Transitional Justice* 70–89 at 73.

11 Ibid.

12 Rhodri C. Williams, *The Contemporary Right to Property Restitution in the Context of Transitional Justice* (International Centre for Transitional Justice 2007) page 1.

13 Par 19 Basic Principles and Guidelines on the Right to a Remedy and Reparation for Victims of Gross Violations of International Human Rights Law and Serious Violations of International Humanitarian Law, U.N. Doc. A/Res/60/147.

14 See Principles on Housing and Property Restitution for Refugees and Displaced Persons, U.N. Doc. E/CN.4/Sub.2/2005/17 (Pinheiro Principles).

either land has been a root cause of the conflict, or there is a protracted and multifarious history of land dispossession.[15] He explained that:

> [G]reater coordination between transitional justice efforts and land tenure reform under the rubric of the rule of law in transitional societies would make for a more effective process of political and economic transition, one that better serves the interests of both justice and development.[16]

Also, a number of recent truth commissions such as those in Kenya[17] and Mauritius[18] have included the land issue in their mandates. These truth commissions have provided the primary platform for a dialogue on land issues within transitional justice processes.[19] They have also raised awareness of the root causes of the land conflict and created a shared narrative on land issues. Further, perpetrators of land violations such as displacement can be prosecuted.[20]

The literature discussed in this section links transitional justice to the land reform policies of restitution, compensation and land tenure. It does not include land redistribution as a transitional justice measure. This is because conventional notions of transitional justice are rooted in Western histories and philosophies. Both transitional justice and restitution are corrective justice measures; that is, they are about the justice administered by the courts in redressing either civil wrongs or crimes. Unfortunately, land restitution starts from the presumption that prior ownership or occupation was a result of just redistribution. Yet, this is not the case in postcolonial polities where land questions stem from colonial and pre-colonial dispossessions, arbitrary colonial borders and forced migration triggered by postcolonial wars. In the case of settler colonies, there is the thorny issue of racially skewed land structures and tenure which is a legacy of colonial rule.

> [P]ostcolonial states are a creation of colonialism and as such are still grappling with issues of nation building . . . in most of these countries land conflicts are associated with the state‘s struggle for permanent sovereignty over its economic and natural resources.[21]

This book recommends postcolonial innovation in conceptualizing transitional justice. A corrective justice measure is not adequate in context where the original distribution was unjust. Transitional justice can fulfil its stated goals if it also has

15 Chris Huggins, *Linking Broad Constellations of Ideas: Transitional Justice, Land Tenure Reform, and Development* (International Centre for Transitional Justice 2009).

16 Ibid.

17 S6(O), Republic of Kenya, The Truth, Justice and Reconciliation Act, No. 6 of 2008.

18 See Chapter 10, Volume 1, Report of the Truth and Justice Commission <www.usip.org/sites/default/files/ROL/TJC_Vol1.pdf>.

19 Huggins (n.15).

20 Roger Duthie and Paul Seils, *The Case for Action on Transitional Justice and Displacement Strategies during and after Conflict* (International Centre for Transitional Justice 2016).

21 Moyo (n.10) at 7*.

a redistributive dimension. How can it strive to deal with the root causes of conflict without distribution when, in most cases, the ideological contestation around justice as redistribution is the root cause of the conflict? It is trite to state that colonialism was a scheme of systematic discrimination, which violated economic, social and cultural rights. This requires a paradigm shift. It means conceptualizing all four land policy options (restitution, redistribution, compensation and land tenure) as transitional justice. Whereas restitution and its alternative compensation can recognize the victimhood of some victims such as refugees and displaced persons, land redistribution can attend to the peculiarities of a postcolonial context by providing redistributive justice. Land tenure reform can be conceptualized as a guarantee of non-recurrence, one of transitional justice's key pillars.

4.3 Zimbabwe: a case study

4.3.1 Background

It is fair to trace the history of juridical state-led appropriations in Zimbabwe to colonialism.[22] This is because tribal land acquisitions which preceded colonial-era appropriations were mainly a product of military conquest. They were also not state-led, since the modern state is a colonial creation.

It is common cause that the colonization of Zimbabwe (formerly called Rhodesia) was impelled by the craving for land and resources.[23] This was achieved through a combination of juridical pilferage and military conquest of the territory's inhabitants.[24] Indeed, the late nineteenth and the twentieth centuries saw the passing of a number of legal instruments which added legitimacy to the forceful acquisition of land by white settlers.[25] These actions were legally validated by English Court in the case of *In Re Southern Rhodesia.*[26] This court approved the appropriation of land from Africans, holding that the land that they lived on and cultivated now vested in the Crown.[27] To the court, the natives' estimation of rights was:

22 For a discussion of the origins of the Zimbabwean land crisis, see Thomas W. Mitchell, 'The Land Crisis in Zimbabwe: Getting Beyond the Myopic Focus upon Black & White' (2000) 11 *Indiana International and Comparative Law Review* 587, Sam Moyo, *The Land Question* (Codesria 1986) and John M. Nading, 'Note, Property under Siege: The Legality of Land Reform in Zimbabwe' (2002) 16 *Emory International Law Review* 737.

23 Michelo Hansungule, 'Who Owns Land in Zimbabwe? In Africa?' (2000) 7 *International Journal on Minority and Group Rights* 305.

24 Ibid.

25 These included; The Lippert Concession (1889), The Native Reserves Order in Council (1898), The Land Apportionment Act (1930), the Natural Resources Act of 1941, the Maize Marketing Act (1930), the Native Land Husbandry Act (1951), the Tribal Trust Lands (TTL) Act (1965) and the 1969 Land Tenure Act (LTA). See also 'Land Issue: Fact Sheet' <www.raceandhistory.com/Zimbabwe/factsheet.html>, and Eric Worby, 'A Redivided Land? New Agrarian Conflicts' (2001) 1(4) *Journal of Agrarian Change* 475–509.

26 *In Re Southern Rhodesia* 1919 AC 211 CD 233–234.

27 Ibid.

> [S]o low in the scale of social organization that their usagesand conception of rights and duties are not to be reconciled with the institutions or the legal ideals of a civilized society.[28]

While this ruling obviously favoured settler-led land seizures, it also became unpopular with the same for its finding that the land belonged to the Crown and not to the British South Africa Company (BSAC).[29] This, among other reasons, prompted the white minority regime of Rhodesia to vie for self-government.[30] In 1925 Rhodesia became a self-governing colony and, in the same year, set up the Morris Carter Land Commission which recommended racial segregation in the apportionment of the colony's land.[31] These recommendations were formalized by the Land Apportionment Act of 1930.[32] Subsequently, fertile land that was situated in high rainfall areas was carved into large-scale farms owned by whites.[33] In contrast, the black majority farming communities were pushed to reserves that received less rainfall and had poor soil quality.[34]

A dualistic land tenure system was thus maintained whereby white settlers, who totalled approximately 5% of the populace, had the best land.[35] This also encompassed good infrastructure, state subsidies, loans and various tax incentives.[36] Huge investments were established to help the settlers create international markets; hence, they were largely export-oriented in their farming.[37] African farming, on the other hand, was either for subsistence purposes or aimed at local markets.[38] Notwithstanding this, few indigenous farmers could make use of local markets since the Maize Marketing Act gave preferential access to white settlers.[39]

These policies had the effect of both marginalizing the production of the indigenous population and ensuring that the black majority remained at the perpetual servitude of the settlers.[40] The struggle for independence and the resulting

28 Ibid. See also Nick Dancaescu, 'Land Reform in Zimbabwe' (2003) 15 *Florida Journal of International Law* 616.

29 Ibid.

30 Ibid.

31 See Report of Presidential Land Review Committee on the Implementation of the Fast Track Land Reform Programme, 2000–2002 ('The Utete Report' 2003) page 11. <https://sarpn.org/documents/d0000622/P600-Utete_PLRC_00-02.pdf>.

32 Ibid.

33 Ibid.

34 Ibid.

35 Ibid.

36 Worby (n.25).

37 Hansungule (n.23).

38 Ibid.

39 Maize Marketing Act (1930). See also Worby (n.25).

40 Ibid. Other strategies included the forced destocking of cattle and other conservation practices in native reserves which were implemented in accordance with the Natural Resources Act of 1941 and the Native Land Husbandry Act (1951). See also Hansungule (n.23).

international isolation created by the United Nations sanctions further exacerbated this skewed inequitable land structure.[41] Trade embargos led white commercial farmers to shift from export-oriented farming to local markets, to the further detriment of peasant production.[42] Thus, at the time of the country's independence in 1980, white farmers produced approximately 90% of the country's marketed food needs.[43]

While this unjust land structure negatively impacted on all Zimbabweans, women's subjugation was worse than that of their male counterparts.[44] Notwithstanding its patriarchal nature, pre-colonial Zimbabwean society guaranteed women's land rights through family and social ties.[45] When the colonialists created a bifurcated legal system with codified customary laws, the traditional safeguards of women's access to land were sidelined.[46] This situation was further worsened by the colonial policies of land tax which were introduced in the early eighteenth century.[47] These tax requirements drove black men to mines and white farms were then used as cheap labour, prompting women to assume the functions of providing food security in the reserves.[48] Although women took up these additional roles, they derived no advantage from the associated power that correlates with such extended duties.[49] For example, when the Native Husbandry Act of 1951 introduced the notion of private property, title to land was given only to African male residents of reserves.[50] Women, on the other hand were relegated to the status of perpetual minors whose enjoyment of land and other resources were subject to their links with men.[51]

Against this background, the war of liberation of Southern Rhodesia was, among other things, inspired by the urge to change the unjust land policies of that colony.[52] In order to ensure a smooth transition, the Lancaster House independence negotiations of 1979 attempted to strike a balance between two competing policy outcomes.[53] These were redressing the axiomatic historical

41 Bertus de Villiers, *Land Reform: Issues and Challenges: A Comparative Overview of Experiences in Zimbabwe, Namibia, South Africa and Australia* (Konrad-Adenauer- Stiftung 2003).
42 Ibid.
43 Ibid.
44 Mildred T. Mushunje, *Women's Land Rights in Zimbabwe* (Broadening Access and Strengthening Input Market Systems (BASIS), Madison 2001) <http://citeseerx.ist.psu.edu/viewdoc/download?doi=10.1.1.465.5950&rep=rep1&type=pdf>.
45 Ibid. Married women were given land by their husbands at marriage, and there were also some customary rules for allocating land to single, divorced and widowed women.
46 Mushunje (n.44).
47 Ibid.
48 Ibid.
49 Ibid.
50 Ibid.
51 Ibid.
52 The Utete Report (n.31).
53 De Villiers (n.41) 7–9.
Ibid.

economic inequalities and promoting economic growth.[54] Thus, the insertion of the following clauses in the peace agreement:

- A ten-year moratorium on the constitutional guarantees to the right to property, which meant that any changes to be made before 1990 had to be made with the approval of a unanimous vote of all the Parliamentarians.[55]
- Property was constitutionally enshrined as a fundamental right. The state could acquire only underutilized land. Any property was to be acquired only on a willing buyer-willing seller basis at its market value.[56]
- The stipulation that the government of Zimbabwe (goZ) had the right of first refusal in all transactions involving land.[57]
- The provision that 'adequate' and 'prompt payment' was to be effected in currencies preferred by the seller in cases of expropriation.[58]
- The requirement that land owners should be given proper notification before land could be acquired.[59]
- The British government gave an undertaking to assist in the land reform process on condition that the goZ matched this funding.[60]

These clauses are of great importance since they continue to dominate the discourse on the Zimbabwean land question. Nonetheless, the extent of the goZ's attempts at implementing these provisions varied at four distinct epochs of the country's history. These periods are 1980–1989, 1990–1999, 2000–2008 and 2008 to date.

a. 1980–1989

For the first ten years, the goZ religiously adhered to the Lancaster House clauses relating to land reform.[61] These terms were clearly given legislative recognition in the *Land Acquisition Act* which enforced the 'willing seller, willing buyer

54 Ibid.
55 Ibid.
56 Ibid.
57 Ibid.
58 Ibid.
59 Ibid.
60 Ibid.
61 See Sam Moyo, *The Land Question in Zimbabwe* (SAPES Books 1995), Sam Moyo, 'The Land Occupation Movement and Democratization in Zimbabwe: Contradictions of Neo-Liberalism' (2001) 30(2) *Millennium Journal of International Studies* 311, Sam Moyo and Paris Yeros, 'Land Occupations and Land Reform in Zimbabwe: Towards the National Democratic Revolution' in S. Moyo and P. Yeros (eds) *Reclaiming the Land; The Resurgence of Rural Movements in Africa, Asia and Latin America* (Zed Books, 2005) and Sam Moyo, 'The Land and Agrarian Question in Zimbabwe' Paper presented at a conference on *The Agrarian Constraints and Poverty Reduction: Microeconomic Lessons for Africa*, Addis Ababa, 17–18 December 2004.

principle' with sellers entitled to 'adequate' and 'prompt' compensation.[62] It should be recalled that the Lancaster House outcome was tilted towards an aspiration of economic growth.[63] An assurance to whites that they would not lose all their privileges was seen as a crucial element of that goal.[64] However, this does not mean that the postcolonial leadership was oblivious to the sensitive nature of the land question.[65] From the onset, it was clearly enunciated that one of the major aims of the land reform programme was to assign the land possessed by whites to blacks so as to abate civil conflict.[66] Thus, the policy of reconciliation was an ostensible tenet of this early land redistribution programme.[67]

The liberal grounding of this land reform programme earned it international acclamation.[68] It was depicted as one of the most advanced land schemes amongst African postcolonial states.[69] However, in reality, the positive outcomes of this exercise were minimal. Perhaps what made the ruling elite and external actors sing from the same hymn sheet was the impressive production of a small number of black farmers.[70] Indeed, at least 300 black farmers, of whom approximately 10 were cabinet ministers, joined the previously all-white Commercial Farmers Union (CFU).[71] Michael Bratton has noted that the emergence of this group bolstered the CFU's influence and ability to lobby the government.[72] This dispelled any insecurity which white commercial farmers might have had in the transition from a white minority regime to black majority rule.[73]

Studies also point to an improvement in women's land rights in resettlements introduced in pursuance of this exercise.[74] This development is attributed to the fall of the extended family and subsequent emergence of nuclear families.[75] This change saw women influencing most of their husband's decisions in issues concerning crops and proceeds from the fields.[76] Also, contrary to traditional

62 Ibid.
63 De Villiers (n.41) 9.
64 Roger Rindell, 'Zimbabwe Land Problem: The Central Issue' in W.H. Morris-Jones (ed) *From Rhodesia to Zimbabwe: Behind and Beyond Lancaster House* (Frank Cass and Company Limited 1980) page 12.
65 See Michael Bratton, 'Ten Years After: Land Redistribution in Zimbabwe, 1980–90' in R.L. Prosterman, N. Temple and T.M. Hanstad (eds) *Agrarian Reform and Grassroots Development* (Lynne Rienner Publishers 1990).
66 Ibid.
67 Ibid.
68 Ibid.
69 Ibid.
70 Ibid.
71 Ibid.
72 Ibid.
73 Ibid.
74 Susie Jacobs, 'Gender Divisions and Land Resettlement in Zimbabwe' *Unpublished DPhil Thesis* (University of Sussex, Institute for Development Studies 1989).
75 Ibid.
76 Ibid.

authorities who usually denied widows and divorcees access to land in communal areas, resettlement officers often permitted these women to stay on the land after the death of their spouses or in the event of a marital breakdown.[77]

It needs to be pointed out, however, that the legislation then was not gender friendly.[78] It exclusively focused on past land injustices associated with race and paid no attention to gender imbalances.[79] This is evidenced by the fact that although the Legal Age of Majority Act (1982) gave women full contractual capacity to purchase and own land on an equal footing with men, S23 of the Constitution maintained the colonial subordination of women's ownership of communal land to men.[80]

Quite significantly, despite the international endorsement of the programme, the land that was actually distributed was merely a third of the government's target of 'nine million hectares or the resettlement of 162000 households'.[81] De Villiers attributes the failure to meet those targets to a number of reasons which include the goZ's lack of resources and capacity.[82] Most of the vast underutilized land which could be easily acquired was not of good quality and was not evenly distributed throughout the country.[83] Noteworthy is that the process had to be led by willing sellers who had to be paid 'promptly and adequately'.

The requirement for 'adequate' and 'prompt' payment is said to have precluded the government from meeting its target. This was more so given the Lancaster House bilateral agreement's stipulation that the goZ had to match whatever was provided by Britain on a pound-for-pound basis.[84] It should be noted that the state's focus during that time was not confined to the mere distribution of land. There were also efforts to improve other socio-economic needs of the population, which included education, health and housing.[85] Consequently, the grant of £33 million provided by the United Kingdom was not enough for the land reform process that was envisaged.[86] While the USAID, the World Bank, the Overseas Development Institute, various think tanks, NGOs, and the EU had shown an interest in funding the land reform programme, limited contributions were made.[87]

Another key concern which retains a contemporary relevance is that the resettlement of people was not combined with programmes for financial, technical,

77 Ibid.
78 Ibid.
79 Ibid.
80 Ibid.
81 Moyo (2001) (n.61) and Lloyd M. Sachikonye, 'The Promised Land' in B. Raftopoulos and T. Savage (eds) *Zimbabwe: Injustice and Reconciliation* (Institute for Justice and Reconciliation 2004).
82 De Villiers (n.41) 12–13.
83 Ibid.
84 Ibid.
85 Ibid.
86 Ibid.
87 Ibid.

educational and infrastructural support.[88] Also, the process's alleviation of over-population in rural areas, where the return of refugees had led to an increase in population, was minimal.[89] Basically, the land reform process which was carried out in the early decade created a façade of inter-racial reconciliation.[90] It embraced liberal notions of capitalism and the nuclear family but did not achieve redistribution.[91]

b. 1990–1999

While the land reform programme embarked on in the first ten years after Zimbabwe's independence can clearly be described as 'state centred but market based', the programme adopted between 1990 and 1999 marked an ideological crisis.[92] This saw an attempt to combine free market dictates with social justice notions.[93]

Soon after the expiration of the constitutional moratorium on the right to property, Section 16 of the Constitution was amended in tandem with the enactment of the Land Acquisition Act of 1992 (hereinafter the Act).[94] This new legal order repealed three key Lancaster House provisions on land, namely, that property could be expropriated only on a 'willing seller, willing buyer' basis; that in the event of an acquisition of land, payment had to be promptly made; and the stipulation that payment was to be effected on any currency preferred by the seller.[95] According to the new law, the market could no longer determine compensation, and parliament was now mandated to enact laws that would stipulate principles for calculating compensation for expropriated land and the duration of payment.[96] The Lancaster House provision of 'prompt payment' in the event of acquisition was replaced by S 19(5) of the Act which stipulated the terms for payment within a 'reasonable' time after acquisition'.[97]

88 Ibid.
89 Ibid.
90 Ibid.
91 Ibid.
92 Moyo (2001) (n 61)
93 Ibid.
94 See Constitution of Zimbabwe Amendment (No. 11) Act, 1990, Act No. 30/1990 and Constitution of Zimbabwe Amendment (No. 12) Act, 1993, Act 4/1993. For the objectives of the 1992 National Land Policy, see Government of Zimbabwe Online: Ministry of Lands, Land Reform and Resettlement <www.gta.gov.zw> (Last visited 10 June 2009).
95 The implementation of the land reform process was now through the Land Acquisition Act of 1992, which laid down the procedures for the compulsory acquisition of rural land.
96 S1 of the Act provided for the creation of a Compensation Committee which had the mandate to determine the value of the property acquired taking into consideration its size, soil type, improvements affected on it infrastructure and other relevant factors. S23 of the Act further provided that disputes on the Compensation Committee's findings had to be handled by the administrative court.
97 The first half was to be paid within a reasonable time following the compensation. Thereafter, half of the balance had to be paid in the two years of the acquisition, and the rest within five years after acquisition.

A critical point worth noting is that land owners no longer led the land purchasing process, as the responsible minister was now empowered to designate certain pieces of land for acquisition.[98] According to the law, service of notice of acquisition on the titleholder of the land designated precluded the same from selling, leasing or otherwise disposing of the property.[99] Pursuant to the Act, 83 white-owned farms were designated for acquisition between 1992 and 1993.[100] As noted in Chapter 3, the constitutionality of this new legal order was tested in *Davies and Others v The Minister of Lands, Agriculture and Water Development.*[101] To re-iterate, five commercial farmers whose farms had been listed for acquisition challenged the constitutionality of the 1992 Act on the basis that the ministerial designation of land was tantamount to expropriation as it restricted the owners' rights to dispose of the land.[102] They also intimated that the designation of their land would reduce its market value.[103] The court, however, rejected their arguments on the basis that designation could not be held to be unconstitutional, as it did not result in the transfer of the right to dispose of the property from the landowner to the state.[104]

Nonetheless, during this decade, both the land acquisition and transfer process were increasingly plagued by controversy and criticism.[105] It was suggested that the process was open to political abuse, as, for example, where a farm owned by a black opposition leader, Reverend Ndabaningi Sithole, was also designated for compulsory acquisition.[106] A second criticism of the programme was that, instead of complying with the 1992 National Land Policy's objective of establishing 'a just, democratic, and efficient land economy', nepotism was rife in land distribution.[107]

In spite of the relaxation in the legal order, fewer than 25,000 peasant households benefitted from the land reform process between 1990 and 1997. This made the total number of resettled households from 1980 to 1997 approximately

98 S14 Land Acquisition Act 1992.
99 Ibid.
100 Dancaescu (n.28).
101 *Davies and Others v Minister of Land Agriculture and Water Development* 1996 SACLR LEXIS 29 (ZS 27 June 1996).
102 Ibid.
103 Ibid.
104 For an elaborate discussion of this case, see Rahman Ford, 'Law History, and the Colonial Discourse: Davies v Commissioner* and Zimbabwe as a Colonialist Case Study' (2001–2002) 45 *Howard Law Journal* 213.
105 See, for example, Marit Stiles, 'Zimbabwe Land Reform: What's Going On?' (1994) 9(5) *Southern African Report* 48 <www.africafiles.org/article.as>
106 The government's rationale for designating Reverend Sithole's farm for acquisition was that the ZANU (Ndonga) party leader's turning his farm into a peri-urban settlement was an illegal act which could well pose a public health risk. See also Ben Hlatshwayo, 'Churu and Ellsworth Farm Designations: Fighting Illegality with Illegality' (1994) 6 *Legal Forum* 11.
107 See Hansungule (n.23).

71,000, which was far below the government's target of 162,000 households.[108] Failure to meet these targets has been largely attributed to successful court challenges by white commercial farmers to the procedural aspects of acquisition.[109]

Notwithstanding the low numbers of resettled households, the land reform programme embarked upon during this period was orderly and peaceful. It is also remarkable to note that by 1997 at least 500 black commercial farmers had emerged.[110] Other positive developments were the adoption of constitutional amendments, one of which prohibited discrimination on the grounds of gender and another which sought to address women's marginalization under inheritance law.[111]

In 1997 the goZ launched its second phase of the land reform and resettlement programme, the objective of which was to resettle 150,000 households within a period of five years. Instead of achieving the stated objectives, the period 1997 to 2000 marked a transition from nonbelligerent and organized land reform process to an allegedly belligerent and haphazard process, termed by the government and its supporters as 'the third Chimurenga/Umvukela' (The third Liberation struggle).[112] The 1980s policy of racial reconciliation was swiftly abandoned.[113]

Several reasons can best explain this policy volte-face. The first of these is related to the country's socio-economic conditions at that time.[114] The 1990s saw a huge population increase that made the demand for land acute.[115] This was compounded by job losses and a decline in the standard of living, which many commentators have linked to the government's capitulation to the World Bank's demands for the introduction of the liberal Economic Structural Adjustment Program (ESAP).[116] The droughts of 1992 and 1993 also made it impossible for the rural areas to continue subsidizing the cities.[117] Kanyeze sees a nexus

108 Sachikonye (n.81) 8–9.

109 Moyo (2004) (n.61) has it that, in the period between 1993 and 1995, court challenges precluded the government from acquiring 130 farms. However, a Commission of Inquiry into Appropriate Agricultural Land Tenure Systems which was commissioned by the President in 1993 observed that the resettlement programme was not adequately funded and also faced planning and administrative problems. For example, in 1994, the allocation for resettlement was equal to only 2.4% of the defence budget. Government of Zimbabwe, *Report of the Commission of Inquiry into Appropriate Agricultural Land Tenure Systems*, 3 volumes (Government Printer 1994).

110 Sachikonye (n.81) 8.

111 See S9 of Constitutional Amendment No. 14, Act No. 14/1996 and Administration of Estates Act, Chapter 6:01 as amended to Act 22/2001. See also Chapter 4, supra notes 994–1002.

112 Sachikonye (n.81) 8.

113 Bratton (n.65).

114 Ibid.

115 Ibid.

116 See, for example, Godfrey Kanyenze, 'Economic Structural Adjustment Program (ESAP): Precursor to Fast Track Resettlement?' in M. Masiiwa (ed) *Post-Independence Land Reform in Zimbabwe* (Friedrich Ebert Stiftung 2004).

117 Ibid.

between the worsening living conditions in the rural areas and the urge on the government to adopt a much more robust land reform process.[118]

The second issue that catapulted the policy change in land reform was the strain in the relations between the government of Zimbabwe and the international community.[119] So far, the Conservatives had handled the Zimbabwe land questions diplomatically, with frequent non-binding promises for financial assistance. In 1997, the UK Labour Party bluntly asserted that their new government had no obligation to fund Zimbabwean land reform.[120] This message was expressed in a letter dated 5 November 1997, which was addressed to the Zimbabwean Minister of Agriculture and Land by Clare Short, the then British minister for overseas development:[121]

> [I] should make it clear that we do not accept that Britain has a special responsibility to meet the costs of land purchase in Zimbabwe. We are a new government from diverse backgrounds without links to former colonial interests. My own origins are Irish and as you know we were colonized not colonizers.[122]

This letter ushered a new era in the Western governments' relationship with Zimbabwe and has been seen as the catalyst for the radical land reform programme.[123] A number of incidents which occurred subsequent to the receipt of this letter substantiate this understanding.

First, 1,471 white-owned farms were slated for acquisition (though with 'full compensation').[124] However, approximately 40% of these were delisted after commercial farmers successfully challenged the acquisition process in the courts.[125] Since European Union citizens largely owned the occupied and expropriated land, EU embassies became involved in the delisting process.[126] This engagement by the EU embassies in the farm delisting process was seen by the goZ as evidence that Western governments' intervention in Zimbabwe's affairs was motivated by the need to preserve the interests of their citizens.[127]

118 Kanyenze (n.116). Ironically, ESAP was introduced in tandem with the 1992 land reform legislation which made the impression that the government was departing from the notion of a market-based economy. For an analysis, see Stiles (n.105).

119 See, for example, B. Ankomah, 'Zimbabwe: The Spark . . . Claire Short's Letter of November 1997' SWANS <www.swans.com/library/art9/ankomah5.html>.

120 Ibid.

121 Ibid.

122 For a full copy of Clare Short's letter, see Ankomah (n.119).

123 Ibid.

124 Moyo (2004) (n.61).

125 Ibid. In 1999, the court further struck off the 847 remaining farms from the expropriation list on the basis that the authorities had not properly complied with the necessary legal and administrative procedures.

126 Ibid.

127 Ibid.

Second, the goZ and the donor community failed to reach an agreement at a conference held in Harare.[128] At the conference the Zimbabwean administration introduced phase two of its land reform process to the donors.[129] The donors expressed an interest in funding the programme, albeit with many in the international community expressing the view that they were in favour only of a less costly market-dictated land reform.[130] The donors thus endorsed the land reform policy presented, on condition that the notions of good governance, poverty reduction, free market, rule of law and sustainable economic policy were taken into consideration in the implementation process.

The goZ possibly saw the imposition of such conditions as a refusal by the former colonial masters to accept their historic responsibilities. Thus, in the wake of the donor conference of 1998, the phenomenon of invading white-owned farms increased. Court orders mandating the police to evict the squatters were largely ignored, with the tacit support of the executive. As a result of the invasions and the state's response, the international community suspended pay-outs of the money pledged at the donor conference. The United Kingdom's official explanation for this default was that the illegal farm invasions were not compatible with the agreements entered into between the government of Zimbabwe and the donors in 1998.

c. 2000–2008

In 2000 both the Constitution and the Land Acquisition Act were amended to legalize the proposed radical land reform programme.[131] These amendments legitimized the government's decision to expropriate land from commercial farmers with compensation only for improvements effected on the land, and not full market value compensation. Invoking the history of dispossession of native land by the settlers during the colonial era, the constitutional amendment obliged Britain, the former colonial master, to establish an adequate fund to compensate the owners for agricultural land acquired for resettlement purposes. However, full compensation was still to be paid for those farms covered by bilateral agreements.[132]

In variance with the 1992 Land Acquisition Act, the 2000 amendments stipulated that only one quarter of the compensation was to be paid at the time of acquisition.[133] Another quarter would be payable within two years, and the balance was to be paid within a five-year period.[134] The Compensation Committee's appellate mandate was also restricted to cases involving non-compliance

128 It was attended by 48 countries and international organizations.

129 Moyo (2004) (n.61).

130 Ibid.

131 Constitution of Zimbabwe Act No. 5 of 2000 (Amendment No. 16). See also De Villiers (n.41).

132 See Zimbabwe: Parliamentary Debates – House of Assembly, 'Second Reading Gazetted Land (Consequential Provisions Bill)' Vol. 33, No. 10, 19 September 2006.

133 See De Villiers (n.41) 21.

134 Ibid.

with the provisions of the Land Acquisition Act.[135] It could also not adjudicate on complaints that the compensation was not fair.[136]

This radical programme for land acquisition, which was referred to as 'fast track', was officially launched in July 2000.[137] It consisted of two methods, namely, the A1 model aimed at giving land to the landless poor, and the A2 model which entailed the creation of black large-scale commercial farmers.[138] Around the same time, the legislature also enacted the Rural Land Occupiers (Protection from Eviction) Act which protected farm occupiers from eviction from the land designated for settlement.[139] As stated in Chapter 3, the issue of the legality of this fast track land reform programme led to the forced resignation of white judges and their replacement with black judges who endorsed the land reform programme.

In 2003, the government enacted a piece of legislation which permitted it to expropriate land from the remaining farmers, including those who only had one farm, had agro-industrial property, were in export processing zones and owned plantations or wildlife conservancies.[140] This was a major departure from the 1998 position, where only land which was derelict, underutilized, owned by foreign property owners and adjacent to communal areas could be acquired.[141] A year later, the Acquisition of Farm Equipment and Materials Act was passed. This stated that the evicted farmers' equipment could be confiscated.[142]

Domestic and international pleas for the re-establishment of the rule of law prompted the government to pass Constitutional Amendment (No. 17) Act in 2005, which nationalized all farmland.[143] It also placed the issue of land acquisition out of the jurisdiction of the Zimbabwean courts and permitted retrospective application of the law relating to the acquisition and conferring of full title of the appropriated land to the state.[144]

The legality of this amendment was unsuccessfully challenged by *Mike Campbell Pvt Ltd and Mr. William Michael Campbell* at the Zimbabwean Supreme Court in March 2007.[145] These applicants alleged that the latest amendment

135 Ibid.

136 Section 29, Land Acquisition Act as amended to Act 15/2000.

137 Amnesty International, 'Zimbabwe: Power and Hunger – Violations of the Right to Food' (2004) AI Index: AFR 46/026/2004 <www.amnesty.ie/wp-content/uploads/2016/05/Zimbabwe-Power-and-hunger-violations-of-the-right-to-food.pdf>.

138 See Moyo (2004) (n.61).

139 Rural Land Occupiers (Protection from Eviction) Act (Chapter 20:26) As amended in s. 4(a)(iii) by s. 30 of the General Laws Amendment Act 2002, from 4 February 2002.

140 See Land Acquisition Amendment Act (2003).

141 Ibid.

142 The Acquisition of Farm Equipment and Materials Act (2004).

143 Constitution of Zimbabwe Amendment (No. 17) Act, 2005 commenced 16 September 2005.

144 S16B Constitution of Zimbabwe 1979 (S.I. 1979/1600 of the United Kingdom) (As amended to No. 17 of 14 September 2005).

145 *Mike Campbell Pvt Ltd & W. M Campbell v Minister of National Security, Lands, Land Reform and Resettlement & Anor* (124/06) [2008] ZWSC 1 (22 January 2008). See also

disregarded the rule of law and also took away the farmers' right to protection of the law.[146] Put simply, the applicants argued that by ousting the judiciary's powers to deliberate on issues relating to land acquisition, the amendment contravened the notion of separation of powers which is a basic structure of the country's Constitution.[147] Much more importantly, they insinuated that the goZ's land reform programme did not meet the customary law limitations on the state's right to expropriate land within its territory.[148] In particular, they contended that there cannot be expropriation without compensation, and that the whole land reform process was racially discriminatory since it targeted only white commercial farmers.[149]

As far as the goZ was concerned, the amendment dealt with the people's fundamental right to land.[150] This is the right to land ownership by the majority of the people which could have been included in the Constitution in the transition from colonial rule if this supreme law had been home grown. While the jurisdiction of the courts could not be removed by a mere act of parliament, the Constitution created an exception, and this did not abrogate the doctrine of separation of powers.[151] In any event, courts still had the jurisdiction to hear matters relating to compensation for land.[152]

The state further argued that expropriation was in the public interest, and therefore the amendment was necessary to stop the endless litigation which had frustrated the necessary land reform programme.[153] The legislation in place could not be said to be discriminatory since it facilitated the expropriating of land from a minority which owned large-scale farms for distribution to the landless majority.[154] It was axiomatic that the land owners were white and the landless were black, and as such, acquisition laws had to be positively discriminatory.[155]

To bring the Land Acquisition Act of 2000 into line with this latest amendment and to deal with unresolved provisions concerning compensation for improvements, the Gazetted Land (Consequential Provisions) Act of 2006 was enacted.[156] The Act also repealed the Rural Land Occupiers (Protection from Eviction) Act which was seen to have served its purpose since offer letters had

---

Mike Campbell (Pvt) Ltd and Others v Republic of Zimbabwe (2/2007) [2008] SADCT 2 (28 November 2008).

146 Ibid.

147 Ibid.

148 Ibid.

149 Ibid.

150 Ibid.

151 *Mike Campbell Pvt Ltd & W. M. Campbell vs. Minister of National Security, Lands, Land Reform and Resettlement & Anor*, SC 124/06.

152 Ibid.

153 Ibid.

154 Ibid.

155 Ibid.

156 Gazetted Land (Consequential Provisions) Act No 8 of 2006.

been issued to all those who occupied state land.[157] Much more significantly, section 3(3) of the Gazetted Land (Consequential Provisions) Act made it a criminal offence to illegally remain on a piece of land which has been gazetted in terms of Constitutional Amendment Number 17.[158] This provision led to the prosecution of a number of white farmers in the magistrates' courts for allegedly occupying land without lawful authority.[159]

Nonetheless, in this phase, more than 11million hectares of land were acquired and distributed to beneficiaries who according to land reform critiques have not been accorded security of tenure, education, credit facilities and all other kinds of services. There have also been particular concerns that the fast track land reform programme violated farm workers' livelihood rights and did not fully respond to women's needs for secure land tenure.[160] It has also been seen as a contributing factor to the undermining of Zimbabwe's food security.[161]

However, the official position was that the land reform process has been a success and has empowered the people of Zimbabwe.[162] In particular, the programme has reduced overpopulation in villages, indigenized the large-scale commercial farming sector and reduced rural poverty.[163] Other alleged successes are the advancement of environmentally sustainable use of land through agriculture and eco-tourism. It is also said to have fostered conditions for sustainable socio-economic and political stability in Zimbabwe.[164] However, the goZ has

157 Clause 7, ibid as read with Zimbabwe: Parliamentary Debates – House of Assembly, 'Second Reading Gazetted Land (Consequential Provisions Bill)', Vol. 33, No. 10, 19 September 2006.

158 Ibid.

159 See, for example, *State v John Eastwood et al.* (November 2007), CRB nos. 1443–1451 (Chegutu Magistrates Court). In defence of the charges against them, the farmers asked for the matter to be referred to the Supreme Court on the basis that Amendment No. 17 erased the rule of law from Zimbabwe, violated the farmers' right to protection of the law and was therefore against the fundamental tenets of international constitutional law. They contended that acquisition of land without compensation is against all democratic rules and is in direct conflict with Article 6 of the Southern African Development Corporation (SADC) treaty to which Zimbabwe is a state party. They also argued that the Gazetted Land (Consequential Provisions) Act is tantamount to an abuse of powers and therefore a breach of Section 18(1) and S18 (9) of the Zimbabwean Constitution. Similar concerns have been raised in regional and international tribunals. See, for example, *Mike Campbell (Pvt) Ltd and Others v Republic of Zimbabwe* (2/2007) [2008] SADCT 2 (28 November 2008).

160 Anne Hellum and Bill Derman, 'Land Reform and Human Rights in Contemporary Zimbabwe; Balancing Individual and Social Justice Through an Integrated Human Rights Framework' (2004) 32(10) *World Development* 1785, see also Human Rights Watch, 'Zimbabwe: Fast Track Land Reform Program' 2002 <www.hrw.org/reports/2002/zimbabwe/>.

161 See Lloyd Sachikonye, 'The Land Is the Economy: Revisiting the Land Question' (2005) 14(3) *African Security Review*.

162 Zimbabwe: Parliamentary Debates – House of Assembly (n.133).

163 Ibid.

164 Ibid.

acknowledged that the payment of compensation to the farmers is still an issue to be dealt with, as is ensuring productive use of land by the beneficiaries.[165] The goZ also pledged 99-year leases to beneficiaries so as to give them security of tenure.[166] Eight audits on the recent land reform programme had been carried out by 2008, and the state has reallocated a number of underutilized A2 farms.[167]

d. 2008–2018

In terms of the Global Political Agreement of 2008, the land reform process is irreversible and the primary obligation to compensate the dispossessed white farmers rests on the United Kingdom.[168] The parties agreed to: (a) conduct a land audit; (b) ensure that all Zimbabweans who applied for land were allocated land without discrimination on any grounds; (c) guarantee security of tenure to all land holders; (d) call upon the former colonial power to accept responsibility to pay compensation for land acquired; and (e) seek international assistance and cooperate in working towards the restoration of all agricultural land's full productivity.[169]

The same language is found in the Constitution of 2013 which states that the following factors might be regarded as crucial when it comes to the compulsory acquisition of agricultural land:

> [u]nder colonial domination the people of Zimbabwe were unjustifiably dispossessed of their land and other resources without compensation; b. the people consequently took up arms in order to regain their land and political sovereignty, and this ultimately resulted in the Independence of Zimbabwe in 1980; c. the people of Zimbabwe must be enabled to re-assert their rights and regain ownership of their land; and accordingly – i. the former colonial power has an obligation to pay compensation for agricultural land compulsorily acquired for resettlement, through an adequate fund established for the purpose; and ii. if the former colonial power fails to pay compensation through such a fund, the Government of Zimbabwe has no obligation to pay compensation for agricultural land compulsorily acquired for resettlement.[170]

165 Ibid.
166 Ibid.
167 Chris Gande, 'Harare Undertaking Another Audit of Agricultural Land Ownership' *Voice of America*, 28 December 2006 <www.voanews.com>. See also Herald Online, 'State Reallocates Under-Utilised A2 Farms' *Herald*, 14 April 2008 <www.herald.co.zw/>.
168 Article V, Land Question, Agreement between the Zimbabwe African National Union Patriotic Front (ZANU PF) and the two Movement for Democratic Change (MDC) formations, on resolving the challenges facing Zimbabwe (Global Political Agreement 2008), <http://constitutionnet.org/sites/default/files/global_political_agreements_2008.pdf>.
169 Ibid.
170 S72 (7) 2013 Constitution of Zimbabwe.

The Constitution also establishes a Land Commission which has a number of functions including carrying out periodic land audits.[171] The Land Commission became operational in February 2018 and embarked on a land audit in October 2018.[172] It is yet to be seen whether it will fulfil its stated objectives. These include ensuring security of tenure and enforcing the law which restricts the amount of land which can be owned by a household.[173]

4.4 The limits of international law: how to read Zimbabwe's experience with land reform

Zimbabwe's experience with land reform resurrects the two legal conundrums. The first is the controversy relating to the scope of the right to property, and the limitations imposed on a sovereign state's right to expropriate and nationalize land within its territory. The second is the identification of an appropriate redress for both colonial and postcolonial expropriations. Both these questions touch on the salient issue of the unresolved question of reparations for colonial injustices.[174]

4.4.1 Scope of the right to property, and limitations imposed on a sovereign state's right to expropriate

International law permits state-led land acquisitions which are for a public purpose, are not discriminatory and are combined with compensation.[175] Thus, expropriations which meet certain conditions are not a violation of the right to property. This view is qualified by customary law where there has been a global consensus that a state can expropriate property which is situated within its territory subject to certain limitations.[176] Unfortunately, there are historic disagreements between Western and postcolonial states on limitations imposed by international law on a state's right to expropriate property within its territory.[177]

Western governments recognize three limitations on a state's entitlement to expropriate property within its borders.[178] In the first instance they note that expropriation must be done for a public purpose.[179] They also recognize that the appropriation process should not be discriminatory and that it should be

171 S296, 2013 Constitution of Zimbabwe as read with the Land Commission Act [Chapter 20:29].
172 The Land Commission Act commenced in February 2018.
173 S297 2013 Constitution of Zimbabwe.
174 Ibid.
175 Peter Malanczuk, *Akehurst's Modern Introduction to International Law* (Routledge 2002), 235.
176 Eduardo M. Penalva, 'Redistributing Property: Natural Law, International Norms and the Property Reforms of the Cuban Revolution' (2000) 52 *Florida Law Review* 107.
177 Malanczuk (n.175) 235.
178 Ibid.
179 Ibid.

combined with 'prompt, adequate and effective' compensation.[180] However, postcolonial states are not in agreement on these limitations.[181]

Indeed, during the Cold War, colonies and former colonies in cohort with the Communist bloc opposed the requirement that a state which wanted to expropriate property had to pay full compensation.[182] Their disagreements were expressed largely through General Assembly resolutions. Of particular significance is paragraph 4 of the General Assembly Resolution 1803 (XVII) on 'Permanent Sovereignty over Natural Resources'.[183] This resolution resembles the Western viewpoint in the sense that it recognizes that expropriation shall be based on public interest and distinguishes itself from the same by replacing full compensation with 'appropriate' compensation.[184] Similar resistance to the Western requirement of full compensation is found in Article 2(2) of the 1974 Charter of Economic Rights and Duties of States, which states that:

> [A]ppropriate compensation should be paid by the (expropriating) state . . . taking into account its relevant laws and regulations and all the circumstances that the State considers pertinent.[185]

Thus, there have always been historic tensions between developing and developed countries on the type of compensation which ought to be paid. These differences are the root causes of the land disputes which Zimbabwe has been attempting to address since the country's independence in 1980.

It is common cause that the goZ's initial policy choice for addressing colonial land injustices was pragmatic and largely influenced by experiences of countries which had attained independence before its own liberation. Two options were really available, the Kenya model and the Mozambique option. When Kenya attained its independence from Britain in 1964, it adopted a liberal land reform programme and maintained remarkable stability (that is, until the issues resurfaced in 2008). This is in contrast to neighboring Mozambique, which miscalculated the power of the master's discourse when it became independent in 1975. The *Frente de Libertaco de Mocambique* (FRELIMO) government declared itself a Marxist Leninist party and vested all land in the state.[186] The liberal notion of the right to property was seen as incompatible with the socialist postcolonial regime's vision of a classless society.[187] Restrictions were put on land's alienability,

180 Ibid.
181 Ibid.
182 Ibid.
183 ¶4 General Assembly Resolution on Permanent Sovereignty over Natural Resources, G.A. Res. 1803 (XVII), 17 U.N. GAOR Supp. (No.17) at 15, U.N. Doc. A/5217 (1962).
184 Ibid.
185 Article 2(2) (c), Charter of Economic Rights and Duties of States, GA Res. 3281(xxix), U.N. GAOR, 29th Sess., Supp. No. 31 (1974) 50.
186 Ibid. See also Preamble, Art 15, 16, 39–31 and 42 *Lei de Terras* 1979 – Land Law of 1979 (Law No. 6/79).
187 Pekka Virtanen, 'The Politics of Law in Mozambique: Customary Authority and Changing Premises of Legal Reform' (2004) 17(1) *International Journal for Semiotics of Law* 53.

and the fundamental land tenure right was characterized as the right of use and enjoyment (*direito de USO e aproveitamento*).[188] Arguably, the result of such policies was economic collapse and a civil war.

Against this background, Zimbabwe initially carried out an imposed liberal market-driven land reform legal framework which *prima facie* embraced the notion of citizenship for all.[189] Expropriations were avoided, and Zimbabwe's relations with the international community were excellent. However, this method was not effective since white farmers were unwilling to make good land available for redistribution.[190] Also, foreign donors were not as generous to Zimbabwe as they had been to Kenya, where they made available 95% of the funding for land reform.[191] In the case of Zimbabwe, many within the international community saw the Zimbabwean land issue as a bilateral dispute between Zimbabwe and the United Kingdom.[192]

The lesser effectiveness of the 'willing seller–willing buyer' model therefore necessitated land expropriation. It can be said the public interest requirement of expropriation in post-2000 Zimbabwe was not contentious, as there seems to be a consensus that land reform was necessary. The same could be said of the issue of 'racial discrimination' which could be attributed to the racially eschewed land holdings.[193] Thus, compensation remains the major contentious issue in the Zimbabwean land reform programmes.

As stated in Chapter 3, international law is state-centric; that is, it is the state which has a responsibility to pay compensation for expropriations carried out by a previous regime. This is a heavy burden for postcolonial societies who have serious resource constraints. As Rajeev Bhargava stated:

> [M]odern colonialism went beyond physical violence, forcible occupation of lands or extraction of tribute and wealth. It forcibly established a relationship between the colonizers and the colonized and inaugurated a flow of human and natural resources that continually fed the economy of the colonizers and impoverished the colonized.[194]

This statement finds support in the fact that all independence constitutions of former British colonies incorporated the right to property as a fundamental right

188 Ibid.

189 The reality, however, is that most landless Zimbabweans (and more so on women) did not fully enjoy their right to social citizenship. For the definition of social citizenship, see T.H. Marshal, *Sociology at the Crossroads and Other Essays* (Heinemann 1963).

190 De Villiers (n.41) 13.

191 Ibid at 12.

192 Ibid.

193 See, however, *Mike Campbell (Pvt) Ltd and Others v Republic of Zimbabwe* (2/2007) [2008] SADCT 2 (28 November 2008).

194 Rajeev Bhargava, 'How Should We Respond to the Cultural Injustices of Colonialism' in J. Miller and S. Kumar (eds) *Reparations: Interdisciplinary Inquiries* (Oxford University Press 2007) page 215.

in addition to other explicit constraints on land acquisition. It should be noted that the right to property does not exist in the ICCPR, ICESCR or even in the first European human rights regional instrument.[195]

4.4.2 *Appropriate redress for both colonial and postcolonial expropriations*

Zimbabwe's 38-year attempt at land reform raises different legal issues and transitional expectations. For example, the white farmers who contend that the fast track land reform's legitimacy was undermined by its discriminatory nature and lack of full compensation might expect restitution. Such expectations could, however, compete with beneficiaries' need for a legal framework, which could secure their tenure.

These are complex questions which the new political order would have to address if it is to restore the rule of law and respect for legal institutions in Zimbabwe. A pragmatic starting point has been the creation of a Land Commission mandated to carry out a land audit so as to determine the compensation needs for previous land owners. This independent audit would identify the beneficiaries and ascertain whether the land that was distributed is actually being put to productive use. Compared to most post-conflict contexts, this exercise might be less tedious in Zimbabwe since land records are still intact and to a larger extent reliable. There is also a need for an institutional framework for handling conflicting 'legitimate' land-related disputes that resulted from the fast track programme.

New understandings of land rights enshrined in non-discriminatory legislation which is compatible with human rights standards are also necessary. A balance is to be struck between respect for the right to property and protecting the rights of less powerful groups. This should be supported by reformed laws on land administration and allocation. Such legislation should also recognize the collateral value of land. As has been stated in Chapter 3, judges can contribute to this process by way of transformative adjudication.

Since 2003, politicians, international non-governmental organizations and individual scholars have all participated in the discussion on how to address land-related questions in post-conflict Zimbabwe.[196] The two factions of Zimbabwe's biggest opposition party, the Movement of Democratic Change (MDC), for example, have already spelt out this issue as one of the concerns which they will address in the event of their assumption of power.[197] It is their view that the

195 See the discussion in, Khanyisela Moyo, 'Justiciable Property Rights and Postcolonial Land Reform: A Case Study of Zimbabwe' in Alice Diver and Jacinta Miller (eds) *Justiciability of Human Rights Law in Domestic Jurisdictions* (Springer 2016) 365–366.

196 See, for example, Movement for Democratic Change, 'Restart Program' <http://mdczw.org/>, International Crisis Group, 'Zimbabwe: An End to the Stalemate?' *Africa Report No. 122*, 5 March 2007 <www.crisisgroup.org> and Markus Scheuermaier, 'Should Land Be Returned to White Farmers in Zimbabwe' (2006) 2 *African Policy Journal*.

197 Movement for Democratic Change, ibid.

Robert Mugabe regime carried out the process in an unlawful and destructive manner, hence their wish to set themselves apart from such lawlessness.[198] Thus they would appoint an independent, all-inclusive Land Commission to investigate the legal transfer of farm ownership and other related matters.[199] In addition, they would create special courts which would handle land-related disputes that resulted from the fast track land reform process.[200]

In 2004, the International Crisis Organization (ICG) also presented a detailed analytical paper on the issue.[201] It recommended the creation of a post-conflict Zimbabwean Land Commission made up of key Zimbabwean stakeholders, with set directives and a sound technocratic grounding.[202] The Commission's role would involve, *inter alia*, carrying out a land audit, arranging tribunals for mediating land claims and generating a compensation method.[203] It is their view that a decision on what is to be done about both the farms and the affected parties ought to be based on whether the land is utilized and on the manner of its acquisition.[204]

Interestingly, the ICG acknowledges that full compensation would not be possible.[205] They have also noted that the issue cannot be resolved in the absence of generous funding from the United Kingdom (UK) and other international donors.[206] This may be enabled by the change of regime since the former Mugabe administration had exhausted the goodwill of Western donors.[207] Ironically, the ICG also notes that the transition could be assisted by the UK's open acknowledgement of its historic responsibility for Zimbabwe's land injustices.[208] This should be augmented by a commitment by the same to technically and financially support Zimbabwe's land reform.[209] Impliedly, reparations for colonial injustices are only payable on the *Self*'s terms.

In the same vein, Markus Scheuermaier has stated that the Zimbabwean land reform process was an affront to both the rule of law and human rights.[210] He also sees the first job of a new regime as being the creation of a national Land Commission which would be composed of major domestic stakeholders and supported by international experts.[211] This body's mandate would be the examination of the land reform process which was implemented since 2000 with a

198 Ibid. See also Movement for Democratic Change, 'Agenda – Land Reform; Agriculture' <http://mdczw.org/>.
199 Ibid.
200 Ibid.
201 International Crisis Group, 'Blood and Soil-Land, Politics and Conflict Prevention in Zimbabwe and South Africa' 2004 <www.crisisgroup.org/home/index.cfm>.
202 Ibid.
203 Ibid.
204 Ibid.
205 Ibid.
206 Ibid.
207 Ibid.
208 Ibid.
209 Ibid.
210 Scheuermaier (n.196).
211 Ibid.

view towards creating a set of property rights appropriate for Zimbabwe.[212] Its terms of reference ought to be wide, to enable it to achieve a balance between vindicating property rights which were disrupted by the outgoing regime and ensuring that a just property rights regime is maintained.[213] Quite significantly, Scheuermaier has noted that the Land Commission has to be augmented by the restoration of a 'Citizenship Compact' between the state and its citizens which incorporates rights and duties of both parties as they relate to property.[214] This is a very important point which recognizes that land conflicts in postcolonial dispensations expose the fluidity of the postcolonial state.

Obviously, some of these suggestions are now largely academic having been overtaken by subsequent events. The goZ has stated that the fast track land reform programme cannot be reversed, and a Land Commission is now operational. Suggestions made by different pundits and actors which were discussed earlier are an effort to emulate policy options from other societies which have had to address land issues in their transitions.[215] Indeed, it is now commonplace for transitional societies to establish either a commission or specialized court (in some cases both) to deal with land questions related to reconstruction and peacemaking. The work of these bodies have included three aspects, namely: investigating and documenting land issues pertinent to the context; acceptance and mediation of claims; and return of property or payment of compensation.[216]

It is also not unusual for transitional societies to provide for land tenure security in their peace agreements. This is seen as a way of both addressing the underlying causes of the conflict and pre-empting struggles for sustainable livelihoods.[217] It is informed by the belief that secure property rights herald economic and political stability.[218] Secure land tenure promotes investment and bestows on those affected equity that they can utilize to access credit and other financial facilities.[219]

212 Ibid.

213 Ibid.

214 Ibid.

215 Similar policies have been pursued in transitions of Kosovo, Bosnia and Herzegovina, Sudan, South Africa, Burundi, Acer, Georgia and Iraq. For a general discussion on post-conflict property rights, see Hans Dans, 'Restoring Property Rights in the Aftermath of War' (2004) 53 *International and Comparative Law Quarterly* 429.

216 Ibid. For example, Annexure 7 of the Dayton Peace Accords set up a Commission for Real Property Claims which adjudicates on claims for return of property or for just compensation in lieu of return. Claims can also be received by the Ombudsman.

217 The African Centre for Technology Studies (ACTS), 'Summary Report on the Conference on Land Tenure and Conflict in Africa: Prevention, Mitigation and Reconstruction' (Kenya: ACTS Press 2004) <www.oxfam.org.uk> (Accessed 10 June 2009).

218 See Dancaescu (n.28).

219 Ibid. In postcolonial Africa this idea became popularized after the groundbreaking work of Hernando De Soto, who claimed that capitalism would also work in Africa if property rights were formalized. Hernando de Soto, *The Mystery of Capital: Why Capitalism Triumphs in the West and Fails Everywhere Else* (Bantam Press 2000).

It is common knowledge that the previous injustices which were addressed by Zimbabwe's land reform programme at independence were carried out by former colonial masters – who, ironically, dictated the terms of the programme.[220] As Rajeev Bhargava put it;

> [B]ecause he can hardly ever be penalized, the colonizer interferes with impunity. He interferes at will because he never waits for an independent legitimating circumstance or motive.[221]

This is qualified by Claire Short's 1997 letter discussed in the previous section, which stated that the UK does not acknowledge its colonial obligation.[222] The UK position is that the funding that it provides to its former colonies for any developmental programme is aid.[223] Africa's economic problems are blamed on corrupt leaders who cannot effectively manage economies.[224] This means that those whose land was expropriated during the colonial encounter can only hope for the master's benevolence to address these injustices.[225] It also means that the Western requirements of poverty eradication and good governance are attached to the provision of such funds.[226]

This is the context which best explains Zimbabwe's post-2000 land reform process which was based on a constitutional framework which calls upon Britain to adequately compensate the expropriated white farmers. Such a direction is obviously weak as it cannot be enforced.[227] Imposing an obligation on another state in a national constitution can be said to be an exercise in futility.[228] Nonetheless, this is a significant development, since it is a direct attack on the state-centric and Eurocentric understanding. It emanates from an understanding that the dominant model was a hindrance to the goZ's attempts at correcting historical injustices in land allocation. The liberal framework was seen as a way of entrenching white privileges.

This view has also been echoed in other postcolonial contexts. An example is the South African model, whereby the state and not the past beneficiaries of apartheid are responsible for the costs of land reform. This is seen as an example of 'victor's justice'.[229] As Olivia L. Zirker put it:

220 Ibid.
221 Bhargava (n.194).
222 Ankomah (n.119).
223 This was expressed at the September 2001 World Congress against racism held in South Africa.
224 Ibid.
225 Ibid.
226 Ibid.
227 Ibid.
228 Ibid.
229 Marcia Barry, 'Now Another Thing Must Happen: Richtersveld and the Dilemmas of Land REFORM in Post-Apartheid South Africa' (2004) 20 *South African Journal of Human Rights* 355.

> [L]and reform in South Africa has been an example of victor's justice. In this instance, the victor appears to be the white minority as they have not been forced to give up the land and their land is now protected under the Constitution.[230]

To their credit, those who coined the South African land reform policy saw restitution as a transitional programme which was essential for nation-building and reconciliation.[231] They also saw restitution as the democratic state's symbolic apology for colonial and apartheid wrongs.[232] In practice, however, the South African restitution programme excused the colonialists for their role in creating a racially skewed land structure.[233] The law called upon everyone who was dispossessed as a result of the racially based laws and practices passed after 19 June 1913 to lodge their claims before 31 December 1998.

Interestingly, the South African government acknowledged that there were removals before 1913 but felt that these could not be reasonably dealt with by the South African Land Commission as there were associated with tribal and colonial military conquest.[234] It then singled out the Natives' Land Act (1913) as the first racially discriminatory law to take land from blacks and give it to whites.[235] This implies that the government's position is that the colonial Glen Grey Act (1894), which created native reserves (areas intended for occupation solely by blacks and used as 'reservoirs of labour'), was not racist.[236]

It is indisputable that to date, white South Africans still enjoy their historic privileges.[237] The revolutionary government has been placed in a difficult position of having to oppose land claims instituted by its partners in land reform.[238] For example, in the *Richtersveld* case, the African National Congress (ANC) government argued that the dispossession of this community was not racially motivated.[239] Concerns have also been raised that the adversarial procedure of the Land Claims Court promotes polarity and differences and not the healing and reconciliation objectives which were envisaged by the interim and final legislative

230 Olivia L. Zirker, 'The Land Is My Land: The Evolution of Property Rights and Land Reform in South Africa' (2003) 18 *Connecticut Journal of International Law* 621, 639.
231 Commission on the Restitution of Land Rights, 'Presentation to the Portfolio Committee on Agriculture and Land Affairs' 29 May 2007, <http://land.pwv.gov.za/restitution>.
232 Commission on the Restitution of Land Rights, ibid.
233 Ibid, as read with Barry (n.229).
234 Ibid.
235 Ibid.
236 For a similar critique, see Fred Hendricks, 'Fault-Lines in South African Democracy: Continuing Crises of Inequality and Injustice' *Discussion Paper 22* (Nordiska Afrikainstitutet 2003).
237 Ibid.
238 *The Richtersveld Community and Others v Alexkor Limited*, 2003 (6) BCLR 583. See also *President of the Republic of South Africa and Anor v Modderklip Boerdery (Pty) Ltd et al.*, Case CCT 20/04.
239 Ibid.

enabling instruments.[240] Quite significantly, restitution claims could be said to be obstructing the government's redistributive agenda as they tend to involve competing claims which are all in the public interest.[241]

Unfortunately, the Zimbabwean form of resistance cannot be said to be a viable model for addressing the limitations in international law. The narrative in Section 4.3 described how the Zimbabwean post-2000 legislative framework facilitated easy transfer of land from whites to blacks regardless of the history of accumulation and entitlement. Such legislation was effective in so far as it enabled the transfer of land from whites to blacks, but it failed to sustain agriculture, exacerbated land ownership conflicts and reduced agriculture investments.[242] It also earned the country a pariah status. From a human rights perspective, the process worked in so far as it gave the natives economic self-determination of their resources. However, it also failed to work as a rights-based method of implementing the state's obligation to *respect, protect and fulfil* individual rights to an adequate standard of living.

4.5 Insights from other postcolonial polities

Land reform programmes which are characterized as liberal are largely pragmatic exercises which combine transitional justice goals and developmental projects. An example is the South African model. Post-apartheid South Africa adopted a Commission on Restitution of Land Rights (South African Land Commission) and a Land Claims Court to give effect to restitution.[243] Restitution is one of the pillars of post-apartheid South Africa's land reform policy, whose other components are redistribution and tenure reform.[244] Its aim is to redress the injustices of the forced removals which were effected after 1913. In contrast to conventional understandings of native entitlement to historically acquired land, claimants in

240 S. Nadssen, 'Restitution, Reconstruction, Reconciliation and Redistribution: Land Reform – Balancing the Interests of the Dispossessed, the Homeless and Development' (1997) 9 *Stellenbosch Law Review* 360.

241 Ibid.

242 See, however, Ian Scoones et al. *Zimbabwe's Land Reform: Myths & Realities* (Currey 2010).

243 These were established in terms of the Restitution of Land Rights Act 22 of 1994 (commenced 2 December 1994).

244 The framework for land reform is stated thus in S25 of the Constitution of the Republic of South Africa, 1996:

> (5) The state must take reasonable legislative and other measures, within its available resources, to foster conditions which enable citizens to gain access to land on an equitable basis.
>
> (6) A person or community whose tenure of land is legally insecure as a result of past racially discriminatory laws or practices is entitled, to the extent provided by an Act of Parliament, either to tenure which is legally secure or to comparable redress.
>
> (7) A person or community dispossessed of property after 19 June 1913 as a result of past racially discriminatory laws or practices is entitled, to the extent provided by an Act of Parliament, either to restitution of that property or to equitable redress.

this country did not have to prove continuous adherence to customary laws and customs in land usage.[245] They were required only to show that they occupied the land for at least ten years between 1913 and 1994, prior to dispossessions through racially motivated laws and practices.

In common with racist Rhodesia, apartheid South Africa had passed a number of legislative instruments which limited ownership and use of land by South African blacks.[246] Rural removals were effected under the Natives' Land Act (1913) which served similar purposes as the Rhodesian Native Reserves Order in Council (1898) and Land Apportionment Act (1898).[247] In particular, it legalized the separation of land between blacks and whites, giving whites control of most areas of South Africa, while blacks were settled in newly established reserves believed to be their historical homes.[248] In reality the process of territorial segregation in South Africa was initiated by the Glen Grey Act (1894) which was led by the English colonialist Cecil John Rhodes. Nonetheless, the application of the Natives' Land Act (1913) was further extended by the Development Trust and Land Act (1936) which gave blacks, who made up 80% of the population, only 13% of South Africa.[249]

Urban apartheid was carried out under the Group Areas Act of 1950 which settled different races in different residential and urban areas.[250] In pursuance of this Act, those blacks who stayed and conducted business in white sections of the urban area were forcefully moved.[251] It is estimated that the number of victims of these apartheid's racially based dispossessions was 3.5 million people.[252] This explains why land reform was one of the key concerns in the struggle against apartheid.[253]

Attempts to correct the effects of these discriminatory pieces of legislation were initiated by the outgoing De Klerk administration in 1990.[254] This regime started

245 Article 2, Restitution of Land Rights Act 22 of 1994 (commenced 2 December 1994). See also Jeremy Gilbert, 'Historical Indigenous people's land claims: A Comparative and International Approach to the common law doctrine on indigenous title' (2007) 56 *International and Comparative Law Quarterly* 583., *The Richtersveld Community and Others v Alexkor Limited and* Barry (n.230) supra note 1530.

246 De Villiers (n.41).

247 Black (or Natives) Land Act No. 27 of 1913 (commenced 19 June 1913).

248 Ibid.

249 Development Trust and Land Act, 1936 Act No. 18 of 1936, published in Government Notice No. 494 of 2 April 1937. Another piece of legislation which was applicable was the Prevention of Illegal Squatting, Act No. 52 of 1951.

250 The Group Areas Act of 1950, Act No. 41 of 1950.

251 Ibid.

252 Commission on Restitution of Land Rights, 'Background to Restitution' 2002 <http://land.pwv.gov.za> (Accessed 2 December 2007).

253 For example, the ANC Freedom Charter of 1955 promised that the 'land shall be shared among those who work it. Restrictions of land ownership on a racial basis shall be ended, and all the land re-divided amongst those who work it to banish famine and land hunger'. *The Freedom Charter, Adopted at the Congress of the People, Kliptown*, on 26 June 1955 <www.anc.org.za>.

254 Anthony J. Christopher, 'Land Restitution in South Africa, 1991–94' (1995) 12(4) *Land Use Policy* 267. See also De Villiers (n.41).

by abolishing key land segregation statutes and thereafter adopted a White Paper on Land Reform which prescribed a minimal policy of restitution whereby only underutilized state-owned land could be restored to its previous owners.[255] A Commission on Land Allocation which investigated claims against the state and made orders for restitution was also established.

Subsequently, and as in Zimbabwe, the peace negotiators struck a compromise between protecting the economy and redressing the legacy of unjust land dispossessions. This was a major climb-down from the radical view articulated by the African National Congress in its Freedom Charter.[256] S121 of the Constitution provided for the right to restitution.[257] S122 authorized the enactment of a statute which would deal with this issue.[258] It was also stipulated that this Act would establish a Commission whose role would be to investigate, mediate and settle land restitution claims.[259] Evidence of unresolved claims was supposed to be submitted to a court of law.[260] Against this background, claims for the restoration of land in South Africa are either mediated by the Commission or settled by the Land Claims Court.[261]

Parallel efforts at redressing the same were also conducted by pressure groups made up of individuals and communities who were victims of past land injustices.[262] Their endeavours were complemented by those of non-governmental organizations who investigated land claims and lobbied for land restitution.[263] These groups largely succeeded in helping poor rural claimants whose cases related to the apartheid-era removals but failed to assist those whose claims stemmed from colonial dispossessions.[264] Although the exercise did not necessarily translate into economic gain for claimants, for most of them, the immeasurable benefit restored their dignity and sense of belonging.[265]

Quite significantly, and from a postcolonial legal perspective, the implementation of South Africa's restitution programme reflects a form of 'agency' or

255 The Abolition of Certain Racially Based Land Measures, Act 108 of 199.

256 In the Freedom Charter it was stated that: 'Restrictions of land ownership on a racial basis shall be ended, and all the land re-divided amongst those who work it to banish famine and land hunger'. See African National Congress (ANC), *Freedom Charter, Adopted at the Congress of the People, Kliptown, on 26 June 1955* <www.anc.org.za> (Accessed 10 June 2009).

257 Constitution of the Republic of South Africa, Act 2000 of 1993 (commenced 27 April 1994).

258 Ibid.

259 Ibid.

260 Ibid. In 1997, chapter 111A was added as an amendment to the Restitution of Land Rights Act. This made it possible for the Land Claim's Court to be used as a court of first instance. Those who opted for this option had to do their own investigative and preparatory work prior to submission of the claim to this tribunal.

261 Chapters 11 and 111, Restitution of Land Rights Act 22 of 1994 (commenced 2 December 1994).

262 Christopher (n.254).

263 Ibid.

264 Ibid.

265 Christopher (n.254).

'negotiation' since it is informed by both liberal legal principles and local context. This can be implied from the state's imposition of conditions which would govern the use of land by its 'historic owners'. As has been stated earlier, one of the stated objectives of both the Zimbabwean and South African land reform processes was the promotion of economic growth which necessitated the transfer of land to both the landless and to those blacks who aspired to be commercial farmers.[266] The latter government, however, recognized that some claimants did not have the required skills for venturing into commercial farming; hence the additional requirement that land could be transferred only to those who agreed to 15-year 'strategic partnerships' with agribusiness.[267] This could be emulated by Zimbabwe, whose radical land reform programme has been widely critiqued for its lack of post-settlement support.[268]

Another innovation of the South African land reform programme is its recognition of the notion of a collective right to property.[269] Thus, claims for restitution can be brought by both individuals and groups.[270] Impliedly, the historic rights holders of land appropriated through apartheid legislation were both groups and individuals. While the notion of group rights to land has led to implementation hurdles and possibilities of gender discrimination, it does reflect the postcoloniality of South Africa's land reform process.

It follows that acceptable expropriations must be moderate or 'within' the master's discourse. The paradigmatic discourse favors the sanctity of property and mostly restricts expropriations to serving public purposes such as building roads. This explains why South Africa's land reform process, which is often hailed for having adhered to the rule of law, was initially premised on interim conformist provisions. These incorporate the right to property and allowed expropriation of land only for public purposes with compensation.[271] This is a stricter application

266 De Villiers (n.41) as read with Bratton (n.65).

267 This issue has been discussed extensively in Alistair Fraser, 'Hybridity Emergent: Geo-History, Learning, and Land Restitution in South Africa' (2007) 38(2) *Geoforum*.

268 De Villiers (n.41).

269 The long title of the Restitution of Land Rights Act states that the act is 'to provide for the restitution of rights in land to persons or communities dispossessed of such rights after 19 June 1913'.

270 See, for example, *The Richtersveld Community and Others v Alexkor Limited* [2004] 3 All SA 244 (LCC).

271 S28 of the 1993 Interim Constitution of South Africa Act 200 of 1993 states that;

a Every person shall have the right to acquire and hold rights in property and, to the extent that the nature of the rights permits, to dispose of such rights.

b No deprivation of any rights in property shall be permitted otherwise than in accordance with a law.

c Where any rights in property are expropriated pursuant to a law referred to in Subsection (2), such expropriation shall be permissible for public purposes only and shall be subject to the payment of agreed compensation or, failing agreement, to the payment of such compensation and within such period as may be determined by a court of law as just and equitable, taking into account all relevant factors, including, in the case of the determination of compensation, the use to which the property is being put, the than the final South African Constitution which permits public interest–based land expropriation. In S25 (4), it is clearly stated that:

> [P]ublic interest includes the nation's commitment to land reform and to reforms to bring about equitable access to all South Africa's natural resources.[272]

This provision and continuing pressure from some sectors that land be expropriated has not influenced the government to follow the Zimbabwean route. So far only one farm has been acquired in this manner.[273] South Africa has largely redistributed land using the willing seller–willing buyer method which derives its legal mandate from the Provision of Land and Assistance Act.[274]

The goal of South Africa's ruling party's Reconstruction and Development Programme (RDP) was to transfer 30% of land within five years of independence through restitution and redistribution.[275] However, in 1999, only 1% had been distributed. This prompted the government to extend the deadline for its 30% target to 2014. By 2007, 13 years after the country's independence, approximately 4% had been transferred via both restitution and redistribution. The slow pace of the programme has been attributed to the now abandoned willing seller–willing buyer principle.[276]

One could say that the slow pace of South Africa's programme would qualify the goZ's position that reliance on market forces would not redress the legacy of colonialism. Yet, for South Africa, Zimbabwe is an example of the perils of a land reform process which is not rights based.[277] Ironically, more than 1,500 South African white farmers have died since the country's independence.[278] This is almost 100 times the recorded number of white farmers' deaths in Zimbabwe since the fast track land reform process began in 2000.[279]

Obviously, the South African model also violates the master's discourse since frustration with the same has led to violations of the right to life. Actually, its willing seller–willing buyer model is not an exact replica of the master's script. To reiterate, the South African government has been largely reluctant to expropriate, preferring to distribute land which has been made available by 'willing sellers'.

---

history of its acquisition, its market value, the value of the investments in it by those affected and the interests of those affected.

272 S25 (4), Constitution of the Republic of South Africa 1996.
273 Commission on the Restitution of Land Rights, supra note 1806.
274 Ibid.
275 Ibid.
276 Africa Research Institute, 'Waiting for the Green Revolution: Land Reform in South Africa' *Briefing Note 1301* (May 2013).
277 Allison Goebbel, 'Is Zimbabwe the Future of South Africa? The Implications for Land Reform in Southern Africa' (2005) 23 *Journal of Contemporary African Studies* 345.
278 Ibid.
279 Ibid.

Yet, the 'willing buyers' are largely hypothetical. It is different from the early willing seller–willing buyer model of Zimbabwe where the 'willing buyer' was easily identified as the state which purchased the land for distribution to its people. In South Africa, the buyers are those groups or individuals whose access to redistribution grants is subject to the approval of the Minister of Land Affairs.[280]

This was initially carried out through a Settlement/Land Acquisition Grant of R16,000 per qualifying household.[281] Since the extension of the deadline for distributing 30% of white-owned land, redistribution is now implemented through the Land Redistribution for Development Program (LRAD) which provides grants of between R20,000 and R100,000 to those who can come up with at least R5,000 in cash or labour.[282] This has meant that land has been largely transferred to few farmers with money, and not exactly to the rural poor.[283] Also, as in Zimbabwe before 2000, South African white farmers have been unwilling to make land available for redistribution.[284]

Another form of 'agency' is in South Africa's evaluation of compensation which is not entirely market-based. It is an attempt to strike a balance between public interest and respect for property rights. In accordance with S25 (3) of the South African Constitution, the amount to be paid, period for payment and payment method must be 'just and equitable'. The market value is just one of the stated appropriate issues which must be factored in. In fact, in some cases it has been difficult to assess the 'market value' of the land since farmers had no opportunity to offer their properties in the 'open market' due to land invasions and informal settlements.[285] It should be recalled that there is no absolute international legal principle on how to assess compensation for expropriated land. As has been shown previously, this is one of the issues which are at the core of Zimbabwe's land debacle.

Nonetheless, a discussion of South African land reform attempts is inconclusive as Zimbabwe has already departed from the market-driven model. Perhaps, lessons can be learnt from Mozambique, which also faced economic decline and unrest after all land was nationalized soon after independence.[286] The framework for the implementation of the Land law in Mozambique was laid in the land regulations of 1987. These contained both provisions for compensation to those who lost their land-use rights and processes for dispute resolution.[287]

280 Edward Lahiff, *Land Reform in South Africa: Is It Meeting the Challenge?* (Programme for Land and Agrarian Studies, University of the Western Cape 2001) <www.plaas.org.za/>.

281 Ibid.

282 Ibid.

283 Ibid.

284 Ibid.

285 Ibid.

286 See Christopher Tanner, 'Law-Making in an African Context: The 1997 Mozambican Land Law' *FAO Legal Papers Online No. 26* (2002) <www.fao.org/fileadmin/user_upload/legal/docs/lpo26.pdf>.

287 Decree no. 16/87 of 15 July.

According to these regulations, a family which was moved was entitled to compensation for improvements and alternative land of similar value.[288] The family also had a right to view the new land before occupying the same.[289] With regard to dispute resolution, the law provided an administrative appeal process within the Ministry of Agriculture.[290] It also offered the possibility of an appeal to the ordinary courts, with the exception that Council of Ministers' decisions were final.[291] Disputes could also be resolved through conciliation, and there were provisions for the composition of a conciliation committee.[292] However, the law lacked precision on the question as to what mechanism was best suited to each particular situation.[293] These regulations were also unenforceable due to tenure insecurity and war-time human movement.[294] Therefore, there was a general expectation that land conflicts would be resolved after the war.[295]

So, when the war finally ended in 1992, different categories of claimants sought restoration of their historic land. According to Jon Unruh, these include, *inter alia*, claims by descendants of those who were dispossessed during the colonial era, those who received land from local administrators after independence, former Portuguese land owners whose land was nationalized in 1975, returning refugees, those who had occupied land abandoned during the war, people who took advantage of the post-war fluidity in property rights to acquire land, war veterans and elites from both RENAMO and FRELIMO who wanted land as part of the peace dividends.[296] With the exception of land rights of returnees, Zimbabwe has similar categories of claimants.

Mozambique's land restitution exercise differed from the South African experience largely because the country lacked resources for pursuing a formal programme.[297] Donor funding was earmarked only for transporting and managing the largely peaceful return of refugees from exile to their original homes.[298] Disputes were initially resolved through customary structures which were seen as legitimate by the local people.[299] Overlapping claims involving locals, elite interests and foreign investors persisted, however, since a number of returnees found

288 Art 52, Decree no. 16/87 of 15 July.
289 Ibid.
290 Article 69, Decree no. 16/87 of 15 July.
291 Article 70, ibid.
292 Article 82, ibid.
293 Steve Boucher, Laurel L. Rose and Michael J. Roth, 'Legal Uncertainty and Land Disputes in the Peri-Urban Areas of Mozambique: Land Markets in Transition' *Research Paper No. 121* (Land Tenure Center, University of Wisconsin-Madison 1995).
294 Ibid.
295 Ibid.
296 Unruh (2005) (n.1).
297 Tanner (n.286).
298 The returnees' right to property restitution was incorporated in the peace accord of 1992. See Protocol III, Section IV, General Peace Agreement (4 October 1992) and Article 5(4) Tripartite Agreement between the Government of the Republic of Mozambique, the Government of Zimbabwe and UNHCR for the Voluntary Repatriation of Mozambican Refugees from Zimbabwe (1993).
299 Tanner (n.286). See also Law no. 4/92 of 6 May.

their land occupied by the latter that were favoured by the legislation of the day and by state practice.[300]

Due to internal and external pressure, the government initiated a land reform programme which sought to create a legal environment for managing these conflicting aspects of restitution.[301] For example, RENAMO officials were advocating for denationalization as a step towards official advancement of restitution.[302] Donors were also calling for a commitment to international human rights standards.[303] Thus, a number of land Commissions were created.

Features of Mozambique's new land law which can be emulated in Zimbabwe's transition are the regulations which allowed different aspects of restitution to be 'self-managed'.[304] The first lesson can be drawn from the much-publicized regulations on formalization of land rights.[305] These called for the renewal of those outstanding land applications which had been previously subjected to competing land claims.[306] Affected parties had to resubmit outstanding land applications within a specified timeframe.[307] Remaining land titles of all those who failed to renew their claims by August 2001 were cancelled, and this became the source of land for restitution to local people who had lost their land before, during and after the war, mostly under contentious circumstances.[308] In the case of Zimbabwe, such land could be given to those landless people who were prevented by the political character of the post-2000 fast track land reform process from applying for land.

However, Mozambique has not adequately dealt with the issue of ex-colonialists' land rights. Joseph Hanlon has it that some Portuguese ex-colonialists successfully relied on colonial-era documents to claim the restoration of their land rights in remote areas of Mozambique.[309] This route could not be said to have been sanctioned by the law since this group's rights were extinguished at independence when all land was nationalized.[310] There are also strong political sentiments against the return of land to the colonialists; hence, the outstanding issue is the question of their entitlement to compensation. This issue which is also pertinent in Zimbabwe is still to be addressed in Mozambique since both the Land law of 1997 and investment law are silent on the issue. Although the investment

300 See Act No. 1/86 of 16 April 1986 which has since been revoked by the Mozambique Land Act (No. 19/97).
301 Unruh (2005) (n.1).
302 Ibid.
303 Ibid.
304 Unruh (2005) (n.1).
305 Land Law (Decree 66/98).
306 Article 46, ibid.
307 Ibid.
308 Unruh (2005) (n.1).
309 Joseph Hanlon, 'The Land Debate in Mozambique; Will Foreign Investors, the Urban Elite, Advanced Peasants or Family Farmers Drive Rural Developments?' *Research Paper Commissioned by Oxfam GB, Regional Management Center for Southern Africa* (2002) <www.oxfam.org>.
310 Preamble, Art 15, 16, 39–31 and 42 *Lei de Terras* 1979.

law does contain provisions on the valuing and timing of compensation for rights which are expropriated in the public interest, its provisions would not apply to the Portuguese ex-colonialists.[311] This is because this law's concern is with those investments which were made after it entered into force.[312]

Against this background, and as in Zimbabwe, former Portuguese settlers and their descendants have approached external forums on the issue of compensation.[313] This prompted the former colonial master, Portugal, to set up a department to deal with their concerns.[314] In 2003, the Export Finance and Insurance Corporation stated that the ex-colonialists are entitled to compensation.[315] As in Zimbabwe, however, concerns have been raised that Mozambique has no capacity to pay such compensation.[316]

Nonetheless, the civil war and droughts plus the collapse of FRELIMO's Soviet ally in 1989 forced the government of Mozambique to officially disassociate itself from Marxist doctrine and to embrace a liberal democratic model.[317] A limited role for the private sector was recognized in 1984, and pressure from Bretton Woods institutions led to fundamental changes in 1986 when the structural adjustment programme was introduced.[318] In 1990, the liberal notions of the rule of law, international human rights and democracy were embraced in the new Constitution, but the land continued to belong to the state.[319] Future investments were protected by the provision that;

> [E]xpropriation may only take place on grounds of public need, use or interest, as defined by law, and there shall be just compensation.[320]

Of particular interest to this section are the findings of Mozambique's 1992 Ad Hoc Land Commission, which was mandated to review state farmland divestiture.[321] This body's research findings indicated the need for a new property rights regime which protected existing customary land tenure arrangements while also promoting investments.[322] This led to the establishment of an Inter-Ministerial Commission for the Revision of Land Legislation in 1995 (Mozambique Land Commission).[323]

311 Article 13, Law on Investment in Mozambique (Law No. 3/93, Approved on 24 June 1993).
312 Article 27, ibid.
313 Mozambique News Agency, 'Prime Minister Defends Nationalization' *AIM Reports, No. 156* (21 April 1999) <www.poptel.org.uk>.
314 Ibid.
315 Unruh (2005) (n.1).
316 Ibid.
317 Tanner (n.286).
318 Ibid.
319 Preamble, Constitution of Mozambique 1990. (Approved and enacted in November 1990).
320 S86 (2), ibid.
321 Ibid.
322 Ibid.
323 Ibid.

The work of this body was complemented by efforts of a number of stakeholders, including non-governmental organizations, academics, donors and foreign interests.[324] The outcome was the Land Policy of 1995, Mozambique Land Law of 1997 – *Lei de Terras* (*Lei No. 19/97*) and regulations to the Land Law (Decree 66/98) which deal with procedures for formalizing new land-use rights.[325] A Technical Annex which is provided for in Articles 9, 10 and 30 of these regulations addresses issues of identification, delimitation and registration of existing community land rights.[326]

This legal framework is remarkable for its departure from the dominant Western understanding that privatization and individual rights to property usher investments and economic growth. The land law was rather informed by and reflected the reality of Mozambique. This is inferred from the law's recognition of verbal evidence as proof of land rights.[327] Land continued to vest in the state and remained non-transferable as this was seen as a way of protecting small holders' access and use of land from domestic and foreign speculators.[328]

This approach raises the question as to whether restrictions on alienability are compatible with the right to property, thus further complicating the uncertainties surrounding the scope of the right to property in international law.[329] It has been demonstrated earlier that there is no international agreement on the scope of the right to property. This friction has often manifested itself on the question of the conditions which need to be fulfilled by a state when it exercises its right to expropriate property within its territory, and not on the issue of restrictions on property transfer.[330] Kendall Burr had this to say on this additional controversy:

> [B]ut as Western ideals of private property rights are incorporated into international documents, alienability may become a central feature of the human right to property, pressuring nations like Mozambique to privatize their land . . . human rights activists (must) rethink their interpretations of 'fundamental' property rights, which risk imposing one's culture's values on another and may in fact hinder economic development.[331]

Thus, the land law of Mozambique does not provide for an absolute right to property.[332] It guarantees individual and collective rights to use and improve

324 Ibid. See also Tanner (n.286).
325 Unruh (2005) (n.1).
326 Ministerial Diploma 29-A/2000.
327 Article 15, *Lei de Terras (Lei No. 19/97)*. See also Hanlon (n.309), and Joseph Hanlon, 'Renewed Land Debate and the "Cargo Cult" in Mozambique' (2004) 30(3) *Journal of Southern African Studies* 603.
328 Article 3, 13, 15 and 24, *Lei de Terras (Lei No. 19/97)* as read with Article 46, Constitution of Mozambique 1990.
329 Kendall Burr, 'The Evolution of the International Law of Alienability: The 1997 Land Law of Mozambique as a Case Study' (2005) 43 *Columbia Journal of Transnational Law* 961.
330 Ibid.
331 Ibid.
332 Ibid.

the land which could be acquired in three different ways.[333] The first manner is through occupation by an individual or community in accordance with customary laws and practices which are compatible with the Constitution.[334] Use rights could also be obtained by a local person who has had peaceful and *bona fide* occupation of the land for a period of ten years or more.[335] Finally, individuals and communities who have had no prior connection to the land in question could acquire these rights through a formal request to the state.[336]

This recognition of both collective and individual tenure is innovative as it reflects the law's postcoloniality. Other significant features of the law are its promotion of gender equality and deference to customary law in land allocation and management.[337] The post-1997 Mozambique land law also ensured that security of tenure was guaranteed only to those formal holders of land rights who put the land to productive use.[338] Article 19 of the 1997 Land Law, in particular, mandated all holders of land-use rights (DUAT), *direto de USO aproveitamento da terra*, to submit a business plan for approval.[339] After two years of the plan's implementation, 50-year use rights, which are renewable for another 50 years, were to be granted to those whose plans were approved.[340]

Land rights of those who did not carry out what they set out to do in the approved business plan were revoked within two years of acceptance of that plan for foreign companies and five years for national companies.[341] This is no different from the land audits which have been conducted by the government of Zimbabwe, but it is noteworthy that the conduct of such an exercise by a regime with recognized democratic credentials might be viewed as legitimate.[342] It should be noted that concerns have been raised by villagers in Zimbabwe that the elite beneficiaries of the A2 farms do not utilize this land.[343]

Zimbabwe can also learn from Mozambique's innovative way of encouraging domestic and foreign companies who require land for commercial purposes to consult or negotiate on their own with local communities.[344] Lessons can also be drawn from the country's laws which allow small-holder community rights of occupation to co-exist with formal investor *Duat* rights.[345] One of the major benefits of this approach, especially in the context of Zimbabwe which has a

333 Article 12, *Lei de Terras* (*Lei No. 19/97*).
334 Article 12(a), ibid.
335 Article 12(b), ibid.
336 Article 12(c), ibid.
337 Articles 16 and 24, *Lei de Terras* (*Lei No. 19/97*).
338 Article 19, *Lei de Terras* (*Lei No. 19/97*).
339 Ibid.
340 Article 17, *Lei de Terras* (*Lei No. 19/97*).
341 Article 25, *Lei de Terras* (*Lei No. 19/97*).
342 See *The Herald* (Zimbabwe), 'Govt Repossesses A2 Farms' 4 February 2008, <www.kubatana.net>.
343 Ibid.
344 Unruh (2005) (n.1).
345 Ibid.

history of unequal tenure arrangements, is that it prevents the country from being divided into subsistence farming areas and commercial areas. This method could be used by some of the Zimbabwe's white farmers who lost land during the post-2000 farm invasions.

4.6 Conclusion

The purpose of this chapter was to explore the relationship between land reform and transitional justice using Zimbabwe as a case study. It was explained that most of the literature on land and transitional justice focuses on restitution and compensation as policy options for dealing with past land injustices. Yet, restitution cannot adequately deal with the large numbers of people who were dispossessed during the colonial encounter. Such an exercise requires redistribution. Is redistribution transitional justice?

Zimbabwe dealt with colonial land injustices by expropriating land from white famers and distributing it to the landless and some blacks who aspired to be commercial farmers. One of the conditions for expropriation to be lawful under international law is the payment of compensation. However, Zimbabwe only paid adequate compensation in the first ten years and later adopted a constitutional provision which states that the government will pay only for improvements on the land. Responsibility for paying the dispossessed farmers the actual value of the land is laid on the United Kingdom, the former colonial master. Zimbabwe is not an isolated case in this regard. Mozambique is yet to resolve the issue of compensation for land nationalized at independence in 1975. South Africa has now abandoned the willing seller–willing buyer method and it is yet to be seen how it would proceed with land reform.

Incidentally, and as the case studies of South Africa and Mozambique demonstrate, the legislation of those countries is not entirely liberal. It rather reflects the ambivalence of the colonial exchange since an inevitable consequence of this contradictory colonial encounter is the adoption of nuanced transitional justice options. For example, some of the transitional land laws have embraced both customary law and civil law. The laws also recognize both individual entitlements to land and collective rights to land. The programmes are state-led, the market is tampered with and, in the case of Mozambique, land's inalienability is even restricted.

In terms of what can be practically done in the current transition, Zimbabwe has already established a Land Commission, which has been mandated to *inter alia* carry out a land audit and deal with issues of security of tenure. As in Kenya and Mauritius, it would be useful if Zimbabwe's truth commission (the National Peace and Reconciliation Commission) could also garner citizens' views on the land issue. This may help uncover the truth about land invasions and assist the dispossessed white farmers in getting closure.

5 Minorities in postcolonial transitions

5.1 Introduction

Regimes that adopt transitional justice mechanisms aspire to move from either armed conflict or authoritarianism to a democratic dispensation based on the rule of law.[1] The rule of law necessitates the enactment and application of laws that proscribe and ultimately punish discrimination against various persons and communities, including minorities.[2] Many transitional societies harbor marginalized ethnic, cultural or religious groups.[3] In postcolonial Africa, attacks on minorities are often the root cause of the armed conflict or authoritarianism.[4] Oftentimes the situation is exacerbated by the fact that minorities' numeric inferiority prevents them from securing their rights through democratic processes.[5]

The previous chapter discussed Zimbabwe's experience with the 'majority's' claim to land that had historically been unlawfully expropriated by the 'white' colonial regime for the benefit of the dominant minority group.[6] Superficially, the racial division suggests that black Zimbabweans are a homogenous unit. Yet the reality, on which this chapter will focus, is that ethnic diversity is an integral cause of conflict in the country.[7]

Disgruntled black minority groupings exist within Zimbabwe. Unfortunately, there is no standardized research that has looked at whether different ethnic groups benefitted equally from the country's various land redistribution schemes.[8] Nonetheless, the Ndebele have persistently complained that they are

1 Mark Arenhovel, 'Democratisation and Transitional Justice' (2008) 15(3) *Democratisation* 570.
2 Guillermo A. O'Donnell, 'Why the Rule of Law Matters' (2004) 15(4) *Journal of Democracy* 32.
3 Chris Chapman, *Transitional Justice and the Rights of Minorities and Indigenous Peoples* (International Centre for Transitional Justice 2009).
4 Abraham Korir Sing'Oei and Laura A. Young, 'Left Behind: Minority Rights, Transitional Justice and Lessons for Kenya' (2010) 5 *Interdisciplinary Journal of Human Rights Law* 49.
5 Khanyisela Moyo, 'Minorities in Postcolonial Transitions: The Ndebele in Zimbabwe' (2011) 1 *African Journal of Legal Studies* 149, 150.
6 Chapter 4.
7 See Terence Ranger, *The Invention of Tribalism in Zimbabwe* (Gweru: Mambo Press, 1985).
8 In its first report to the Committee on CERD, the GoZ of Zimbabwe promised to give statistics on land distributed to Ndebele and Shonas in its next report, but it did not do so. See ¶ 9, Summary Record of the 1132 meeting: Zimbabwe. 12/04/96 CERD/C/SR.1132.

being denied economic and social benefits.[9] Some groups within the Ndebele want to exercise the right to external self-determination.[10] Even though these concerns may be deemed peripheral to the conflict of the day, a history of violations of rights may preclude members of such groups from being part of a shared narrative of the conflict, and this gives rise to their demands for pre-emptive measures. Left unattended, these concerns can forestall the peace process.[11] Such issues are bound to surface in transitional periods since these are times when various stakeholders are involved in mapping the destiny of their society. This is an exercise described by Ruti Teitel as both 'backward' and 'forward' looking.[12] Hurst Hannum has explained that demands for group accommodation and for some form of autonomy are based on three legitimate needs.[13] These are the protection of minority rights, an expression of self-determination and the quest for democratic governance.[14]

Against this background, this chapter examines the relationship between transitional justice and postcolonial minorities' quest for either internal or external self-determination. It begins by discussing the relationship between transitional justice and minorities. Then it analyses the distinctive features of postcolonial minorities. The chapter then details the story of the Ndebele in Zimbabwe. This is followed by an analysis which looks at the limitations of international law and its potential for facilitating the gradual move towards peace. This section includes comparative materials from those postcolonial societies which have had to address similar concerns. The chapter concludes with viewpoints which are of relevance not only to Zimbabwe but also to other postcolonial societies.

5.2 Minorities and transitional justice

The relationship between transitional justice and minority rights is contradictory.[15] Protection of minorities and fulfilment of the right to self-determination can

9 See Minority Group International, 'The Ndebele Profile' <https://minorityrights.org/minorities/ndebele/>. See also Brilliant Mhlanga, 'Devolution – The "Ticklish" Subject: The "Northern Problem" and the National Question in Zimbabwe' (2012) 1(2) *Ubuntu Journal of Conflict Transformation* 206.

10 An example is the Mthwakazi Republic Party <https://mthwakazirepublicparty.org/>. Some of the other groups fighting for external self-determination are discussed in Mhlanga (n.9).

11 For example, the concerns of Chief Buthelezi's Inkatha Freedom Party nearly threatened South Africa's transition to black majority rule. See Hercules Booysen, 'South Africa: In Need of a Federal Constitution for its Minority Peoples' (1997) 19 *Loyola International and Comparative Law Review* 789, Hennie A. Strydom, 'Minority Rights Issues in Post-Apartheid South Africa' (1997) *19 Loyola of Los Angeles International and Comparative Law Journal* 873 and Barbara Oomen, 'Group Rights in Post-Apartheid South Africa – The Case of the Traditional Leaders' (1999) 31(44) *The Journal of Legal Pluralism and Unofficial Law* 73.

12 Ruti G. Teitel, *Transitional Justice* (Oxford University Press 2000).

13 Hurst Hannum, *Autonomy, Sovereignty, and Self-Determination: The Accommodation of Conflicting Rights* (University of Pennsylvania Press 1990).

14 Ibid.

15 See Michael Freeman, 'National Self-determination, Peace and Human Rights' (1998) 10(2) *Peace Review*.

be defined as prerequisites for a peaceful democratic establishment, but they can also be seen as an impediment to the same.[16] According to Sing'Oei and Young, there is

> [A] tension between nationalism and perceived separation, a tension between individualistic and commutarian frames of reference and a tension between formal legalistic and traditional, or indigenous processes.[17]

Nonetheless, some transitional societies have removed discriminatory provisions from their constitutions and introduced mechanisms for inclusion in truth commissions and peace agreements as part of their policy of guarantees of non-recurrence.[18] For example, the Guatemalan Peace Accord underscored the need to constitutionally define the country as multi-ethnic, multi-cultural, and multi-lingual.[19] In Burundi, the Arusha Peace and Reconciliation Accord (2000) prohibited all political or other associations from advocating for ethnic, religious or gender discrimination, and provided the foundation for a consociational power-sharing agreement.[20]

It is axiomatic that concerns of minorities need to be a key aspect of the transitional agenda if the conflict or war has been caused by the state's violation of their rights.[21] In 1993, the then Special Rapporteur on minorities, Asbjørn Eide, referred to this context as a 'situation involving minorities'.[22] According to him, such situations occur when there is a general feeling of discontent within those who belong to minority groups, and this is connected to their group membership.[23] The nature of their grievances can be assessed in terms of the demands that they make.[24]

The first demand is for equality of treatment.[25] For example, in Northern Ireland prior to the Good Friday Agreement of 1998, the minority Catholic community claimed that successive Unionist governments had subjected them to various forms of social, political and economic discrimination.[26] The Northern Ireland example is very interesting because it also introduces a second set of demands which have been made by minority groups. This is the legally contro-

16 Ibid.
17 Sing'Oei and Young (n.4) 61–68.
18 Paragraphs 62–64 Report of the Special Rapporteur on the promotion of truth, justice, reparation and guarantees of non-recurrence, Pablo de Greiff, 2015, A/HRC/30/42.
19 Paragraph 64, ibid.
20 Paragraph 63, ibid.
21 See Christie Bell, *On the Law of Peace: Peace Agreements and the Lex Pacificatoria* (Oxford University Press 2008) pages 109–128.
22 Paragraph 44, Asbjørn Eide, Possible Ways and Means of Facilitating the Peaceful and Constructive Solution of Problems Involving Minorities U.N. Doc. E/CN.4/Sub.2/1993/34 and Add.1–4 (1993).
23 Ibid.
24 Ibid.
25 ¶45, ibid.
26 See Joseph Ruane, *The Dynamics of Conflict in Northern Ireland: Power, Conflict and Emancipation* (Cambridge University Press 1996).

versial and extreme claim for secession. In this context, groups will be demanding that they join their fellow members in another state or create their own new state in the area which they occupy.

Also, some governments have imposed rigid identities on people and have quashed any dissent by way of ethnic cleansing.[27] Thus, the third set of demands is for conditions which enable the minority to preserve their identity.[28] These groups often seek the use of their language, religion and other aspects of cultural identity to maintain their culture.[29] Some of these claimants have tied such requirements to the need for a degree of non-territorial autonomy, for example, the use of their own laws based on their own culture in family law matters.[30]

Finally, there are some minorities who have demanded territorial autonomy.[31] As stated earlier, this is a fundamental feature of polities where regions are accorded local self-government.[32] Popular examples of these structures include classic federalism, consociation, and arrangements of confederation, devolution and decentralization.[33] This has been illustrated in the outcome of the 1995 Dayton Peace Agreement, which restructured Bosnia and Herzegovina along ethnic and religious lines.[34]

Similarly, a number of recent peace agreements include provisions for advancing self-determination claims of minorities.[35] Notable examples include the already-mentioned General Framework Agreement for Peace in Bosnia and Herzegovina (1995 Dayton Agreement), the Northern Ireland Peace Agreement (1998 Good Friday Agreement), the Bougainville Peace Agreement (2001) and the Constitutional Framework for Provisional Self-government in Kosovo (2001). This state practice, which has shaped comparative constitutional law, can be construed as a legal justification for addressing minority concerns in transition.[36] Indeed, in post-conflict societies, constitutions are often used to either facilitate the integration of disgruntled minorities or to accord them some degree of autonomy.[37]

The question, then, is whether concerns of minorities are a priority in other transitional contexts, where the cause of the conflict is not necessarily an ethnic conflict or 'situation involving minorities'.[38] Should societies transitioning from

27 For a definition of ethnic cleansing, see ¶130, Final Report of the Commission of Experts Established Pursuant to Security Council Resolution 780, U.N. Doc. S/1994/674 (1992).
28 ¶ 46, Eide (n.22).
29 Ibid.
30 Ibid.
31 ¶ 47, Eide (n.22).
32 Charles E. Ehrlich, 'Democratic Alternatives to Ethnic Conflict: Consociationalism and Neo-Separatism' (2000) 26 *Brook Journal of International Law* 447.
33 Ibid.
34 Dayton Agreement on Implementing the Federation of Bosnia and Herzegovina, Dayton, 10 November 1995, *35 I.L.M. 170 (1996)*.
35 Bell (n.21).
36 Ibid at 200–238.
37 Ibid.
38 See Lawrence Schlemmer, 'The Challenge of Political Transition in South Africa: Majority vs. Minority Rights' (1991) 22(1) *South African Journal of Sociology* 16.

authoritarian rule focus on minimal guarantees which facilitate a society's move to peace and defer such special rights?[39] Should the immediate concern be the move to a unitary democratic state which treats everyone equally?[40] Are minority issues a time-wasting distraction that puts an additional strain on the already limited resources of transitional societies?[41]

Two counter-arguments to this can be made.[42] First, although the most apparent transitional priorities are democratization and economic advancement, transitional societies have in fact accorded legal recognition to the language and culture of majorities before prescribing any liberal democratic reforms. Only minorities are told that their own concerns ought to come second to those of the majorities. Deferral of the issue of special rights for minorities is often a means for assimilating those minorities, thus making it difficult for them to make demands in future.

Second, even if one agrees that transitional priorities are minimal guarantees which restore security, so that the state can move to an economically advanced democracy, the focus on minority rights cannot be said to be idle or superfluous. It ensures that nation-building is an inclusive process.

It can also be argued that ignoring minority claims can be detrimental to the security that the transition aims for, as this may prompt radical members of minority groups to resort to violence. Indeed, failure to respect the special characteristics of minorities has often created apprehensions by the groups concerned that they would be subsumed by majority communities. Thus, some of these groups have resorted to preservative measures which include violence. As Deon Geldenhuys and Johann Rossouw put it:

> [W]here minority groups believe that they lack the means to secure their survival as a group, alienation and instability could be the inevitable consequences.[43]

Given all of this, the legal justification for addressing minority concerns in transition are the 'hard' and 'soft' law human rights standards which establish an intricate link between minority rights, self-determination and democratic governance. Another legal basis is state practice observed from recurrent provisions on minorities in post-war international, regional and domestic peace agreements. Indeed, it has been common practice for constitutional designs to respond to an affected group's quest for 'self-determination' and democratic governance.

39 Ibid.

40 Ibid.

41 Judy Barsalou has argued that 'resource constraints and mandate limits are inevitable features of transitional justice mechanisms and trauma relief programs'. Judy Barsalou, *Trauma and Transitional Justice in Divided Societies* (Diane Publishing 2008).

42 Will Kymlicka, 'Justice and Security in the Accommodation of Minority Nationalism' in Alan Dieckhoff (ed) *The Politics of Belonging: Nationalism, Liberalism and Pluralism* (Lexington Books 2004).

43 Deon Geldenhuys and Johann Rossow, 'The International Protection of Minority Rights' *A Special Report Compiled for F W de Klerk Foundation* (2001), <www.cassrccp.com/>.

5.3 The distinctive features of postcolonial transitional minority questions

5.3.1 The postcolonial context

As shown previously, in the paradigmatic human rights discourse, minority concerns become a transitional issue in two contexts. The first of these is those circumstances where the conflict is of an ethnic nature or has been caused by the state's failure to represent everyone without discrimination. The second context is those cases where inclusion of minorities in the transitional agenda is part of the broad democratization process. This simplistic understanding, which often starts with the state as the reference point, has its limitations as it ignores an axiomatic cause of conflict in postcolonial societies.[44] In these societies, ethnic conflict is often traced back to the colonial encounter which involved serious ethnocide.[45]

The roots of postcolonial ethnic conflicts can be explained through an analysis of these countries' three historic epochs.[46] The first of these is the period when the colonialists created the postcolonial state.[47] In order to create institutions for governance, the colonialists relied on ethnographic knowledge of the territories over which they had assumed power to govern each group along racial or ethnic lines.[48] Absolute power was used to subordinate and incorporate diverse groups that had previously existed separately; yet in some cases, there had been long-standing tensions between these groups.[49]

In most cases, colonialists even fostered enmity between indigenous native ethnic groups by placing favoured minorities in positions of power.[50] Examples of this practice are the Belgian policies which bestowed superiority status to the Tutsi in Burundi, the British alliance with the Sunni in colonial Iraq and France's policies which favoured the Alawi minorities in colonial Syria.[51] As shown in the previous chapter, in the partially settled African colonies of Zimbabwe, South

44 See Mai-linh K. Hong, 'A Genocide by Any Other Name: Language, Law and the Response to Darfur' (2008) 49 *Virginia Journal of International Law* 235.

45 Ibid.

46 For a background to the challenges of postcolonial Southern Africa, see Leroy Vail, *The Creation of Tribalism in Southern Africa* (University of California Press 1989).

47 Ibid as read with Hong (n.44).

48 Daniel P.S. Goh, 'From Colonial Pluralism to Postcolonial Multiculturalism: Race State Formation and the Question of Cultural Diversity in Malaysia and Singapore' (2008) 2(1) *Sociology Campus* 232.

49 Ibid.

50 See the Kateka dissenting opinion in Armed Activities, Kooijmans separate opinion, 2005 I.C.J. 116, 9.

51 Matthias Goldmann, 'Does Peace Follow Justice or Vice Versa? Plans for Post-Conflict Justice in Burundi' (2006) 30 *Fletcher Forum of World Affairs* 137, Makau Mutua, 'The Iraq Paradox: Minority and Group Rights in a Viable Constitution' (2006) 54 *Buffalo Law Review* 927 at 939 and Daniel Pipes, 'The Alawi Capture of Power in Syria' (1989) *Middle Eastern Studies* <www.danielpipes.org>.

Africa and Mozambique, the dominant minorities were the white settlers.[52] In all these cases, discontent with the privileges and coercive policies of these dominant minorities were a rallying point for the majorities' nationalist struggles, which largely evolved along communitarian religious, linguistic or ethnic lines.

Thus, the second epoch which explains ethnic rivalry is the democratization processes and the transition from minority to majority rule.[53] As explained in previous chapters, the quest for development added to concerns amongst the postcolonial elite that their new states would be destabilized led to the adoption of the *uti possidentis* doctrine.[54] This principle, which maintained the borders that had been inherited from colonialism, was initially adopted during the gaining of independence of the former Spanish colonies of Latin America. It was also incorporated into the Charter of the Organisation of African Unity (OAU) during the African decolonization process, together with the principles of state sovereignty and territorial integrity.[55]

Uti possidentis served two purposes, namely to prevent frontier disputes among new states and to warn potential colonialists that there was no territory which was *terra nullius.* Groups which had previously existed separately were expected to live together in harmony. The prevailing view then was that discrimination was only an attribute of colonialism.[56] This understanding had an added weight in former settler colonies where attempts at promoting difference had a sad resonance with the racist past where minority rights were inimical to democracy and associated with the entrenchment of white privileges.[57]

Notwithstanding these good intentions, the shift of power from dominant minorities to majorities did not necessarily usher peace in postcolonial societies.[58] This is because the terms of decolonization were a product of elite pacts.[59] The effects of this in postcolonial Africa has been explained by Chinedu Reginald Ezetah in his view that:

> [T]he practical consequence of absence of consent in the amalgamation of the post-colonial African state has been the legitimization of coerciveassimilation of nations, tyranny and violent repression of liberation movements. The specter of failed states has been attributed to the tyranny and authoritarianism of the contrived states in Africa and their concocted citizenry. This

52 Chapter 4.

53 See Anthony Anghie, 'Representing Culture, Translating Human Rights Symposium: Nationalism, Development and the Postcolonial State: The Legacies of the League of Nations' (2006) 41 *Texas International Law Journal Summer* 441.

54 See Enver Hasani, 'International Law under Fire, Uti Possidetis juris: From Rome to Kosovo' (2003) 27 *Fletcher Forum of World Affair* 85.

55 Ibid.

56 Strydom (n.11).

57 Ibid, for the South African example.

58 Chinedu R. Ezetah, 'International Law of Self-Determination and the Ogoni Question: Mirroring Africa's Post-Colonial Dilemma' (1996) 19 *Loyola of Los Angeles International Law and Comparative Law Journal* 811.

59 Ibid.

> is the heritage of colonialism and Africa's post-colonial burden which will remain a recurring decimal to the international law of self-determination.[60]

This failure to recognize and legally manage plurality has largely contributed to the classification of these states as being characterized by war, authoritarianism and dictatorship.[61] This is because ethnic conflicts and the state's tendency to use force to quash dissent was a common feature of the period after decolonization.[62]

Thus, the third era in postcolonial contexts which created disgruntlement among minority groups and their related demands is the postcolonial era. Most of the grievances expressed by minorities are a protest against the effects of the policies of postcolonial states which had the effect of marginalizing or violating minority rights.[63] Famous illustrations of this are the Rwandan genocide and the Ogoni's quest for self-determination.[64] The latter was prompted partly by environmental degradation and partly by the Nigerian's state's violation of the Ogoni people's physical integrity rights.[65]

Over and above all these concerns, there are specific issues which affect females within postcolonial minority communities.[66] In addition to being subjected to the same injustices as their male counterparts during the colonial era, they also had to endure further subjugation from their men who treated them thus as a way of regaining their lost power.[67] After colonization, these women also experienced multiple forms of discrimination.[68] For example, postcolonial governments are on record for having used women as targets of ethnic cleansing usually through systematic rape and sexual slavery.[69] Unfortunately, the usual reaction to real or perceived ethnocide by patriarchs within the minority communities has been to subject their women to harmful cultural practices.[70] As Darini Rajasingham put it;

> [W]ithin the dialectics of post-colonial nationalism, women have figured as the idealized preservers of pre-colonial culture and tradition. They are seen to be: a) untainted by colonialism; b) the bearers and nurturers of custom,

60 Ibid at 853.
61 Ibid.
62 For example, Nigeria and Congo experienced civil wars which were aimed at stopping a minority group from seceding soon after they became independent in 1960.
63 For the Darfur example, see Hong (n.44).
64 See Goldmann (n.51) as read with Ezetah (n.58).
65 Ezetah (n.58).
66 Darini Rajasingham, 'On Mediating Multiple Identities: The Shifting Field of Women's Sexualities within the Community, State and Nation' in Margaret A. Schuler (ed) *From Basic Needs to Basic Rights: Women's Claim to Human Rights* (Women, Law and Development International 1995) pages 233–248.
67 Ibid.
68 Ibid.
69 See Final Report of Special Rapporteur on Contemporary Forms of Slavery on Systematic rape, sexual slavery and slavery-like practices during armed conflict, U.N. Doc. E/CN.4/Sub.2/1998/13 (1998).
70 Rajasingham (n.66).

> tradition and culture within the household . . . c) the mothers of the nation who literally reproduce and maintain the purity of the ethnic/racial/national community.[71]

All these issues are illuminated by the concerns of the Ndebele people of Zimbabwe to be presented next.

5.4 The story of the Ndebele of Zimbabwe

The Ndebele of Zimbabwe, who are mainly concentrated in the southern and western parts of the country, have a strong group identity, born out of a culture and language that is fundamentally different from that of the majority Shona ethnic group.[72] Their existence in this territory is not unusual, as in common with other postcolonial states, Zimbabwe is artificial in that it harbors distinct minorities who are inadequately represented in dominant narratives of its contested conflict.[73] This is constitutionally a 'God-fearing' country, though issues of religion do not belong to the political arena as there are largely left to individual conscience.[74] Thus, the most relevant fault lines in any credible discussion on minority concerns in Zimbabwe are ethnic, cultural and linguistic.

Within and in addition to two major ethnic groups, of approximately 82% Shona speakers, 17% Ndebele speakers and tiny white and Asian populations, the country has 16 constitutionally recognized official languages, namely Chewa, Chibarwe, English, Kalanga, Koisan, Nambya, Ndau, Ndebele, Shangani, Shona, sign language, Sotho, Tonga, Tswana, Venda and Xhosa.[75] English is the principal language of instruction all over the country, while Ndebele and Shona are also taught in areas where there are majority languages.[76] There is an explicit constitutional reference to the preservation and promotion of cultural values and practices as a national objective.[77] Also, the Constitution states that everyone has

71 Ibid.
72 See Minority Rights Group, World Directory of Minorities <www.minorityrights.org>.
73 Juliet Thondlana, 'Using Indigenous Languages for Teaching and Learning in Zimbabwe' (2002) <http://jan.ucc.nau.edu/>. The issue of minority culture and language rights in Zimbabwe was raised in par 27 of the concluding observations of the Human Rights Committee in its consideration of the initial and last report of the government of Zimbabwe to the Committee in 1998; ICCPR/C/SR.1649, CCPR/C/SR.1650. See also Summary record of the 1375th meeting: Zimbabwe. 14/03/2000. CERD/C/SR.1375. See also James Muzondidya, 'Invisible Subject Minorities and the Quest for Justice and Reconciliation in Post-Colonial Zimbabwe' in Brian Raftopoulos and Tyrone Savage (eds) *Zimbabwe: Injustice and Political Reconciliation* (Weaver Press 2004) and Teresa Barnes, 'Reconciliation, Ethnicity and School History in Zimbabwe 1980–2002' in Brian Raftopoulos and Tyrone Savage (eds) *Zimbabwe: Injustice and Reconciliation, Institute for Justice & Reconciliation* (Weaver Press 2004).
74 The preamble of Zimbabwe's Constitution acknowledges the supremacy of God.
75 S6 Constitution of Zimbabwe.
76 ¶ 4 Summary record of the GoZ initial report to Committee on CERD (n.73).
77 S16 Constitution of Zimbabwe.

the right to use the language of their choice and to participate in the cultural life of their choice.[78]

Zimbabwe's Constitution includes a declaration of rights, which protects individuals against different forms of discrimination.[79] Thus, the Zimbabwean Constitution provides the legal framework for a society where the law is applied equally to everyone and where there is universal suffrage. It has two key shortcomings, however. First, it does not explicitly provide for collective rights. It is largely liberal and individualistic. Neither has it been a useful tool for the legal protection of minorities who are marginalized politically and economically. This explains why this section will contribute to the collective claim by the Ndebele that they have something to contribute to Zimbabwe's governance but are excluded by the political system from doing so. This group's concerns can be explained through an analysis of four epochs, namely, the colonial era (1840–1980), the period after independence (1980–1987), the period after Gukurahundi (1988–2008) and the current epoch (2008–2019).

5.4.1 1840–1980

Many academic renditions on the subject have traced both the Ndebele deep sense of place and the historic background to their animosity with the majority Shona population to the arrival of King Mzilikazi from Zululand in present-day Zimbabwe around 1840.[80] On arrival in the territory that was inhabited by the Shona under different chieftainships, King Mzilikazi founded the Ndebele state, which assimilated people of different origins, including some Shona.[81] In the process, he is alleged to have raided and pillaged these tribes, stealing their cattle and women, and thus giving rise to the traditional antipathy between the Shona and the Ndebele.[82]

The colonialists relied on this ethnographic knowledge in their approach to the group as they used both force and fraudulent treaties to conquer the Ndebele Kingdom. They also manipulated this history to divide and rule the two major ethnic groups. This was done through a number of ways, including ensuring that the legacy of Ndebele pillage and brutality was portrayed in Rhodesian history books.[83] In the Rhodesian narrative, the Shona were depicted as a weak and disorganized group that had not resisted imperialism as they needed protec-

78 S63 Constitution of Zimbabwe.
79 Chapter 4 Constitution of Zimbabwe.
80 See Julian R.D. Cobbing, 'The Ndebele under the Khumalo, 1820–1896' *Unpublished PhD Thesis* (University of Lancaster 1976), Sabelo J. Ndlovu-Gatsheni, 'Dynamics of Democracy and Human Rights among the Ndebele of Zimbabwe' *Unpublished PhD Thesis* (University of Zimbabwe 2003) and Rahman Ford, 'Law, History, and the Colonial Discourse: Davies v Commissioner and Zimbabwe as a Colonialist Case Study' (2001) 32 *Howard Law Journal* 213.
81 Ibid.
82 Ibid.
83 Barnes (n.73).

tion from the better-organized but militaristic and brutal Ndebele.[84] This in turn allowed the white settlers to portray themselves as the civilized ushers of peace, Christianity and order under the flag of the Union.[85]

These constructs fostered ethnic differences which were evident before and during the war of liberation against colonialism. Indeed, a number of Ndebele traditional leaders openly opposed the colonialists' decision to combine their kingdom with the various Shona chieftainships in 1900.[86] This resentment manifested itself as early as 1914 when the Matabele National Home Society was established to mobilize for an autonomous Ndebele homeland.[87]

Subsequently, there was a convergence of interests in the struggle against the white minority's occupation, seen in the formation of a united main liberation movement, Zimbabwean African People's Union (ZAPU), under the leadership of Joshua Nkomo in 1961.[88] However, notions of separate identity were not dispensed with, as in 1963 the party was split into two and the Zimbabwe African National Union (ZANU) was created.[89] While both parties included Shona and Ndebele speakers, mutual resentment and regional recruitment practices led to the identification of ZAPU with Ndebele speakers and the strong alignment of ZANU with the Shona speakers.[90]

The unifying nature of the fight against racist rule also made it possible for ZANU and ZAPU leaders to frequently present joint positions at crucial conferences held in Lusaka (Commonwealth), Havana (Non-Aligned Movement) and lastly at the decisive London, Lancaster Constitutional Conference in the transition to majority rule.[91] Nonetheless, there were still calls for a federation or separate existence which were championed by the party led by Chief Kayisa Ndiweni, who was seen as a paramount chief for Matebeleland.[92]

Unfortunately, the Lancaster House's deliberations considered only post-independence race relations between black and white, and not any disagreements that existed between native groups. The issue of minority rights was therefore only scrutinized in so far as it conferred citizenship, property rights, entrenched overrepresentation in parliament for seven years and guaranteed civil service pensions to the economically significant white minority.

84 Ibid.
85 Ibid.
86 See Centre for International Development and Conflict Management (CIDCM) (2007), 'Data; Chronology for Ndebele in Zimbabwe' <www.cidcm.umd.edu>.
87 Ibid.
88 Ibid.
89 Ibid.
90 Ngwabi Bhebe and Terence O. Ranger (eds), *Soldiers in Zimbabwe's Liberation War: Volume One* (James Currey 1995). See also Ngwabi Bhebe, *The ZAPU and ZANU Guerrilla Warfare and the Lutheran Evangelical Church in Zimbabwe* (Mambo Press 1999).
91 This became possible after a unified alliance (Patriotic Front) of ZANU and ZAPU, which was jointly led by Joshua Nkomo and Robert Mugabe, was formed in 1976.
92 Wole Olaleye, 'Political Parties and Governance in Zimbabwe' *EISA Occasional Paper No. 18*.

5.4.2 1980–1987

In spite of the two parties' unity at the negotiating table, the first independent elections held in February 1980 were fought separately and culminated in victory for Robert Mugabe's ZANU PF.[93] Even though these elections are viewed mostly as the country's first democratic elections, they were marred by intimidation and electoral violence.[94] Most significantly, there was a tacit acceptance by key political actors that the country was divided into two nations.[95] For example, when Mugabe was confronted about the intimidation of Joshua Nkomo's campaigners in certain Shona-dominated constituencies, he stated that:

> [T]hat's my part of the country, Manicaland, that's mine. The fact that Nkomo can't campaign there is down to the fact that I control it; I've had a cell there for five years. Is it surprising that people don't turn out there for Nkomo? Would I go to Nkomo's country (Matabeleland) and expect to raise a crowd there? Of course I wouldn't.[96]

In line with Mugabe's notion of his country and 'Nkomo's country', the distribution of seats by province showed that voters elected their candidates on regional, linguistic and ethnic lines.[97] For example, ZANU PF swept all seats in the Shona-speaking areas of Manicaland, Mashonaland Central, Mashonaland East and Victoria.[98] Nkomo's ZAPU won all seats in Matabeleland South and lost only one out of ten seats in Matabeleland North.[99]

In spite of all this glaring reality of ethnic differences, the post-independence review of national policies and legislation was confined to racially discriminatory laws.[100] There were also a number of measures adopted for ending racial discrimination.[101] While these efforts were progressive, it is unfortunate that the new regime was merely preoccupied with creating a multi-racial society and eliminating tensions between whites and blacks.[102] There was no similar drive towards pre-empting ethnic tensions amongst the indigenous population.[103]

93 For thorough discussions on this issue, see Douglas G. Anglin, 'Zimbabwe: Retrospect and Prospect' (1980) 35 *International Law Journal* 663, and Robert O. Matthews, 'From Rhodesia to Zimbabwe: Prerequisites of a Settlement' (1990) 45 *International Law Journal* 292.
94 David Smith, Colin Simpson and Ian Davies, *Mugabe* (Pioneer Head 1981) page 181.
95 Ibid at 187.
96 Ibid.
97 Anglin (n.93) and Matthews (n.93).
98 Ibid.
99 Ibid.
100 Mhlaba, L. (1999), supra notes 2242.
101 Ibid.
102 Ibid.
103 Ibid.

While the government became popular abroad for extending a hand of forgiveness and reconciliation to the ex-colonialist, it clearly did not entertain any dissenting voices from the Ndebele minority group.[104] This is seen in that soon after independence, there was apparent discontent by the Ndebele that they, and particularly the former ZAPU liberation war heroes, were being discriminated against and not given meaningful political positions.[105] These concerns were compounded by the perception that the central government ignored the community's economic or developmental needs.[106] For example, notwithstanding the fact that the region has been subjected to chronic droughts and water shortages since 1985, the government has committed no resources to the Matabeleland Zambezi Water Project, which had been seen as the solution to regional water shortage for decades.[107]

Perhaps the greatest moment when the goZ alienated itself from the Ndebele community is when it unleashed terror in their region on the basis that Nkomo's party led dissidents or terrorists who were attacking white farmers and were the South African apartheid regime's agents for destabilizing a new black government. In the period 1983–1987, the government deployed a North Korean-trained army unit in the Ndebele-speaking areas leading to the massacres of approximately 20,000 Ndebeles. This episode is widely referred to as the Gukurahundi, a Shona word which means 'the rain that washes away the chaff from the last harvest, before the spring rains'.[108] According to Sabelo Ndlovu-Gatsheni:

> [I]t seemed the last harvest was the achievement of independence, the 'Matebeleland region and the Ndebele were the chaff that was supposed to be washed away and the 'spring rain' was the establishment of the one-party state in Zimbabwe.[109]

This view is widely held and is the basis for a growing movement which is campaigning for the massacres to be officially recognized as a genocide. The

104 See Edwin Mkwananzi, 'Responsibility for Enforced Disappearances under International Law: The Case of Matebeleland 1983–1987' *Unpublished PhD Thesis* (University of Zimbabwe 1997).

105 Catholic Commission for Justice and Peace (CCJP) and the Legal Resources Foundation (LRF), *Breaking the Silence, Building the Peace: Report on the Disturbances in Matebeleland and the Midlands, 1980 to 1988* (CCJP and LRF 1997). See also Norma Kriger, 'Veterans' Pensions in Zimbabwe; Dispute Resolution and Nation-building' (2005) 20 *Ohio State Journal on Dispute Resolution* 249.

106 See Ammon Mutembwa, 'Water and the Potential for Resource Conflicts in Southern Africa' *Occasional Paper No. 3, Global Security Fellows Initiative* (University of Cambridge 1998).

107 Ibid.

108 Sabelo Ndlovu-Gatsheni, 'The Post-Colonial State & Matebeleland: Regional Perceptions of Civil-Military Relations, 1980–2002' in Rocklyn Williams, Gavin Cawthra, and Diane Abrahams (eds) *Ourselves to Know: Civil-Military Relations and Defence Transformation in Southern Africa* (Institute of Security Studies 2003).

109 Ndlovu-Gatsheni, ibid.

interpretation is based on the 1948 Convention on the Prevention of Genocide. In addition to violations of the rights of the Ndebele to existence, other liberty and physical integrity rights violated during this time include reports of torture, arbitrary detentions, rape, mass beatings and a number of incidents of enforced or involuntary disappearances.[110]

The formal end of these disturbances was brought about by the unity accord of December 1987 (1987 GNU).[111] This agreement issued a general amnesty to the dissidents, put Nkomo in the position of a half vice-president and merged other ZAPU leaders into ZANU PF, thereby creating a one-party state.[112] Although the 1987 GNU facilitated the move from violence to peace, it failed to promote reconciliation between the two communities since a blanket amnesty was imposed without any state acknowledgement of culpability.[113] It has also been difficult for the victims and their families to forgive and forget, since no official truth about the reasons for, or the extent and nature of, the atrocities committed has been established.[114] These grievances were further exacerbated by the fact that during the disturbances, the goZ disseminated propaganda to the effect that it was the ZAPU dissidents who had terrorized their communities.[115]

Yet, the truth according to the narratives of the victims is that it was the 'Shona speaking' state security agents who brutalized them.[116] Thus, while most renditions would conveniently document the issue as a question of the Ndebele grievances against the regime of that era, the Ndebele group resentment has been towards both the majority Shona tribe and government.[117] The widely held view in the region is that:

> [T]he Gukurahundi wasn't a dissident war, it was a war between the Shona and the Ndebele.[118]

Two critical issues have to be highlighted about these disturbances. First, as is typical of male-dominated Eurocentric discourses, gender-related crimes committed during Gukurahundi and the regime's use of food as a political tool against the Ndebele people do not receive adequate attention in scholarly works.[119] Sec-

110 CCJP and LRF (n.105) as read with Mkwananzi (n.104).
111 Ibid.
112 The one-party state came about because the government of national unity coincided with the end of the seven-year constitutional moratorium on white overrepresentation in parliament.
113 CCJP and LRF (1997) (n.105).
114 Ibid.
115 Ibid.
116 See the narratives provided as appendixes in CCJP and LRF (n.105).
117 Vigdis Broch-Due, 'Violence and Belonging: Analytical Reflections' in Vigdis Broch-Due (ed) *Violence and Belonging: The Quest for Identity in Post-Colonial Africa* (Routledge 2005).
118 Ibid.
119 CCJP and LRF (1997), supra notes 2257.

ond, the amnesty which followed the Gukurahundi atrocities gave rise to the perception that the goZ can act with impunity, and thus to a fear among the Ndebele that similar acts may be perpetrated against them again.

5.4.3 1988–2008

Indeed, the 1987 GNU was not fully embraced by the Ndebele community. This observation is supported by the axiomatic fact that the region became a stronghold for the Movement for Democratic Change (MDC) which was formed in 1999, out of a coalition of dissenting voices. The region was further alienated by the fact that just before the 2002 presidential elections, the ruling ZANU PF party threatened some Ndebele areas with starvation if they supported the opposition party.[120] In the same year, Shona-speaking election monitors were deployed to the region to monitor elections in Matebeleland to the chagrin of the locals.[121]

The MDC split on 12 October 2005, and in a self-evident ingenuity aimed at garnering the support from the majority Shona group, the leadership of the largely Ndebele splinter group scouted for a Shona speaker, Professor Arthur Mutambara, to lead their faction.[122] This decision confirmed fears held by many in Matebeleland that they will always be marginalized politically. This is more so since the power-sharing deal signed on 15 September 2008 did not have a Ndebele signatory.

Two political parties from Matebeleland, namely the Patriotic Union of MaNdebeleland (PUMA) and Mthwakazi People's Convention (MPC), were formed in this era. These groups' aspirations were quite significant as they made demands which are not peculiar to the case of Zimbabwe. They were both born out of discontent with the colonial state formation, postcolonial state's marginalization of the Ndebele, the legacy of state violations of this group's rights and a genuine fear that Matebeleland would be absorbed into Shona identity and culture. While both groups required territorial autonomy, they differ in the sense that MPC's quest was for external self-determination.

In addition to demands for accountability and autonomy, there are also demands that the region be administered by local civil servants instead of the current Shona administrators.[123] Economically speaking, claims are for increased opportunities

120 Amnesty International, *Zimbabwe Power and Hunger – Violations of the Right to Food* (London: Amnesty International, International Secretariat 2004) and Khanyisela Moyo, 'Just Ends, Just Means . . . Is Starving a Nation for Political Gain a Crime against Humanity? The Zimbabwean Case 2000–2003' *Unpublished Master's Thesis* (University of Oslo 2003).

121 See Centre for International Development and Conflict Management (CIDCM), 'Assessment for Ndebele in Zimbabwe' <www.mar.umd.edu/assessment.asp?groupId=55203>.

122 See Movement for Democratic Change (UK), 'Bulawayo Welcomes Professor Mutambara; MDC President' <www.mdcuk.com/Starrally.htm>.

123 CIDCM, 'Data: Assessment for Ndebele in Zimbabwe' <www.cidcm.umd.edu>.

and more public spending in the region.[124] Culturally, many would like to see the promotion of and respect for the Ndebele lifestyle and language rights with a change in the perceived Shona bias of civil servants who administer the area.[125]

5.4.4 2008–2019

As stated in previous chapters, highlights for the period 2008–2019 included the GNU of 2009, the adoption of a new Constitution in 2013, the end of the GNU in 2013 and the 2017 coup which saw Robert Mugabe's resignation as president and his replacement by Emerson Mnangagwa. During the constitutional outreach exercise, six out of ten provinces stated that they wanted devolution of power.[126] This became a contentious issue, as some thought that calls for devolution of power were an excuse for Matebeleland' s secession.[127] Nonetheless, devolution was included in the Constitution, but the preamble to the relevant section states that:

> [w]hereas it is desirable to ensure the preservation of national unity in Zimbabwe and the prevention of all forms of disunity and secessionism.[128]

However, advocacy for external self-determination persists. For example, the Mthwakazi Republic Party (MRP) was formed in 2014.[129] The party's objective is to fight for the restoration of the Mthwakazi state; that is, the state of the Ndebele which was founded by King Mzilikazi around 1840. Other groups currently fighting for the restoration of the Ndebele state include the Mthwakazi National Party (MNP), the Matabeleland Liberation Front (MLF) and the 1893 Mthwakazi Restoration Movement.[130]

5.5 How to read Zimbabwe's experience with the Ndebele question

The Ndebele demands invoke two legal conundrums. The first is the definition of minorities as it affects the nature of rights conferred on this group. The second is the controversial question as to whether minorities have a right to self-determination, or indeed a legal right to autonomy.

124 Ibid.
125 Ibid.
126 See Norman T. Nhede, 'Devolution of Power and Effective Governance: The Zimbabwean Constitutional Debate' (2013).
127 Ibid.
128 Preamble Chapter 14, Constitution of Zimbabwe.
129 See <https://mthwakazirepublicparty.org/>.
130 For the 1893 Human Rights Movement see <http://1893mrm.org/>.

5.5.1 Are the Ndebele a 'minority' in international law?

There is no agreed legal definition of minorities which is of universal application.[131] However, most scholarship on the subject draws from a working definition proposed by the then Special Rapporteur on minorities, Francesco Caportoti, in 1977.[132] Caportoti explained that four requirements are to be met for a group composed of a state's nationals to be characterized as a minority by law. First, the group must be numerically lesser than the rest of the state's inhabitants. Second, it must inhere in a non-dominant position. Third, the group must have common ethnic, linguistic or religious features that set it apart from the rest of the population. Fourth, the group has to directly and indirectly exhibit a perception that it is united in its bid to preserve its collective group identity.[133]

In 1985, Jules Deschênes also made a proposal which repeated all the requirements in the Caportoti definition but differed in its claim that the group should be that of 'citizens' who also have an objective of attaining both *de jure* and *de facto* equality with the rest of the population.[134] However, the Human Rights Committee made it clear in its General Comment No. 23 that minorities who are to be protected by state parties are not necessarily citizens of a country.[135] Rights provided for in Article 27 of the ICCPR are for all individuals within a state.[136] These cannot be restricted to citizens as, for example, political rights which are provided for in Article 25.[137]

The issue of non-dominance also needs to be clarified.[138] Frustrations which may lead minorities to seek equal treatment with the rest of society are varied; that is, they can either be political or economic, and in some cases dominant communities can exist as minorities.[139] As was illustrated in the previous chapter, prior to 2000 and the start of Zimbabwe's fast track land reform programme, the white minority were in an economically dominant position.[140] Yet, in the transition from colonialism in 1980, it was considered necessary for them to be accorded

131 In Europe what is close to be a legal definition is that which was offered by the Council of Europe in 1993 but since the focus of this study is on postcolonial contexts, no attention will be given to this understanding. See Council of Europe Parliamentary Recommendation 1201 (1993).

132 Francesco Capotorti, 'Study on the Rights of Persons Belonging to Ethnic, Religious and Linguistic Minorities' U.N. Doc E/CN.4/Sub.2/384/Rev.1 (1977).

133 Ibid. Note that the definition restricts the ambit of minority protection to 'nationals', thus all refugee protection is excluded since most refugees and migrant workers are often not nationals.

134 Jules Deschênes, 'Proposal Concerning a Definition of the Term "Minority"' U.N. Doc. E/CN.4/Sub.2/1985/31 (1985).

135 Paragraph 5.1 General Comment 23 of the Human Rights Committee U.N. Doc. CCPR/C/21/Rev.1/Add.5.

136 Ibid.

137 Ibid.

138 See Richard A. Schermerhorn, *Comparative Ethnic Relations: A Framework of Theory and Research* (Random House 1970).

139 See Chapter 4 in relation to the Zimbabwean white minority.

140 Ibid.

special measures to protect them from political marginalization in the country's move from white minority rule to black majority rule. This was also the case with minorities in South Africa's transition from apartheid.

Another definition worth noting is the working definition of minorities coined in 1993 by Asbjørn Eide.[141] This definition incorporates Caportoti's two elements and excludes the issue of non-dominance and his fourth requirement that this has to consist of persons who manifest solidarity in their wish to preserve a group identity.[142]

Given the fact that minorities can also dominate some societal aspects, this work does not distinguish between dominant minorities and less influential groups.[143] Thus, the chapter construes the Ndebele as a minority in international law. They are a group which resides in a sovereign state, are numerically inferior to the rest of the state's population, have members who have common attributes of an ethnic, religious or linguistic nature which set them apart from the rest of the population and which manifests unity in its desire to maintain and preserve its group identity.

On this note, a distinction which Western pundits have made between minorities and indigenous peoples ought to be highlighted as it has an added significance in postcolonial contexts.[144] The most cited examples of indigenous peoples are American Indians and Aborigines in Canada. In the case of postcolonial Africa, groups which have been classified as marginalized indigenous peoples include the Berber of North Africa, Batwa of Central Africa and San of Botswana. Examples of minorities would be the Zulu of South Africa, Scottish of the United Kingdom and the North African immigrants of France.

The term indigenous peoples refers to aboriginal marginalized persons who were originally in the state before the arrival of the dominant group.[145] These are the people who do not want to be integrated and have collectively sought to preserve their culture and traditions.[146] Self-identification as indigenous and members' acceptance of an individual's indigeneity is seen as the most significant

141 Asbjørn Eide, 'Possible Ways and Means of Facilitating the Peaceful and Constructive Solution of Problems Involving Minorities' U.N. Doc. E/CN.4/Sub.2/1993/34 and Add.1–4 (1993).

142 Ibid.

143 For example, the Zimbabwean white minority discussed in the previous chapter were dominant economically.

144 Par 4.3 Report of the African Commission on Human and Peoples' Rights Working Group of Experts on Indigenous Populations/Communities E/CN.4/Sub.2/AC.5/2005/WP.3.

145 Sarah Pritchard, 'The Rights of Indigenous People to Self-determination under International Law' (1992) *Aboriginal Law Bulletin*. Characteristics of indigenous peoples are derived from; Par 50, Jose R.M. Cobo (Study on the Problem of Discrimination against Indigenous Populations, U.N. Doc. E/CN.4/Sub.2/1983/21/Add. 8, art. 1(1) (b), ILO 169 (1983) and Erica-Irene Daes, 'Working Paper On the Concept of "Indigenous People"', U.N. Doc. E/CN.4/Sub.2/AC.4/1996/2 (1996).

146 Ibid.

criterion for establishing groups who can be said to be indigenous.[147] This notion of individual self-identification as a member of the minority group has also been proposed by UN practitioners as a way of ensuring that cultures and traditions are not imposed on the unwilling. This is of utmost importance in issues dealing with indigenous peoples because the whole essence of their legal protection is based on an understanding that they face extinction because of the modern policies of ethnocide.[148]

According to Asbjørn Eide and Erica-Irene Daes, minorities and indigenous peoples have two different claims.[149] First, minorities allegedly seek to exercise individual rights, but indigenous peoples want collective rights.[150] Second, minorities' demands are said to be for non-discrimination, and indigenous peoples' quest is for autonomy.[151] This understanding by UN practitioners is also reflected in relevant international standards and is related to the question as to whether a minority group has a right to self-rule within or without the state's borders, if this is the best way of preserving its entity.[152]

5.5.2 *Is the Ndebele quest for autonomy and self-determination legitimate?*

Groups that are calling for the restoration of the Ndebele state (Mthwakazi) claim that their demands for autonomy are a pursuit of a right to self-determination.[153] The legal validity of these claims is questionable, although some pundits have stated that minorities have a right to autonomy. Jane Wright, for example, has argued that autonomous arrangements for minorities are an appropriate mechanism through which states can fulfil their international legal obligation to extend a right to self-determination to all its peoples.[154] In her view, the *UN Declaration on Principles of International Law Concerning Friendly Relations and Co-operation among States in Accordance with the Charter of the United Nations* calls

147 Ibid.

148 Robert A. Williams, 'Frontier of Legal Thought III: Encounters on the Frontiers of International Human Rights Law: Redefining the Terms of Indigenous Peoples' Survival in the World' (1990) *Duke Law Journal* 660.

149 Asbjørn Eide and Erica-Irene Daes, 'Working Paper on the Relationship and Distinction between the Rights of Persons Belonging to Minorities and Those of Indigenous Peoples' E/CN.4/Sub.2/2000/10 (2000).

150 For an understanding of group and peoples' rights in human rights law, see Peter Jones, 'Human Rights, Group Rights and Peoples' Rights' (1999) 21(1) *Human Rights Quarterly* 80.

151 Ibid.

152 Ibid.

153 For meanings of self-determination, autonomy and the relationship between the two, see Marc Weller, 'Towards a General Comment on Self-determination and Autonomy' Working Paper submitted to the UN Working Group on Minorities, 11th Session/25 May 2005. E/CN.4/Sub.2/AC.5/2005/WP.5.

154 Jane Wright, 'Minority Groups, Autonomy, and Self-Determination' (1999) 19 *Oxford Journal of Legal Studies* 606.

for positive steps for correcting the inequitable distribution of power between majority and minority groups.[155] On that basis, she argues that:

> [A]utonomy should be regarded as a constructive tool by which the proper aspirations of minority groups may be realised. Moreover autonomy reflects the principle of 'equality' of peoples and is a vehicle through which the obligation on states to respect the right of self-determination may be fulfilled.[156]

The consociationalist/autonomist model seeks to limit extremist politics by recognizing difference and ensuring that numerically inferior groups participate in government.[157] This is achieved through elite power-sharing arrangements which may include proportional representation.[158] Cultural or political autonomous arrangements for groups within the national borders are also favoured.[159]

Nonetheless, Wright's view is rather simplistic for two broad reasons. First, autonomy is not always an appropriate policy for giving minorities a voice in the administration of their society.[160] For example, Tom Hadden proposed integration with diversity in policing, security and the criminal justice sector rather than autonomy, since the former has higher prospects of fostering peace and stability.[161] In previous studies he had explained that there are three different methods of dealing with disgruntled minorities, namely the autonomist, integrative and assimilative approaches.[162] Of these three approaches, assimilation is not promoted by the United Nations as it denies the group effective participation in its society's cultural, economic and political life.[163]

Assimilation and integration are similar in so far as they are based on a fear that empowering difference might foster conflict.[164] Unity is seen as a key necessity in the nation-building project.[165] However, assimilative measures are aimed at elim-

155 Declaration on Principles of International Law Concerning Friendly Relations and Co-operation among States in accordance with the Charter of the United Nations, G.A. Res. 2625, Annex, 25 U.N. GAOR, Supp. (No. 28), U.N. Doc. A/5217 at 121 (1970), as read with the preamble to the UN Charter.

156 Wright (n.154).

157 Arend Lijphart, *Democracy in Plural Societies: Comparative Exploration* (Yale University Press 1977) as read with Samuel Issacharoff, 'Democracy and Collective Decision Making' (2008) 6(2) *International Journal of Constitutional Law* 231.

158 Ibid.

159 Ibid.

160 For different approaches, see Tom Hadden, 'International and National Actions for the Protection of Minorities – The Role of the Working Group on Minorities' E/CN.4/Sub.2/AC.5/2004/WP.3 (2004). See also Tom Hadden and Ciarán O. Maolain, 'Integrative Approaches to the Accommodation of Minorities' E/CN.4/S ub.2/AC.5/2001/WP.6 (2001).

161 Par 3, Tom Hadden, 'Working Paper on the Integration with Diversity in Security, Policing and Criminal Justice' U.N. Doc. E/CN.4/Sub.2/AC.5/2006/WP.1 (2006).

162 Ibid.

163 Ibid.

164 Hadden (n.160).

165 Ibid.

inating minorities' special characteristics and absorbing them into the majority identity and culture.[166] This is different from integration, which is popular with Western diplomats who favour policies which, while reflecting the will of the majority, are also supported by a strong minority rights system.[167]

Second, Wright's assertions are problematic as they are too dismissive of the international legal distinction between minorities and 'peoples', yet this issue has a tremendous influence on who can demand autonomy as a right.[168] This legal conundrum was examined by Asbjørn Eide in 2001.[169] He explained that there is merit in the argument that groups living within a state have a right to internal self-determination and not external self-determination or secession.[170] In his view, the *Declaration of Friendly Relations* defines the need for a representative government and implies that all the people within a state have a right to elect their government.[171] This is the democratic element of the right to internal self-determination.[172]

This cannot be taken as a basis for autonomous arrangements since by this definition minorities cannot be said to 'peoples' who are entitled to external self-determination.[173] 'Peoples' who are entitled to external self-determination are the 'demos' and not the distinct 'ethnoses', the former term referring to all the inhabitants of a sovereign state who have a right to fully establish their territory.[174] Obviously, this applies to peoples who were colonized or subjected to foreign occupation, but the same cannot be said of 'a group' within a state.[175] As has been said earlier, there is also a difference between persons belonging to minorities and indigenous peoples who are entitled to autonomy.[176]

166 Ibid.

167 As Tom Hadden has explained, 'integration may be taken to cover structures and policies aimed at securing full recognition of the identity and culture of members of minority communities and their full participation as such in national or regional society' (¶ 31 ibid).

168 To this argument, Jane Wright has responded that 'distinctions drawn between minorities and peoples are more apparent than real and are self-evidently driven by political considerations rather than functional reality'. Wright (n.154).

169 See Asbjørn Eide, 'Cultural Autonomy and Territorial Democracy: A Recipe for Harmonious Group Accommodation' U.N. Doc. E/CN.4/Sub.2/AC.5/2001/WP.4 (2001); and Geoff Gilbert, 'Autonomy and Minority Groups – A Legal Right in International Law?' U.N. Doc. E/CN.4/Sub.2/AC.5/2001/CRP.5 (2001).

170 Ibid.

171 Ibid.

172 A right to democracy is inherent in Article 21 of the UDHR, Article 25 of the ICCPR and in relevant regional conventions which gives everyone a right to take part in the government of his or her country.

173 Eide (n.169).

174 Ibid.

175 Ibid.

176 As Eide and Daes have stated, 'the principal legal distinction between the rights of minorities and indigenous peoples in contemporary international law is with respect to internal self-determination: the right of a group to govern itself within a recognized geographical area, without State interference (albeit in some cooperative relationship with State authori-

Nevertheless, Eide also clarified in his 2001 study that minority groups who live in a sovereign state, including inhabitants from former colonies who claim that the government of a state is not representing all the people without discrimination, can approach the Committee on ICERD.[177] With respect to ethnic groups' demands for autonomy, the Committee on ICERD explained in General Comment 21 that the territorial integrity of states is jealously guarded in international law.[178] In its view:

> [A] fragmentation of States may be detrimental to the protection of human rights, as well as to the preservation of peace and security. This does not, however, exclude the possibility of arrangements reached by free agreements of all parties concerned.[179]

Therefore, there is no sound international legal basis for the view that minorities' autonomous arrangements derive from the right to self-determination. Neither is there any legal consensus as to whether minorities are also 'peoples' who have a right to freely establish their society or that there is an obligation on states to grant minorities any degree of autonomy. Nevertheless, there is wide acceptance of the notion that autonomous arrangements that are implemented in good faith can be a mechanism for reducing conflict.

5.6 Postcolonial agency in transitions

The paradigmatic legal understanding is that minorities have no right to external self-determination and they have no group right to internal self-determination, although they can enjoy this individual right via democratic processes. As the earlier discussion indicated, in postcolonial contexts the application of these legal rules can be detrimental to peace and even to the legal system itself. However, complete disobedience to the master's discourse can work only in limited contexts where such conduct is in the interest of Western states. Thus post-conflict postcolonial societies have attempted a delicate balance whereby international law is made to fit the society's circumstances. Telling examples of such agency are the experiences of South Africa and Northern Ireland.[180]

---

ties, as in any federal system of national government)'. ¶ 43 Eide and Daes (2000), supra notes 2094.

177 Article I of the ICERD included ethnic groups in its definition of those who are not supposed to be racially discriminated against.

178 General Comment 21 of the Committee on the Elimination of Racial Discrimination (CERD Committee) U.N. Doc. A/51/18.

179 Paragraph 6, ibid.

180 See Christine Bell and Kathleen Cavanaugh, 'Constructive Ambiguity' or Internal Self-Determination? Self-Determination, Group Accommodation, and the Belfast Agreement' (1998) 22 *Fordham International Law Journal* 1345, Bell (n.21), Kristin Henrad, *Minority Protection in Post-Apartheid South Africa: Human Rights, Minority Rights and Self-*

Christine Bell and Kathleen Cavanaugh have commented thus of Northern Ireland's 1998 Good Friday Agreement:

> Examination of the Belfast Agreement from the perspective of international law indicates an example of an agreement that embraces and embodies the suggested re-workings of the self-determination norm.[181]

This work recognized this as evidence of postcolonial *agency*. For sure, the agreement contains both clauses which are steeped in the master's discourse and those which are quite innovative in the sense that they go beyond conventional understandings of what international law is prepared to accord to minorities. Of significance is the provision that:

> [I]t is for the people of the island of Ireland alone, by agreement between the two parts respectively and without external impediment, to exercise their right of self-determination on the basis of consent, freely and concurrently given, North and South, to bring about a united Ireland, if that is their wish, accepting that this right must be achieved and exercised with and subject to the agreement and consent of a majority of the people of Northern Ireland.[182]

On the face of it, it could be said this clause is still entrenched in international law since it makes it clear that Northern Ireland questions of external self-determination will be determined by 'demos' of Northern Ireland and not by a minority group within Northern Ireland. It can also be said that the agreement also conforms to the contemporary international legal framework in its inclusion of clauses on equal rights for women and the protection for minorities within an individual human rights framework.

Similarly, and in accordance with the UN Declaration and the Council of Europe Framework Convention for the Protection of National Minorities (Framework Convention), the agreement established a consociational government in the form of an assembly with power-sharing and mutual vetoes, to ensure that minorities effectively participate in decision making. Further adherence to the Framework Convention is also seen in the institutionalization of cross-border contacts between Northern Ireland and the Republic of Ireland.

However, a close scrutiny of the agreement reveals that it is in fact *mimicry* of the master's discourse, since it offers a possibility for the deviation from the principle of territorial integrity. In fact, the 'demos' who are given possibilities for external self-determination are homeland minorities within the United Kingdom. It also breaches the sacred notion of sovereignty by embracing the idea of

---

Determination. Perspectives on the Twentieth Century Series (Praeger 2002) and Strydom (n.11).

181 Bell and Cavanaugh (n.180).

182 Constitutional Issues; Belfast Agreement (1998) <www.c-r.org>.

shared sovereignty between the Republic of Ireland and the United Kingdom.[183] There are also special rights to ensure substantive and procedural equality. Further, power is also disaggregated by the mainstreaming of civil society in the governance of society.

Agency in the approach to minority-related self-determination disputes also features in South Africa's constitutional framework which facilitated its transition from apartheid. Although the process was itself an exercise in self-determination by the majority black population who have had a negative experience with programmes aimed at promoting difference, concessions were still made to those who wanted to maintain their different identities. This is different from the Zimbabwean decolonization process, where special rights were accorded only to the white minority whose continued presence in the country was considered to be of economic importance.

It has already been pointed out that as in Zimbabwe prior to black majority rule, South Africa has a history of a centralized racialized state with power concentrated on the white minority. Similarly, the South African black community was united in so far as they resisted 'white rule' but were far from being homogenous. This fact was acknowledged in the interim Constitution, which officially recognized 11 languages.[184]

Basically, South Africa adopted a constitutional model which has a liberal tenor in its passage from apartheid to black majority rule.[185] This formula was, however, modified in two ways. First, special rights were accorded to linguistic, cultural and religious minorities. As this is not the principal focus of this section, it suffices to point out that the South African Constitution provides that:

> [P]ersons belonging to a cultural, religious or linguistic community may not be denied the right, with other members of that community – to enjoy their culture, practice their religion and use their language; and to form, join and maintain cultural, religious and linguistic associations and other organs of civil society.[186]

Second, South African transitional negotiators extended the possibility for autonomy or self-government to groups which are not the typical 'peoples' for

183 Bell and Cavanaugh (n.180).

184 Article 3, Constitution of the Republic of South Africa, Act 200 of 1993.

185 Oomen (n.11) and Booysen (n.11).

186 S31, Constitution of the Republic of South Africa, 1996. The exercise of those rights ought to be compatible with the rest of the constitutionally enshrined rights. Unfair discrimination by both the state or any other person on the basis of, *inter alia*, race, ethnic or social origin, colour, language religion and so on is prohibited. There is also a constitutional requirement for the establishment of a mechanism for the promotion of such special rights for minorities so as to ensure peace and community cohesion. Furthermore, there was a constitutional requirement (which has since been complied with) for the enactment of legislation for the prohibition and prevention of discrimination by non-state actors.

whom international law extends the right to self-determination.[187] In fact, the present South African Constitution offers two forms of self-determination to minorities. These are possibilities for self-government and the limited right to cultural self-determination.[188]

This approach was a product of a process of attempting to strike a delicate balance between competing aspirations of self-determination which took place in the period between Nelson Mandela's release from prison in 1990 and the democratic elections of 1994.[189] In that epoch, the majority ANC party aspired for a democratic, multi-racial centralized state.[190] On the other hand, minorities' opposition parties, which included right-wing Afrikaner parties and the Zululand-based party led by the Inkatha Freedom Party, vowed for autonomy within or without the existing borders.[191]

In the initial stages the law was to a large extent in conformity with the dominant discourse in the sense that its emphasis was still on equality and democracy. This is evidenced by the substance of the initial Constitutional Principles (CP) on self-determination which were inserted into the South African Transitional/ Interim Constitution of 1993.[192] These include the CP which provided that:

> [C]ollective rights of self-determination informing, joining and maintaining organs of civil society, including linguistic, cultural and religious associations, shall, on the basis of non-discrimination and free association, be recognized and protected.[193]

Another one stated that:

> [P]rovision shall be made for participation of minority political parties in the legislative process in a manner consistent with democracy. Further, a transitional government of national unity was formed to ensure effective political participation by minority groups at national and regional levels.[194]

As in Zimbabwe in the passage to black majority rule, the first concessions to be made to minorities were to appease the economically important white groups.[195] Thus, white civil and security force members were given job and pension guarantees.[196] There was also amnesty for atrocities committed during the

187 Oomen (n.11) and Booysen (n.11).
188 Ibid.
189 Oomen (n.11).
190 Ibid.
191 Ibid.
192 Ibid. See also Constitutional Principles, Constitution of the Republic of South Africa, Act 200 of 1993.
193 Ibid.
194 CP XIV, ibid.
195 Ibid.
196 Oomen (n.11).

apartheid era.[197] The major difference between the two countries guarantees to the white minorities could be attributed to the fact that during the negotiation stage the right-wing Afrikaner parties boycotted the negotiation process on the basis that it had not factored in their quest for a territorially based homeland (Volkstaat).[198] This might have also given impetus to the Zulu's demands for a tribal kingdom.[199]

When it became apparent that the Zulu and Afrikaner demands would threaten the peace process, last-minute amendments were inserted to the Interim Constitution.[200] Thus, S160 of the Interim Constitution was amended to include a provision that:

> A provincial constitution may; (a) provide for legislative and executive structures and procedures different from those provided for in this Constitution in respect of a province; and (b) where applicable, provide for the institution, role, authority and status of a traditional monarch in the province, and shall make such provision for the Zulu Monarch in the case of the province of KwaZulu/Natal.[201]

In addition, CP XXXIV provided for:

> The right to self-determination by any community sharing a common language and cultural heritage, whether in a territorial entity within the Republic or in any other recognized way.[202]

The adequacy and acceptability of these principles have been discussed elsewhere. For the purposes of this work, it suffices to point out that South Africa did not hold firm to the notion of territorial integrity, nor did it restrict the right to internal self-determination to indigenous peoples. Thus, its transitional constitutionalism was *mimicry* of the master's discourse. This form of *agency* could be exported to neighboring Zimbabwe so as to pre-empt the instability which was likely to be caused by the Ndebele marginalization.

5.7 Conclusion

This chapter has demonstrated that the current thrust of international law as seen in the definition of minorities is to integrate the new Western minorities who are the immigrants. The definition of indigenous people also shows the law's emphasis on correcting historical land injustices which were perpetrated by the

197 Ibid.
198 Ibid.
199 Ibid.
200 Ibid.
201 S160 Constitution of the Republic of South Africa, Act 200 of 1993.
202 CP XXXIV, ibid.

descendants of the majority groups in Western society against the autochthonal peoples. Existing legal standards do not confer external self-determination to postcolonial minorities; neither do they give them a collective right to internal self-determination. At the same time, it is a fact that the postcolonial nation state was imposed on the minorities.

Nonetheless, minorities exist in postcolonial societies even though this nomenclature is unpopular with both postcolonial governments and those communities which are presumed to be such in international law. As stated previously, some postcolonial governments deny the existence of this community because they are afraid that any promotion of difference would point to both their illegitimacy and their authoritarian tendencies. Minorities also resist this classification because its only benefits are the state-centric, weak individual rights entitlements, which in most cases facilitate the postcolonial states' preference for assimilation as a way of managing diversity. The categorization as numerically inferior has also been confused with *de facto* citizenship inferiority.

The Ndebele experiences which have been presented do illuminate these concerns. Indeed, in common with their compatriots in other postcolonial societies, those who champion the Ndebele cause have cited the colonial history and post-independence human rights abuses as the basis for their demands. Further, even though the Ndebele issue might be deemed to be at the periphery of the current Zimbabwean crisis, it cannot be cursorily thrust aside since a plethora of organizations fighting this cause are already in existence. Their demands are fortified by the fact that both the opposition and the ZANU PF government do not seem to prioritize the need to endorse an unbiased historic record of the Gukurahundi genocide which might give closure to the Ndebele.

This legacy of impunity and state-sanctioned amnesia has bolstered this community's demands for internal and external self-determination. In an international legal system which applies equally to all, secession would be ideal since the group has a shared culture and is territorially based. In any event, a Ndebele monarchy which was divorced from the rest of the Shona territory existed before colonialism. Further, there are fewer prospects for effective participation in the country's governance by this community. Of course, what is envisaged is a modernized Ndebele state and not traditional leadership, since such style of administration tends to be inimical to the rights of women.

The international legal reality, however, is that beyond colonization, the collective right to internal self-determination has been extended only to indigenous peoples and not to minorities. In addition, notwithstanding the inroads which globalization has made to the principles of sovereignty and territorial integrity, these notions are still sacred. There is a general resistance to any efforts that seek to disrupt the international order. Thus, lessons could be borrowed from hybrid self-determination methods employed in the South African and Northern Ireland transitional case studies which are *mimicry* of the dominant discourse. It has in fact been said that this is an emerging norm for dealing with ethnic conflict in postcolonial transitions.

Therefore, it is unfortunate that the master's discourse does not allow postcolonial minorities similar opportunities to the European experience when group protection under the League of Nations, facilitated the nation-building exercises of states which emerged after World War I. This need is imperative, since postcolonial states have demonstrated that they would not hesitate to violate both minority physical integrity rights and economic, social and cultural rights in their bid to reign in those communities seen as a threat to both the state's stability and their rule. This is the subject matter of the next chapter.

6 Dealing with the legacy of impunity

6.1 Introduction

The previous chapter stated that the government of Zimbabwe (goZ) resorted to violence and other violations of human rights in a bid to assimilate the Ndebele minority. This was not an isolated case; Zimbabwe has a long history of impunity dating back to the pre-colonial era. In fact, gross violations of rights are still being committed with impunity at the time of writing.[1] The country is not an exception in this regard.[2] Although facile comparisons are to be eschewed, incidents of systematic violations of rights are common to postcolonial nation-building efforts. Unfortunately, frequent application of this method has led to a dehumanizing and iniquitous cycle of brutality which begets the characterization of these states as unjust.

In the past, it was quite acceptable for these polities to give amnesties as a way of peace-building whilst correcting their deficit of legitimacy.[3] Nowadays, however, the global reach of human rights law has given credence to the notion that amnesties perpetuate a culture of impunity, and also to the view that exonerated atrocities will always afflict a nation's inner morality.[4] This has heralded contemporary attempts at striking a balance between accountability for past atrocities and securing peace.[5]

The issue is of added importance to economically disadvantaged postcolonial societies where post-conflict reconstruction packages are often contingent on

1 See Zimbabwe Human Rights Commission, 'Monitoring Report in the Aftermath of the 14 January to 16 January 2019 "Stay Away" and Subsequent Disturbances' <www.zhrc.org.zw>.

2 See, for example, the case of Nigeria discussed in Chinedu R. Ezetah, 'International Law of Self-Determination and the Ogoni Question: Mirroring Africa's Post-Colonial Dilemma' (1996) 19 *Loyola of Los Angeles International Law and Comparative Law Journal* 811.

3 See Jessica Gavron, 'Amnesty in the Light of Developments in International Law and the Establishment of the International Criminal Court' (2002) 51 *International and Comparative Law Quarterly* 91.

4 Ibid. See also Naomi Roht-Arriaza (ed), *Impunity and Human Rights in International Law and Practice* (Oxford University Press 1995). See also Mo Bleeker and Neil J. Kritz, *Dealing with the Past: Critical Issues, Lessons Learned and the Challenges for Future Swiss Policy* (Swiss Peace 2004).

5 Ibid.

the new dispensation's commitment to a justice mechanism.[6] Yet, an insistence in bringing perpetrators to account can hinder peace-making efforts in contexts when there is no regime change or when the old regime still controls either the economic or security apparatus.[7]

This is related to the exceptionalism with which powerful states apply pressure on relevant states to punish human rights atrocities. The exemption of 'friendly' states from such commitments has led to perceptions that transitional justice is used as an instrument in pursuit of strategic goals.[8] Similarly, inconsistencies in foreign policies have ushered perceptions that the law of accountability is a tool for regime change aimed at modelling all states in the master's image.[9]

At the same time, it is facile to state that the quest for justice is imperialism. Postcolonial victims of human rights abuses want redress, but not always from Eurocentric mechanisms which are individualistic and give women's rights secondary importance.[10] Against this backdrop, and noting the crucial role of donor funding in peacebuilding efforts, postcolonial societies have had to resort to ingenious means. They have attempted to strike a balance between adherences to the master's demands for certain types of justice mechanisms and also to local justice understandings.

This chapter describes Zimbabwe's experience of justice and peace issues with a view to examining broader international polemics. As explained in Chapter 2, Zimbabwe can be described as a pre-transition country, that is, there has not been a 'definite transition from one regime to the next, nor a clear move from conflict to peace'.[11] To re-iterate, apart from the period 2008–2013, when the country had an inclusive government, Zimbabwe has been ruled, since 1980, by one political party (ZANU PF). The country has been wracked by conflict since the colonial era and has adopted transitional justice mechanisms at different epochs. This chapter will thus give a background to dealing with the past in Zimbabwe. It covers the relevant epochs requiring attention, past attempts at dealing with the past, the main obstacles in history and an overview of future opportunities and threats to dealing with the past in Zimbabwe. The chapter

6 Jane Stromseth, David Wippman and Rosa Brooks, *Can Might Make Rights? Building the Rule of Law after Military Interventions* (Cambridge University Press 2006).

7 See Matthias Goldman, 'Does Peace Follow Justice or Vice Versa? Plans for Post Conflict Justice in Burundi' (2006) 30 *Fletcher Forum of World Affairs* 137.

8 Catherine Turner, 'Delivering Lasting Peace, Democracy and Human Rights in Times of Transition; The Role of International Law' (2008) 2(2) *International Journal of Transitional Justice* 126.

9 Chapter 2, see also Stromseth, Wippman and Brooks (n.5).

10 In the case of Zimbabwe, see Shari Eppel, 'A Tale of Three Dinner Plates: Truth and the Challenges of Human Rights Research in Zimbabwe' (2009) 35(4) *Journal of Southern African Studies* 967, See also Mai-Linh K. Kong, 'A Genocide by Any Other Name: Language, Law and the Response to Darfur' (2008) 49 *Virginia Journal of International Law Association* 235 and Guy Fiti Sinclair, '"The Ghosts of Colonialism in Africa": Silences and Shortcomings in the ICJ 2005 Armed Activities Decision' (2007) 14 *ILSA Journal of International and Comparative Law* 121.

11 Joanna R. Quinn, 'Whither the Transition of Transitional Justice' (2014–2015) 8(1) *Interdisciplinary Journal of Human Rights Law* 63.

also looks at current prospects for dealing with the past as laid down in the new Constitution.

6.2 Zimbabwe: the context

6.2.1 Pre-independence Zimbabwe: a laconic historical narrative[12]

The recorded history of the territory now called Zimbabwe is characterized by great violence.[13] This is largely traced back to the arrival of Mzilikazi and his entourage around 1840.[14] In keeping with the times, Mzilikazi is said to have forcefully assumed control over the already-existing Shona people in the process of establishing the Ndebele nation in the south west of present-day Zimbabwe.[15]

The next main epoch was the creation of the state of Rhodesia, and again the use of violence was central to its inception.[16] The sequence of historical events starts with Cecil John Rhodes's British South Africa Company (BSAC)'s fraudulent treaties with the King of the Ndebele which led to the natives' uprisings of 1893 and 1896.[17] Both uprisings were stopped by private sector force, which led to the conquest and annexation of the territory into the British empire.[18]

As explained in Chapter 4, the colonial regime used both the law and force to expropriate land. Chapter 5 highlighted that the Ndebele kingdom was forcefully combined with the rest of the Shona-inhabited territory in 1900. Thus, for the purposes of this chapter, it suffices to point out that racially based capitalistic exploitation of resources, which was validated by law, intensified in 1922 when political power was handed to the white settler population.[19]

As stated in Chapter 4, Britain's commitment to the decolonization process was resisted by the Rhodesian white settlers who unilaterally declared Rhodesia

12 For the colonial history of Zimbabwe, see Cannan S. Banana (ed), *Turmoil and Tenacity: Zimbabwe 1890–1990* (The College Press 1989).

13 The Redress Trust, 'Zimbabwe: From Impunity to Accountability, Are Reparations Possible for Victims of Gross and Systematic Human Violations?' (2004), The Redress Trust, 'Torture in Zimbabwe, Past and Present: Prevention, Punishment, and Reparation? A Survey of Law and Practice' (2005) <www.redress.org/>.

14 See Minorities at Risk Project, 'Chronology for Ndebele in Zimbabwe' (2004) <www.refworld.org/docid/469f38f81e.html>.

15 Ibid.

16 See Arthur Keppel-Jones, *Rhodes and Rhodesia: The White Conquest of Zimbabwe, 1884–1902* (McGill–Queen's University Press 1983).

17 Minorities at Risk Project (n.14).

18 Ibid.

19 The principal statutes that facilitated the exploitation were the Land Apportionment Act of 1930 which marginalized the production of the indigenous population, hence ensuring that the black majority remained at the perpetual servitude of the settlers; and the 1934 Labour laws which stipulated that Africans could not enter skilled trade and professions. This resulted in most Africans working either as cheap labour on white farms or under poor conditions in white-owned factories and mines. For a discussion of the land legislation, see Roger Rindell, 'Zimbabwe Land Problem: The Central Issue' in W.H. Morris-Jones (ed) *From Rhodesia to Zimbabwe: Behind and Beyond Lancaster House* (Frank Cass and Company Limited 1980).

to be independent (UDI) in 1965.[20] This UDI regime, which faced international isolation, was under the leadership of Ian Douglas Smith.[21] It declared a state of emergency which was renewed 49 times and remained in force until 1990.[22] This was ten years after majority rule had been established.[23] Thus, the application of certain fundamental rights, including freedom of association, assembly and movement, were suspended for 25 years.

Nonetheless, the Smith regime adopted harsher measures and rigorously implemented racial segregation.[24] The greatest incidents of widespread and systematic violence occurred after 1972, during the civil war between Zimbabwean liberation movements and the Rhodesian forces.[25] It is said that other tactics employed included the use of food as a political weapon, strict control over access to land, propaganda, censorship and the use of biological warfare.[26]

6.2.2 The transition from Rhodesia

Economic pragmatism in the Lancaster House agreement necessitated the inclusion of sweeping amnesty provisions.[27] This was typical of negotiated settlements that were part of Britain's process of decolonization.[28] These provisions covered both infringements of rights by the Rhodesian regime and those committed by

20 See Douglas G. Anglin, 'Unilateral Independence in Southern Rhodesia' (1964) 19(4) *International Law Journal* 551, and Douglas G. Anglin, 'Zimbabwe: Retrospect and Prospect' (1980) 35 *International Law Journal* 666.

21 For an insight into the international attitude towards Ian Smith's UDI, see the following resolutions: 'Resolutions on Sanctions against Southern Rhodesia and Measures to Assist Zambia' (1973) 12 *International Legal Materials* 454, 'Security Council Resolution on Sanctions against Southern Rhodesia' (1973) 12 *International Legal Materials* 1014, 'U.N. Security Council Resolutions on Assistance to Mozambique during Its Application of Sanctions against Southern Rhodesia' (1976) 15 *International Legal Materials* 718, 'U.N. Security Council Resolutions on Sanctions against Southern Rhodesia' (1976) 15 *International Legal Materials* 720, 'Commonwealth of Nations: Communiqué on Rhodesia' (1966) *International Legal Materials* 1158, 'Organization of African Unity: Resolution on Rhodesia' (1967) *International Legal Materials* 130, 'United States: Executive Order on Trade with Rhodesia' (1967) *International Legal Materials* 100, 'United Nations: General Assembly Resolution on Rhodesia' (1967) *International Legal Materials* 144, 'United Kingdom: Proposals for Settlement of Rhodesia Problem' (1967) *International Legal Materials* 134, 'United Nations: Security Council Resolution Imposing Mandatory Sanctions on Trade with Rhodesia' (1967) *International Legal Materials* 141.

22 Geoff Feltoe, 'Towards a Stronger Human Rights Culture in Zimbabwe: The Special Role of Lawyers' (1989–1990) 7–8 *Zimbabwe Law Review* 134.

23 Ibid.

24 Michael G. Bochenek, 'Compensation for Human Rights Abuses in Zimbabwe' (1994) 26 *Columbia Human Rights Law Review* 483.

25 Ibid. Agents of the white minority government are said to have killed between 30,000 and 80,000 people, and those assassinated included leaders of the black liberation movements.

26 Ibid.

27 Richard Carver, 'Zimbabwe: Drawing a Line through the Past' (1993) 37(1) *Journal of African Law* 69.

28 O.N. Musamirapamwe, 'The Evian Agreements on Algeria and the Lancaster Agreements on Zimbabwe: A Comparative Analysis' (1982) 12 *Georgia Journal of International and Comparative* Law 153.

the nationalists in attempts to overthrow it. The British government was also excused from any liability in tort and reparations proceedings. Public debts accrued by Rhodesia, including war debts, were not extinguished, however, and accordingly inherited by the new Zimbabwean state.[29]

It is noteworthy that this decision to draw a line through the past was negotiated amongst three sets of elites who had in one way or another all been complicit in Rhodesian human rights abuses.[30] Victims were not consulted. After his electoral victory in 1980, Robert Mugabe stated that for the sake of nation-building and reconciliation, Zimbabwe had now forgiven and forgotten the human rights atrocities committed in Rhodesia.[31] As will be briefly shown in this chapter, this post-Rhodesia amnesia was to be the preferred strategy of independent Zimbabwe in dealing with human rights abuses that occurred during its periods of unrest. In this regard, four post-independence epochs can be analyzed.

6.2.3 1980–1988

To re-iterate, human rights abuses committed in the colonial era were not punished, investigated or even publicly acknowledged. Enabling legislation was adopted to facilitate the 'forgive and forget' strategy.[32] Senior Rhodesian army, police and security officials who had operated in a state of emergency and participated in the widespread and systematic human rights abuses were retained.[33] The state of emergency that had existed since 1965, together with the legal framework that had enabled the Rhodesian government to illegally detain without trial and to torture, execute and cause the forced disappearances of its opponents was maintained during the first ten years of independence.[34]

However, peace and stability did not immediately ensue after independence.[35] This was initially attributed to the difficulties of trying to integrate three former rival armies into one national army.[36] The ZANU PF government's reaction to dissent was to unleash the retained institutions that the Rhodesians had dedicated to the abuse of human rights of its opponents, thereby legitimizing a tradition of human rights abuse and a culture of impunity.[37] This reaction can be illustrated by two examples. First, the Rhodesian army was used to commit atrocities against the perceived ZAPU dissidents in the Bulawayo's Entumbane Township barely a year after independence.[38] The integration of the former Rhodesian army was not

29 Ibid, Ord. 3/1979, Amnesty Act (Chapter 9.02).

30 See Report of the Southern Rhodesia Constitutional Conference held at Lancaster House, London, September–December 1979, <https://peacemaker.un.org/sites/peacemaker.un.org/files/ZW_791221_LancasterHouseAgreement.pdf>.

31 Carver (n.27).

32 Ord. 12/1980, Amnesty (General Pardon) Act (Chapter 9:03).

33 Carver (n.27).

34 Ibid.

35 Bochenek (n.24).

36 Ibid.

37 Ibid.

38 See Catholic Commission for Justice and Peace (CCJP) and the Legal Resources Foundation (LRF), *Breaking the Silence, Building the Peace: Report on the Disturbances in Matebeleland*

problematic largely due to the fact that this force continued to enjoy favorable working conditions during the transitional phase. However, bringing together the military wings of ZANLA (ZANU) and ZIPRA (ZAPU), who were housed in makeshift camps, proved to be difficult.

Therefore, grievances over poor conditions fuelled differences between ZIPRA and ZANLA in Entumbane Township, which culminated in an open conflict in November 1980 and February 1981. In a bid to quash the fighting in February 1981, ZANU PF deployed former Rhodesian forces including the air force against ZIPRA-perceived dissidents. More than 100 people died, including civilians, prisoners and children. When faced with allegations of these harrowing atrocities in Entumbane, the government reacted by setting up a judicial commission of inquiry which investigated the events but was precluded from publicizing its findings.[39] In 1983, another commission was established to look into reports of killings of civilians by the army in Matebeleland, and again the report was not published.[40]

Second, in the advent of increased military action against the perceived dissidents of Matebeleland and Midlands, the government took advantage of the existence of a state of emergency to issue regulations that exculpated its officials and security forces from any consequent criminal and civil acts.[41] In this environment, and in particular between 1983 and 1987, there were reports of mass killings, torture, burning, bayoneting, rape, destruction of property and enforced 'disappearances' perpetrated by the North Korean-trained Fifth Brigade that was deployed by ZANU PF.[42] It is estimated that approximately 20,000 people lost their lives.[43] Of significance is the fact that some of the tactics used in the military action against the Ndebele dissidents had been employed by the colonial regime in its campaign against the nationalists' forces.[44]

A related critical point worth underlining is the inheritance of the Rhodesian culture of impunity and the normalization of the Lancaster House precedent of judicial amnesia.[45] This is exemplified in the way in which the state dealt with human rights violators after the Matebeleland atrocities. After the unity accord of 27 March 1987, an amnesty for dissidents was deemed imperative for the

---

and the Midlands, 1980 to 1988 (CCJP and LRF 1997). See also Norma Kriger, 'Veterans' Pensions in Zimbabwe; Dispute Resolution and Nation-building' (2005) 20 *Ohio State Journal on Dispute Resolution* 249.

39 The Dumbutshena Commission of Inquiry.

40 The Chihambakwe Commission of Inquiry.

41 See Section 4 (1), Emergency Powers (Security Forces Indemnity) Regulations 1982(SI) 487/1982 as amended by SI 159/1983.

42 CCJP and LRF (n.38).

43 Mphathisi Ndlovu, 'Speaking for the Dead: Testimonies, Witnesses and the Representations of Gukurahundi Atrocities in New Media' (2018) 30(3) *Journal of African Cultural Studies* 293 at 294.

44 Carver (n.27).

45 In Rhodesia, the Indemnity and Compensation Act 45/1975 exonerated the state personnel involved in the fight against terrorism from any liability for civil proceedings and human rights violations.

sake of peace.[46] In June, this amnesty was extended to the army and other state actors.[47] Seventy-five security force members who either had been sentenced or were awaiting trial for several human rights violations, and four Fifth Brigade soldiers who were on death row for committing murder in Matebeleland, were amongst those who escaped justice.[48] A pattern of impunity was thus set.

6.2.4 1989–1999

If there was ever a time when Zimbabweans enjoyed a semblance of peace, it was during the period from 1990 to 1996.[49] After the state of emergency ended in 1990, the goZ ratified a number of international conventions and even collaborated with non-governmental organizations in providing human rights training to the police and prison officers.

However, the culture of impunity still manifested itself on three occasions, when the government was faced with allegations of human rights violations perpetrated by its state machinery. First was through the granting of amnesty to alleged perpetrators of human rights abuses after the 1990 and 1995 elections, which were considered to be marred by state-orchestrated political violence.[50] Second, in the wake of the 1998 food riots, the government ignored human rights organizations' calls for the creation of an independent inquiry, which would look at reported abuses.[51] Similarly, the UN Human Rights' Committee's recommendations that an impartial inquiry be set up were not acted upon.[52] Third, when faced with a court action initiated by domestic human rights organizations in 1999 compelling the release of the report on the 1983–1987 Matebeleland atrocities, the government simply stated that the document had been misplaced.[53]

Nevertheless, in 1999, a formidable opposition party, the Movement for Democratic Change (MDC) was born, and ZANU PF ceased to be politically secure. It became extremely hostile to both human rights organizations and the opposition party as it saw them as vicarious agents of foreign ideologies.[54] It thus stopped making any pretence at taking responsibility for alleged human rights

46 Clemency Order No. 1 of 1988, published in Government Gazette Extraordinary (GN 257A/1988) on 3 May 1988.

47 Carver (n.27) 261. See also comment by Anthony P. Reeler, 'Can You Have a Reparations Policy without Justice?' (2000) 12(4) *Legal Forum (Harare)*.

48 Ibid.

49 Several factors contributed to this state of affairs, namely, the existence of a *de facto* one-party state, the end of the Cold War and the demise of the apartheid regime in neighboring South Africa.

50 General Notice 42A/1990 and Clemency Order No. 1/1995.

51 Zimbabwe Human Rights NGO Forum, 'Consolidated Report on the Food Riots 19–23 January 1998' (1998) <www.hrforumzim.com/>.

52 Ibid.

53 Amnesty International, *Zimbabwe: Toll of Impunity* (Amnesty International Secretariat 2002) <http://web.amnesty.org/>.

54 Amnesty International, *Zimbabwe* (London: Amnesty International Secretariat 2005) <http://web.amnesty.org/>.

violations.[55] Against this background, the culture of impunity became firmly entrenched, and this will be demonstrated by the subsequent narrative.

6.2.5 2000–2008

In October 2000, an amnesty for politically motivated crimes was announced.[56] This was after allegations of state-orchestrated violence that had occurred both before and after the constitutional referendum of February 2000. This amnesty covered the period of violent invasions of white-owned commercial farms and the parliamentary elections in June 2000 which were marred by violence.[57] It was not extended to those who had committed crimes such as 'murder, robbery, rape, indecent assault, statutory rape, theft, possession of arms and any offence involving fraud or dishonesty'.[58] However, those responsible for other egregious offences, including torture, were also excused from any liability.[59]

Throughout this period there was an increasing level of repression.[60] This was mostly manifested in unabated, widespread and systematic human rights violations during the presidential elections of 2002 and also in local, mayoral and parliamentary by-elections held in 2003.[61] Other human rights violations included attacks on human rights defenders, infringements on freedom of association and assembly, censorship of the independent media, excessive use of force by the Zimbabwe Republic Police, including torture and ill-treatment, and violations of the right to food and housing.[62]

It is fair to state that the country's human rights abuses mainly occurred before and after elections and were also associated with the state's excessive use of force when responding to demonstrations.[63] This does not mean that there was no crisis, since in 2008 the country faced the worst economic challenges ever since its formation.[64] It is thus fair to state that the worst violations during this epoch were those of economic, social and cultural rights.[65]

55 Ibid.
56 Clemency Order of No. 1 October 2000; General Noticc 457/A/2000.
57 This issue was covered in Chapter 4.
58 See Section 2 and 4(a) Clemency Order of No. 1 October 2000 (n 55).
59 For a detailed discussion, see Zimbabwe Human Rights NGO Forum, 'Torture in Zimbabwe' (2004) 34 *Human Rights Monitor* <www.hrforumzim.com/>.
60 Insights on these can be found from the reports of the Zimbabwe Human Rights NGO Forum <www.hrforumzim.com/>.
61 Ibid.
62 Amnesty International (n.54).
63 By way of illustration, according to the statistical reports of the Zimbabwe Human Rights NGO Forum, politically motivated and state-orchestrated violence which occurred in 2007 included 19 cases of abductions, 855 of assaults, 3,477 violations on freedoms of expression, association and movement, 586 cases of torture, 3,352 cases of unlawful arrest and detention and 3 murders. These figures have dropped drastically since the signing of the Memorandum of Understanding by the country's main parties on 21 July 2008.
64 See Nelson Banya, 'Zimbabwe Inflation Hits New Record at 66,212.3 Percent' *Reuters*, 14 February 2008 <http://africa.reuters.com/>.
65 Ibid.

Of significance is the gender dimension of the country's crisis, evidenced by the fact that the impact of the economic decline has been felt more acutely by women who have openly protested against the same.[66] Of course, women in Zimbabwe have also suffered physical rights violations in common with men, an example being Women of Zimbabwe Arise (WOZA) – a group which has been at the forefront of demonstrations – which has frequently been physically assaulted by the police.[67]

Nonetheless, other recorded gender-based violations include sexual violence perpetrated by those identified to be supporters of ZANU PF during the election periods in the years 2000 and 2002.[68] Furthermore, women are said to have been more affected by the internal displacement which occurred during the farm invasions of 2000–2005 and the urban clean-up operation known as Operation Murambatswina.[69] Approximately 700,000 people were displaced during the latter exercise, and a number of homes were destroyed.[70] Most women who were involved in the informal trading sector also lost their means of livelihood.[71] However, the classification of Operation Murambatswina as a human rights violation is contentious, since this exercise could be interpreted as a state policy for implementing Zimbabwe's international obligation to *protect* the enjoyment of the right to health.[72]

It has to be pointed out that whilst the state publicly denied any violations of human rights, it conceded liability in the confines of judges' chambers.[73] This fact has been confirmed in the analysis of civil proceedings that the Zimbabwe Human Rights NGO Forum (the Forum) has been instituting on behalf of victims of state-orchestrated violence since 1998.[74] According to their June 2006 report, in 90% of their completed cases, either the cases were settled out of court or the court's findings favoured the victims.[75] This, however, cannot be seen as effective redress for victims of human rights violations in Zimbabwe, since these are only those cases which were brought to the attention of the Forum. There has also not been any public acknowledgement of wrongdoing by the state. The cycle of impunity may continue since the main opposition party has also demonstrated an inclination towards violence when faced with dissent.[76] Despite the

66 Zimbabwe Human Rights NGO Forum, '"A Woman's Place Is in the Home?" – Gender-based Violence and Opposition Politics in Zimbabwe' (2006) *Report Produced by the Zimbabwe Human Rights NGO Forum as a Contribution Towards 16 Days of Activism against Gender Based Violence* <www.hrforumzim.com/>.

67 Ibid.

68 Ibid.

69 Ibid.

70 Ibid.

71 Ibid.

72 Most of the homes destroyed were in areas which are not serviced, and it is common cause that there is a high risk of cholera in places where sewage and drinking water are not treated.

73 Zimbabwe Human Rights NGO Forum, 'An Analysis of the Human Rights NGO Forum Legal Cases, 1998–2006' *Special Report* (June 2006) <www.hrforumzim.com/>.

74 Ibid.

75 Ibid.

76 See Zimbabwe Human Rights NGO Forum, 'Political Violence Report of the Month of July 2006' (2006) <www.hrforumzim.com/>.

vibrancy of the country's civil society, together with international attention on the political negotiations of 2008, combating impunity does not appear to be a priority of the GPA.

6.2.6 2008–2019

As stated in previous chapters, following violence, social and economic collapse, Zimbabwe's key political parties signed a Global Political Agreement (GPA) on 15 September 2008.[77] Noteworthy are Articles 6 and 7 of the GPA. Article 6 provided for the creation of a Parliamentary Select Committee, which would lead the process of producing a 'people driven' Constitution and Article 7 dealt with the promotion of 'equality, national healing, cohesion and unity'. In particular, Article 7.1 (c) stated that the parties:

> [S]hall consider the setting up of a mechanism to properly advice on what measures might be necessary and practicable to achieve national healing, cohesion and unity in respect of victims of pre and post-independence political conflicts.[78]

When the power-sharing agreement ended with ZANU PF's victory in the 2013 harmonized elections, both Articles 6 and 7 of the GPA had been implemented. An Organ for National Healing, Reconciliation and Integration (ONHRI) was established, and the country had a new Constitution.[79] One of the achievements of the ONHRI was in ensuring that the 2013 Zimbabwean Constitution included provisions on a mechanism for dealing with the past.

Part 6 of the Zimbabwean Constitution of 2013 established a National Peace and Reconciliation Commission (NPRC) and provided for its composition, functions and reports.[80] This is supposed to be a temporary body led by an experienced lawyer, which would last for ten years. Commissioners were appointed in 2016, and the NPRC was made operational in 2018.[81] This body has a broad mandate and is intended to be both forward and backward looking.[82] In particular, the NPRC

77 Agreement between the Zimbabwe African National Union Patriotic Front (ZANU PF) and the two Movement for Democratic Change (MDC) formations, on resolving the challenges facing Zimbabwe (GPA), <www.copac.org.zw/phocadownload/GNU/gpa.pdf>.

78 Art 7.1(c) GPA, ibid.

79 For a critique of the work of the ONHRI, see Moreblessing Mbire, 'Seeking Reconciliation and National Healing in Zimbabwe: Case of the Organ on National Healing, Reconciliation and Integration (ONHRI)' *Master's Thesis* (Institute of Social Studies, 2011).

80 Part 6, Constitution of Zimbabwe Amendment (No. 20) Act, 2013 <www.parlzim.gov.zw/attachments/article/56/constitution.pdf>.

81 The National Peace and Reconciliation Commission Act came into force on 5 January 2018.

82 According to S252 of the 2013 Constitution, the duties of the NPRC are to: ensure post-conflict justice, healing and reconciliation; to develop and implement programmes to promote national healing, unity and cohesion in Zimbabwe and the peaceful resolution of disputes; to bring about national reconciliation by encouraging people to tell the truth about the past and facilitating the making of amends and the provision of justice; to develop procedures and institutions at a national level to facilitate dialogue among political parties, communities, organizations and other groups, in order to prevent conflicts and disputes arising in the

has to recover the truth about past atrocities, facilitate the provision of reparations, resolve disputes and pre-empt future conflict. On the face of it, the constitutional provisions are progressive as they factor the four key areas which a state has to address so that it can adequately deal with its past. These are the right to know, right to justice, right to reparation and guarantees of non-recurrence.[83] However, given Zimbabwe's experience with state-led truth recovery processes, it remains to be seen whether there will be a genuine public acknowledgement of past human rights violations. Public acknowledgement of human rights abuses is necessary for peace, national healing and reconciliation as it establishes trust and accountability.

6.3 How to read Zimbabwe's legacy of impunity

The Zimbabwean experience brings to the fore the old debate on the permissibility of domestic amnesties. It also raises the issue of appropriate justice mechanisms for redressing the injustices caused to the people of Zimbabwe both during colonization and in the 39 years of ZANU PF rule. Inherent in the latter issue is the vexed question of colonial accountability.

6.3.1 Blanket amnesty legislation as lex injusta non est lex

The history of regular amnesty proclamations is not peculiar to Zimbabwe. In the past, other African postcolonial societies, which include Uganda, South Africa and Sierra Leone, have also resorted to amnesties as instruments for reconciliation and peace building.[84] On the face of it, the approach may be consistent with Arti-

---

future; to develop programmes to ensure that persons subjected to persecution, torture and other forms of abuse receive rehabilitative treatment and support; to receive and consider complaints from the public and to take such action in regard to the complaints as the Commission considers appropriate; to develop mechanisms for early detection of areas of potential conflicts and disputes, and to take appropriate preventive measures; to do anything incidental to the prevention of conflict and the promotion of peace; to conciliate and mediate disputes among communities, organizations, groups and individuals; and to recommend legislation to ensure that assistance, including documentation, is rendered to persons affected by conflicts, pandemics or other circumstances.

83 See Report of the Special Rapporteur on the promotion of truth, justice, reparation and guarantees of non-recurrence, Pablo de Greiff, 'United Nations General Assembly' A/HRC/21/46 (9 August 2012) <www.ohchr.org/Documents/HRBodies/HRCouncil/RegularSession/Session21/A-HRC-21-46_en.pdf>.

84 See Truth and Reconciliation Commission Act of 22 February 2000 (Sierra Leone) and art XXVI of the 1999 Lomé Peace Agreement. The Amnesty Act of 2000 offers pardon to all Ugandans engaged or engaging in acts of rebellion against the government of Uganda since 26 January 1986. See Refugee Law Project 2005, 'Whose Justice? Perceptions of Uganda's Amnesty Act 2000: The Potential for Conflict Resolution and Long-term Reconciliation' *Working Paper No. 15* (4 February 2005). The South Africa National Unity and Reconciliation Act 34 of 1995 established a mechanism for granting broad amnesties to those who had committed politically motivated crimes during the apartheid regime and who made full disclosure The amnesty was to exempt individuals from both criminal and civil liability. Further, for Sierra Leone, see Article 14, Peace Agreement between the Government of the Republic

cle 6(5) of Protocol 11 to the 1969 Geneva Convention which states that broad amnesties are to be given to those who have been punished or detained on the basis of their participation in the hostilities.[85] Nonetheless, the International Committee of the Red Cross (ICRC) explained in 1995 that the purpose of this provision is to facilitate the end of hostilities and not to excuse violations of humanitarian law.[86]

Human rights law, customary international law and international criminal law do not condone blanket amnesties. Legally permissible amnesties do not cover crimes against humanity, the international crime of genocide, war crimes and other violations of humanitarian law. International human rights law also reflects on a positive duty to investigate, prosecute and even punish the perpetrators of human rights abuses. The question, then, is whether the Zimbabwean amnesties were permissible.

An obvious starting point would be the pre-independence amnesties, but these will be given special attention under the heading of colonial accountability. Thus, this section focuses on postcolonial atrocities. It has to be pointed out that the regime which has monopolized the Zimbabwean political arena since independence has to some extent often complied with its international obligation to investigate although findings of two Commissions of inquiry have never been made public.[87] Thus, there is no official truth for the 1980s Gukurahundi and Entumbane atrocities, and fact-finding has been largely confined to efforts of non-government organizations and academics.[88]

It can be said that most of the violations of civil and political rights documented by credible sources in Zimbabwe between 2000 and 2008 are not serious enough to be classified as grave war crimes, genocide or crimes against humanity. Therefore, it could be said that the amnesties from this era are permissible. The same however, cannot be said of the Gukurahundi atrocities of 1983–1987, which could be classified as an international crime of genocide since the target of these abuses was a defined ethnic group. Moreover, even though a state of emergency existed at the time of the human rights violations, rights violated during this era are not subject to derogation.

Unfortunately, the case of the Rwandan genocide and the experience of Darfur in Sudan have taught us that this label is likely to be resisted by international actors who prefer the terms 'war crimes' and 'crimes against humanity'.[89] Indeed,

---

of Sierra Leone and the Revolutionary United Front of Sierra Leone, signed at Abidjan on 30 November 1996, <www.usip.org/>. In the case of South Africa, see Indemnity Act 35 of 1990 and Indemnity Act 151 of 1992.

85 This line of thinking was advanced in *The Azanian Peoples Organization (AZAPO) v The President of the Republic of South Africa and Ors.* 1996 4 SA 671 (CC).

86 Christine Bell, *On the Law of Peace: Peace Agreements and the Lex Pacificatoria* (Oxford University Press 2008) 245.

87 See B. Rafttopoulos and S. Eppel, *Political Crisis, Mediation and the Prospects of Transitional Justice in Zimbabwe* (Institute for Democracy in Africa [IDASA] 2008) <www.idasa.org.za> (Accessed 10 June 2009).

88 Ibid.

89 Mai-Linh K. Hong, 'A Genocide by Any Other Name: Language, Law and the Response to Darfur' (2008) 49 *Virginia Journal of International Law Association* 235.

although there were noticeable ethnic features which were central to the recent abuses in Darfur, the UN Security Council, International Criminal Court (ICC), European Union (EU) and African Union (AU) were not keen to identify the events as an act of genocide.[90] The explanation for this position has been given by David Luban:

> [W]ith headlines such as Murder – But no Genocide, the motivation to intervene was gone. . . . Genocide sounds like it might be our business, but 'mere' murder is theirs.[91]

Therein lies the problem, which is the inherent politics of *othering* in the discourse of international law.[92] The *Self* wants to maintain a moral high ground in comparison to the *Other*; thus the term 'genocide' is seen as problematic as it is apt to generate a moral obligation in public perceptions. This is likely to be the case with the Gukurahundi in the case of Zimbabwe, since the international community failed to recognize or acknowledge these events as an act of genocide at the time of their occurrence. Nevertheless, and notwithstanding the semantics, there is a good case for the waiver of the amnesty given in 1987 since violations of this era can be described as an act of genocide.

The passage of time will pose no barrier to such prosecutions since in international law, grave crimes are not prescribable. Also, as explained in Chapter 2, the obvious legal issue of retroactivity will be mediated by international law which provides continuity through norms on accountability. In fact, there is postcolonial precedent of such waivers in the cases of Argentina and Chile.[93] However, in Zimbabwe such a problem might harm the peace-building efforts, since the Mnangagwa regime and a number of those who are said to have masterminded the 1980s atrocities still control the security apparatus.

Therefore, a second question which arises is whether there could be a role for the International Criminal Court (ICC), as the current government is both unable and unwilling to deal with the 1983–1987 Gukurahundi atrocities. This raises axiomatic jurisdictional hurdles since the ICC's jurisdiction is limited to those crimes committed after its establishment in 2002.[94] As stated previously, the Zimbabwean post-2002 violations can hardly be referred to as serious crimes which can be dealt with by the ICC. Furthermore, Zimbabwe is not a state party

90 Ibid.

91 David Luban, 'Calling Genocide by Its Rightful Name: Lemkin's Word, Darfur and the UN Report' (2006) 7 *Chicago Journal of International Law* 303.

92 The idea of 'othering' derives from the groundbreaking work of Edward W. Said, *Orientalism* (Pantheon Books 1978).

93 In 2001, in an obvious instance of self-adjudication, the courts of Argentina found the amnesty laws which were passed between 1988 and 1989 to be in breach of both international law and the victims' constitutional rights. Similarly, in 2000, a Chilean court held that the 1978 amnesty law which precluded the prosecution of the Pinochet regime was not consistent with international law and human rights standards.

94 Article 11 (1), Rome Statute of the International Criminal Court (hereinafter Rome Statute), <www.icc-cpi.int/>.

to the ICC, and in the absence of a regime change, there is little chance that the jurisdiction of the ICC will be accepted by domestic political actors.

Mark Ellis, however, has persistently argued that the Robert Mugabe regime's crimes ought to be investigated and prosecuted by the ICC and that such an action could be made possible by a referral from the UN Security Council.[95] In his view, the regime could be prosecuted for 'other inhumane acts' which include its systematic and widespread use of food as a political weapon.[96] This raises a very important issue on the limitations of international law with regard to enforcement of violations of economic social and cultural rights. It can be said that ever since the country received international attention, most deaths in Zimbabwe have been caused by the state's failure to *respect, protect and fulfil* its citizens' rights to economic, social and cultural rights and not politically motivated violence. Unfortunately, international law is unable to deal with such violations since they also implicate Western international intervention.

Similarly, and on the face of it, the involvement of international organizations may appear to be a means for ensuring that victims of political violence obtain justice.[97] Yet, in political practice, such an action is mostly reserved for poor postcolonial states.[98] According to Max Pensky, this:

> [a]llows powerful and wealthy Western European states, which have pushed for the ICC's existence and continue to define its institutional rationale to demand legal limits to state members' sovereign control over their own domestic policy . . . but at the same time to direct (poor, postcolonial, Southern) states to remain the presumptive first recourse for high risk and high-cost prosecutions.[99]

Thus the anti-impunity initiative raises questions on the character and ambit of postcolonial states' sovereignty and especially in the application of the principle of universal jurisdiction.[100] This is a customary international law rule which allows domestic courts to prosecute grave crimes which amount to crimes against humanity without considering the nationality of either the victim or the perpetrator.[101] Those who support this rule state that it assists victims to obtain justice in contexts where their governments are unable or unwilling to pursue justice and in circumstances where the offender is out of reach of the courts in the country where the offence was committed because

95 Mark S. Ellis, 'The World vs Robert Mugabe' *International Herald Tribune*, 2 April 2004.

96 Ibid.

97 Max Pensky, 'Amnesty on Trial: Impunity, Accountability and the Norms of International Law' (2008) 1(2) *Ethics and Global Politics* 1.

98 Ibid.

99 Ibid.

100 See Lee K. Boyd, 'Universal Jurisdiction and Structural Reasonableness' (2004) *40 Texas International Law Journal* 1, and Anthony Sammons, 'The 'Under-Theorization of Universal Jurisdiction: Implications for Legitimacy on Trials of War Criminals by National Courts' (2003) 21 *Berkeley Journal of International Law* 111.

101 Ibid.

they have sought a safe haven elsewhere.[102] However, current examples of the application of universal jurisdiction suggest that its exercise is often politically motivated and that it succeeds only in incidents involving nationals of poor postcolonial states.[103]

6.3.2 Appropriate justice mechanisms for redressing Zimbabwe's past human rights abuses

> [J]ustice cannot be captured simply by identifying the wrongdoers, taking them to court, and sentencing them to serve time in jail. We must ask: what form of justice is due to the victims of the crimes, especially those who suffered severe physical or psychological injury, or whose economic means have been severely disrupted, such as through the loss of a breadwinner? What would be an appropriate form of justice for whole communities that ha3ve suffered or been completely destroyed? While criminal justice is critical – and I would like to underline that is should always be considered as a vital component – other approaches should also be considered.[104]

Transitional justice scholars have identified a number of methods for dealing with past human rights abuses, and these include trials, truth-seeking methods, reparations and memorialization programmes. None of these mechanisms are a novelty to postcolonial Zimbabwe, notwithstanding its history of amnesty legislation.[105] In the past, the goZ has employed some truth-finding, reparatory, institutional transformation and memorialization programmes.[106] The legal system has also been used to selectively prosecute some perpetrators, with the latest attempt targeted at those alleged to have been involved in corrupt practices.

This cannot be taken to mean that perpetrators have not enjoyed both *de jure* and *de facto* immunity, since most of these mechanisms have either been piecemeal or tantamount to rewards to the victors of the liberation struggle.[107] In particular, the findings of the country's two formal commissions of inquiry into disturbances in Matebeleland in the 1980s have never been made public, even

102 Ibid.

103 See Paul Chevigny, 'Limitations of Universal Jurisdiction' *Global Policy Forum*, March 2006 <www.globalpolicy.org>.

104 Priscilla Hayner, 'Justice in Transition: Challenges and Opportunities' Presentation to the *55th Annual DPI/NGO Conference on Rebuilding Societies Emerging from Conflict: A Shared Responsibility*, United Nations, New York, 9 September 2002 <www.un.org/dpi/ngosection>.

105 Zimbabwe Human Rights NGO Forum, 'Exploring Transitional Justice Options in Contemporary Zimbabwe' (2006) <www.hrforumzim.com/>.

106 Ibid.

107 Zimbabwe Human Rights NGO Forum (n.105).

though the country's human rights organizations have applied pressure on the government to do so.[108]

Reparatory programmes carried out so far have included the contentious land reform programme discussed in Chapter 4 and the compensation schemes which were abused by the ruling elite and war veterans from the liberation struggle.[109] In particular, the government enacted, in the year the country attained its independence, the War Victims Compensation Act of 1980 to compensate injury and death which occurred during the war of liberation.[110] In its actual implementation, this act was treated as a social welfare scheme for the ruling elite and their associates, and not a reparatory programme for victims of the colonial era.[111]

A government doctor who assessed the claimants' degrees of disability diagnosed some of them, who were government ministers, to be about 98% disabled.[112] After the exposure of this scandal, some war veterans pressured the government to give them compensation packages as well, and later this scheme was extended to facilitate the compensation of those who had been detained or abused during the liberation war of the 1970s.[113] It will be recalled from previous chapters that these groups are largely aligned to ZANU PF. Thus, the credibility of these measures as a justice mechanism for repairing the colonial past is in doubt.

Similar sentiments can be made in respect to the government-led memorialization programmes.[114] These have been reduced to propaganda tools for reminding the nation of the role played by the ruling elite and their supporters in the struggle against white minority rule.[115] As Chapter 4 explained, this exclusive focus was instrumental in the support which the ruling party received for its land reform process.[116] Norma Kriger has noted that state-led collective memory programmes have been used largely to legitimate a group's claim to power and resources while de-legitimizing others' rights to the same.[117] Herein lies the major limitation of international legal mechanisms which are blind to the struggle for resources in postcolonial societies.[118]

108 Ibid. See also *Zimbabwe Lawyers for Human Rights and Anor v President of Zimbabwe and Anor*, S-12-03 (Civ App 311/99).

109 Ibid, as read with also Norma Kriger, 'Veterans' Pensions in Zimbabwe: Dispute Resolution and Nation-building' (2005) 20 *Ohio State Journal on Dispute Resolution* 249.

110 Kriger, ibid.

111 Ibid.

112 Ibid.

113 Ibid. See also The 2004 Ex-Political Prisoners, Detainees and Restrictees Act (No 24/2004).

114 Zimbabwe Human Rights NGO Forum (n.105).

115 Ibid, as read with Centre for the Study of Violence and Reconciliation (CSVR), 'Memorialisation and Reconciliation in Transitional Southern African Societies' (2005) <www.csvr.org.za>.

116 See Norma Kriger, 'From Patriotic Memories to Patriotic History in Zimbabwe, 1990–2005' (2006) 27(6) *Third World Quarterly* 1151.

117 Ibid.

118 Ibid.

Nevertheless, in addition to state-led initiatives, parallel efforts have been made by the country's opposition parties and civic society.[119] They have documented allegations of political violence, pursued civil claims against the state and examined possible justice options. Civil society has also attempted domestic and international litigation on behalf of victims of post-independence human rights violations.

Indeed, domestic and international organizations have played a fundamental fact-finding role in reporting alleged human rights abuses. The Catholic Commission for Justice and Peace in Zimbabwe (CCJPZ), formally called the Catholic Commission for Justice and Peace in Rhodesia, has actually consistently done so since the 1970s when it documented abuses by the Rhodesian security forces.[120] It was also a lone fact-finding body during the Gukurahundi massacres of the early 1980s.

These initiatives, however, are inadequate since there are led by elites who are based mainly in the country's two capital cities. Thus, there is insufficient ethnographic knowledge of those communities mostly affected by the violence. Although some of the civic groups engaged in documentation claim to have provincial offices, their effectiveness in the villages where violent incidents have been known to be prevalent is still to be tested.[121]

Much more significantly, whilst civic society reports might be a useful lobby tool, they do not also present a complete and accurate historic account. For example, the statistical figures of the CCJP report of the Matebeleland atrocities are disputed.[122] According to the authors, this is largely attributed to the fact that during the disturbances, most of the affected areas were inaccessible.[123] The state's propaganda also laid the bulk of the blame on the so-called dissidents.[124]

Also, obtaining redress for violations of economic, social and cultural rights may be practically impossible in Zimbabwe. Despite the fact that the notion of indivisibility and interdependence of rights is now recognized, Zimbabwean human rights documentation is still largely Eurocentric in that its principal focus is on civil and political rights.[125] This issue has added importance when it comes to gender-based violence.

119 Zimbabwe Human Rights NGO Forum (n.105). See also Khanyisela Moyo, 'Forbidden Truth? – Background to Truth Recovery in Zimbabwe, Challenges, Opportunities and Threats' *Conference Report, Zimbabwe Human Rights NGO Forum* (Zimbabwe Human Rights NGO Forum & The Institute of Justice and Reconciliation 2014) pages 19–32.

120 Zimbabwe Human Rights NGO Forum (n.105).

121 An example of such an organization is the Zimbabwe Civic Education Trust (ZIMCET); <www.zimcet.org>. See also Shari Eppel, *Transitional Justice for Villagers in Zimbabwe* (Institute for Democracy in South Africa [IDASA] 2008).

122 CCJP and LRF (n.38).

123 Ibid.

124 Ibid.

125 Ibid. See, however, Amnesty International, 'Zimbabwe: Power and Hunger – Violations of the Right to Food' 15 October 2004. See also K. Moyo, 'Just Ends, Just Means . . . Is Starving a Nation for Political Gain a Crime against Humanity? The Zimbabwean Case 2000–2003' *Unpublished Thesis* (University of Oslo 2003).

NGO reports on this topic reveal an interface between violations of bodily integrity rights and breaches of economic social and cultural rights. For example, women whose source of livelihood was destroyed during the urban clean-up are alleged to have been more vulnerable to sexual exploitation and abuse.[126] Similarly, the women-led protests against economic challenges have been brutally suppressed by the state, which has in the process violated women's bodily integrity rights.[127] Some of these women have been arrested and subjected to inhumane and degrading treatment due to the country's poor prison conditions. Their situation has been exacerbated by the state's inability to provide sanitary towels to the incarcerated.[128]

Nonetheless, since 2001 a number of proposals have been made by the opposition party, the Zimbabwean civil society and some academics on potential justice mechanisms for the anticipated transition.[129] Although different options have been considered, it seems that those who believe something has to be done prefer a bifurcated approach which involves selective trials and a truth commission.[130] This marks a departure from the language of the 1990s, when legal debates on accountability in Zimbabwe concentrated largely on how the Zimbabwean legal system was a barrier to compensation for individual's human rights abuses.[131]

It has to be pointed out that initial efforts at pursuing compensation for victims of past human rights atrocities were led by well-meaning, Western-trained, white human rights activists who unfortunately had no appreciation of the context.[132] This explains these actors' preference for individual compensation schemes; yet in view of the scale of poverty and violence in Matebeleland in the 1980s and the whole of Zimbabwe post-2000, it might be expected that almost every family would have a legitimate right to compensation.[133] Awarding compensation to individuals when the vast majority of the people in the country are poor cannot be equated to the advancement of justice, and this explains the number of false human rights abuse allegations.[134] Against this background, Brian Raftopoulos and Shari Eppel have submitted that:

> [A] system of making people individually responsible for recounting their abuses, especially in a situation of dire poverty, will more or less invite

126 Zimbabwe Human Rights NGO Forum (n.66).

127 Ibid.

128 Ibid.

129 Some of these have been discussed in Max du Plessis and Jolyon Ford, 'Justice and Peace in a New Zimbabwe: Transitional Justice Options' (2008) *Institute for Security Studies Papers* 164.

130 Ibid.

131 See Feltoe (n.22) and Bochenek (n.24).

132 Examples of such work are that of the Catholic Commission for Justice and Peace in Zimbabwe and AMANI Trust.

133 Shari Eppel and Brian Raftopoulos, *Political Crisis, Mediation and the Prospects for Transitional Justice in Zimbabwe* (Cape Town: IDASA 2008).

134 Ibid.

> fraudulent claims and invented histories, which will confound our efforts to reach any kind of 'forensic' truth in terms of violations in the future.[135]

It is said that in a research exercise carried out in the Lupane area of Zimbabwe, a headman alerted the interviewers to the fact some of the allegations of violence were not true.[136] These falsehoods stemmed from people's assumptions that the researchers were conducting a registration exercise for compensation.[137] This advances the case for communal reparations, which can take the form of developments in the educational, health and housing sector of affected regions. The case against individual reparations is further strengthened by Zimbabwe's bad record with individual compensation schemes.

Nonetheless, the case for and against the use of certain mechanisms for addressing Zimbabwe's past human rights abuses has been examined elsewhere.[138] Issues of methodology have also been considered by others.[139] Whilst the usefulness of these exercises cannot be disputed, this work is wary of the contemporary excitement at replicating the experiences of other countries without any interrogation of the country's exigencies or immediate priorities. This view is based on a number of observations.

First, notwithstanding the establishment of the NPRC as a transitional justice mechanism for Zimbabwe, there is little evidence that this is what the victims want, or of any prospects that the commission will establish the truth.[140] According to Eppel, in a survey which looked at the urgent needs of the people in Matebeleland, most people considered food security to be their immediate priority, and 80% of them put water as their second urgent need.[141] Much more importantly, when asked about a specific mechanism for redressing the past, 80% of the respondents are said to have wanted exhumations and memorialization of their deceased relatives who are still in mass graves. This is in comparison to the 5% who said truth-telling was important.[142]

This indicates the popularity of a restorative justice approach among those who are truly acquainted with the country's conflict.[143] This story of Zimbabwe is a story of most postcolonial societies. For example, Rosalind Shaw's ethnographic study of ordinary Sierra Leonese perceptions of the TRC, which was established after the country's 11-year civil war, observed that this mechanism was popular

135 Ibid.
136 Ibid.
137 Ibid.
138 Du Plessis and Ford (n.129).
139 Ibid.
140 As stated earlier, if compensation is given as an incentive for people to tell their stories, the chances are high that a lot of people will fabricate their stories.
141 Eppel (n.121).
142 Ibid.
143 Ibid.

only with politicians and NGOs, and not with the victims.[144] In her opinion, which is shared by this author:

> [I]deas concerning the conciliatory and therapeutic efficacy of truth telling are the product of Western culture of memory deriving from North American and European historical processes.[145]

On the same note, research conducted by Timothy Sizwe Phakathi and Hugo van der Merwe found that even the most celebrated South African TRC was not seen as a success by most victims.[146] Interestingly, Priscilla Hayner, an expert on the subject, conceded in 2001 that the majority of TRCs which had then been established had not been successful.[147] The reasons for this failure have been lack of public involvement and resource constraints. There are also doubts that some TRCs can even meet their core objective of correcting history. Yet, most Western-sponsored NGOs still prefer a TRC as the core transitional justice mechanism for postcolonial transitions. This leads to the question as to whose justice is being promoted by these actors. Could it be that the whole purpose of these mechanisms is to foist Western culture on the postcolonial?

The same logic extends to the preference for trials as a transitional justice mechanism as it derives its precedent from placing human rights violators on trial in the aftermath of a Western war.[148] It should be noted that that the Nazi atrocities which set this precedent cannot be paralleled to the Zimbabwean contemporary conflict. Nonetheless, Western-sponsored NGOs and other agents of the civilization mission have been persistent in trying to establish a basis for prosecution.

In this regard, and in the case of Zimbabwe, Eppel noted that a direct line of command from senior security personnel cannot be established in respect of the 2008 political violence in rural areas.[149] Most of the brutal acts were either at an intra-community level, involving neighbours, and some were cases of family members attacking each other.[150] Community leadership has also been implicated

144 Rosalind Shaw, 'Rethinking Truth and Reconciliation Commissions: Lessons from Sierra Leone' *Special Report 130* (United States Institute of Peace 2005). See also Gearoid Millar, 'Between Western Theory and Local Practice: Cultural Impediments to Truth-telling in Sierra Leone' (2011) 29(2) *Conflict Resolution Quarterly* 177.

145 Ibid.

146 Timothy S. Phakathi and Hugo van der Merwe, *The Impact of the TRC's Amnesty Process on Survivors of Human Rights Violations* (CSVR 2008).

147 Priscillar B. Hayner, *Unspeakable Truths: Confronting State Terror and Atrocity* (Routledge 2001).

148 On the genealogy of transitional justice see Ruti G. Teitel, 'Transitional Justice Genealogy' (2003) 16 *Harvard Human Rights Journal* 69.

149 Eppel (n.121).

150 Ibid.

in these rifts.[151] Thus, she suggests that a restorative justice approach may be the best way of dealing with atrocities at this level.[152] Professor Ruti Teitel has, however, explained that the state does have a degree of responsibility for those atrocities attributed to private individuals.[153] According to her:

> Even when past evil is perpetrated by private actors, the state is often, nevertheless, still implicated, whether in policies of persecution, by acts of omission in failing to protect its citizens, or finally, in the cover up of criminal acts and impunity.[154]

Against this background, this work acknowledges that there might be a need for the trial of those elites who bear the greatest responsibility for the atrocities committed during the 1980s. It is also believed that traditional and restorative justice mechanisms are best suited to most of the violent acts committed after 2000.[155]

Ironically, even Western feminists, who have much in common with postcolonial theorists, are very suspicious of this model as they fear further subjugation of women within traditional structures.[156] The tendency is to marginalize non-Western ideas of justice with a perception that they are either not good enough or unimportant.[157] For example, Professor Fionnuala Ní Aoláin's critique of Bacholi's notion that Western ideas of accountability might be different from African or Mozambican ideas is that this issue requires further refinement on what those mechanisms might be.[158]

Overall, all the issues raised in the section confirm this work's submission that international law is based on Western history and that it treats the *Other* as being devoid of a useful past. Therefore, there is a need for serious and committed engagement with pre-colonial accountability mechanisms. The matters discussed also add validity to this work's view that conventional justice mechanisms are individualistic and mostly suited to violations of civil and political rights. This means that they cannot adequately deal with postcolonial challenges. However, in view of the donor community's lack of confidence in local mechanisms, an exclusively traditional and restorative justice approach might not be useful. This is more so since the alternative restorative justice approach has a Marxist tone to it as it targets the material bases of a society.

151 Ibid.
152 Ibid.
153 Ruti G. Teitel, *Transitional Justice* (Oxford University Press 2000) 28.
154 Ibid.
155 Ibid.
156 Fionnuala Ní Aoláin, 'Political Violence and Gender in Times of Transition' (2006) 15(3) *Columbia Journal of Gender and the Law* 829.
157 Ibid.
158 Ibid as read with Andrea Bartoli, 'Learning from the Mozambique Peace Process the Role of the Community of Sant'Egidio' in Ronald J. Fisher (ed), *Paving the Way: Contributions of Interactive Conflict Resolution to Peacemaking* (Lexington Books 2005).

6.3.3 *Colonial responsibility for the contemporary culture of impunity*

Both civic society and academics have noted that in addition to ZANU PF's excesses, the culture of impunity in Zimbabwe can be attributed to the influence and history of colonialism.[159] It has already been pointed out that colonialists committed serious human rights violations during both the formation of the state of Rhodesia and the time when they suppressed nationalist resistance to their racist rule. It has also been explained that economic considerations impelled the independence negotiators to grant blanket amnesties for colonial-era violations.

This fact was acknowledged by the participants of a civil society symposium held in South Africa in 2003 which suggested that colonial human rights abuses can be addressed by a TRC.[160] They proposed the separation of pre-1960 and post-1960 (Rhodesian) crimes. This was based on a perception that the period after 1960 represented the living memory of Zimbabweans. The accuracy of this view is still to be tested, and this work is of the view that the participants in the symposium were aware of the fact that Western governments are not likely to commit their resources to a project which has the effect of undermining their position as champions of human rights. Thus, in the case of Zimbabwe, focus on those atrocities committed after Ian Smith's UDI has the effect of shifting the blame from Britain, the colonial master, to a small group of individuals who governed Rhodesia during that time.

In fact, there may be practical difficulties in attempting to seek individual redress for violations committed in former British colonies. The creation of a generally accepted historical account of colonialism can be impeded by the fact that records from this era were either expunged or are held as confidential. In any event, such an exercise in Zimbabwe might be of little use since most of the key perpetrators from the colonial era are too old, dead or no longer residing in the country.[161]

Much more importantly, focus on individual responsibility exposes the limitations of international law which attends to physical rights violations and not the far-reaching effects of colonialism in postcolonial societies.[162] A common proclivity in Western legal renditions is to offer a universalistic positivist approach to international legal issues. Yet, in addition to the failure to account for violations of bodily integrity rights, there are a number of indirect ways in which colonialism fostered the culture of impunity in former colonies.

The first manner, which was discussed in Chapter 3, is the establishment of the 'janus-faced' state subject to one hegemonic power. Western modern law,

159 See Penny Morrel and Piers Pigou, *Civil Society and Justice in Zimbabwe: Proceedings of a Symposium held in Johannesburg 11–13 August 2003* (Themba Lesizwe 2003).

160 Ibid.

161 In Zimbabwe, for instance Cecil John Rhodes, the founder of the colonial state of Rhodesia, died in 1902, and UDI leader Ian Smith died in November 2007.

162 Rena L. Scott, 'Moving from Impunity to Accountability in Post-War Liberia: Possibilities, Cautions and Challenges' (2005) 33 *International Journal of Legal Information* 345.

which contains the discourse of universal human rights, was administered by white judges in urban centers. On the other hand, customary law, which was associated with culture and accorded an inferior status, was dispensed by the tribal leadership in the villages. Nonetheless, the evolution of the political pith through the sacrifice of those external to the dominant discourse meant that those in the villages could not hold the administration developed in the centre to account.

The second issue, which in the case of Zimbabwe is exemplified by the land question and one of the lasting legacies of colonialism, is the legalization of inequalities. Through the bifurcated state, urban authority spoke the language of property rights, and rural authority spoke the language of communal and traditional possession of land. In the case of settler colonial Rhodesia, South Africa and Namibia, this duality had a racial component to it. This system, which continued after independence, enabled the new occupiers of the centre, who were the black elite, to also monopolize the economic activities. This meant that those at the periphery could not hold independent political views since the source of their financial support was either Western benevolence or patronage at a domestic level.

The third question, which Chapter 5 demonstrated in the case of Zimbabwe, is the artificial multi-cultural nature of the postcolonial state. This fact has fostered conflicts in postcolonial states since leaders who do not feel responsible for other tribes or might have historic grievances against a minority group often nurture their own clans. This leads to perceptions by other groups that they are not being treated equally.

This fact has presented additional challenges to the state-building attempts and is exacerbated by the fact that the indirect rule system of the colonial era did not make any efforts to make the centre accountable to those at the periphery. The Ndebele grievances which were covered in the previous chapter are a product of the goZ's lack of accountability to those who inhabit areas which are further from the capital. Indeed, access to resources and opportunities have been granted on kinship and party patronage. This has been particularly so given that at independence, Zimbabwe, in common with other postcolonial states, was left economically weak such that it could not survive without good relations with the colonial state. This explains the ruling elite's arrogation to itself and its supporters the little of whatever is left from the national resources.

Rena Scott, who has raised similar arguments with respect to Liberia, has suggested that one way of dealing with these issues in postcolonial Africa is through leadership reform.[163] However, this work is of the view that the leadership style is merely a symptom of postcolonial impunity, which has everything to do with the postcolonial artificial state and the biases of the discourse of international law. However, the rapid Zimbabwean economic meltdown which was largely caused by the goZ's direct attack on the master's discourse through its radical land reform programme is a warning that any attempt at redressing the colonial past ought to remain located within the master's discourse.

163 Ibid.

6.4 Insights from other postcolonial polities

6.4.1 The legality of blanket amnesties

It has been explained previously that the regulatory reach of international law has led to an understanding that domestic amnesties for the most serious crimes are unjust.[164] Yet, retributive justice may be an antithesis to peace in contexts like Zimbabwe where alleged perpetrators are part of the transitional process. Thus, postcolonial societies which have been in a similar situation have had to adopt innovative ways of ensuring that they foster peace and also avoid blanket amnesties. South Africa offers a good example of such ingenuity.

As in Zimbabwe's independence negotiations, amnesty was seen as an important facilitator of peace in South Africa's transition from apartheid since this was a case of political compromise and not regime change.[165] Thus, the differences between the two countries' independence negotiations was not in the issue of whether there was to be an amnesty, but in the nature and extent of the same.[166] Part of the differences could be attributed to the timing of the two countries' independence.[167] Zimbabwe made its passage from Rhodesia between 1979 and 1980, which was the Cold War period and when human rights enforcement at the UN level was passive. On the other hand, South Africa made its move from apartheid to black majority rule in the post-Cold War era when transitional justice had burgeoned.

Nonetheless, in the case of South Africa, the proclamation of conditional amnesties was enshrined in the 1993 Interim Constitution.[168] The mechanism for implementing these amnesty provisions was the TRC, which dealt with applications on the basis of a formula stipulated in the *Promotion of National Unity and Reconciliation Act of 1995*.[169] Applicants could be granted amnesty only after they had fully disclosed details of each individual politically motivated crime which they had committed during the mandate period. They also had to show that their actions were proportional to the desired intent.

164 Max Pensky, 'Amnesty on Trial: Impunity, Accountability and the Norms of International Law' (2008) 1(2) *Ethics and Global Politics* 1.

165 On South Africa's transition to black majority rule, see Allister Sparks, *Tomorrow Is Another Country: The Inside Story of South Africa's Road to Change* (University of Chicago Press 1996).

166 Note, however, that prior to the TRC, conditional amnesties two pieces of indemnity legislation granted temporal immunities to individuals for the sake of peace. See Indemnity Act 35 of 1990 and Indemnity Act 151 of 1992.

167 It is a fact that the regulatory reach of human rights norms has not been consistent historically.

168 Chapter 15, South African Interim Constitution, Act 200/1993.

169 S(20)(2)(c) *Promotion of National Unity and Reconciliation Act* 34 of 1995 as amended by Act 87 of 1995. See also Brandon Hamber, 'Rights and Reasons: Challenges for Truth Recovery in South Africa and Northern Ireland' (2003) 24(4) *Fordham International Law Journal* 1074 and Sparks (n.165).

It has to be noted that the TRC's work was consistent with international law in its avoidance of blanket amnesties which satisfied to a degree the requirements for individual accountability. It was, however, *mimicry* of the same since it fell short of the obligations to investigate, prosecute and punish the serious crime of apartheid. Nonetheless, the process did offer the postcolonial an opportunity to input into the master's discourse as it departed from the existing view that a TRC was a method of fact-finding or of obtaining historic justice, moving to a combined approach which heralded an understanding that this mechanism can serve multifaceted purposes, which include reparations, accounting, restorative justice, healing and reconciliation.[170]

Subsequent to South African's ingenuity, a number of other recent postcolonial methods of creativity have shaped international law. The first approach, which is exemplified by the cases of Cote d'Ivoire, Sierra Leone and Burundi, has been to restrict prosecutions to grave atrocities and the worst perpetrators whilst granting blanket amnesties or employing a restorative justice approach in cases concerning low-level perpetrators. The second way, which has been promoted in Uganda, is also a bifurcated approach. This is the idea of preserving the use of domestic criminal justice or retribution to the most serious crimes whilst resorting to traditional justice as a way of promoting reconciliation in dealing with less serious abuses.

Finally, the third means of adhering to the master's discourse's demands for accountability while taking into consideration the postcolonial context is to void compromises on criminal justice in cases where there is a return to violence. This is what has been done by Sierra Leone when it indicted Charles Taylor, even though he had previously been granted amnesty. An analogous clause also exists in the Belfast Agreement which made prisoners' indemnities conditional to guarantees of non-violence.

6.4.2 *Appropriate justice mechanism for redressing Zimbabwe's past human rights abuses*

This work has explained that Western models of redress are not always suitable for postcolonial contexts. For example, individual reparations in the form of financial compensation may not be an appropriate vehicle for delivering justice in the case of Zimbabwe, since the country's experience with such an approach has already demonstrated that fraudulent claims cannot be avoided. Furthermore, offering compensation to victims of state-sponsored violence may not be fair to others whose human rights violations do not fit within the conventional definitions of

170 See Charles Villa-Vicencio, 'Restorative Justice: Dealing with the Past Differently' in Charles Villa-Vicencio and W.J. Verwoerd (eds) *Looking Back, Reaching Forward: Reflections on the Truth and Reconciliation Commission of South Africa* (Zed Books Ltd 2000), and Warren Buford and Hugo van der Merwe, 'Reparations in Southern Africa' (2004) 44(1–2) *Cahiers d'études africaines.*

breaches covered by reparatory programmes. Yet, their victimhood may also be a consequence of the political situation.

These include gender-based violations and breaches of economic social and cultural rights. Consider, for example, the case of a family whose breadwinner has died of diabetes compounded by the health sector's inability to provide insulin.[171] Consider also deaths caused by cholera, which are an obvious case of the state's inability to *protect*, *respect* and *fulfil* economic, social and cultural rights; and also women who contracted AIDS after being driven by the economic situation to engage in prostitution.[172] Thus, individual compensation schemes are not appropriate in the context of the Zimbabwean crisis, of which all are victims.[173]

This is not the first time that the suitability of individual compensation as a method of obtaining reparatory justice has been questioned in a postcolonial context. In an indirect response to critiques that individual financial awards which were given in pursuance of South Africa's reparatory justice programmes were inadequate, Thabo Mbeki expressed sentiments which this work believes ought to apply to Zimbabwe's NPRC.[174] In Mbeki's view, the TRC should have been about:

> The continuing challenge of reconstruction and development: deepening democracy and the culture of human rights, ensuring good governance and transparency, intensifying economic growth and social programmes, improving citizens' safety and security and contributing to the building of a humane and just world order.[175]

In the case of Zimbabwe, it is argued that the anti-impunity principle can be championed through the use of domestic or international trials for offences committed in the 1980s and a restorative or even traditional justice approach to the post-2000 violations. Actually, in Zimbabwe there have been informal attempts at restorative justice approaches in the form of exhumations and memorialization.

This is also not the first proposal for the adoption of local justice approaches.[176] Shari Eppel, for example, has highlighted the three stratums where this is necessary.[177] First is at a community level, where relationships ought to be mended so that people will not be easily used as instrumental tools in future

171 On challenges to Zimbabwe's health sector, see Khameer K. Kilda, 'The Future of Health in Zimbabwe' (2018) 11(1) *Global Health Action.*

172 The Zimbabwe humanitarian crisis has been highlighted in K.E. Boon, 'Coining a New Jurisdiction: The Security Council as Economic Peacekeeper' (2008) 41 *Vanderbilt Journal of Transnational Law* 991, supra note 2645.

173 Supra notes 2563–2660.

174 Statement by Thabo Mbeki to the National Houses of Parliament and the Nation during the tabling of the Report of the TRC in Cape Town on 15 April 2003, reproduced in Buford and van der Merwe (n.170).

175 Ibid.

176 Eppel (n.121).

177 Ibid.

political agendas.[178] Second is at a grassroots level, in empowering citizens to understand that their leaders ought to be accountable to them.[179] Third, the notion of accountability and responsible leadership ought to be extended to local councils and traditional leadership.[180]

Of course, restorative justice approaches do not have complete approval in human rights discourses.[181] Inherent in that disapproval is the fear of the threat that restorative justice mechanisms pose to the state. Restorative justice methods perceive criminality not only as breach of state law, but an infringement on humanity and relationships between people. The focus is on the consequences of the criminal act and not legal enforcement.

The Zimbabwean legal culture largely views the exploration of non-Western conflict resolution mechanisms as a marginal and inappreciable constituent of Western discourse. There is an inherent Western bias which views law as being made up of two forms of regulations: domestic law and public international law. Yet, the postcolonial reality is that the principal method of ordering the actions of those peripheral to the centre is customary law, which is administered by the traditional leaders.

Interestingly, restorative justice and traditional justice notions can gain acceptance if situated within the master's discourse. For example, the South African TRC embraced the local spirit of *ubuntu/humaneness*. It also promoted the perception that this otherwise Western mechanism was a restorative justice process for restoring the victims' human and civil dignity.[182]

Another axiomatic example of postcolonial mimicry is the Rwandan GNU's inclusion of the gacaca courts as part of tripartite legal mechanisms for dealing with its 1994 genocide legacy.[183] Originally a community-based dispute resolution mechanism preserved for property, theft and family law disputes, the gacaca was introduced as a way of filling the gap when it was realized that the other two mechanisms could not cope with the caseloads. Gacaca trials conformed to the master's discourse in the sense that they promoted the anti-impunity principle yet fell short of the same since they did not adhere to the international due process standards.

Much more significantly, Ariel Meyerstein has noted that this legalistic critique of gacaca impedes its recognition as a *sui generis* postcolonial hybrid model.[184] This confirms this work's submission that there is an inherent bias

178 Ibid.

179 Ibid.

180 Ibid.

181 See John Braithwaite, 'Restorative Justice: Assessing Optimistic and Pessimistic Accounts' (1999) 25 *Crime and Justice* 1.

182 Villa-Vicencio (n.170) as read with *South Africa Truth and Reconciliation Commission Report* (Macmillan Reference 1999) 126.

183 See Toran Hansen, *The Gacaca Tribunals in Post-Genocide Rwanda* (University of Minnesota 2005) and Alana E. Tiemessen, 'After Arusha: Gacaca Justice in Post-Genocide Rwanda' (2003) 8(1) *African Studies Quarterly*.

184 Ariel Meyerstein, 'Between Law and Culture: Rwanda's Gacaca and Postcolonial Legality' (2007) 32(2) *Law & Social Inquiry* 467.

in human rights discourse which sees non-Western traditions as marginal and inessential. Nonetheless, the introduction of gacaca to the transitional justice discourse does add credence to Homi Bhabha's notion of the 'third space of enunciation'.[185]

Indeed, inclusion of gacaca in the fight against impunity in Rwanda has set a precedent for other postcolonial transitional societies to consider the involvement of their own traditional methods of dispute settlement.[186] For example, in Burundi, ubushingantahe, a dispute-resolving method administered by revered men of the community, has been proposed.[187] Similarly, there have been suggestions that 'Mato Put' be used in Uganda.[188] Thus, transitional contexts have accorded the postcolonial an opportunity to input into the dominant discourse. Against this background, it is hoped that a study of pre-colonial accountability measures in Zimbabwe should be carried out. Of course, the writer is aware that some of these mechanisms may not be suitable for modern times and may even destroy the gains which have been made so far in gender rights.

6.4.3 *Dealing with colonial atrocities*

It has been noted that an attempt to hold individuals accountable for atrocities committed during the colonial era may not always be possible or practical. Of course, dilemmas of amnesties and the passage of time can be dealt with, as the legacy of Nuremberg has set the precedent that there are some heinous crimes for which prosecution is not constrained by time limits. As explained previously, certain amnesties are not permissible in international law and can thus be waived. It has been stated, however, that there may be difficulties in obtaining reliable evidence for establishing a *prima facie* case for colonial crimes and the identification of suitable individual perpetrators for colonial atrocities may also pose problems.

So far in Zimbabwe, there is the NPRC and memorialization.[189] It can be argued that the NPRC may not be effective in a context where the appropriate abusers cannot be easily located. Memorialization will also add no value in the Zimbabwean case where heroes and independence day celebrations already commemorate the colonial legacy. On the same note the colonial past ought to be confronted; otherwise, this history will continue to offer the ruling elite a good excuse for failures in governance.[190]

Nonetheless, other postcolonial subjects have resorted to reparatory justice as an innovative attempt at holding the colonialists accountable for the colonial

185 Homi Bhabha, 'Cultural Diversity and Cultural Differences' in Bill Ashcroft et al. (eds) *The Post-Colonial Studies Reader* (Routledge 1995).
186 See Barney Afako, 'Reconciliation and Justice: "Mato Oput" and the Amnesty Act' (2002) 11 *Accord: An International Review of Peace Initiatives* 67.
187 See Agnes Nindorera, 'Ubushingantahe as a Base for Political Transformation in Burundi' (2003) *Boston Consortium.*
188 Afako (n.186).
189 See, for example, Morrel and Pigou (n.159). See also du Plessis and Ford (n.129).
190 Chapter 4 highlighted this issue as it relates to the Zimbabwean land question.

past. The focus of reparations is not on the individual wrongdoers, but on the descendants of the same, and on those who are perceived to have been beneficiaries of colonialism. These actions can be divided into those which address specific elements of physical rights violations and those that attend to the ubiquitous experience of colonialism, which this work noted as including indirect rule, domination and economic exploitation.

The first approach is illustrated by developments in Namibia and Kenya. The former concerns a lawsuit which was filed in the United States by the Herero against the German government for the genocidal annihilation of its people in 1904.[191] The later involves the successful multi-million-pound compensation claim against Britain filed by the Mau Mau freedom fighters that were allegedly tortured and subjected to inhuman and degrading punishment during their war of independence.[192] In the case of the Herero action, Germany has apologized, acknowledged that this was genocide and attended a ceremony which commemorated this brutal past.[193] However, it has refused to pay compensation on the basis that relevant international legal standards were not in existence at the time of the genocide.[194] This is a very interesting argument which is likely to be used by Britain if such a lawsuit was to be filed by Zimbabweans.

Much more importantly, Mark Gibney et al. have interpreted apologies by Western governments to both their citizens and those who inhabit foreign territories as the *Self*'s own model of a TRC.[195] The difference in the approach in which the West deals with those human rights abuses attributed to itself has an impact on the relationship between developed countries and less developed countries. Also, apologies which are offered by states and not individual perpetrators may be less meaningful. This raises the issue of the role of the state in dealing with the legacy of past injustices.

It is conceded that on their own, apologies may not adequately redress colonial wrongs. This is particularly so since the discourse around history and the colonial experience is still largely controlled by colonial powers who have been reluctant to make archival materials relating to the colonial era publicly available. Nonetheless, it is submitted that if offered by a former colonial master to a postcolonial society, the significance of an apology lies not in interstate relations but in the discourse of engagement between the postcolonial state and its own citizenry.[196] An apology can provide closure to postcolonial citizenry and thus preclude a false

191 Rachel Anderson, 'Redressing Colonial Genocide: The Hereros' Cause of Action against Germany' (2005) 93 *California Law Review* 1155.

192 Jennifer Balint, 'The "Mau Mau" Legal Hearings and Recognizing the Crimes of the British Colonial State: A Limited Constitutive Moment' (2016) 3(2) *Critical Analysis of Law*.

193 Anderson (n 191)

194 Ibid.

195 Mark Gibney et al. (eds), *The Age of Apology: Facing Up to the Past* (University of Pennsylvania Press 2008).

196 This is a counter argument to Mark Gibney et al. (2007) supra note 2921's argument that an apology given by the state may be less meaningful.

mirror of correcting historic imbalances from being used as a tool for avoiding accountability by the postcolonial ruling elite.[197] According to Bill Rolston and Fionnuala Ní Aoláin,

> [a]n apology can provide something which is usually missing in the experience of colonized people, namely acknowledgement. The value of this cannot be underestimated. Central to the experience of colonialism is the denial of harms, the rejection of the victims' narrative and above all the demonization of any subaltern resistance. To name colonial conquest, genocide and dispossession for what they were is to go some way towards reinstating the colonized to dignity.[198]

The second manner in which the colonial past has been confronted is exemplified by the 2008 bilateral relationship agreement signed by Italy and Libya.[199] This treaty addresses, *inter alia*, the colonial past. Italy agreed to pay $5 billion in compensation to be paid in installments of $250 million for a period of 25 years in the form of investments in infrastructure and developmental projects.[200] Italy also apologized for the colonial-era exploitation and atrocities.[201] It also returned the statue of Venus which had been illegally taken to Rome during the era of imperialism.[202] Of course, it would be naïve to expect that this compensation will be specifically directed to communities and aspects directly connected to the destruction caused by colonialism. Nonetheless, it is fair to argue that the targeting of certain communities or issues is unnecessary since the effects of colonialism extend to all facets of postcolonial societies.

However, it would be ambitious to expect that the Libyan/Italian development will easily be replicated elsewhere in postcolonial Africa since most of these societies are too poor and do not possess the same bargaining power as Colonel Muammar Qaddafi's Libya. It is common cause that most postcolonial societies receive aid from their former colonial masters. It is this work's view that the benevolence tag ought to be removed and these amounts should be accompanied by a full moral acceptance of the implication of colonialism in the contemporary postcolonial culture of impunity. This move may put the colonial epoch behind and offer the *Other* an opportunity to focus on its nation-building efforts.

197 As stated before, the fact that the colonialists have never been made to account can explain why there are no domestic calls for the outgoing regime to be held to account in Zimbabwe.

198 Bill Rolston and Fionnuala Ní Aoláin, 'Colonialism, Redress and Transitional Justice: Ireland and Beyond' (2018) 7(2) *State Crime Journal* 328, 343.

199 See also Natalino Ronzitti, 'The Treaty on Friendship, Partnership and Cooperation between Italy and Libya: New Prospects for Cooperation in the Mediterranean?' (2009) 1(1) *Bulletin of Italian Politics* 125.

200 Ibid.

201 Ibid.

202 Ibid.

6.5 Conclusion

To sum up, according to the recorded history of the territory which is now called Zimbabwe, in around 1840 Mzilikazi, the King of the Ndebele, arrived in the southern part and used force against the existing Shona people to establish his kingdom. The white settlers came four decades later and violently established the country of Rhodesia. Nationalists also resorted to force in their war of liberation. After independence and throughout ZANU PF's 39-plus years in power, they have deployed the security apparatus to violently deal with anyone perceived to be an opponent.

A culture of impunity exists in Zimbabwe as evidenced by the proclamation of amnesties for politically related crimes after different episodes of conflict. It is this work's argument that while most of the amnesties were permissible, those for the Gukurahundi atrocities are not, as the Gukurahundi can be said to be a genocide. It is therefore yet to be seen how the country's NPRC will be able to deal with the country's past injustices.

The story of Zimbabwe is the story of most countries with a colonial past that have to address a legacy of impunity, which was largely fostered by the colonial encounter. Unfortunately, these countries' challenges defy conventional transitional justice approaches. At the same time, resort to traditional justice might not be supported by those who fund transitional justice. It may also not be a progressive move for any country since the application of some pre-colonial accountability mechanisms may not be consistent with the legal victories of the feminist movements.

Nonetheless, Zimbabwe has the opportunity to input into a discourse which to date has been largely influenced by colonial powers. Already, precedents of successful forms of *agency* exist in, *inter alia,* South Africa's experience with the TRC, Rwanda's use of *gacaca,* Namibia's victory in getting an apology for colonial atrocities from Germany and Libya's success in getting Italy to pledge compensation for the colonial past.

7 Conclusion

7.1 Overview and contribution to transitional justice

This work has used the challenges presented by issues of transitional justice in Zimbabwe to illuminate the complexities of such questions in postcolonial societies. It began by asserting that the boundaries of the subject of transitional justice are still to be defined, yet its dominant discourse gives attention to and commits greater resources to delineating mechanisms for punishing or exposing past human rights abuses. To borrow from Nancy Fraser's thesis, conventional justice discourses prioritize justice as recognition and not justice as redistribution.[1] An examination of this through the lens of feminist and postcolonial theory suggests that this restricted focus serves the purposes of preserving a status quo where powerful states and men have created a discourse framework that is not easily accessible to other groups.[2] However, the ambivalence in the dissemination of this knowledge creates opportunities for resistance which enable the postcolonial and women to have an input into a discourse which, as already stated, is largely masculine and controlled by powerful states.

To qualify these assertions, this work used four issues which need to be addressed in Zimbabwe's transition, to demonstrate three broad submissions. The first of these is the idea that transitional justice is a broad subject. The second is a rebuttal of the presumption that international law is neutral and has fixed rules which can easily mediate domestic rule of law challenges. The third is the view that the complex issues which arise in postcolonial transitions have led to the creation of soft law standards which are evidence of these states' contribution to a discourse which was largely produced and shaped by the histories of former colonial masters. All these issues embraced the gender dimension. Perhaps this work's contribution to the debate on the nexus between transitional justice and feminist concerns is its departure from the proclivity to associate women's experiences of conflict with only sexual abuses to encompass an understanding that

1 Nancy Fraser, *Justice Interruptus: Critical Reflections on the 'Postsocialist' Condition* (Routledge 1997).

2 Khanyisela Moyo, 'Feminism, Postcolonial Legal Theory and Transitional Justice: A Critique of Current Trends' (2012) 1(2) *International Human Rights Law Review* 237.

women's experiences can be included in all topics of transitional justice. A general description of this work is that it is critical of transitional justice but not in an entirely negative sense, as it gives illustrations of both challenges and possibilities of postcolonial transitions.

7.2 The definitional issue

Chapter 2 pushed the contours of transitional justice, and in doing so it relied on legal and political science literature. It was explained that justice measures that are employed in transitional times not only create a culture of accountability, but also are a form of political restructuring. They are not permanent as they include both provisional measures and those which will be entrenched with time. They limit governmental power and also construct the transition. This fosters peace, thereby restoring or establishing a 'liberal' democracy.

The four critical areas of research were positioned within the field of transitional justice. Drawing from, among others, the cutting-edge work of Professor Ruti G. Teitel, Rama Mani and the Special Rapporteur on the promotion of truth, justice, reparation and guarantees of non-recurrence, this work explained that restoring the rule of law is a core objective of transitional justice initiatives. In the same vein, since the judiciary is the custodian of the rule of law, the existence of a compromised and impartial judiciary is an indication that laws are no longer being applied fairly and equally. Transitional justice measures which are employed to reform a tainted or compromised judiciary are a part of guarantees of non-recurrence. The chapter positioned transitional land reform programmes within all four pillars of transitional justice, namely, truth, justice, reparations and guarantees of non-recurrence. It also noted that transitional minority rights issues are an example of guarantees of non-recurrence. Furthermore, the study explained that combating impunity is an issue of truth, justice and reparations.

7.3 The limitations of international law

At the heart of the Zimbabwean crisis is a clash of values between former colonial masters and postcolonial societies which puts to the test international law's universality and neutrality. Yet, conventional legal transitional discourses confine themselves to choices of mechanisms for combating the legacy of impunity. Their starting point is that there are established legal rules which prescribe that those who violated rights during war or a period of authoritarianism ought to be held accountable. Such accountability is said to be desirable for the promotion of the rule of law and the strengthening of legal institutions. This is also presumed to usher a democratic liberal state that respects minority rights and the right to property.

This viewpoint was challenged in Chapter 2 of this study, which produced the work's main argument. To re-iterate, it was argued that human rights law was not originally intended for the postcolonial and its discourse is often used to 'civilize' postcolonial societies. Nonetheless, transitional contexts create opportunities for postcolonial *agency* which is made possible by both the ambivalence of the master's discourse and the *Other's* resistance to hegemony. To develop this argument, Chapters 3–6 engaged with both the content of the Zimbabwean crisis and the complex international law questions presented by the same.

7.3.1 Rule of law and judicial independence

In Chapter 3, it was shown that the rule of law is a phrase which embodies a number of objectives and approaches. For example, while academics may focus on the legal values which are advanced by the rule of law, practitioners may be concerned with the creation of an environment where the rule of law can be upheld. These varied aspirations and strategies have an impact on understandings of what constitutes judicial independence. Consequently, academics are focused on the judiciary's ability to impartially produce good enforceable rulings. On the other hand, practitioners look at factors which might hinder the judiciary from arriving at objective rulings.

In addressing this issue, this work attempted to merge both concerns of academics and practitioners by evaluating both contentious judgements of Zimbabwe's judiciary and the country's institutional framework. It also examined the international discourse of judicial independence which focuses on separation of powers, financial mechanisms, security of tenure, sufficient remuneration appointments and removal of judges. There are also issues of judicial disciplining, removal and accountability. All these universal measurements are abstract and do not consider the major challenge to judicial independence in poor postcolonial societies, namely limited resources. Consequently, focus on separation of powers is inadequate since the state may not be the major threat. Postcolonial judiciaries can easily be influenced by private business and external actors.

A related crucial issue in those societies, especially in cases where there is a constitutional democracy, is the complicity of the legal institutions in the conflict. This raises conflicting perspectives on the necessities and possibilities for judiciary reform. The transitional justice discourse's yardstick for measuring this is to look at the extent to which the judiciary managed to uphold the rule of law in times of crisis.

The case of Zimbabwe challenges this simplistic approach. At independence, Zimbabwe inherited a judiciary that had endorsed and served under Ian Smith's racist regime. This judiciary was very progressive in its rulings and even made improvements in the country's protection of women's rights, yet it clashed with the government on issues relating to the death penalty and land reform. This raised disagreements as to who was served by this judiciary, and particularly so since it was headed by a white Chief Justice. It is fair to also state that a large number of the domestic population perceived the white judges as vicarious agents of Western values since land rights issues in the country revolved around race relations. This explains why there was no public outcry when land-related judgements were not enforced. Yet, those with an international outlook commended the judiciary for its independence.

After the resignation of the white Chief Justice and other white judges, they were replaced by an almost exclusively black but equally qualified judiciary under the leadership of someone with liberation war credentials. The reform also saw a change in the interpretation of land rights and a new understanding that notions of property rights should embrace social justice. The international media and Western-sponsored human rights activists condemned the judiciary for its lack of independence. The Zimbabwean judiciary was said to be under siege, and this was especially so in the wake of allegations that the new judges had benefitted from the country's controversial land reform programme.

This creates a perspective of a perverted judiciary which championed a certain party ideology. Yet, there is evidence that these judges did uphold the law in non-contentious cases and actually opposed the government in cases which did not relate to land reform. Also, a study of judicial independence in Southern Africa suggested that, in comparison to neighboring countries, the Zimbabwean public still had faith in its judiciary. In this backdrop, a crucial task in the transitional moment would be the creation of a national narrative so as to reach a consensus on the legitimacy of the judiciary.

7.3.2 Land reform in transition

As stated previously, in Zimbabwe the issue of a compromised judiciary arose in relation to land reform judgements. As stated in Chapter 4, previous commentators on the subject have touched on the effects of the state-led radical programme and not the controversial issues of the right to property and expropriation. Thus, this work engaged with these issues and highlighted that in international law there is no global consensus on the scope of the right to property. Neither is there an agreement on the limitations to be imposed on a sovereign state's right to expropriate land within its territories.

Nonetheless, land reform is a cross-cutting issue, which is relevant to all four pillars of transitional justice, namely, truth, justice, reparations and guarantees of non-recurrence. In particular, recent truth commissions have included the land issue in their mandates. Perpetrators of land injustices such as displacement can be prosecuted. Reparations for land injustices take the form of restitution and compensation. Finally, land tenure reform can be said to be a guarantee of non-recurrence.

Chapter 4 also looked at the issue of an appropriate redress for colonial and postcolonial land injustices and offered pragmatic solutions which are not necessarily grounded in international law. It noted that the major limitation in international law is that it privileges restitution as a mechanism for dealing with past land injustices, yet the case of Zimbabwe and other postcolonial societies demonstrates that the legitimacy of both colonial and postcolonial title to land is contentious. The international legal framework is also not exactly suited to postcolonial circumstances because it is in the form of individual reparations programmes which target clear past perpetrators and land owners, yet these parties cannot be identified in postcolonial dispensations.

7.3.3 Minority rights in transition

The reference to racial divisions in Chapters 3 and 4 may have suggested that the only challenges to the postcolonial state of Zimbabwe were external and racial. Thus Chapter 5 sought to do away with this notion of homogeneity and to focus on ethnic diversity as a source of conflict in postcolonial societies. It explained that the relevant international legal framework has been largely shaped by Western nation-building episodes, and this explains why the existing legal framework, including the definition of minorities, is not suited for postcolonial challenges. In particular, while postcolonial minorities' quest is for autonomy, international law would rather offer them integration; yet this strategy is appropriate only for groups defined as minorities in Western societies. Unfortunately, this prescription means that postcolonial minorities will continue to be subjected to the violence of the postcolonial state. Also, the experiences of the Ndebele of Zimbabwe suggest that where claims of postcolonial minorities are directed to a state which does not pose a threat to Western values, then the discourse of transitional justice is less likely to be invoked.

7.3.4 Combating the legacy of impunity

The transitional justice discourse uses the Nuremberg legacy to promote an anti-impunity standard. Yet, postcolonial Zimbabwe's civil and political rights abuses are relatively less serious and can hardly be paralleled to events which led to the Nazi trials. This misapplication of precedent is also evidenced by the exceptionalism with which pressure to punish past wrongdoers is applied. The Zimbabwe experience is very revealing in this regard and even suggests that the anti-impunity drive can be an impediment to peace-building efforts and urgent priorities of economic revival. Exclusive focus on the conduct of the immediate outgoing regime is also not sufficient, since the history of violence in postcolonial states can be traced to the colonial encounter. Those few interventions which have attempted to address the colonial legacy have a limited outlook, since they focus on particular physical human rights violations and not on the broad impact of the colonial experience in the contemporary culture of the lack of accountability in the postcolonial world.

This book also noted that almost all mechanisms for redressing past human rights violations are based on the idea of individual responsibility and are suited only for violations of civil and political rights. The notion of the indivisibility of rights is not given serious consideration.[3] Zimbabwe's past experiences with compensation schemes and fact-finding exercises reveal that individualistic measures cannot work in situations where almost everyone can be seen as a victim. Similarly, exclusive focus on civil and political rights violations is not appropriate in circumstances where victims, particularly women, were subjected to widespread

3 See Lisa J. Laplante, 'On the Indivisibility of Rights: Truth Commissions, Reparations, and the Right to Development' (2007) 10 *Yale Human Rights and Development Law Journal* 141.

and systematic violations of economic, social and cultural rights. Thus in Zimbabwe, victims of violations of economic, social and cultural rights are not included in paradigmatic transitional justice discourses.

It has been stated that a NPRC is currently operational in Zimbabwe. Arguably, the idea of truth-telling as a method for promoting healing and forgiveness is a Western construct which does not adequately deal with postcolonial challenges. Indeed, its efficacy as such in postcolonial dispensations is still to be proven. On the same note, while trials can be an appropriate measure for dealing with senior perpetrators of state-orchestrated violence who are based in urban areas, these may not be suited for those at the periphery where the main source of ordering is customary law. As stated in Chapter 3, postcolonial societies inherited a dual legal system whereby Western law, which contained the discourse of human rights, was administered by white judges and the black elite in urban areas; whilst in rural areas, customary law, which spoke the language of indigenous culture, was applied by traditional leaders. Thus, restorative justice measures may be well suited for past injustice which occurred in the villages. It needs to be clarified that this work is proposing not absolute powers for traditional authorities, but their application in a manner which is consistent with women's rights.

7.4 Hybridity

In addition to highlighting complex legal issues, Chapters 3–6 used the experiences of other postcolonial societies to demonstrate a notion of a third space where supplementary discourses move in to disrupt the bipolar exchange. This eventuality is desirable as it rids us of the binarisms which have allowed essentialized perspectives of culture to be often appropriated by both former colonial masters and elites in postcolonial administrations for different agendas.

7.4.1 Rule of law and judicial independence

Chapter 3 found that policy makers in postcolonial societies have realized that one of the causes of rule of law deficits in their societies is the inadequacy of legal frameworks which were imposed during the decolonizing stage. This explains the rise of the concept of the new constitutionalism which embraced an idea of the rule of law which not only focused on preserving law and order, but also championed the goal of economic independence. Judges have also played a role in this transformation by taking positions in Constitutional Commissions.

As has already been stated, the traditional yardstick for judicial independence is the extent to which this body upheld the rule of law in terms of crisis. Thus, transitional mechanisms for purging or dealing with judges in transitional times are based on the individual judge's record. This becomes a complex question in instances when the legal questions which were to be examined in difficult times are controversial in international law.

Against this background, postcolonial transitional societies have introduced innovative ways of restoring the rule of law. In Africa, this was embedded within the idea of new constitutionalism and implemented by way of Constitutional Commissions leading to the adoption of home-grown Constitutions. In Zimbabwe and South Africa, this notion led to the adoption of a postcolonial Constitution which included justiciable economic, social and cultural rights. As stated in Chapter 3, the effect of that constitutional framework in South Africa was to promote a relationship of accountability, transparency and responsiveness between the three arms of the state.

There have also been innovative ways of ensuring that judges also take part in instilling public faith in their role. In South Africa, this has taken the form of transformative adjudication, and in Tanzania and other postcolonial societies, judges have been involved in legal literacy programmes. There have also been training programmes for the judiciary including a curriculum in gender awareness. The judiciary has also dealt with the domestic financial challenges by directly courting Western donors. To pre-empt accusations that by receiving such assistance they will promote external agendas, judges have ensured that donor funding is targeted, open and effective. There has also been an attempt to include the concerns of women and other marginalized groups in donor-funded projects, especially those which deal with customary forms of adjudication.

Other nuanced postcolonial forms of dealing with domestic challenges have included the subjection of the international legal requirement for sufficient resources for the judiciary to international assistance. Codes of Ethics which deal with corruption and limit judges' participation in activities which limit their independence have also been adopted in Rwanda's transition from the genocide and during Ghana and Tanzania's in-house judicial reform processes. Last but not least, transitional times have also been used to create innovative ways of securing adequate representation of women in the judiciary.

7.4.2 Land reform in transition

It has been said that international law cannot adequately deal with postcolonial land-related complex issues. The first of these is the scope of the right to property and legal restrictions put on a state's right to expropriate land within its territory. The second is the legal basis for redressing past land injustices. Chapter 4 demonstrated how South Africa and Mozambique introduced nuanced forms of dealing with these issues without completely dismantling the master's discourse.

In the transition from apartheid, South Africa adopted a 'willing seller–willing buyer' land reform programme which, while appearing to be market-based, was not exactly liberal. For example, the willing buyers were hypothetical as they were those individuals whose applications for redistribution grants were approved by the state. Compensation was also not market based.

Similarly, when Mozambique abandoned socialism, it embraced liberal notions of the rule of law while not conforming to Western notions of privatization as land continued to vest in the state. There was an attempt to strike a balance between the promotion of investment and protection of customary land tenure arrangements. The peculiarities of the state of Mozambique were considered, since oral evidence was accepted as proof of land ownership and land alienability was restricted. There was also an attempt to promote gender equality whilst deferring to customary law in land acquisition. Small holder land acquisition was allowed to co-exist with formal investor holdings, and this could be a good lesson for Zimbabwe, where segregation between farming areas persists.

In terms of postcolonial redress for past land injustices, while there have been many pragmatic efforts in other postcolonial dispensations, South Africa and Mozambique give good illustrations of 'agency'. In both cases, there was recognition of a collective right to land. South Africa averted the issue of title to land by embracing a nuanced notion of native title to land. It also recognized that there might be competence issues and thus merged liberalism and local content when it imposed conditionalities on the uses of land by historic owners. However, the issue of former white farmers' land rights persistently defies domestic innovation and can be dealt with only by way of bilateral arrangements and not legal rulings which are less likely to be enforced.

7.4.3 *Minority rights in transition*

It has been explained that the international legal definition of minorities limits postcolonial groups' demands for autonomy and self-determination. This fact has actually been recognized by such groups who have resorted to self-identification as indigenous. In postcolonial transitions, this limitation has been addressed through nuanced forms of constitutionalism. The South Africa and Northern Ireland experiences give useful insight in this regard. In both cases, their temporary constitutional frameworks accorded minorities rights which they do not otherwise have in international law. In both cases, there was recognition of a collective right to self-determination and a possibility for external self-determination which is a deviation from the principle of *uti possidentis*. Northern Ireland even went further to include a notion of shared sovereignty.

7.4.4 *Combating the legacy of impunity*

Chapter 6 identified a number of complex issues which make the discourse of accountability less suited to postcolonial transitions. The first was its focus on retributive justice, which may be an antithesis to peace. Thus, some postcolonial societies have circumvented the duty to investigate, prosecute and punish whilst appearing to adhere to the anti-impunity standard. The South African TRC is a good example. Traditionally a historic justice mechanism, it was modified in the transition from apartheid to include conditional amnesties that served the purposes of creating a culture of accountability. Similar creativity in other postcolonial societies have been in the form of selective prosecutions and bifurcated approaches where only senior perpetrators are prosecuted and other offences are dealt with by way of traditional or restorative justice mechanisms.

The second issue concerns the adaptability of Western mechanisms to postcolonial circumstances. For example, in South Africa, a truth commission which was otherwise a Western historic justice mechanism was appropriated and presented to the public as a mechanism for promoting the local spirit of *ubuntu* or humanness. Also, the Rwandan experience with gacaca has been presented in this study as a demonstration of a third space in which the local engages with the Western. This traditional mechanism was used to advance both the Western duty to prosecute and domestic needs for restorative justice. However, while these mechanisms have tried to deal with gender-based sexual violence, it remains to be seen how such creativity will be extended to dealing with violations of economic, social and cultural rights.

The third question relates to colonial responsibility for the contemporary postcolonial culture of impunity. There has been very little postcolonial creativity in this regard. Successful attempts have been alive to the practical hurdles of individual responsibility and thus they have taken the form of lawsuits against a former colonial power, addressing physical violations of rights. To date, the most effective way of dealing with broader effects of colonialism have been by way of bilateral relationship treaties, as exemplified by the agreement between Libya and Italy.

7.5 Further research

This study is cognizant of the impossibility of focused research to deal with all of the questions which emanate from the process of analysis. In terms of detailed factual accounts this research has focused primarily on the Zimbabwean experience as a means of illuminating the predominant issues. Postcolonial comparative studies are used to glean insights into possible solutions for common problems. It is submitted that this approach has been effective and has also created opportunities for further research into, *inter alia*, three key areas. The first of these is the question of legal values which arose in the discussion of the struggle of Zimbabwean judges with the contentious land question. This necessitates a comparative study of postcolonial judicial rulings in terms of crisis. The second derives from this study's assertions that economic, social and cultural rights are marginalized in the dominant transitional justice discourse. This calls for an inquiry into the extent to which the notion of indivisibility of rights is advanced in postcolonial transitions. The third issue arises from this work's submission that paradigmatic forms of addressing past human rights violations are rooted in Western culture and that there is a proclivity to marginalize non-Western measures. There is therefore scope for further research on pre-colonial or indigenous accountability mechanisms.

Bibliography

Books and articles

Abbink J, 'Ethnicity and Constitutionalism in Contemporary Ethiopia' (1997) 41 *Journal of African Law* 159

Abeyesekera S, 'A Women's Human Rights Perspective on War and Conflict' (2003) *Women Human Rights Net* <www.whrnet.org/>

Ackerman B A, *The Future of Liberal Revolution* (Yale University Press 1992)

Adam H and Moodley K, *The Opening of the Apartheid Mind: Options for a New South Africa* (University of California Press 1993)

Adler G W, 'Challenging Transition Theory-The Labour-Movement, Radical Reform, and Transition to Democracy in South-Africa' (1995) 23(1) *Politics and Society* 75

Ado M K, 'Political Self-Determination within the Context of the African Charter on Human and People's Rights' (1988) 32 *Journal of African Law* 182

Afako B, 'Reconciliation and Justice: "Mato Oput" and the Amnesty Act' (2002) 11 *Accord: An International Review of Peace Initiatives* 6

African National Congress, 'The Reconstruction and Development Programme' *African National Congress* (1994) <www.anc.org.za>

Aginam O, 'The Nineteenth Century Colonial Fingerprints on Public Health Diplomacy: A Postcolonial View' (2003) 1 *Law, Social Justice & Global Development Journal (LGD)* <www2.warwick.ac.uk/>

Akhavan P, 'Punishing War Crimes in the Former Yugoslavia: A Critical Juncture for the New World Order' (1993) 15(2) *Human Rights Quarterly* 262

———, 'The International Criminal Tribunal for Rwanda: The Politics and Pragmatics of Punishment' (1996) 90(3) *American Journal of International Law* 501

———, 'The Yugoslav Tribunal at a Crossroads: The Dayton Peace Agreement and Beyond' (1996) 18(2) *Human Rights Quarterly* 259

———, 'Justice and Reconciliation in the Great Lakes Region of Africa: The Contribution of the International Criminal Tribunal for Rwanda' (1997) 7(2) *Duke Journal of Comparative and International Law* 325

———, 'Justice in The Hague, Peace in the Former Yugoslavia? A Commentary on the United Nations War Crimes Tribunal' (1998) 4(20) *Human Rights Quarterly* 73

Akinsanya A A, *The Expropriation of Multinational Property in the Third World* (Praeger 1980)

Alexander N, *Some Are More Equal Than Others: Essays on the Transition in South Africa* (Buchn Books 1993)

Al-Jarbou A M, 'Judicial Independence: Case Study of Saudi Arabia' (2004) 19(1) *Arab Law Quarterly* 5

Altiparmak K, 'The Application of the Concept of Continuing Violation to the Duty to Investigate, Prosecute and Punish under International Human Rights Law' (2003) 21–25 *Turkish Yearbook of Human Rights* 3

Alvarez J E, 'Judging the Security Council' (1996) 90(1) *American Journal of International Law* 1

———, 'Nuremberg Revisited: The Tadic Case' (1996) 7(2) *European Journal of International Law* 245

———, 'Crimes of States/Crimes of Hate: Lessons from Rwanda' (1999) 24(2) *Yale Journal of International Law* 365

Ambos K, 'The Legal Framework of Transitional Justice' Study prepared for the International Conference '*Building a Future on Peace and Justice*', Nuremberg, 25–27 June 2007 <www.peace-justice-conference.info/>

Amnesty International, *Zimbabwe: Toll of Impunity* (Amnesty International, International Secretariat 2002)

———, *Afghanistan: Re-establishing the Rule of Law* (Amnesty International Secretariat August 2003)

———, *Zimbabwe Power and Hunger – Violations of the Right to Food* (Amnesty International Secretariat 2004)

———, *Somalia: The Need for Effective Human Rights Protection under the New Transitional Government* (Amnesty International Secretariat 2005)

Amstutz M R, *The Healing of Nations: The Promise and Limits of Political Forgiveness* (Rowman & Littlefield Publishers 2005)

Anand R P, *Confrontation or Cooperation? International Law and the Developing Countries* (Kluwer Law International 1987)

Anderson B, *Imagined Communities: Reflections on the Origin and Spread of Nationalism* (Verso 1991)

Anderson R J, 'Redressing Colonial Genocide: The Hereros' Cause of Action against Germany' (2005) 93 *California Law Review* 1155

Angell A, 'The Transition to Democracy in Chile: A Model or an Exceptional Case?' (1993) 46(4) *Parliamentary Affairs* 563

Anghie A, 'Finding the Peripheries: Sovereignty and Colonialism in Nineteenth-Century International Law' (1999) 40 *Harvard International Law Journal* 1

———, *Imperialism, Sovereignty and the Making of International Law* (Cambridge University Press 2005)

———, 'Representing Culture, Translating Human Rights Symposium: Nationalism, Development and the Postcolonial State: The Legacies of the League of Nations' (2006) 41 *Texas International Law Journal Summer* 441

Anghie A and Chimni B S, 'Third World Approaches to International Law and Individual Responsibility in Internal Conflicts' (2003) 2 *Chinese Journal of International Law* 78

Anglin D G, 'Unilateral Independence in Southern Rhodesia' (1964) 19 *International Law Journal* 551

———, 'Zimbabwe: Retrospect and Prospect' (1980) 35 *International Law Journal* 663

Appiagyei-Atua K, 'Nominal Democracy for Development in Africa: A Workable Concept?' (2002) 1 *Law, Social Justice & Global Development Journal (LGD)* <Http://elj.warwick.ac.uk/>

Archibugi D, 'A Critical Analysis of the Self-determination of Peoples: A Cosmopolitan Perspective' (2003) 10(4) *Constellations* 488

Arsanjani M H, 'The Rome Statute of the International Criminal Court' (1999) 93(1) *American Journal of International Law* 22

Arthur P, 'Some Thoughts on Transition – A Comparative View of the Peace Processes in South-Africa and Northern-Ireland' (1995) 30(1) *Government and Opposition* 48

Ashcroft B, Griffiths G and Tiffin H, *The Post-colonial Studies Reader* (Routledge 1995)

———, *Key Concepts in Post-Colonial Studies* (Routledge 1998)

———, *Post-Colonial Studies: The Key Concepts* (Routledge 2000)

Ashdown P, 'What I Learned in Bosnia', *The New York Times*, 28 October 2002> <www.ohr.int/ohr-dept/>

Askin K D, *War Crimes against Women: Prosecutions in International War Crimes Tribunals* (Martnus Nijhoff 1997)

———, 'Gender Crimes Developments in the ICTR: Positive Developments' (2005) 3(4) *Journal of International Criminal Justice* 1007

Asmal K, *The Chorley Lecture* (London School of Economics 1999)

Atlas P M and Licklide R, 'Conflict among Former Allies after Civil War Settlement: Sudan, Zimbabwe, Chad and Lebanon' (1999) 1(36) *Journal of Peace Research* 35–54

Atuahene B, 'Property and Transitional Justice' (2010) 58 *UCLA Law Review Discourse* 65

———, 'The Importance of Conversation in Transitional Justice: A Study of Land Restitution in South Africa' (2014) 39(4) *Law & Social Inquiry* 902

———, *We Want What's Ours: Learning from South Africa's Land Restitution Program* (Oxford University Press 2014)

Aukerman M J, 'Extraordinary Evil, Ordinary Crime: Framework for Understanding Transitional Justice' (2002) 15 *Harvard Human Rights Journal* 39

Baffour A, 'Zimbabwe: The Spark . . . Claire Short's Letter of November' *SWANS* (1997) <www.swans.com/>

Balint J, 'The 'Mau Mau' Legal Hearings and Recognizing the Crimes of the British Colonial State: A Limited Constitutive Moment' (2016) 3(2) *Critical Analysis of Law*

Banda F, 'Meaningless Gestures? African Nations and the Convention on All Forms of Discrimination against Women' in Eekelar J and Nhlapo T (eds) *The Changing Family: Family Forms and Family Law* (Hart Publishing 1998)

———, *Women, Law and Human Rights: An African Perspective* (Hart Publishing 2005)

Banya N, 'Zimbabwe Inflation Hits New Record at 66,212.3 Percent' *Reuters*, 14 February 2008 <http://africa.reuters.com/>

Barahona de Brito A, *Human Rights and Democratization in Latin America: Uruguay and Chile* (Oxford University Press 1997)

Barkan E, 'Reparation; A Moral and Political Dilemma' in Miller J and Kumar S (eds) *Reparations: Interdisciplinary Inquiries* (Oxford University Press 2007)

Barnes T, 'Reconciliation, Ethnicity and School History in Zimbabwe 1980–2002' in Raftopoulos B and Savage T (eds) *Zimbabwe: Injustice an Reconciliation, Institute for Justice and Reconciliation* (Cape Town: Institute for Justice and Reconciliation 2004)

Barry M, 'Now Another Thing Must Happen: Richtersveld and the Dilemmas of *Land* Reform in Post-apartheid South Africa' (2004) 20 *South African Journal of Human Rights* 355

Barsalou J, *Trauma and Transitional Justice in Divided Societies, Special Report 135* (United States Institute of Peace 1995)

———, 'Trauma and Transitional Justice in Divided Societies' *Special Report No. 135* (United States Institute of Peace 2005)

Bartoli A, 'Learning from the Mozambique Peace Process: The Role of the Community of Sant'Egidio' in Fisher R J (ed) *Paving the Way: Contributions of Interactive Conflict Resolution to Peacemaking* (Lexington Books 2005)

Bass G J, *Stay the Hand of Vengeance: The Politics of War Crimes Tribunals* (Princeton University Press 2000)

Bassiouni M C, *Crimes against Humanity in International Criminal Law* (Kluwer Law International 1999)

Bauer P, *Equality, The Third World and Economic Delusion* (Weidenfield and Nicolson 1981)

Beasley C, *What Is Feminism?: An Introduction to Feminist Theory* (Sage Publications 1999)

Beetham D, 'Democracy and Human Rights: Contrast and Convergence' Seminar on the *Interdependence between Democracy and Human Rights*, Office of the High Commissioner for Human Rights, United Nations, Geneva, 25–26 November 2002 <www.unhchr.ch/>

Bell C, 'Dealing with the Past in Northern Ireland' (2003) 26 *Fordham International Law Journal* 1095

———, *Peace Agreements and Human Rights* (Oxford University Press 2003)

———, 'Women and the Problems of Peace Agreements: Strategies for Change' in Coomeraswamy R (ed) *Women, Peacemaking and Constitutions* (Women Unlimited 2004)

———, *Negotiating Justice: Human Rights and Peace Agreements* (International Committee on Human Rights Policy 2006)

———, 'Liberal Multiculturalism and the Limits of International Law' (2007) 6(4) *Ethnopolitics* 599

———, 'The "New Law" of Transitional Justice' Study prepared for the *International Conference 'Building a Future on Peace and Justice'*, Nuremberg, 25–27 June 2007 <www.peace-justice-conference.info/documents.asp>

———, *On the Law of Peace: Peace Agreements and the Lex Pacificatoria* (Oxford University Press 2008)

———, 'Transitional Justice, Interdisciplinarity and the State of the "Field" or "Non-Field"' (2009) 3(1) *International Journal of Transitional Justice* 5

Bell C, Campbell C and Ní Aoláin F, 'Justice Discourses in Transition' (2004) 13 *Social and Legal Studies* 306

———, 'The Battle for Transitional Justice: Hegemony, Iraq and International Law' in McEvoy K, Morrisson J and Anthony G (eds) *Judges, Transition and Human Rights Cultures: Essays in Honour of Stephen Livingstone* (Oxford University Press 2006)

Bell C and Cavanagh K, 'Constructive Ambiguity or Internal Self-determination? Self-determination, Group Accommodation and the Belfast Agreement' (1998) 22 *Fordham International Law Journal* 1345

Bell C and O'Rourke C, 'Does Feminism Need a Theory of Transitional Justice?' (2007) 1(1) *International Journal of Transitional Justice* 23

Bell V and Kirstein C, 'Out of Conflict: Peace, Change and Justice' (2004) 13(3) *Socio-Legal Studies* 300

Benjamin W, 'Theses on the Philosophy of History' in *Illuminations* (Schocke 1969)

Berkerley B, *Zimbabwe: Wages of War* (Lawyers Committee for Human Rights 1986)

Beth L, 'Discourse in Development: Viewing the United Nations Committee on Human Rights through the Post-Colonial Lens' (September 2003) *Working Paper 11*, Villanova University School of Law Working Paper Series <http://law.bepress.com/>

Bhabha H K, 'Of Mimicry and Man: The Ambivalence of Colonial Discourse' in Bhabha H K (1994) *The Location of Culture* (Routledge 1984)

———, 'Cultural Diversity and Cultural Differences' in Ashcroft B, Griffiths G and Tiffin H (eds) *The Post-Colonial Studies Reader* (Routledge 1995)

Bhargava R, 'How Should We Respond to the Cultural Injustices of Colonialism' in Miller J and Kumar S (eds) *Reparations: Interdisciplinary Inquiries* (Oxford University Press 2007)

Bickford L, 'Transitional Justice' (2004) 3 *Encyclopaedia of Genocide and Crimes against Humanity* <www.ictj.org/en/tj/>

Biel R, *The New Imperialism: Crisis and Contradictions in North /South Relations* (Zed Books 2000)

Bigge D M and von Briesen A, 'Conflict in the Zimbabwean Courts: Women's Rights and Indigenous Self-Determination in Magaya v. Magaya' (2000) 13 *Harvard Human Rights Journal* 289

Bilateral.org, 'Zimbabwe Admits Breach of Law against Dutch Farmers' 16 November 2007 <www.bilaterals.org/>

Biti T, 'A Predatory State and the Rule of Law in Zimbabwe' (1999) 1 *Zimbabwe Human Rights Bulletin* 97

Bleeker M and Sisson J, 'Dealing with the Past: Critical Issues, Lessons Learned and the Challenges for Future Swiss Policy' (2004) *Working Paper*, Bern: Swiss Peace <www.swisspeace.org/koff/>

Bochenek M G, 'Compensation for Human Rights Abuses in Zimbabwe' (1994) 26 *Columbia Human Rights Law Review* 483

Bolocan M J, 'Rwandan Gacaca: An Experiment in Transitional Justice' (2004) *Journal of Dispute Resolution* 355

Bond P, 'Competing Explanations of Zimbabwe's Long Economic Crisis' (2007) 8(2) *Safundi the Journal of South African and American Studies* 149

Bondzie-Simpson E, 'A Critique of the African Charter on Human and People's Rights' (1998) 31 *Howard Law Journal* 643

Boon K E, 'Open for Business': International Financial Institutions, Post-conflict Economic Reform and the Rule of Law' (2007) 39 *New York University Journal of International Law and Politics* 513

———, 'Coining a New Jurisdiction: The Security Council as Economic Peacekeeper' (2008) 41 *Vanderbilt Journal of Transnational Law* 991

Booysen H, 'South Africa: In Need of a Federal Constitution for Its Minority Peoples' (1996) 19 *Loyola International and Comparative Law Review* 789

Booysen S, 'The Dualities of Contemporary Zimbabwean Politics: Constitutionalism Versus the Law of Power and the Land' (2003) 7(2 and 3) *African Studies Quarterly*

Boraine A, 'Transitional Justice as an Emerging Field' Presented at the *'Repairing the Past: Reparations and Transitions to Democracy' Symposium*, Ottawa, Canada, 11 March 2004

Bosire L, 'Overpromised, Underdelivered: Transitional Justice in Sub-Saharan Africa' *Occasional Paper Series* (International Centre for Transitional Justice 2006)

Boucher S, Rose L L and Roth M J, 'Legal Uncertainty and Land Disputes in the Peri-Urban Areas of Mozambique: Land Markets in Transition' *Research Paper No. 121* (Land Tenure Center, University of Wisconsin-Madison 1995)

Boyd K, 'Universal Jurisdiction and Structural Reasonableness' (2004) 40 *Texas International Law Journal* 1

Brahm E, 'Rule of Law' in Burgess G and Burgess H (eds) *Beyond Intractability* (Conflict Research Consortium, University of Colorado 2005)

Braithwaite J, 'Restorative Justice: Assessing Optimistic and Pessimistic Accounts' in Tonry M (ed) *Crime and Justice: A Review of Research* (University of Chicago Press 1999)

Bratton M, 'Ten Years After: Land Redistribution in Zimbabwe; 1980–1990' in Prosterman R L, Temple M N and Hanstad T M (eds) *Agrarian Reform and Grassroots Development: Ten Case Studies* (Lynne Rienner Publishers 1990)

Brazier R, *Constitutional Reform: Reshaping the British Political System* (Oxford University Press 1998)

Brems E 'Enemies or Allies? Feminism and Cultural Relativism as Dissident Voices in Human Rights Discourse' (1997) 19 *Human Rights Quarterly* 136

Brighouse H, *Justice* (Polity Press 2004)

Brinks D, 'Judicial Reform and Independence in Brazil and Argentina: The Beginning of a New Millennium' (2004) 40 *Texas International Law Journal* 595

Brito de A B, Gonzalez-Enriquez C and Aguilar P (eds), *The Politics of Memory: Transitional Justice in Democratizing Societies* (Oxford University Press 2001)

Broch-Due V, 'Violence and Belonging: Analytical Reflections' in Broch-Due V (ed) *Violence and Belonging: The Quest for Identity in Post-Colonial Africa* (Routledge 2005)

Brophy A L, 'Reconsidering Reparations' (2006) 81 *Indiana Law Journal* 811

Brown M M, 'Rule of Law and Transitional Justice in Conflict and Post-Conflict Societies' *UNDP Administrator Statement to the Security Council* (New York: United Nations 6 October 2004) <www.undp.org/>

Bruce J W, 'Land Reform in Zimbabwe?' (2000) 79 *Land Tenure Centre Newsletter* <www.ies.wisc.edu>

Buford W and van der Merwe H, 'Reparations in Southern Africa' (2004) 1–2 *Cahiers d'études Africaines* 44

Bunting A, 'Theorizing Women's Cultural Diversity in Feminist International Human Rights Strategies' (1993) 20(1) *Journal of Law and Society* 6

Burr K, 'The Evolution of the International Law of Alienability: The 1997 Land Law of Mozambique as a Case Study' (2005) 43 *Columbia Journal of Transnational Law* 961

Byers M (ed), *The Role of Law in International Politics: Essays in Law and International Relations* (Oxford University Press 2000)

Call C T, 'Is Transitional Justice Really Just?' (2004) 11(1) *Brown Journal of World Affairs* 101

Callaghy T, *The State-Society Struggle: Zaire in Comparative Perspective* (Columbia University Press 1984)

Campbell C, 'Wars on Terror', and Vicarious Hegemons: The UK, International Law, and the Northern Ireland Conflict' (2005) 54 *International Comparative Law Quarterly* 321

Campbell C and Ní Aoláin F, 'Local Meets Global: Transitional Justice in Northern Ireland' (2003) 26 *Fordham International Law Journal* 871

Campbell C, Ní Aoláin F and Harvey C, 'The Frontiers of Legal Analysis: Reframing the Transition in Northern Ireland' (2003) 66 *Modern Law Review* 317

Campbell H, *Reclaiming Zimbabwe: The Exhaustion of the Patriarchal Model of Liberation* (David Phillip Publishers 2003)

Cappelletti M, 'Repudiating Montesquieu? The Expansion and Legitimacy of Constitutional Justice' (1985) 35(1) *Catholic University Law Review* 1

Carew G M, *Democratic Transition in Postcolonial Africa: A Deliberative Approach* (Edwin Mellen Press 2006)

Carlos S, 'Economic Reform and Judicial Governance in Brazil: Balancing Independence with Accountability' (2003) 10(4) *Democratization* 161

Carothers T, 'The Rule of Law Revival' (1998) *Foreign Affairs*

———, *Aiding Democracy Abroad: The Learning Curve* (Carnegie Endowment for International Peace 1999)

———, 'How Democracies Emerge: The "Sequencing" Fallacy' (2007) 18(1) *Journal of Democracy* 12

———, 'Rebuilding Developmental States: From Theory to Practice Judicial Reform and the Rule of Law' *Oversees Development Agency, Meeting Series: January–April 2006* <www.odi.org.uk/speeches/>

Carver R, *Zimbabwe: A Break with the Past? Human Rights and Political Unity* (An Africa Watch Report 1989)

———, 'Zimbabwe: Drawing a Line through the Past' (1993) 37(1) *Journal of African Law* 69

Casper G, 'Rule of Law? Whose Law?' in Lorenz S et al. (eds) *Festschrift fur Andreas Heldrick Zum 70. Geburtstag* (Verlag C.H. Beck 2005)

Cassese A, 'Modern Constitutions and International Law' (1985) 192 *Hague Recueil* 331

———, *Self-Determination of Peoples: A Legal Reappraisal* (Lauterpacht Memorial Lectures 1995)

———, 'On the Current Trends Towards Criminal Prosecution and Punishment of Breaches of International Humanitarian Law' (1998) 9(1) *European Journal of International Law* 2

Castellino J, 'Order and Justice: National Minorities and the Right to Secession' (1999) 6 *International Journal on Minority and Group Rights* 389

Castellino J and Gilbert J, 'Self-Determination, Indigenous Peoples and Minorities' (2003) 3 *Macquarie Law Journal* 155

Catholic Commission for Justice and Peace (CCJP) and the (Legal Resources Foundation (LRF), *Breaking the Silence, Building the Peace: Report on the Disturbances in Matebeleland and the Midlands, 1980 to 1988* (CCJP and LRF 1997)

Centre for International Development and Conflict Management (CIDCM), 'Data; Chronology for Ndebele in Zimbabwe' (2007) <www.cidcm.umd.edu>

Centre for the Study of Violence and Reconciliation (CSVR), 'Memorialisation and Reconciliation in Transitional Southern African Societies' (2005) <www.csvr.org.za>

Cepl V, 'The Transformation of Hearts and Minds in Eastern Europe' (1997) 17(2) *Cato Journal* 229

Chabvuta T, 'Exploring Transitional Justice for Past Human Rights Violations: The Case of Zimbabwe' *Unpublished LL.M Dissertation* (Transitional Justice Institute, University of Ulster 2006)

Charlesworth H et al., 'Feminist Approaches to International Law' (1991) 85 *American Journal of International Law* 613

Charlesworth H and Chinkin C, *The Boundaries of International Law: A Feminist Analysis* (Manchester University Press 2000)

Cheater A, 'Human Rights in Zimbabwe July–December 1999: A Baseline Report' (1999) 2 *Zimbabwe Human Rights Bulletin* 2

Chesterman S, 'Justice under International Administration: Kosovo, East Timor and Afghanistan' (2002) *International Peace Academy*

———, *You the People: The UN, Transitional Administration, and State-Building* (Oxford University Press/International Peace Academy 2004)

———, 'Building Up or Building Down the State: State Building and Humanitarian and Development Assistance' *SSRC Humanitarian Action Seminar*, 8 February 2005

———, 'Ownership in Theory and in Practice: Transfer of Authority in UN State-Building Operations' (2007) 1(1) *Journal of Intervention & State-Building*

———, 'An International Rule of Law' (2008) 56 *American Journal of Comparative Law* 331

Chesterman S, Ignatieff M and Thakur R C, *Making States Work: State Failure and the Crisis of Governance* (United Nations University Press 2005)

Chevigny P, 'Limitations of Universal Jurisdiction' (2006) *Global Policy Forum* <www.globalpolicy.org>

Chigara B, 'From Oral to Recorded Governance: Reconstructing Title to Real Property in 21st Century Zimbabwe' (2001) 30 *Common Law World Review* 36

———, *Amnesty in International Law: The Legality under International Law of National Amnesty Laws* (Longman 2002)

Chinkin C, 'East Timor: A Failure of Decolonization' (1999) 20 *Australian Yearbook of International Law* 35

———, 'Gender, Human Rights, and Peace Agreements' (2003) 18 *Ohio State Journal on Dispute Resolution*

Christopher A J, 'Land Restitution in South Africa, 1991–94' (1995) 12(4) *Land Use Policy* 267

Chukwudi E E, 'Transition and the Reasons of Memory' (2004) 102(4) *The South Atlantic Quarterly* 755

Chun L, 'Human Rights and Democracy: The Case for Decoupling' (2001) 5(3) *International Journal of Human Rights* 19

Claxton H, 'Land and Liberation: Lessons for the Creation of Effective Land Reform Policy in South Africa' (2003) 8 *Michigan Journal of Race and Law* 529

Cnossen C and Sith V M, 'Developing Legal Research Methodology to Meet the Challenge of New Technologies' (1997) 2 *The Journal of Information, Law and Technology (JILT)* <www2.warwick.ac.uk/>

Cobban H, 'Notes on the Development of Transitional Justice since 1995' (2005) *Just World News* <http://justworldnews.org/archives/notes><

Cobbing J R, 'The Ndebele under the Khumalo' 1820–1896' *Unpublished PhD Thesis* (University of Lancaster 1976)

Cohen S, 'State Crimes of Previous Regimes Knowledge, Accountability, and the Policing of the Past' (1995) 20(1) *Law & Social Inquiry* 7

Coles C M, 'Land Reform for Post- Apartheid South Africa' (1993) 20 *Boston College Environmental Affairs Law Review* 699

———, 'Justice in Transition? Prospects for a Palestinian– Israel Truth Commission' *Middle East Report*, May–August 1995

Commission on the Restitution of Land Rights, 'Presentation to the Portfolio Committee on Agriculture and Land Affairs' 29 May 2007 <http://land.pwv.gov.za/restitution>

Cook R J, 'Accountability in International Law for Violations of Women's Rights by Non-State Actors' (1993) 25 *Studies in Transnational Legal Policy* 93

Cooke E (ed), *Modern Studies in Property Law, vol II* (Hart Publishing 2003)

Corder H, 'Judicial Policy in a Transforming Constitution' in Morison J, McEvoy K and Anthony G (eds) *Judges, Transition, and Human Rights* (Oxford University Press 2007)

Costea P, 'The Legal System and the Judiciary in the Marxist Leninist Regimes of the Third World' (1990) 16 *Review of Socialist Law* 225

Cotterrel R, *The Sociology of Law* (Butterworths 1984)

Cox M and Garlick M, *The Politics of Jurisprudence: A Critical Introduction to Philosophy* (University of Pennsylvania Press 1989)

———, 'Musical Chairs: Property Repossession and Return Strategies in Bosnia and Herzegovina' in Leckie S (ed) *Returning Home: Housing and Property Restitution Rights of Refugees and Displaced Persons* (Transnational Publishers 2003)

Crocker C A, Hampson F O and Aall P (eds), *Grasping the Nettle: Analyzing Cases of Intractable Conflict* (USIP Press 2005)

Czarnota A W, 'Law as Mnemosyne and as Lethe: Quasi-Judicial Institutions and Collective Memories' in Christodoulidis E and Veitch S (eds) *Lethe's Law: Justice, Law and Ethics in Reconciliation* (Hart Publishing 2001)

Czarnota A W, Krygier M and Sadurski W, *Rethinking the Rule of Law after Communism* (Central European University Press 2005)

D'Amato A, 'The Neo-Positivist Concept of International Law' (1965) 59 *American Journal of International Law* 321

———, 'On Consensus' (1970) 8 *Canadian Yearbook of International Law* 104

D'Amato T, *Book Review: Cook, B 1994 (ed), Human Rights of Women: National and International Perspectives* (University of Pennsylvania Press 1995)

Dancaescu N, 'Land Reform in Zimbabwe' (2003) 15 *Florida Journal of International Law* 616

Darnolf S and Laakso L (eds), *Twenty Years of Independence in Zimbabwe: From Liberation to Authoritarianism* (Palgrave Macmillan 2003)

Dashwood H S, 'Social Welfarism, Poverty Alleviation and Political Stability in Zimbabwe' (1999) 3 *Canadian Journal of Development Studies* 567

———, 'Inequality, Leadership and the Crisis in Zimbabwe' (2002) 57 *International Law Journal* 209

Dashwood H S and Pratt C, 'Leadership, Participation and Conflict Management: Zimbabwe and Tanzania' in Matthews R O and Ali T (eds) *Civil Wars in Africa* (McGill Queen's University Press 1999)

Davidson L and Purohit R, 'The Zimbabwean Human Rights Crisis: A Collaborative Approach to International Advocacy' (2004) 7(1) *Yale Human Rights and Development Journal* 108

de Bourbon A, 'Human Rights Litigation in Zimbabwe: Past, Present and Future' (2003) 3 *African Human Rights Law Journal* 195

de Brito A B, González E C and Aguilar F P, *The Politics of Memory: Transitional Justice in Democratizing Societies* (Oxford University Press 2001)

de Bruin J, 'Zimbabwe's Place in the Commonwealth' *Advocacy Programme, Commonwealth Human Rights Initiative* (CHRI New 2004)

Decker S, 'Postcolonial Transitions in Africa: Decolonization in West Africa and Present Day South Africa' (2010) 47(5) *Journal of Management Studies* 791
De Greiff P, 'Justice and Reparations' in Miller J and Kumar R (eds) *Reparations: Interdisciplinary Inquiries* (Oxford University Press 2007)
———, 'Theorizing Transitional Justice' (2012) 51 *Nomos* 31
De Soto H, *The Mystery of Capital: Why Capitalism Triumphs in the West and Fails Everywhere Else* (Black Swan 2000)
De Villiers B, *'Land Reform: Issues and Challenges' A Comparative Overview of Experiences in Zimbabwe, Namibia, South Africa and Australia* (Konrad-Adenauer-Stiftung 2003)
De Waal V, *The Politics of Reconciliation, Zimbabwe's First Decade* (Hurst & Co 1999)
De Wit P, 'Land Conflict Management in Mozambique: Case study of Zambézia Province' *Paper Prepared for the Land Tenure Service* (FAO 2001) <www.fao.org>
Diamond L, Linz J and Lipset S M (eds), *Democracy in Developing Countries Africa* (Lynne Rienner Publishers 1988)
Dias R W M, 'Legal Politics: Norms behind The Grundnorm' (1968) 26 *Cambridge Law Journal* 233
Dickinson L A, 'Transitional Justice in Afghanistan: The Promise of Mixed Tribunals' (2002) 31 *Denver International Journal of Law and Policy* 23
Dlamini M A, 'African Legal Philosophy': A Southern African View' (1997) 2 *Journal for Juridical Science* 22
Donnelly J, *Universal Human Rights in Theory and Practice* (Cornell University Press 1989)
Douzinas C, *Human Rights and Empire: The Political Philosophy of Cosmopolitanism* (Routledge Cavendish 2007)
Douzinas C and Gearey A, *Critical Jurisprudence: The Political Philosophy of Justice* (Hart Publishing 2005)
Dugard J, 'The Quest for a Liberal Democracy in South Africa' (1987) 4 *Acta Juridica* 237
Duncanson I, 'Writing in the Postcolonial: Postcolonial Legal Scholarship' (2003) 1 *Law, Social Justice & Global Development Journal (LGD)* ><www2.warwick.ac.uk/>
Du Plessis M and Ford J, 'Justice and Peace in a New Zimbabwe; Transitional Justice Options' (2008) *ISS Occasional Paper 164*
———, 'Transitional Justice: A Future Truth Commission for Zimbabwe?' (2009) 58(1) *International and Comparative Law Quarterly* 73–117
Duthie R and Seils P, *The Case for Action on Transitional Justice and Displacement Strategies during and after Conflict* (International Centre for Transitional Justice 2016)
Dworkin R, *Taking Rights Seriously* (Duckworth 1978)
———, *Law's Empire* (Harvard University Press 1986)
Eggers A, 'When Is a State a State? The Case for Recognition of Somaliland' (2007) 30 *Boston College International and Comparative Law Review* 211
Ehrlich C E, 'Democratic Alternatives to Ethnic Conflict: Consociationalism and Neo-Separatism' (2000) 26 *Brook Journal of International Law* 447
Eide A, 'Preventing Impunity for the Violator and Ensuring Remedies for the Victim' ((2000) 69(1) *Nordic Journal of International Law* 1
Eisgruber C L, 'The Living Hand of the Past: History and Constitutional Justice' (1996) 65 *Fordham Law Review* 1611
Elich G, *Strange Liberators: Militarism, Mayhem, and the Pursuit of Profit* (Llumina Press 2006)

Ellis M S, 'Case for Mugabe ICC Trial' *NewZimbabwe.com*, 1 April 2004 <www.newzimbabwe.com>

Elster J, 'Coming to Terms with the Past. A Framework for the Study of Justice in the Transition to Democracy' (1998) 39 *European Journal of Sociology (Archives Européenes de sociologie)* 7

———, *Closing the Books: Transitional Justice in a Historical Perspective* (Cambridge University Press 2004)

———, 'A Framework for the Study of Transitional Justice' *Rettsoppgjøret etter 1945 – et forskningsprosjekt: Artikler* <www.media.uio.no>

Enwezor O, *Experiments with Truth: Transitional Justice and the Processes of Truth and Reconciliation: Documenta11_Platform 2* (Hatje Cantz, Ostfildern-Ruit, 2002)

Eppel S, 'Gukurahundi: The Need for Truth and Reparations' in Raftopoulos B and Savage T (eds) *Zimbabwe: Injustice and Political Reconciliation* (Weaver Press 2004)

———, *Transitional Justice for Villagers in Zimbabwe* (Institute for Democracy in South Africa 2008)

Eppel S and Raftopoulos B, *Political Crisis, Mediation and the Prospects for Transitional Justice in Zimbabwe* (Solidarity Peace Trust 2009)

Escobar A, *Encountering Development: The Making and Unmaking of the Third World* (Princeton University Press 1995)

Evans G, 'Zimbabwe: Is There Any Way Out?' Notes for *Panel Presentation by Gareth Evans, President, International Crisis Group, to Royal Commonwealth Society Conference, Zimbabwe: Preparing for Change*, London, 2 July 2007 <www.crisisgroup.org/>

Evans M, *Transformative Justice: Remedying Human Rights Violations beyond Transition: Transitional Justice Series* (Routledge 2018)

Ezetah C R, 'International Law of Self-Determination and the Ogoni Question: Mirroring Africa's Post-Colonial Dilemma' (1996) 19 *Loyola of Los Angeles International Law and Comparative Law Journal* 811

Falk R, 'Sovereignty and Human Dignity: The Search for Reconciliation' in Deng F M and Lyons T (eds) *African Reckoning a Quest for Good Governance* (Brookings Institution Press 1997)

Fan H, 'The Missing Link between Self-determination and Democracy: The Case of East Timor' (2007) 6 *Northern Western University Journal of International Human Rights* 176

Fancher M P and Richardson H J, 'Government Land Acquisition in Zimbabwe: An Essential Element of the Right to Self-Determination' (2002) 59 *Guild Practice* 186

Fanon F, *The Wretched of the Earth* (Penguin 1963)

Farrelly A, 'Foreign Policy in the Courts – The ATCA and in Re South African Apartheid Litigation: What SOSA Makes Courts Do' (2005) 30 *Seton Hall Legislative Journal* 437

Feltoe G, 'Towards a Stronger Human Rights Culture in Zimbabwe: The Special Role of Lawyers' (1990) 7–8 *Zimbabwe Law Review* 134

———, 'Report of the Internal Security Forces in Zimbabwe' (1996) *Third World Legal Studies* 21

———, 'The Rule of Law in Zimbabwe – A Façade of Democracy' in Morrel P et al. (eds) *Civil Society and Justice in Zimbabwe: Proceedings of Symposium Held in Johannesburg 11–13 August 2003* (Themba Lesizwe 2003)

Fermandois J and Morris M A, 'Democracy in Chile. Transition and Consolidation 1987–2000' (1995) 279 *Conflict Studies* 1

Findlay I M, 'Working for Postcolonial Legal Studies: Working with the Indigenous Humanities' (2003) 1 *Law, Social Justice and Gobal Development Journal* <http://elj.warwick.ac.uk/>

Fine R and Rai S (eds), *Civil Society: Democratic Perspectives* (Frank Cass 1997)

Fineman M A and Zinsstag E, *Feminist Perspectives on Transitional Justice* (Intersentia 2013)

Fitzpatrick P and Darian-Smith E, 'The Laws of the Postcolonial: An Insistent Introduction' in Darian-Smith E and Fitzpatrick P (eds) *Laws of the Postcolonial* (University of Michigan Press 1999)

Fletcher L E and Weinstein H M, 'Violence and Social Repair: Rethinking the Contribution of Justice to Reconciliation' (2002) 24 *Human Rights Quarterly* 573

Fletcher L E, Weinstein H M and Rowen J, 'Context, Timing and the Dynamics of Transitional Justice: A Historical Perspective' (2009) 31(1) *Human Rights Quarterly* 163

Ford R, 'Law History, and the Colonial Discourse: Davies v Commissioner* and Zimbabwe as a Colonialist Case Study' (2001) 45 *Howard Law Journal* 213

Forsythe D P, 'Human Rights in a Post-Cold War World' (1991) 15 *Foreign World Affairs* 55

Foucault M, *The Archaeology of Knowledge, and the Discourse on Language* (Pantheon Books 1972)

Fox G H, 'International Law and the Entitlement to Democracy after War' (2003) 9 *Global Governance* 179–197

Fox G H and Roth B R (eds), *Democratic Governance and International Law* (Cambridge University Press 2000)

Franck T M, 'The Emerging Right to Democratic Governance' (1992) 86(1) *America Journal of International Law* 46

———, '"The Powers of Appreciation": Who Is the Ultimate Guardian of UN Legality?' (1992) 86 *American Journal of International Law* 519

Franke K M, 'Gendered Subjects of Transitional Justice' (2006) 15(3) *Columbia Journal of Gender and Law*

Fraser A, 'Hybridity Emergent: Geo-history, Learning, and Land Restitution in South Africa' (2007) 38(2) *Geoforum*

Fraser N, *Justice Interruptus: Critical Reflections on the 'Postsocialist' Condition* (Routledge 1997)

Freeman M, 'National Self-determination, Peace and Human Rights' (1998) 10(2) *Peace Review* 157

———, *Human Rights: An Interdisciplinary Approach* (Polity Press 2002)

Fritz F, 'Sound of Sanity in a Mad Season' *The Southern Africa Litigation Centre Newsroom*, 8 August 2006 <www.southernafricalitigationcentre.org>

Fuller L L, 'Positivism and Fidelity to Law – A Reply to Professor Hart' (1958) 71 *Harvard Law Review* 630

———, *The Morality of Law* (Yale University Press 1964)

Gande C, 'Harare Undertaking Another Audit of Agricultural Land Ownership' (2006) *Voice of America*, 28 December 2006 <www.voanews.com>

Garcia B M, 'Compensation for Human Rights Abuses in Zimbabwe' (1995) 26(2) *Columbia Human Rights Law Review* 483

Gardam J and Jarvis M, 'Women and Armed Conflict: The International Response to the Beijing Platform for Action' (2000) 32 *Columbia Human Rights Law Review* 1

Gathii J, 'Dispossession through International Law: Iraq in Historical and Comparative Context' in Jones B G (ed) *Decolonizing International Relations* (Rowman & Littlefield Publishers 2006)

Gavron J, 'Amnesty in the Light of Developments in International Law and the Establishment of the International Criminal Court' (2002) 51 *International and Comparative Law Quarterly* 91

Geldenhuys D and Rossouw J, 'The International Protection of Minority Rights' (2001) *A Special Report Compiled for F W de Klerk Foundation* <www.fwdklerk.org.za>

Georgiev D, 'Politics or Rule of Law: Deconstruction and Legitimacy in International Law' (1993) 4 *Journal of European International Law* 1

Gewirth A, 'The Basis and Content of Human Rights' in Pennock J R and Chapman J W (eds) *Human Rights* (New York University Press 1981)

Gibney M, Howard-Hassmann R E, Coicaud J-M and Steiner N, *The Age of Apology: Facing Up to the Past* (University of Pennsylvania Press 2007)

Gilligan C, *In a Different Voice* (Harvard University Press 1982)

Glass A, 'A Review of PostColonial Liberalism by Duncan Ivison' (2003) *Australian Humanities Review*

Gledhill J, 'Liberalism, Socio-Economic Rights and the Politics of Identity: From Moral Economy to Indigenous Rights' in Wilson R A (ed) *Human Rights Culture and Context: Anthropological Perspectives* (Pluto Press 1996)

Gloppen S, 'Reparatory Justice, a Road to Reconciliation? On the Role of Reparations in Transitional Justice Theory' in Ulrich G and Krabbe L B (eds) *Human Rights in Development Yearbook 2001: Reparations: Redressing Past Wrongs* (Kluwer Law International 2003)

Goh D P S, 'From Colonial Pluralism to Postcolonial Multiculturalism: Race State Formation and the Question of Cultural Diversity in Malaysia and Singapore' (2008) 2(1) *Sociology Campus* 232

Goldman M, 'Does Peace Follow Justice or Vice Versa? Plans for Post Conflict Justice in Burundi' (2006) 30 *Fletcher Forum of World Affairs* 137

Goredema C, 'Whither Judicial Independence in Zimbabwe' in Raftopoulos B and Savage T (eds) *Zimbabwe: Injustice and Reconciliation* (Institute for Justice & Reconciliation 2004)

Gormally B, 'Community Restorative Justice in Northern Ireland – An Overview' (2007) *Restorative Justice Online* <www.restorativejustice.org<>

Graham S, 'The Truth Commission and Post-apartheid Literature in South Africa' (2003) 34(1) *Research in African Literatures*

Gready P, 'Reconceptualising Transitional Justice: Embedded and Distanced Justice' (2005) 5(1) *Conflict. Security and Development* 3

Gready P and Robins S, 'From Transitional to Transformative Justice: A New Agenda for Practice' (2014) 8 *International Journal of Transitional Justice* 339

Grewal K, 'Rape in Conflict, Rape in Peace: Questioning the Revolutionary Potential of International Criminal Justice for Women's Human Rights' (2010) 33(1) *Australian Feminist Law Journal* 57

———, 'International Criminal Law as a Site for Enhancing Women's Rights? Challenges, Possibilities, Strategies' (2015) 23(2) *Feminist Legal Studies* 149

Griffiths A, 'Customary Law in a Transnational World: Legal Positivism Revisited' Paper Presented for *Conference on Customary Law in Polynesia*, 12 October 2004

Gross O, 'Chaos and Rules Should Responses to Violent Crises Always Be Constitutional?' (2003) *Yale Law Journal* 112

———, 'The Concept of "Crisis": What Can We Learn from the Two Dictatorships of L. Quinctius Cincinnatus?' *17th International Conference*, Italy, 20 May 2005

Gross O and Ní Aoláin F, *Law in Times of Crisis – Emergency Powers in the Theoretical and Comparative Perspective* (Cambridge University Press 2006)

Grovogui S N, *Sovereigns, Quasi Sovereigns, and Africans: Race and Self-Determination in International Law* (University of Minnesota Press 1996)

Gubbay A R, 'The Protection of Fundamental Human Rights: The Zimbabwean Experience' (1997) 19 *Human Rights Quarterly* 228

Guha R (ed), *Subaltern Studies Reader 1986–1995* (University of Minnesota Press 1997)

Gutto S, 'Current Concepts, Core Principles, Dimensions, Processes and Institutions of Democracy and the Inter-Relationship between Democracy and Modern Human Rights' Seminar on the *Interdependence between Democracy and Human Rights*, Office of the High Commissioner for Human Rights, United Nations, Geneva, 25–26 November 2002 <www.unhchr.ch/democracy/seminar.>

Hagopian F and Mainwaring S, 'Democracy in Brazil: Prospects and Problems' (1987) 4 *World Policy Journal* 48

Halberstam M, 'Belgium's Universal Jurisdiction Law: Vindication of International Justice or Pursuit of Politics' (2003) 25 *Cardozo Law Review* 247

Hamber B, 'Rights and Reasons: Challenges for Truth Recovery in South Africa and Northern Ireland' (2003) 26 *Fordham International Law Journal* 1074

Hanlon J, 'The Land Debate in Mozambique; Will Foreign Investors, the Urban Elite, Advanced Peasants or Family Farmers Drive Rural Developments'? *Research Paper Commissioned by Oxfam GB, Regional Management Center for Southern Africa* (2002) <www.oxfam.org.uk>

———, 'Renewed Land Debate and the "Cargo Cult" in Mozambique' (2004) 30(3) *Journal of Southern African Studies* 603

Hannum H, *Autonomy, Sovereignty, and Self-Determination: The Accommodation of Conflicting Rights* (University of Pennsylvania Press 1990)

Hansen T, *The Gacaca Tribunals in Post-Genocide Rwanda* (University of Minnesota 2005)

Hans-Joachim H, 'An Independent Judiciary in Crisis Regions: Challenges for International Law in Cases of State Failure and Armed Conflicts' in Debiel T and Klein A (eds) *Fragile Peace: State Failure, Violence and Development in Crisis Region* (Zed Books 2002)

Hansungule M, 'Who Owns Land in Zimbabwe? In Africa?' (2000) 7 *International Journal on Minority and Group Rights* 305

Harris D J, *Cases & Materials on International Law* (Sweet & Maxwell 1998)

Hart H L A, 'Positivism and the Separation of Law and Morals' (1958) 71 *Harvard Law Review* 593

Hart V, 'Constitutional Making and the Transformation of Conflict' (2001) 26(2) *Peace and Change* 15

Hatchard J, 'Detention without Trial and Constitutional Safeguards in Zimbabwe' (1985) 29 *Journal of African Law* 39

Hayden P (ed), *The Philosophy of Human Rights* (Paragon House 2001)

Hayek F A, *The Road to Serfdo* (University of Chicago Press 1944)
Hayner P, *Unspeakable Truths: Confronting State Terror and Atrocity* (Routledge 2001)
———, 'Justice in Transition: Challenges and Opportunities' Presentation to the *55th Annual DPI/NGO Conference 'Rebuilding Societies Emerging from Conflict'*, United Nations, 2002
Head M, 'A Victory for Democracy? An Alternative Assessment of the Republic of Fiji v Prasad' (2001) *Melbourne Journal of International Law* 20
Hegarty A, 'The Government of Memory: Public Inquiries and the Limits of Justice in Northern Ireland' (2003) 26 *Fordham International Law Journal* 114
Held V, *Feminist Morality: Transforming Culture, Society and Politics* (University of Chicago 1993)
Hellum A, 'Changing Law and Gender Relations in Post-colonial Africa: Options and Limits for the Subjects of Legal Pluralism' (2000) 2 *Law and Social Enquiry*
Hellum A and Derman B, 'Land Reform and Human Rights in Contemporary Zimbabwe; Balancing Individual and Social Justice through an Integrated Human Rights Framework' (2004) 32(10) *World Development* 1785
Henrad K, *Minority Protection in Post- Apartheid South Africa: Human Rights, Minority Rights and Self-Determination. Perspectives on the Twentieth Century Series* (Praeger 2002)
Hermansen G F, 'Democracy and Accountability – The Human Rights Discourse on Future Democracy and Past Abuses in Regime Transition' Dissertation submitted in *Pursuance of a Master of Art in the Theory and Practice of Human Rights* (Norwegian Institute of Human Rights, Faculty of Law University of Oslo 2002)
Hesse C and Post R, *Human Rights in Political Transitions: Gettysburg to Bosnia* (Zone Books 1999)
Heywood A, *Political Ideologies: An Introduction* (McMillan Press 1992)
Hill J, 'Beyond the Other? A Postcolonial Critique of the Failed State Thesis' (2005) 3(2) *African Identities* 139
Hirschman A, 'The Search for Paradigms as a Hindrance to Understanding' in Rabinow P and Sullivan W M (eds), *Interpretative Social Science: A Second Look* (University of California Press 1987)
Hlatshwayo B, 'Churu and Ellsworth Farm Designations; Fighting Illegality with Illegality' (1994) 6 *Legal Forum* 11
Hohe T, 'Justice without Judiciary in East Timor' (2003) 3(3) *Conflict, Security and Development*
Holmes S, 'The End of Decommunization' (1994) 3 *East European Constitutional Review*
Hong M K, 'A Genocide by Any Other Name: Language, Law and the Response to Darfur' (2008) 49 *Virginia Journal of International Law* 235
Hooker M, *Legal Pluralism: An Introduction to Colonial and Neo-Colonial Laws* (Oxford University Press 1975)
Horowitz R S, 'International Law and State Transformation in China, Siam, and the Ottoman Empire During the Nineteenth Century' (2004) 15(4) *Journal of World History*
Howe S, *Ireland and Empire: Colonial Legacies in Irish History and Culture* (Oxford University Press 2002)
Huggins C, *Linking Broad Constellations of Ideas: Transitional Justice, Land Tenure Reform, and Development* (International Centre for Transitional Justice 2009)

Hughes K, 'Operation "Operation Drive Out the Trash": The Case for Imposing Targeted United Nations Sanctions against Zimbabwean Officials' (2007) 76 *Fordham Law Review October* 323

Human Rights Watch, *An Approach to Reparation* (Human Rights Watch 2001)

———, *Zimbabwe: Food Used as Political Weapon* (Human Rights Watch 2003)

———, *Not Eligible: The Politicization of Food in Zimbabwe* (Human Rights Watch 2003)

Huntington S P, *The Third Wave: Democratization in the Late Twentieth Century* (University of Oklahoma Press 1991)

Hurst H, *Autonomy, Sovereignty, and Self-Determination: The Accommodation of Conflicting Rights* (University of Pennsylvania Press 1996)

Huyce L, 'Justice after Transition: On the Choices Successor Elites Make in Dealing with the Past' (1995) 20(1) *Law & Social Inquiry* 51

———, 'Zimbabwe: Why Reconciliation Failed' *International Institute for Democracy and Electoral Assistance* (2005) <www.idea.int/>

Iliff A R, 'Arresting Impunity: Toward a Transitional Justice Paradigm for Zimbabwe' Dissertation Prepared in *Partial Fulfillment for a Degree with Honours – Bachelor of Arts* (Harvard College 2004)

Inder S A, *Democracy, Ethnic Diversity and Security in Post-Communist Europe* (Praeger 2001)

International Bar Association, 'Report Highlighting the Critical Situation Faced by Judges and Lawyers in Zimbabwe' (April 2001) <www.ibanet.org>

———, Press Release, 'Lawyers from Southern Africa Call on African Countries and the UN Security Council to Support the ICC' (2008) <www.ibanet.org>

International Council on Human Rights Policy, *Negotiating Justice? Human Rights and Peace Agreements* (Versoix 2006)

International Crisis Group, 'Rwanda at the End of the Transition: A Necessary Political Liberalization' *ICG Africa Report No. 53*, 13 November 2002

———, 'Afghanistan: Judicial Reform and Transitional Justice' *ICG Asia Report No. 45*, 28 January 2003

———, 'Blood and Soil: Land, Politics and Conflict Prevention in Zimbabwe and South Africa' *Africa Report No. 85*, 17 September 2004 <www.crisisgroup.org/>

———, 'Zimbabwe: An End to the Stalemate?' *Africa Report No. 122*, 5 March 2007 <www.crisisgroup.org>

———, 'Zimbabwe: Prospects from a Flawed Election' *Africa Report No. 138*, 2008 <www.crisisgroup.org>

International Media, 'Opposition Splits While Zimbabwe Continues to Slip' (2005) <www.idu.org>

Iorns C J, 'Indigenous Peoples and Self Determination: Challenging State Sovereignty' (1992) 24 *Case Western Reserve Journal of International Law* 199

Irigaray L, *Thinking the Difference: For a Peaceful Revolution*. Translated by K Montin (Athlone Press 1994)

Issacharoff S, 'Democracy and Collective Decision Making' (2008) 6 *International Journal of Constitutional Law April* 231

Jacobs S, 'Gender Divisions and Land Resettlement in Zimbabwe' *Unpublished D.Phil Thesis* (University of Sussex: Institute for Development Studies 1989)

Jeary J H, 'The Structure, Composition and Jurisdiction of Courts and Authorities Enforcing the Criminal Law in British African Territories' (1960) 9 *International and Comparative Law Quarterly* 396

Jeater D, 'Speaking Like a Native: Vernacular Languages and the State in Southern Rhodesia, 1890–1935' (2001) 42(3) *Journal of African History* 449

Jones B G (ed), *Decolonizing International Relations* (Rowman & Littlefield Publishers 2006)

Jones P, 'Human Rights, Group Rights and Peoples' Rights' (1999) 21(1) *Human Rights Quarterly* 80

Jovanovic M, 'Recognising Minority Identities through Collective Rights' (2005) 27 *Human Rights Quarterly* 625

Kagoro B, 'Constitutional Reform as Social Movement: A Critical Narrative of the Constitution-making Debate in Zimbabwe, 1997–2000' in Raftopoulos B and Savage T (eds), *Zimbabwe: Injustice and Reconciliation, Institute for Justice and Reconciliation* (Institute for Justice and Reconciliation 2004)

Kalley J A, *South Africa's Road to Change, 1987–1990: A Select and Annotated Bibliography* (Greenwood Press 1991)

Kambale P, 'The Development of the Habré Case in Senegal' Transcript of remarks presented at *The Pinochet Precedent: Individual Accountability for International Crimes*, sponsored by American University, Washington College of Law and the Institute for Policy Studies, 26 March 2001 <www.ips-dc.org/>

Kanyenze G, 'Economic Structural Adjustment Programme (ESAP): Precursor to Fast Track Resettlement?' in Masiiwa M (ed), *Post-Independence Land Reform in Zimbabwe* (Friedrich Ebert Stiftung 2004)

Kanyongolo F E, 'The Constitution and the Democratization Process in Malawi' in Sichone O (ed) *The State and Constitutionalism in Southern Africa* (SAPES Books 1998)

Kapoor I, 'Acting in a Tight Spot: Homi Bhabha's Postcolonial Politics' (2003) 25(4) *New Political Science* 561

———, 'Capitalism, Culture, Agency: Dependency Versus Postcolonial Theory' (2002) 23(4) *Third World Quarterly* 647

Kapur R, 'The Tragedy of Victimisation Rhetoric: Resurrecting the "Native" Subject in International/Post-Colonial Feminist Legal Politics' (2002) 15 *Harvard Human Rights Journal* 1

Kariuki S, 'Failing to Learn from Failed Programmes? South Africa's Communal Land Rights Act (CLRA 2004)' (September 2004) *ASC Working Paper No. 58*, Leiden: African Studies Centre

Kautz S, 'Liberty, Justice and the Rule of Law' (1999) 11 *Yale Journal of Law and the Humanities* 435

Kazuyuki T, 'Contemporary Democracy in a Parliamentary System' (1990) 53 *Law & Contemporary Problems* 105

Kennedy D, 'International Law and the Nineteenth Century: History of an Illusion' (1996) 65 *Nordic Journal of International Law* 385

Kent L, 'Local Memory Practices in East Timor: Disrupting Transitional Justice Narratives' (2011) 5(3) *International Journal of Transitional Justice* 434

Kenya Land Alliance (KLA), 'The National Land Policy in Kenya: Addressing Historical Injustices' *KLA Issue Paper No. 2/2004* <www.kenyalandalliance.or.ke>

Keppel-Jones A, *Rhodes and Rhodesia: The White Conquest of Zimbabwe, 1884–1902* (McGill–Queen's University Press 1983)

Kiss E, 'Moral Ambition within and beyond Political Constraints: Reflections on Restorative Justice' in Rotberg R I and Thompson D (eds) *Truth v. Justice* (Princeton University Press 2002)

Kleinfeld R, 'Competing Definitions of the Rule of Law: Implications for Practitioners' (January 2005) *Carnegie Endowment; Carnegie Paper No. 55*

Klug H, 'Amnesty, Amnesia, and Remembrance: International Obligations and the Need to Prevent the Repetition of Gross Violations of Human Rights' (1998) 92 *American Societies of International Law Proceedings* 316

Kofele-Kale N, 'Asserting Permanent Sovereignty over Ancestral Lands: The Bakweri Land Litigation against Cameroon' (2007) 13 *Annual Survey of International and Comparative Law* 103

Kolarova R, 'Tacit Agreements in the Bulgarian Transition to Democracy: Minority Rights and Constitutionalism' (1993) 1(1) *The University of Chicago Law School Roundtable* 2

Kommers D P, 'Transitional Justice in Eastern Germany' (1997) 22 *Law and Social Inquiry* 830

Kong M K, 'A Genocide by Any Other Name: Language, Law and the Response to Darfur' (2008) 49 *Virginia Journal of International Law Association* 235

Koskenniemi M, *From Apology to Utopia: The Structure of International Legal Argument* (Finnish Lawyers 1989)

Koskenniemi M, 'The Politics of International Law' (1990) I *European Journal of International Law* 4

Kriger N, 'Veterans' Pensions in Zimbabwe; Dispute Resolution and Nation-building' (2005) 20 *Ohio State Journal on Dispute Resolution* 249

———, 'From Patriotic Memories to Patriotic History in Zimbabwe 1990–2005' (2006) 27(6) *Third World Quarterly* 1151

Krisch N, 'International Law in Times of Hegemony: Unequal Power and the Shaping of the International Legal Order' (2005) 16 *European Journal of International Law* 369

Kritz N J, *Transitional Justice: How Emerging Democracies Reckon with Former Regimes Vols 1–3* (United States Institute of Peace Press 1995)

———, 'The Rule of Law in the Post-Conflict Phase: Building a Stable Peace' in Crocker C A, Hampson F O and Aall P (eds) *Managing Global Chaos: Sources of and Responses to International Conflict* (USIP Press 1996)

———, 'Where We Are and How We Got Here: An Overview of Developments in the Search for Justice and Reconciliation' in Henkin A (ed) *The Legacy of Abuse: Confronting the Past, Facing the Future* (The Aspen Institute 2002)

Kuhn T S, *The Structure of Scientific Revolutions* (University of Chicago Press 1970)

Kumar V, 'A Proleptic Approach to Post-colonial Legal Studies? A Brief Look at the Relationship between Legal Theory and Intellectual History' (2003) 2 *Law, Social Justice and Global Development Journal* <www2.warwick.ac.uk/>

Kymlicka W, 'Justice and Security in the Accommodation of Minority Nationalism' in Dieckhoff A (ed) *The Politics of Belonging: Nationalism, Liberalism and Pluralism* (Lexington 2004)

———, 'The Internationalization of Minority Rights' (2008) 6 *International Journal of Constitutional Law* 1

Ladley A, 'Changing the Courts in Zimbabwe: The Customary Law and Primary Courts Act' (1982) 26 *Journal of African Law* 95

Lahiff E, *Land Reform in South Africa: Is It Meeting the Challenge?* (University of the Western Cape 2001)

———, 'Land and Livelihoods: The Politics of Land Reform in Southern Africa' (2003) 34(3) *IDS Bulletin* 54

Lamba S, *A Post-Colonial Theory of Justice: Towards the New Constitution of Kenya* (Mazingira Institute 1982)

Laplante L J, 'On the Indivisibility of Rights: Truth Commissions, Reparations, and the Right to Development' (2007) 10 *Yale Human Rights and Development Law Journal* 141

Larbi G A, 'Between Spin and Reality: Examining Disclosure Practices in Three African Countries' (2007) 27 *Public Administrations and Development* 205

Lauren P G, 'From Impunity to Accountability: Forces of Transformation and the Changing International Human Rights Context' in Thakur R and Malcontent P (eds) *From Sovereign Impunity to International Accountability: The Search for Justice in a World of States* (United Nations University Press 2004)

Lee R S (ed), *The International Criminal Court: The Making of the Rome Statute-Issues, Negotiations, Results* (Kluwer Law International 1999)

Leiter B, 'Legal Realism' in Patterson D (ed) *A Companion to Philosophy of Law and Legal Theory* (Clarendon Press 1996)

Lenta P, 'The Tikoloshe and the Reasonable Man: Transgressing South African Legal Fictions' (2004) 16 *Law and Literature* 353

Levin R and Weiner D (eds), *Struggles for Land in Mpumalanga, South Africa* (Africa World Press 1997)

LeVine V T, *The Cameroons: From Mandate to Independence* (University of California Press 1964)

Lijphart A, *Democracy in Plural Societies: Comparative Exploration* (Yale University Press 1977)

Lindholm T, 'Article 1' in Alfredsson G and Eide A (eds) *The Universal Declaration of Human Rights* (Kluwer Law International 1999)

Linz J J and Alfred C, *Problems of Democratic Transition and Consolidation: Southern Europe, South America, and Post-Communist Europe* (Johns Hopkins University Press 1996)

Luban D, 'Calling Genocide by Its Rightful Name: Lemkin's Word, Darfur and the UN Report' (2006) 7 *Chicago Journal of International Law* 303

Luu Tien D, 'Judicial Independence in Transitional Countries' *United Nations Development Programme* (Oslo Governance Centre 2003)

Lyon B, 'Discourse in Development: A Post-Colonial Theory "Agenda" for the UN Committee on Economic, Social and Cultural Rights' (2003) 10 *Journal of Gender, Social Policy and the Law* 3

Machakanja P, *National Healing and Reconciliation in Zimbabwe: Challenges and Opportunities* (Institute for Justice and Reconciliation 2010)

Macpherson C B, *The Political Theory of Possessive Individualism: Hobbes to Locke* (Clarendon Press 1962)

Maddison S and Shepherd L J, 'Peacebuilding and the Postcolonial Politics of Transitional Justice' (2014) 2(3) *Peacebuilding* 253

Madhuku L, 'Constitutional Protection of the Independence of the Judiciary: A Survey of the Position in Southern Africa' (2002) 46(2) *Journal of African Law* 232

Mahoso T P, 'Lawyers' Body Fights for Return of Rhodesia' (2006) *African Focus*, 6 August 2006

Makamure K, 'Introductory Remarks: Human Rights and Democracy in the African Context Today: A Historical Setting' in Nherere P and d'Engelbronner-Kolff M (eds) *The Institutionalisation of Human Rights in Southern Africa* (Nordic Human Rights Publications 1993)

Malanczuk P, *Akehurst's Modern Introduction to International Law* (Routledge 2002)

Mallinder L, 'Can Amnesties and International Justice Be Reconciled?' (2007) 1(2) *International Journal of Transitional Justice* 208

———, 'Exploring the Practice of States in Introducing Amnesties' in *Building a Future on Peace and Justice*, pp. 127–171 (Springer, Berlin, Heidelberg 2009)

Maluwa T, *International Law in Postcolonial Africa* (Kluwer Law International 1999)

Mani R, *Beyond Retribution: Seeking Justice in the Shadows of War* (Blackwell Publishers 2002)

Marker S, 'Effects of Colonization' in Burgess G and Burgess H (eds) *Beyond Intractability* (Conflict Research Consortium, University of Colorado 2003)

Marong A B M, 'Toward a Normative Consensus against Corruption: Legal Effects of the Principles to Combat Corruption in Africa' (2002) 30 *Denver Journal of International Law and Policy* 99

Marsden P, *Afghanistan: Minorities, Conflict, and the Search for Peace* (Minority Rights Group International 2001)

Marshal T H, *Sociology at the Crossroads and Other Essays* (Heinemann 1963)

Martenczuk B, 'The Security Council, the International Court and Judicial Review: What Lessons from Lockerbie?' (1999) 10 *European Journal of International Law* 517

Matthews R O, 'From Rhodesia to Zimbabwe: Prerequisites of a Settlement' (1990) 45 *International Journal* 292

May R A and Milton A K, *(UN) Civil Societies: Human Rights and Democratic Transitions in Eastern Europe and Latin America* (Lexington Books 2005)

Mazrui A A, 'Planned Governance and the Liberal Revival in Africa: The Paradox of Anticipation' (1992) 26 *Cornell International Law Journal* 541

Mbaku J M, 'Constitutionalism and Governance in Africa' (2004) *West Africa Review* 6

McAdams A J and Helen Kellogg Institute for International Studies, *Transitional Justice and the Rule of Law in New Democracies* (University of Notre Dame Press 1997)

McCandless E, 'Reconciling Relationships While Pursuing Justice: The Case of Land Redistribution in Zimbabwe' (2000) 25(2) *Peace and Change* 225

———, 'The Case of Land in Zimbabwe. Cause of Conflict, Foundation of Sustained Peace' in Abu-Nimer M (ed) *Reconciliation, Justice, and Peace in Interethnic Conflict* (Rowman and Littlefield Publishers 2001)

McClintock A, *The Angel of Progress: Pitfalls of the Term 'Post-Colonialism' Colonial Discourse and Postcolonial Theory* (Columbia University Press 1994)

McEvoy K and Mallinder L, 'Amnesties in Transition: Punishment, Restoration, and the Governance of Mercy' (2012) 39(3) *Journal of Law and Society* 410

McGoldrick D, *The Human Rights Committee: It's Role in the Development of the International Covenant on Civil and Political Rights* (Clarendon Press 1991)

McKeever G, 'Citizenship and Social Exclusion: The Re-Integration of Political Prisoners in Northern Ireland' (2006) 47(3) *British Journal of Criminology* 423

Meijer M B (ed), *Dealing with Human Rights: Asian and Western Views on the Value of Human Rights* (Kumarian Press 2001)

Meintjes S, Turshen M and Pillay A, *The Aftermath: Women in Post-conflict Transformation* (Zed Books 2001)

Meister R, 'Forgiving and Forgetting: Lincoln and The Politics of National Recovery' in Hesse C and Post R (eds) *Human Rights in Political Transition: Gettysburg to Bosnia* (Zone Books 1999)

———, 'Human Rights and the Politics of Victimhood' (2002) 16(2) *Ethics & International Affairs* 91
Mendez J E, 'Accountability for Past Abuses' (1997) 19 *Human Rights Quarterly* 255
———, 'In Defence of Human Rights' in McAdams A (ed) *Transitional Justice and the Rule of Law in New Democracies* (University of Notre Dame Press 1997)
Meredith M, *Robert Mugabe and the Tragedy of Zimbabwe* (Public Affairs 2002)
Merry S, 'Legal Pluralism' (1988) 22 *Law and Society Review* 869
Meyerstein A, 'Between Law and Culture: Rwanda's Gacaca and Postcolonial Legality' (2007) 32(2) *Law & Social Inquiry* 467
Midgley E D F, *The Natural Law Tradition and the Theory of International Relations* (Barnes & Noble Books 1975)
Mignolo W, *Local Histories/Global Designs: Coloniality, Subaltern Knowledges, and Border Thinking* (Princeton University Press 2012)
Miller J and Kumar S (eds), *Reparations: Interdisciplinary Inquiries* (Oxford University Press 2007)
Mills C W, *The Racial Contract* (Cornell University Press 1997)
Minow M, *Between Vengeance and Forgiveness* (Beacon Press 1998)
Mitchell T W, 'The Land Crisis in Zimbabwe: Getting Beyond the Myopic Focus upon Black & White' (2000) 11 *Indiana International and Comparative Law Review* 587
Mittlebeeler E V, 'Race and Jury in Rhodesia' (1968) 15 *Howard Law Journal* 181
Mkwananzi E, 'Responsibility for Enforced Disappearances under International Law: The Case of Matebeleland 1983–1987' *Unpublished PhD Thesis* (University of Zimbabwe 1997)
Mohanty C T, 'Under Western Eyes: Feminist Scholarship and Colonial Discourses' in Mohanty C T, Russo A and Torres L (eds) *Third World Women and the Politics of Feminism* (Indiana University Press 1991)
Mohanty C T, Russo A and Torres L (eds), *Third World Women and the Politics of Feminism* (Vol. 632) (Indiana University Press 1991)
Moore-Gilbert B, *Postcolonial Theory: Contexts, Practices, and Politics* (Verso 1997)
Morison J, McEvoy K and Anthony G (eds) *Judges, Transition, and Human Rights* (Oxford University Press 2007)
Morrel P and Pigou P, *Civil Society and Justice in Zimbabwe – Proceedings of a Symposium Held in Johannesburg 11–13 August 2003* (Themba Lesizwe 2003)
Morris M H, 'International Guidelines against Impunity: Facilitating Accountability' (1996) 59 *Law and Contemporary Problems* 29
Moslund S, 'Literature as Discourse: An Analysis of the Discursive Strategies in Salman Rushdie's *The Satanic Verses*' (2006) 61(4) *Orbis Litterarum* 291
Movement for Democratic Change, 'Restart Program' <http://mdczw.org/>
Moyo J N, 'Democratization and the Prospects for Human Rights' in Nherere P and d'Engelbronner-Kolff M (eds) *The Institutionalisation of Human Rights in Southern Africa* (Nordic Human Rights Publications 1993)
Moyo K, 'Just Ends, Just Means. . . ., Is Starving a Nation for Political Gain a Crime against Humanity? The Zimbabwean Case 2000–2003' *Unpublished M.A Thesis* (University of Oslo 2003)
———, 'Minorities in Postcolonial Transitions: The Ndebele in Zimbabwe' (2011) 4(2) *African Journal of Legal Studies* 149
———, 'Feminism, Postcolonial Legal Theory and Transitional Justice: A Critique of Current Trends' (2012) 1(2) *International Human Rights Law Review* 237

———, 'Forbidden Truth? – Background to Truth Recovery in Zimbabwe, Challenges, Opportunities and Threats in Conference Report' (Zimbabwe Human Rights NGO Forum & The Institute of Justice and Reconciliation 2014), pp. 19–32

———, 'Mimicry, Transitional Justice and the Land Question in Racially Divided Former Settler Colonies' (2015) 9(1) *International Journal of Transitional Justice* 70

———, 'Timing and the Implementation of Transitional Justice in Zimbabwe' (National Transitional Justice Working Group, Zimbabwe 2015) <www.ntjwg.org/article.php?id=147>

Moyo S, *The Land Question in Zimbabwe* (SAPES Books 1995)

———, 'The Land Occupation Movement and Democratization in Zimbabwe: Contradictions of Neo-liberalism' (2001) 30(2) *Millennium Journal of International Studies* 311

——— 'The Land and Agrarian Question in Zimbabwe' Paper Presented at the Conference on *'The Agrarian Constraint on Poverty Reduction: Macroeconomic Lessons for Africa'*, Addis Ababa, 17–18 December 2004

Moyo S and Yeros P, 'Land Occupations and Land Reform in Zimbabwe: Towards the National Democratic Revolution' in Moyo S and Yeros P (eds) *Reclaiming the Land; The Resurgence of Rural Movements in Africa, Asia and Latin America* (Zed Books 2005)

Mugabe R G, 'Statement by President of the Republic of Zimbabwe to the 58th Session of the UN General Assembly' 26 September 2003 <www.un.org/>

Mukasa S, 'Addressing Women' s Demands in the Transition Process: Paper Presented at the Launch of the Women's Minimum Demands to Political Parties' 4 October 2004 ><www.wougnet.org</>

Musamirapamwe O N, 'The Evian Agreements on Algeria and the Lancaster Agreements on Zimbabwe: A Comparative Analysis' (1982) 12 *Georgia Journal of International and Comparative Law* 153

Mutembwa A, 'Water and the Potential for Resource Conflicts in Southern Africa' (1998) *Occasional Paper No. 3*, Global Security Fellows Initiative, University of Cambridge

Muzondidya J, 'Invisible Subject Minorities and the Quest for Justice and Reconciliation in Post-colonial Zimbabwe' in Raftopoulos B and Savage T (eds), *Zimbabwe: Injustice and Reconciliation* (Institute for Justice and Reconciliation 2004)

Myers G W, 'Competitive Rights, Competitive Claims: Land Access in Post-War Mozambique' (1994) 20(4) *Journal of Southern African Studies* 603

Nadassen S, 'Restitution, Reconstruction, Reconciliation and Redistribution Land Reform – Balancing the Interests of the Dispossessed, the Homeless and Development' (1997) 8 *Stellenbosch Law Review* 360

Nagy R, 'Transitional Justice as Global Project: Critical Reflections' (2008) 29(2) *Third World Quarterly* 275

Nalder N, 'A Guest of Convenience?: What Happened to the Rule of Law in Zimbabwe' (2001) 5 *Newcastle Law Review* 99

Nathan L, 'Consistency and Inconsistencies in South African Foreign Policy' (2005) 2 *International Affairs* 81

National Reconciliation and Transitional Justice Processes in West Africa (2004), *CDD-Ghana*, Accra

Ncube W, 'Dealing with Inequities in Customary Law: Action, Reaction and Social Change in Zimbabwe' (1991) 5 *International Journal of Law and Family* 59

Ndlovu-Gatsheni S, 'Dynamics of Democracy and Human Rights among the Ndebele of Zimbabwe' *Unpublished PhD Thesis* (University of Zimbabwe 2003)

———, 'The Post-Colonial State and Matebeleland: Regional Perceptions of Civil-Military Relations, 1980–2002' in Williams R, Cawthra G and Abrahams D A (eds) *Ourselves to Know: Civil-Military Relations and Defence Transformation in Southern Africa* (Institute of Security Studies 2003)

———, 'Do Zimbabweans Exist?' The Ferguson Centre for African and Asian Studies, 7 February 2008 <www.open.ac.uk

Ndlovu F, 'Is there Anything Minor about Minority Languages? Another Look at the Politics of Languages in Zimbabwe' Paper presented at the *Fourth International Conference on Preserving African Languages, Organized by the African Language Research Project*, University of Maryland Eastern Shore, 4–7 November 2004 <www.umes.edu/>

Nesiah V, 'Discussion Lines on Gender and Transitional Justice: An Introductory Essay Reflecting on the ICTJ Bellagio Workshop on Gender and Transitional Justice' (2006) 15 *Columbia Journal of Gender and Law* 799

———, 'The Ground Beneath Her Feet: "Third World" Feminisms' (2013) 4(3) *Journal of International Women's Studies* 30–38

News24 Special Report, 'Bush Blasts "Illegitimate" Bob' 22 November 2008 <www.news24.com>

Ng'ong'ola C, 'The Post-colonial Era in Relation to Land Expropriation Laws in Botswana, Malawi, Zambia and Zimbabwe' (1992) 41 *International Comparative Law Quarterly* 118

Ní Aoláin F, *The Politics of Force: Conflict Management and State Violence in Northern Ireland* (Blackstaff Press 2000)

———, 'Political Violence and Gender During Times of Transition' (2006) 15 *Columbia Journal of Gender and Law* 829

———, 'Advancing Feminist Positioning in the Field of Transitional Justice' (2013) 6(2) *International Journal of Transitional Justice* 1

Ní Aoláin F and Campbell C, 'The Paradox of Transition in Conflicted Democracies' (2005) 27 *Human Rights Quarterly* 172

Nickel J W, 'Rethinking Indivisibility: Towards a Theory of Supporting Relations between Human Rights' (2008) 30(4) *Human Rights Quarterly* 984

Nielsen K, 'Liberal Nationalism, Liberal Democracies, and Secession' (1998) 48 *University of Toronto Law Journal* 253

Nino C S, 'The Duty to Punish Past Abuses of Human Rights Put Into Context: The Case of Argentina' (1991) 100(8) *Yale Law Journal* 2619

Nozick R, *Anarchy State and Utopia* (Basic Books 1974)

Ntsebeza L and Hall R (eds) *The Land Question in South Africa: The Challenge of Transformation and Redistribution* (Human Sciences Research Council 2007)

Nyamu-Musembi C I, 'Achieving Gender Equality in a Plural Legal Context: Custom and Women's Access to and Control of Land in Kenya' (1998) *Third World Studies* 21

———, 'Ruling Out Gender Equality? The Post-Cold War Rule of Law Agenda in Sun-Saharan Africa' (2006) 27(7) *Third World Quarterly* 1193

Obarrio J, 'Legal Pluralism and Peace Process: The Ambiguous Reemergence of "Customary" Law in Mozambique' (Grant: SSRC Peace and Global Security 2002) ><www.iisce.org/obarriossrcpeace.htm<>

O'Donnell G, 'Transition to Democracy: Some Navigation Instruments' in Paster R (ed) *Democracy in the Americas: The Swing in the Pendulum* (Holmes and Meier 1989)

O'Donnell G, Schmitte P and Arnson C, *Transitions from Authoritarian Rule: Tentative Conclusions about Uncertain Democracies* (Johns Hopkins University Press 2013)

O'Donovan K, 'Engendering Justice, "Women's Perspectives and the Rule of Law"' (1989) 39 *University of Toronto Law Journal* 129

O'Flynn I and Russell D, *Power Sharing: New Challenges for Divided Societies* (Pluto 2005)

Okafor F U, 'Legal Positivism and the African Legal Tradition' (1984) 24 *International Philosophical Quarterly* 157

Okello M S, Dolan C and Mncwabe N (eds), *Where Law Meets Reality: Forging African Transitional Justice* (Pambazuka Press 2012)

Okoth-Ogendo H W O, 'Constitutions without Constitutionalism: Reflections on an African Political Paradox' in Greenberg D et al. (eds) *Constitutionalism & Democracy: Transitions in the Contemporary World* (Oxford University Press 1993)

Oladosu J, 'Choosing a Legal Theory on Cultural Grounds: An African Case for Legal Positivism' (2001) 2(2) *West Africa Review*

O'Leary B and McGarry J G, *The politics of Antagonism: Understanding Northern Ireland* (The Athlone Press 1993)

Oloka-Onyango J, 'Heretical Reflections on the Right to Self-determination: Prospects and Problems for a Democratic Global Future in the New Millennium' (1999) 15 *American University International Law Review* 151

———, 'Reinforcing Marginalized Rights in An Age of Globalization: International Mechanisms, Non-State Actors, and the Struggle for People's Rights in Africa' (2002) 18 *American University International Law Review*851

Olson M, 'Dictatorship, Democracy and Development' (1993) 87(3) *American Political Science Review* 567

Onwudiwe E, 'A Critique of Recent Writings on Ethnicity and Nationalism' (2001) 32(3) *Research in African Literatures* 213

Oomen B, 'Group Rights in Post-Apartheid South Africa – The Case of the Traditional Leaders' Paper Presented at the *14th International Congress of Anthropological and Ethnological Sciences in Williamsburg, Virginia* 1998

———, *Chiefs in South Africa: Law, Power and Culture in the Post-apartheid Era* (Palgrave 2005)

———, 'Justice Discourses and the Question of Legitimacy' Study Prepared for the International Conference *'Building a Future on Peace and Justice'*, Nuremberg, 25–27 June 2007 <www.peace-justice-conference>

Orentlicher D F, 'Settling Accounts: The Duty to Prosecute Human Rights Violations of a Prior Regime' (1991) 100 *Yale Law Journal* 2537

Orford A, 'Locating the International: Military and Monetary Interventions after the Cold War' (1997) 38 *Harvard International Law Journal* 443

———, 'Feminism, Imperialism and the Mission of International Law' (2002) 71 *Nordic Journal of International Law* 275

O'Rourke C, *Gender Politics in Transitional Justice* (Routledge 2013)

Otto D, 'Subalternity and International Law: The Problems of Global Community and the Incommensurability of Difference' (1996) 5 *International Journal of Social and Legal Studies* 337

Pahuja S, 'The Postcoloniality of International Law' (2005) 45 *Harvard International Law Journal* 459

Palley C, *The Constitutional History and Law of Southern Rhodesia, 1888–1965* (Clarendon Press 1966)

———, 'The Judicial Process: UDI and the Southern Rhodesian Judiciary' (1967) 30 *Modern Law Review* 263

Pankhurst D, 'Unraveling Reconciliation and Justice? Land and the Potential for Conflict in Namibia' (2000) 25(2) *Peace and Change* 239

Pannikar R, 'Is the Notion of Human Rights a Western Concept' (1982) 120 *Diogenes* 76

Patman R G, *Universal Human Rights* (St. Martin's Press 2000)

Paulson S, 'Classical Legal Positivism at Nuremberg' (1975) 4(2) *Philosophy and Public Affairs*

Pazvakavambwa S, 'Land Redistribution in Zimbabwe' Paper presented at '*Land Redistribution: Towards a Common Vision, Regional Course, Southern Africa*', 9–13 July 2007 <www.sarpn.org.za/documents>

Penalva E M, 'Redistributing Property: Natural Law, International Norms and the Property Reforms of the Cuban Revolution' (2000) 52 *Florida Law Review*

Pensky M, 'Amnesty on Trial: Impunity, Accountability and the Norms International Law' (2008) 1(2) *Ethics and Global Politics*

Phakathi T S and van der Merwe H, *The Impact of the TRC's Amnesty Process on Survivors of Human Rights Violations* (CSVR 2003)

Pipes D, 'The Alawi Capture of Power in Syria' (1989) *Middle Eastern Studies* <www.danielpipes.org>

Posner E A and Vermeule A 'Transitional Justice as Ordinary Justice' (2004) 117(3) *Harvard Law Review* 761

Posner R A, 'An Economic Approach to the Law of Evidence' (1999) 51 *Stanford Law Review* 1477

———, *Economic Analysis of Law* (Aspen 2003)

Preece J J, 'Democracy, Minority Rights and Plural Societies: Pus ca Change?' (2008) 2(2) *Sociology Campus* 609

Prempeh H K, 'African Judges, in Their Own Cause: Reconstituting Independent Courts in Contemporary Africa' (2006) 4 *International Journal of Constitutional Law* 592

Przeworski A, 'Democracy as a Contingent Outcome of Conflicts' in Elster J and Pue W, 'Editorial' (2003) 1 *Law, Social Justice and Global Development* <www2.warwick.ac.uk/>

Radin M J, 'Reply: Please Be Careful with Cultural Feminism' (1993) 45 *Stanford Law. Review* 1567

Raftopoulos B and Eppel S, *Political Crisis, Mediation and the Prospects of Transitional Justice in Zimbabwe* (Institute for Democracy in Africa 2008)

Raftopoulos B and Savage T (eds), *Zimbabwe: Injustice and Reconciliation* (Institute for Justice & Reconciliation 2004)

Rajagopal B, 'International Law and Social Movements: Challenges of Theorizing Resistance' (2003) 41 *Columbia Journal of Transnational Law* 397

Rajasingham D, 'On Mediating Multiple Identities: The Shifting Field of Women's Sexualities within the Community, State and Nation' in Schuler M A (ed) *From Basic Needs to Basic Rights: Women's Claim to Human Rights* (Women, Law and Development International 1995)

Ranger T, 'Growing from the Roots: Reflections on Peasant Research in Central and Southern Africa' (1978) 5 *Journal of Southern African Studies* 119

———, *The Invention of Tribalism in Zimbabwe* (Mambo Press 1985)

———, *Historical Dimensions of Democracy and Human Rights in Zimbabwe* (University of Zimbabwe Publications 2004)

Ratner S R and Abrams J S, *Accountability for Human Rights Atrocities in International Law: Beyond the Nuremberg Legacy* (Clarendon Press 2001)

———, 'Overcoming Temptations to Violate Human Dignity in Times of Crisis: On the Possibilities for Meaningful Self-Restraint' (2004) 5(1) *Theoretical Inquiries in Law* 81

Rawe M, 'Transitional Policing Arrangements in Northern Ireland: The Can't and Won't of the Change Dialectic' (2003) 26 *Fordham International Law Journal* 871

Rawls J A, *A Theory of Justice* (Oxford University Press 1973)

———, *Political Liberalism* (Columbia University Press 2005)

The Redress Trust, 'Zimbabwe: From Impunity to Accountability, Are Reparations Possible for Victims of Gross and Systematic Human Violations?' (2004) <www.redress.org.>

———, 'Torture in Zimbabwe, Past and Present: Prevention, Punishment, and Reparation? A Survey of Law and Practice' (June 2005) <www.redress.org>

Reeler A P, 'Can You Have a Reparation Policy without Justice?' (2000) 12(4) *Legal Forum* 202

Report of the Presidential Land Review Committee on the Implementation of the Fast Track Land Reform Programme, 2000–2002 ('The Utete Report') <www.sarpn.org.za/>

Rex J, 'Pluralism and Multiculturalism in Colonial and Post-Colonial Society – Thematic Introduction' (2003) 5(2) *International Journal of Multicultural Societies* 106

Reyntjens F, 'Authoritarianism in Francophone Africa: From the Colonial State to the Postcolonial State' (1988) *Third World Legal Studies* 59

Rindell R 'Zimbabwe Land Problem: The Central Issue' in Morris-Jones W H (ed), *From Rhodesia to Zimbabwe: Behind and beyond Lancaster House* (Frank Cass and Company Limited 1980)

Risse T, Ropp S C and Sikkink K, *The Power of Human Rights: International Norms and Domestic Change* (Cambridge University Press 1999)

Robinson A, 'Escaping the Colonial Trap: Resistance, Postcolonial Theory and Rhizomatic Politics' (Asia Research Study Group, Nottingham, Nottingham University 2003) <www.nottingham.ac.uk>

Rodley N S, 'Conceptual Problems in the Protection of Minorities: International Legal Developments' (1995) 17(1) *Human Rights Quarterly* 48

Roht-Arriaza N, 'State Responsibility to Investigate and Prosecute Grave Human Rights Violations in International Law' (1990) 78 *California Law Review* 44

——— (ed), *Impunity and Human Rights in International Law and Practice* (Oxford University Press 1995)

———, 'The Developing Jurisprudence on Amnesty' (1998) 20 *Human Rights Quarterly* 843

Rolston B and Ní Aoláin F, 'Colonialism, Redress and Transitional Justice: Ireland and Beyond' (2018) 7(2) *State Crime Journal* 328

Ronzitti N, 'The Treaty on Friendship, Partnership and Cooperation between Italy and Libya: New Prospects for Cooperation in the Mediterranean?' (2009) 1(1) *Bulletin of Italian Politics* 125

Rooney E, 'Women's Equality in Northern Ireland's Transition: Intersectionality in Theory and Place' (2006) 14(3) *Feminist Legal Studies* 353

Rosenblum P, 'Save the Tribunals; Salvaging the Movement, A Response to Makau Mutua' (1997) 11 *Temple International & Comparative Law Journal* 190
Ross A, *On Law and Justice* (University of California Press 1959)
Rotberg R, 'Africa's Mess, Mugabe's Mayhem' (2000) 79 *Foreign Affairs* 47
Sachikonye L M, 'The Promised Land' in Raftopoulos B and Savage T (eds) *Zimbabwe: Injustice and Reconciliation* (Institute for Justice and Reconciliation 2004)
Sadurski W and European University Institute Law Dept, *'Decommunisation', 'Lustration', and Constitutional Continuity: Dilemmas of Transitional Justice in Central Europe* (European University Institute 2003)
Said E, *Orientalism* (Pantheon Books 1978)
Saideman L, 'Do Palestinian Refugees Have a Right of Return to Israel – An Examination of the Scope of and Limitations on the Right of Return' (2003) 44 *Virginia Journal of International Law* 829
Saki O and Chiware T, 'The Law in Zimbabwe' (2007) *Globalex* <www.nyulawglobal.org>
Sammons A, 'The Under-theorization of Universal Jurisdiction: Implications for Legitimacy on Trials of War Criminals by National Courts' (2003) 21 *Berkeley Journal of International Law* 111
Sandusky S R, 'Women's Political Participation in Developing and Democratizing Countries: Focus on Zimbabwe' (1999) 5 *Buffalo Human Rights Review* 253
Santiso C, 'Economic Reform and Judicial Governance in Brazil: Balancing Independence with Accountability' (2003) 10(4) *Democratization* 161
Sarat A, Douglas L and Umphrey M M, *The Limits of Law* (Stanford University Press 2005)
Scharf M, 'Swapping Amnesty for Peace: Was There a Duty to Prosecute International Crimes in Haiti?' (1996) 31 *Texas International Law Journal* 1
Schauer F, 'Legal Transitions: Is There an Ideal Way to Deal with the Non-Ideal World of Legal Change? Legal Development and the Problem of Systemic Transition' (2003) 13 *Journal of Contemporary Legal Issues* 261
Scheuermaier M, 'Should Land Be Returned to White Farmers in Zimbabwe' (2006) 2 *African Policy Journal* 1
Schmid E and Nolan A, '"Do No Harm"? Exploring the Scope of Economic and Social Rights in Transitional Justice' (2014) 8(3) *International Journal of Transitional Justice* 362
Schmitt C, *The Concept of the Political* (University of Chicago Press 1996)
Schuler M (ed), *From Basic Needs to Basic Rights: Women's Claim to Human Rights* (Women, Law & Development International 1995)
Schweickar D, 'A Democratic Theory of Economic Exploitation Dialectically Developed' in Gottlieb R (ed) *Radical Philosophy: Tradition, Counter-Tradition, Politics* (Temple University Press 1993)
Scott R L, 'Moving from Impunity to Accountability in Post-war Liberia: Possibilities, Cautions and Challenges' (2005) 33 *International Journal of Information* 345
Seidman R B, 'To What Extent Can We Use Experience to Decide What Is Just? A Case Study from Zimbabwe' (1984) 29 *The American Journal of Jurisprudence* 1
Shameem N, 'The Rule of Law and the Independence of the Judiciary in Fiji' Paper Presented to the *International Commission of Jurists Queensland*, 21 July 2004 <www.courts.qld.gov.au/publications>

———, 'Maintaining Judicial Independence in Fiji' Paper presented at the *International Association of Women Judges, 8th Biennial Conference*, Sydney, Australia, 3–7 May 2006 <www.iawj.org>

Sharp D N, 'Interrogating the Peripheries: The Preoccupations of Fourth Generation Transitional Justice' (2013) 26 *Harvard Human Rights Journal* 149

Shaw W S, '"They Stole Our Land": Debating the Expropriation of White Farms in Zimbabwe' (2003) 41(1) *Journal of Modern African Studies* 75

Shirley J, 'The Role of International Human Rights and the Law of Diplomatic Protection in Resolving Zimbabwe's Land Crisis' (2004) 27 *Boston College International and Comparative Law Review* 161

Shivji I G, *The Concept of Human Rights in Africa* (Codesria Book Series 1989)

———, 'Law's Empire and Empire's Lawlessness: Beyond Anglo–American Law' (2003) 1 *Law, Social Justice and Global Development Journal (LGD)*> <www2.warwick.ac.uk>

Sinclair G F, 'The Ghosts of Colonialism in Africa: Silences and Shortcomings in the ICJ 2005 Armed Activities Decision' (2007) 14 *ILSA Journal of International and Comparative Law* 121

Sithole M, 'Zimbabwe's Eroding Authoritarianism' (1998) 8(1) *Journal of Democracy* 127

Skogly S, 'Crimes against Humanity Revisited: Is There a Role for Economic and Social Rights' (2001) 5 *International Journal of Human Rights*

Smiley M, 'Democratic Justice in Transition' (2001) 99 *Michigan Law Reviews* 1332

Smiley X, 'Zimbabwe, Southern Africa and the Rise of Robert Mugabe' (1979) 58 *Foreign Affairs* 1061

Smith R K M and van den Banker C, *The Essentials of Human Rights* (Hodder Arnold 2005)

Snyder J L, 'Trials and Errors: Principle and Pragmatism in Strategies of International Justice' (2004) 28(3) *International Security* 5

Somerville K, 'The U.S.S.R. and Southern Africa Since 1976' (1984) 22(1) *Journal of Modern African Studies* 73

Soyinka-Airewele P, 'Subjectivities of Violence and the Dilemmas of Transitional Governance' (2004) 6 *West Africa Review*

Sparks A, *Tomorrow Is Another Country: The Inside Story of South Africa's Road to Change* (Hill & Wang 1995)

Speech by the Hon. Mrs. Justice Rita Makarau Judge President of the High Court of Zimbabwe on the Occasion of the Opening of the 2007 Legal Year, Harare High Court, 15 January 2007 <www.kubatana.net/>

Spencer R, 'Optimism of the Intellect and Optimism of the Will: The Unseasonable Art of Ngugi wa Thiong'o' (2003) 2 *Electronic Law Journals – LGD* ><www2.warwick.ac.uk<>

Spivak G C, 'Can the Subaltern Speak?' in Nelson C and Grossberg L (eds) *Marxism and the Interpretation of Culture* (University of Illinois Press 1988)

———, *A Critique of Postcolonial Reason: Toward a History of the Vanishing Present* (Harvard University Press 1999)

Sriram C L, *Confronting Past Human Rights Violations: Justice vs. Peace in Times of Transition* (Frank Cass 2004)

Stahn C, 'Complemantarity, Amnesties and Alternative Forms of Justice: Some Interpretative Guidelines for the International Criminal Court' (2005) 3 *Journal of International Criminal Justice* 695

Steiner J H, 'Political Participation as a Human Right' (1988) 1 *Harvard Human Rights Yearbook* 77

———, 'Ideals and Counter Ideals in the Struggle Over Autonomous Regimes for Minorities' (1991) 66 *Notre Dame Law Review* 1539

Steiner J H and Alston P, *International Human Rights in Context: Law, Politics, Morals* (Oxford University Press 2000)

Sterio M, 'On the Right to External Self-Determination: Selfistans, Secession, and the Great Powers' Rule' (2010) 19 *Minnesota Journal of International Law* 137

Stockwell A J, 'British Decolonisation: The Record and the Records' (2006) 15(4) *Contemporary European Histories* 573

Stromseth J E, Wippman D and Brooks R, *Can Might Make Rights?: Building the Rule of Law after Military Interventions* (Cambridge University Press 2006)

Strydom H A, 'Minority Rights Issues in Post-Apartheid South Africa' (1997) 19 *Loyola of Los Angeles International and Comparative Law Journal* 873

Sundhya P, 'Comments: Power and the Rule of Law in the Global Context' (2004) 28 *Melbourne University Law Review* 232

Tanner C, *Law – Making in an African Context: The 1997 Mozambican Land Law* (FAO Legal Papers Online 2002)

Teitel R G, 'How Are the New Democracies of the Southern Cone Dealing with the Legacy of Past Human Rights Abuses' in Kritz N J (ed) *Transitional Justice: How Emerging Democracies Reckon with Former Regimes, Vol 1* (US Institute of Peace Press, 1995)

———, 'Bringing the Messiah through the Law' in Post R and Hesse C (eds) *Human Rights in Transition: From Gettysburg to Bosnia* (Zone Press 1999)

———, *Transitional Justice* (Oxford University Press 2000)

———, 'Humanity's Law: Rule of Law in the New Global Politics' (2002) 35 *Cornell International Law Journal* 352

———, 'The Future of Human Rights Discourse' (2002) 46 *Saint Louis University Law Journal* 449

——— 'Global Rule of Law: Universal and Particular' 10th Annual Conference on *'The Individual vs. the State Central European University'*, Budapest, 14–16 June 2002

———, 'Transitional Justice Genealogy' (2003) 16 *Harvard Human Rights Journal* 69

———, 'Transitional Justice in the New Era' (2003) 26 *Fordham International Law Journal* 893

———, 'The Law and Politics of Contemporary Transitional Justice' (2005) 38 *Cornell International Law Journal* 837

———, 'Transitional Justice: Post-war Legacies' (2006) 27 *Cardozo Law Review*

———, 'Transitional Jurisprudence: The Role of Law in Political Transformation' (1996) 106 *Yale Law Journal* 2009

———, *Globalizing Transitional Justice* (Oxford University Press 2014)

Thakur R and Malcontent P (eds) *From Sovereign Impunity to International Accountability: The Search for Justice in a World of States* (United Nations University Press 2004)

Thompson C, 'Zimbabwe; Intersection of Human Rights Land Reform and Regional Security' (2000) *Foreign Policy in Focus* <www.fpif.org/commentary/zimbabwe.html>

Thuo G J, 'Foreign and Other Economic Rights upon Conquest and under Occupation: Iraq in Comparative and Historical Context' (2004) 25 *University of Pennsylvania Journal of International Economic Law* 491

Tiemessen A E, 'After Arusha: Gacaca Justice in Post-Genocide Rwanda' (2003) 8(1) *African Studies Quarterly*

Tolley H Jr, 'The Concealed Crack in the Citadel: The United Nations Commission on Human Rights Response to Confidential Communications' (1984) 6 *Human Rights Quarterly* 420

Turner C, 'Postwar Land Dispute Resolution: Land Tenure and the Peace Process in Mozambique' (2001) 18 *International Journal of World Peace* 3

———, 'Local Land Tenure in the Peace Processes' (2002) 14 *Peace Reviews* 337

———, 'Land Tenure and Legal Pluralism in the Peace Process. Peace and Change' (2003) 28 *Journal of Peace Research* 352

———, 'Land and Property Rights in the Peace Process' in Burgess G and Burgess H (eds) *Beyond Intractability* (Conflict Research Consortium, University of Colorado 2004)

———, 'Property Restitution Laws in a Post-war Context: The Case of Mozambique' (2005) 1 *African Journal of Legal Studies* 147

———, 'Delivering Lasting Peace, Democracy and Human Rights in Times of Transition; The Role of International Law' (2008) 2 *International Journal of Transitional Justice* 126

———, *Violence, Law and the Impossibility of Transitional Justice* (Routledge 2016)

Van Deer Merwe C G and Du Plessis J E, *Introduction to the Law of South Africa* (Kluwer Law International 2004)

Van der Walt J, 'Blixen's Difference: Horizontal Application of Fundamental Rights and the Resistance to Neocolonialism' (2003) 1 *Law, Social Justice & Global Development Journal (LGD)* <http://elj.warwick.ac.uk>

Van de Vijver L (ed), *The Judicial Institution, in Southern Africa, a Comparative Study of Common Law Jurisdictions* (Democratic Governance and Rights Unit, University of Cape Town 2006)

Van Horn A, 'Redefining "Property": The Constitutional Battle Over Land Redistribution in Zimbabwe' (1994) 38 *Journal of African Law* 144

Verdeja E, 'A Normative Theory of Reparations in Transitional Democracies' (2006) 37(5) *Metaphilosophy* 740

Vijapur A P, 'International Protection of Minority Rights' (2006) 43(4) *International Studies* 367

Villa-Vicencio C, 'Restorative Justice: Dealing with the Past Differently', in Villa-Vicencio C and Verwoerd W J (eds), *Looking Back, Reaching Forward: Reflections on the Truth and Reconciliation Commission of South Africa* (Zed Books Ltd 2000)

Vines A, *Renamo: Terrorism in Mozambique* (Indiana University Press 1991)

Virtanen P, 'The Politics of Law in Mozambique: Customary Authority and Changing Premises of Legal Reform' (2004) 17(1) *International Journal for Semiotics of Law* 53

Vyas Y, 'The Independence of the Judiciary: A Third World Perspective' (1992) *Third World Legal Studies* 127

Wacks R, *Understanding Jurisprudence: An Introduction to Legal Theory* (Oxford University Press 2017)

Waldorf L, 'Anticipating the Past: Transitional Justice and Socio-Economic Wrongs' (2012) 21(2) *Social and Legal Studies* 171

Waldorf L, Shaw R and Hazan P (eds), *Localizing Transitional Justice: Interventions and Priorities after Mass Violence* (Stanford University Press 2010)

Waldron J, 'Why Is Indigeneity Important' in Miller J and Kumar S (eds) *Reparations: Interdisciplinary Inquiries* (Oxford University Press 2007)

wa Mutua, M, 'Conflicting Conceptions of Human Rights: Rethinking the Post-Colonial State' (1995) 89 *American Society of International Law Proceedings* 488

———, 'Why Redraw the Map of Africa: A Moral and Legal Inquiry' (1995) 16 *Michigan Journal of International Law* 111

———, 'Hope and Despair for a New South Africa: The Limits of Rights Discourse' (1997) 10 *Harvard Human Rights Journal* 63

———, 'Never Again: Questioning the Yugoslav and Rwanda Tribunals' (1997) 11 *Temple International & Comparative Law Journal* 167

———, 'Politics and Human Rights: An Essential Symbiosis' in Byers M (ed) *The Role of Law in International Politics: Essays in International Relations and International Law* (Oxford University Press 2000)

———, 'Savages, Victims, and Saviors: The Metaphor of Human Rights' (2001) 42 *Harvard International Law Journal* 201

———, 'The Iraq Paradox: Minority and Group Rights in a Viable Constitution' (2006) 54 *Buffalo Law Review* 927

Warbrick C and McGoldrick D, 'The Northern Ireland Peace Agreement, Minority Rights and Self-determination' (1998) 47 *International and Comparative Law Quarterly* 943

Weinstein W, 'Africa's Approach to Human Rights at the United Nations' (1976) 6(4) *A Journal of Opinion* 14

Welhengama G, '"The Legitimacy of Minorities" Claim for Autonomy through the Right to Self-determination' (1999) 68 *Nordic Journal of International Law* 413

Welsh H A, 'Dealing with the Communist Past: Central and East European Experiences after 1990' (1996) 48 *Europe-Asia Studies* 419

Wheatley S, 'Deliberative Democracy and Minorities' (2003) 14(3) *European Journal of International Law* 507

Wheaton H, *Elements of International Law* (Little Brown 1855)

White N D, 'On the Brink of Lawlessness: The State of Collective Security Law' *Hilaire McCoubrey Memorial Lecture*, University of Hull, 15 May 2002

———, *The United Nations System: Toward International Justice* (Lynne Rienner Publishers 2002)

Whitford W, 'The Rule of Law' (2000) *Wisconsin Law Review* 723

Widner J A, *Building the Rule of Law: Francis Nyalali and the Road to Judicial Independence in Africa* (W.W. Norton & Company 2001)

———, 'Courts and Democracy in Postconflict Transitions: A Social Scientist's Perspective on the African Case' (2001) 95(1) *American Journal of International Law* 64

Williams R A, 'Frontier of Legal Thought III: Encounters on the Frontiers of International Human Rights Law: Redefining the Terms of Indigenous Peoples' Survival in the World' (1990) *Duke Law Journal* 660

Williams R C, 'The Contemporary Right to Property Restitution in the Context of Transitional Justice' (2007) *International Center for Transitional Justice* <www.ictj.org>

Wisborg P, 'It Is Our Land': Human Rights and Land Tenure Reform in Namaqualand, South Africa. Land Tenure as a Human Rights Issue: Evidence from South

Africa' *PhD Thesis* (Norwegian University of Life Sciences: Noragric, Department of International Environment and Development Studies 2007)

Worby R, 'A Redivided Land? New Agrarian Conflicts and Questions in Zimbabwe' (2001) 1(4) *Journal of Agrarian Change* 475

Wright J, 'Minority Groups, Autonomy, and Self-Determination' (1999) 19 *Oxford Journal of Legal Studies* 606

Wright S, *International Human Rights, Decolonization and Globalization: Becoming Human* (Routledge 2000)

Yarwood L (ed), *Women and Transitional Justice: The Experience of Women as Participants* (Routledge 2012)

Young R J C, *Colonial Desire: Hybridity in Theory, Culture and Race* (Routledge 2005)

———, *Postcolonialism: A Historical Introduction* (John Wiley & Sons 2016)

Yusuf H O, *Transitional Justice, Judicial Accountability and the Rule of Law* (Routledge 2010)

Yuval–Davis N, *Gender and the Nation* (Sage 1997)

Ziemele I, *Reservations to Human Rights Treaties and the Vienna Convention Regime: Conflict, Harmony or Reconciliation* (Martinus Nijhoff Publishers 2004)

Zimbabwe Human Rights Commission, 'Monitoring Report in the Aftermath of the 14 January to 16 January 2019 "Stay Away" and Subsequent Disturbances' <www.zhrc.org.zw>

Zimbabwe Human Rights NGO Forum, 'Torture in Zimbabwe' (2004) 34 *Human Rights Monitor* <www.hrforumzim.com/>

———, 'Exploring Transitional Justice Options in Contemporary Zimbabwe' *Special Report* (January 2006) <www.hrforumzim.com/>

———, '"A Woman's Place Is in the Home?" Gender-based Violence and Opposition Politics in Zimbabwe' Report produced by the *Zimbabwe Human Rights NGO Forum as a Contribution towards 16 days of Activism against Gender Based Violence* 2006 <www.hrforumzim.com/>

———, 'An Analysis of the Human Rights NGO Forum Legal Cases, 1998–2006' *Special Report* (June 2006) <www.hrforumzim.com/>

———, 'Transitional Justice Options for Zimbabwe' (2007) <www.hrforumzim.com>

———, 'Political Violence Report of the Month of July 2006' <www.hrforumzim.com/>

———, 'Political Violence Report for the Month of September 2008' <www.hrforumzim.com/>

———, 'Second International Conference on Transitional Justice in Zimbabwe 9–11 October 2013' *Conference Report* (2014) <www.hrforumzim.com/>

Zimbabwe: Parliamentary Debates – House of Assembly, 'Second Reading Gazetted Land (Consequential Provisions Bill)' Vol. 33, No. 10, 19 September 2006

Zimmerli C H, 'Human Rights and the Rule of Law in Southern Rhodesia' (1971) 20 *International Law and Comparative Law Quarterly* 239

Zirker O L, 'The Land Is My Land: The Evolution of Property Rights and Land Reform in South Africa' (2002) 18 *Connecticut Journal of International Law* 621

Table of cases

Zimbabwe/Rhodesia

- Adams v. Adams (1971) P. 188
- Baron v. Ayre, N.O. and Others, NN.O., 1968(2) S.A. 284 (R.A.D.)
- Chihowa v. Mangwende (1987) 1 ZLR 228 (SC)
- Claudious Marimo & Movement for Democratic Change v the Minister of Justice Legal and Parliamentary Affairs & Ors, SC25/06, Constitutional Application No. 160/05
- Etheredge case SC 194/07
- Fieldsend A.J.A. in Madzimbamuto v Larder-Burke N.O. and Another, N.O.
- Igudu Farm (Pvt) Ltd v Commissioner of Police & Ors HH-143-01
- Jenah v Nyemba (1986) 1 ZLR 138 (SC)
- Madzimbamuto v Larder-Burke N.O. and another, N.O., Baron v. Ayre, N.O. and Others, NN.O. 1968(2) S.A. 284 (R.A.D)
- Magaya v Magaya, SC NO. 210–98 (1999) 3 LRC 35
- Mike Campbell Pvt Ltd & W. M Campbell vs. Minister of National Security, Lands, Land Reform and Resettlement & Anor 124/06) ((Pvt)) [2008] ZWSC 1 (21 January 2008)
- Minister of Home Affairs v York & Another 1982 2 ZLR 48(SC)
- Minister of Lands, Resettlement & Ors v Commercial Farmers Union S-111-01
- Murisa v Murisa (1991) S-41-91
- Pf-ZAPU v Minister of Justice 1985 (1) ZLR 305
- Re Southern Rhodesia 1919 AC 211 CD
- Richard Mapolisa v R (Southern Rhodesia, Privy Council Appeal No. 19 of 1964, judgement delivered on 10 November 1964)
- Rushwaya v Minister of Local Government 1987 (1) ZLR (5)
- S v Ncube and Others 1987 (2) ZLR 246(S)
- S v Slatter & Others 1983 (2) ZLR 144(H)
- The Commercial Farmers Union v Comrade Border Gezi and Others HC3544/2000

- Trustees of Roper Trust v District Administrator, Hurungwe & Ors (1) HH-192-2001
- Trustees of Roper Trust v. District Administrator, Hurungwe & Ors (2) HH-200-2001
- York v The Minister of Home Affairs and Others, HC-H-264-82
- Zimbabwe Lawyers for Human Rights and Anorvs. President of Zimbabwe and Anor, S-12-03 (Civ App 311/99)

Regional and international tribunals

- Armed Activities, Kooijmans separate opinion, 2005 I.C.J. 116, 9
- Department of Land Affairs and Others v Goedgelegen Tropical Fruit (Pty) Limited, Case CCT 69/06 (South Africa) (decided on 6 June 2007)
- Ex parte Former Highlands Residents: In Re Ash and Others v Department of Land Affairs, 2000 (2) All SA 26–64 (LCC)
- Factory at Chorzow, Judgment No. 13, 1928 PCIJ (Series a No. 17, p. 47)
- Government of the Republic of South Africa and Others v Irene Grootboom and Others, CCT 11/00 (2000)
- In re South African Apartheid Litigation 346 F Supp. 2d 538 case
- Judgment, Akayesu (ICTR 96-4-T), Trial Chamber 1, 2 September 1998
- Legal Consequences of the Construction of a Wall in the Occupied Palestinian Territory, 2004 ICJ REP. 131 (9 July)
- Mike Campbell (Pvt) Ltd and Others v Republic of Zimbabwe [2008] SADCT 2 (28 November 2008), SADC Tribunal (SADC)
- President of the Republic of South Africa and Anor vs. Modderklip Boerdery (PTY) LTD et al, Case CCT 20/04 (South Africa)
- The Azanian Peoples Organization (AZAPO) v The President of the Republic of South Africa and Ors. 1996 4 SA 671 (CC)
- The Richtersveld Community and Others v Alexkor Limited Case No. 488/2001 (South Africa)
- Velasquez-Rodriguez Case, Inter-Am. Ct. H.R. (ser. C) No. 4 Para 166

Table of statutes

Zimbabwe

- Administration of Estates Act (Chapter 6:01) as amended to Act 22/2001.
- Criminal Law (Codification and Reform) Act (Chapter 9:23), Act 24/2004.
- Land Acquisition Act (Chapter 20:10) (1985).
- Communal Land Act (1981).
- Constitution of Zimbabwe Amendment, (No. 7) Act, 1987.
- Constitutional Amendment (No. 13), Act No. 9 (1993).
- Constitution of Zimbabwe Amendment (No. 16), Act No. 5/2000.
- Constitution of Zimbabwe Amendment (No. 17), Act No. 5/2005.
- Constitution of Zimbabwe Amendment (No. 20) Act, 2013.
- Customary Law and Local Courts Act (Chapter 7:05).
- Emergency Powers Act (Chapter 83).
- Gazetted Land (Consequential Provisions) Act No. 8 of 2006.
- High Court Act (Chapter 7:06).
- Land Apportionment Act (1930).
- The Land Acquisition Act (1992).
- Land Acquisition Act (2000).
- Land Acquisition Amendment Act (2003).
- Law and Order Maintenance Act (Chapter 65).
- Lippert Concession (1889).
- Magistrates Court Act, (Chapter 7:10).
- Maize Marketing Act (1930).
- National Peace and Reconciliation Commission Act (Chapter 10:32).
- Native Land Husbandry Act (1951).
- Native Reserves Order in Council (1898).
- Natural Resources Act of 1941.
- Public Order Act, 1955.
- Rural Land Occupiers (Protection from Eviction) Act (Chapter 20:26) (2002).
- Small Claims Court Act (Chapter 7:12).
- Southern Rhodesia Constitution Order, 1965 (S.I. 1965 No. 1952. United Kingdom).
- Sedition Act, 1936.

- Subversive Activities Act, 1950.
- Supreme Court Act (Chapter 7:13).
- The Acquisition of Farm Equipment and Materials Act (2004).
- The Gazetted Land (Consequential Provisions) Act (2006).
- Tribal Trust Lands (TTL) Act (1965).
- Unlawful Organisations Act (Chapter 91).

Regional and international

- Black (or Natives) Land Act No. 27 of 1913 (commenced 19 June 1913) (South Africa).
- Communal Land Rights Act of 2004 (South Africa).
- Communal Property Associations Act 28 of 1996 (South Africa).
- Conversion of Certain Rights into Leasehold or Ownership Act 81 of 1988 (South Africa).
- Chile Law of Amnesty, No. 2.191 (18 April 1978), reprinted from *Diario Oficial, No 30.042.*
- Development Facilitation Act 67 of 1995 (South Africa).
- Development Trust and Land Act, 1936 (Act No. 18 of 1936) (South Africa).
- Constitution of the Republic of Ghana (1992).
- Constitution of Malawi (1994) S165(1).
- Constitution of the Republic of South Africa (1996).
- Ethics Law 1998 (Mozambique).
- Interim Constitution of South Africa Act 200 of 1993.
- Interim Protection of Informal Land Rights Act 31 of 1996.
- Land Reform (Labour Tenants) Act 3 of 1996.
- Leadership Code (Act No. 8) of 1991 (Uganda).
- Prevention of Corruption Act 1965 (Kenya).
- Public Office Holders (Declaration of. Assets and Disqualification) Act 550/1998 (Ghana).
- Public Leadership Code of Ethics (No. 13) of 1995 (Tanzania).
- Restitution of Land Rights Act 22 of 1994 (commenced 2 December 1994) (South Africa).
- Republic of Kenya, The Truth, Justice and Reconciliation Act, No. 6 of 2008.
- South African Promotion of National Unity and Reconciliation Act, No. 34 of 1995.
- The Abolition of Certain Racially Based Land Measures Act 108 of 1991.
- The Upgrading of Land Tenure Rights Act 112 of 1991 (South Africa).
- Truth and Reconciliation Commission Act of 22 February 2000 (Sierra Leone).

Table of regulations, treaties, international resolutions and key reports

- African [Banjul] Charter on Human and Peoples' Rights, adopted June 27, 1981, OAU Doc. CAB/LEG/67/3 rev. 5, 21 I.L.M. 58 (1982), entered into force 21 October 1986.
- Agreement between the Zimbabwe National Union Patriotic Front (ZANU PF) and the two Movement for Democratic Change (MDC) Formations, on Resolving the Challenges Facing Zimbabwe, Done in Harare on the 15th of September 2008, Available at; <http://peacemaker.un.org/zimbabwe-resolving-challenges2008>
- Bassiouni M C (2000), Revised set of basic principles and guidelines on the right to reparation for victims of gross violations of human rights and humanitarian law, U.N. Doc. E/CN.4/2000/62.
- Beijing Declaration and Platform for Action, Fourth World Conference on Women, A/CONF.177/20 (1995) and A/CONF.177/20/Add.1 adopted 15 September 1995.
- Capotorti F (1977) 'Study on the Rights of Persons Belonging to Ethnic, Religious and Linguistic Minorities', U.N. Doc. E/CN.4/Sub.2/384/Rev.1.
- Charter of Economic Rights and Duties of States, G.A. Res. 3281 (xxix), U.N. GAOR, 29th Sess., Supp. No. 31 (1974) 50.
- Commonwealth of Nations: Communiqué on Rhodesia. *International Legal Materials* 1158 (1966).
- Commonwealth Secretariat (1991), 'Harare Commonwealth Declaration'.
- Concluding observations of the Committee on the Elimination of Racial Discrimination: Zimbabwe, CERD/C/304/Add.92, 4 April 2000.
- Dakar Declaration and Recommendations on the Right to Fair Trial in Africa, adopted by Resolution on the Right to Fair Trial and Legal Aid in Africa (1999): ACHPR/Res 41(XXVI) 99.
- Declaration on Apartheid and its Destructive Consequences in Southern Africa, G.A. Res. S-16/24, secs. 5, 6(a), U.N. Doc. A/RES/S-16/1 (1990).
- Declaration on the Granting of Independence to Colonial Countries and Peoples,(1960) G.A. res. 1514 (XV), 15 U.N. GAOR Supp. (No. 16).
- Declaration on the Rights of Persons Belonging to National or Ethnic, Religious and Linguistic Minorities (1992), G.A. Res. 47/135, 47 U.N. GAOR Supp. (No. 49), at 210, U.N. Doc. A/Res/47/135.

- Deschênes J (1985) 'Proposal Concerning a Definition of the Term 'Minority', U.N. Doc. E/CN.4/Sub.2/1985/31 (1985).
- Draft Declaration on the Rights of Indigenous Peoples, U.N. Doc. E/CN.4/Sub.2/1994/2/Add.1 (1994).
- Eide, A (1993), 'Possible ways and means of facilitating the peaceful and constructive solution of problems involving minorities' U.N. Doc. E/CN.4/Sub.2/1993/34 and Add.1-4.
- European Charter on the Statute for Judges and Explanatory Memorandum, Strasbourg, 8 10 July 1998.
- European Convention for the Protection of Human Rights and Fundamental Freedoms 213 U.N.T.S. 222, entered into force 3 September 1953, as amended by Protocols Nos 3, 5, and 8 which entered into force on 21 September 1970, 20 December 1971 and 1 January 1990 respectively.
- Final Report of Special Rapporteur on Contemporary Forms of Slavery on systematic rape, sexual slavery and slavery-like practices during armed conflict, U.N. Doc. E/CN.4/Sub.2/1998/13 (1998).
- Final Report of the Commission of Experts Established Pursuant to Security Council Resolution 780 (1992) U.N. Doc. S/1994/674.
- General Assembly Resolution on Permanent Sovereignty over Natural Resources, G.A. res. 1803(XVII), 17 U.N. GAOR Supp. (No. 17) at 15, U.N. Doc. A/5217 (1962).
- General Comment 12 of the Committee on Economic, Social and Cultural Rights (ESCR Committee), U.N. Doc. E/C.12/1999/5.
- General Comment 23 of the Human Rights Committee U.N. Doc. CCPR/C/21/Rev.1/Add.5.
- General Comment 15 of the Committee on Economic, Social and Cultural Rights (ESCR Committee). U.N. Doc. E/C.12/2002/11.
- Geneva Convention relative to the Protection of Civilian Persons in Time of War, 75 U.N.T.S. 287 (21 October 1950).
- Government of Zimbabwe (1982), *Transitional National Development Plan 1982–3 to 1984–5*, Volume 1 (Harare: Government Printers).
- Government of Zimbabwe Report to the 41st Ordinary Session of the African Commission on Human and People's Rights, ACCRA: Ghana, May 2007; www.achpr.org/english>
- Government of Zimbabwe (1994) 'Report of the Commission of Inquiry into Appropriate Agricultural Land Tenure Systems' (Harare: Government Printers).
- Hadden T (2004) 'International and national actions for the protection of minorities – the role of the working group on minorities', E/CN.4/Sub.2/AC.5/2004/WP.
- Hadden T and Maolain C O (2001) 'Integrative Approaches to the Accommodation of Minorities', E/CN.4/Sub.2/AC.5/2001/WP.6.
- Hague Convention IV – Laws and Customs of War on Land: Oct,18 1907, 36 Stat. 2277, 1 Bevans 631, 205 Consol. T.S. 277, 3 Martens Nouveau Recueil (ser. 3) 461, (Jan. 26, 1910).

- International Convention on the Elimination of All Forms of Discrimination against Women, G.A. res. 34/180, 34 U.N. GAOR Supp. (No. 46) at 193, U.N. Doc. A/34/46, entered into force 3 September 1981.
- International Convention on the Elimination of All Forms of Racial Discrimination G.A. res. 2106 (XX), Annex, 20 U.N. GAOR Supp. (No. 14) at 47, U.N. Doc. A/6014 (1966), 660 U.N.T.S. 195, entered into force 4 January 1969.
- International Convention on the Rights of the Child, G.A. res. 44/25, annex, 44 U.N. GAOR Supp. (No. 49) at 167, U.N. Doc. A/44/49 (1989), entered into force 2 September 1990.
- International Covenant on Civil and Political Rights, G.A. res. 2200A (XXI), 21 U.N. GAOR Supp. (No. 16) at 52, U.N. Doc. A/6316 (1966), 999 U.N.T.S. 171, entered into force 23 March 1976.
- International Covenant on Economic, Social and Cultural Rights, G.A. res. 2200A (XXI), 21 U.N. GAOR Supp. (No. 16) at 49, U.N. Doc. A/6316 (1966), 993 U.N.T.S. 3, entered into force 3 January 1976.
- Joinet L, *The Administration of Justice and the Human Rights of Detainees: Question of the Impunity of Perpetrators of Human Rights Violations (Civil and Political)*, Revised Final Report presented to the Sub-Commission on Prevention of Discrimination and Protection of Minorities, United Nations Economic and Social Council: E/CN.4/Sub.2/1997/20/Rev.1, October 1997, 3.
- Office of the United Nations High Commissioner for Human Rights (2006), *Rule of Law Tools for Post-Conflict States, Mapping the Justice Sector* (New York and Geneva: United Nations).
- Office of the United Nations High Commissioner for Human Rights (2006), *Rule of Law Tools for Post-Conflict States, Vetting: An Operational Framework* (New York and Geneva: United Nations).
- Organization of African Unity: Resolution on Rhodesia. *International Legal Materials* 130 (1967).
- Recommendation No. R (94) 12 of the Committee of Ministers to Member States on the Independence, Efficiency and Role of Judges (Adopted by the Committee of Ministers on 13 October 1994 at the 518th meeting of the Ministers' Deputies).
- Report of the Secretary-General on the causes of conflict and the promotion of durable peace and sustainable development in the continent, U.N. Doc. A/52/871-S/198/318 (13 April 1998).
- Report of the Secretary-General on the effective promotion of the Declaration on the Rights of Persons Belonging to National or Ethnic, Religious and Linguistic Minorities, 6 September 2005, U.N. Doc. A/60/333.
- Report of the Secretary-General on the rule of law and transitional justice in conflict and post-conflict societies. S/2004/613, 30 July 2004.
- Report of the Special Rapporteur on the promotion of truth, justice, reparation and guarantees of non-recurrence, A/HRC/36/50, 21 August 2017.

- Report of the Special Rapporteur on the promotion of truth, justice, reparation and guarantees of non-recurrence, A/HRC/30/42, 7 September 2015.
- Report of the Special Rapporteur on the promotion of truth, justice, reparation and guarantees of non-recurrence on his global study on transitional justice, A/HRC/36/50/Add.1, 21 August 2017.
- Resolution on the Establishment of an Effective African Court on Human and Peoples' Rights: ACHPR/Res. 76 (XXXVII) 05.
- Resolution on the Respect and the Strengthening on the Independence of the Judiciary (1996), ACHPR/Res. 21 (XIX) 96.
- Resolution on the Right to Fair Trial and Legal Aid in Africa (1999), ACHPR/Res. 41 (XXVI) 99.
- Resolution on the Right to Recourse and Fair Trial, ACHPR/Res.4 (XI) 92.
- Resolutions on Sanctions against Southern Rhodesia and Measures to Assist Zambia 12 *International Legal Materials* 454 (1973).
- Rhodesia: Cease-Fire Agreement, 16 Africa Research Bull 5511–12 (1979)
- Rome Statute of the International Criminal Court, U.N. Doc. 2187 U.N.T.S. 90, entered into force 1 July 2002.
- Security Council Resolution on Sanctions against Southern Rhodesia, 12 *International Legal Materials* 1014 (1973).
- Singhvi L M (1985), 'The Administration of Justice and the Human Rights of Detainees: Study on the Independence and Impartiality of the Judiciary, Jurors and Assessors and the Independence of Lawyers', *Final Report*. Geneva: United Nations, U.N. Doc. E/CN.4/Sub.2/1985/18 and Add. 1–6, 1985.
- South Africa Truth and Reconciliation Commission of South Africa Report (Macmillan Reference 1999).
- Southern Rhodesia – Report of the Constitutional Conference, Lancaster House, London, September-December 1979" (Lancaster House, 21 December 1979).HMSO, 1980 Command *Paper No. 7802* ISBN: 0-101780206.
- The Council of Europe's Framework Convention for the Protection of National Minorities ETS 157; 2 IHRR 217 (1995).
- The Universal Declaration of Human Rights (1948), G.A Res. 217A(111), U.N. Doc, A/810.
- United Kingdom: Proposals for Settlement of Rhodesia Problem. *International Legal Materials* 134 (1967).
- United Nations Commission on Human Rights, Basic principles and guidelines on the right to a remedy and reparation for victims of gross violations of international human rights law and serious violations of international humanitarian law, U.N. Doc. E/CN.4/2005/L.48, 13 April 2005.
- United Nations Economic and Social Council, E/CN.4/2004/60/Add .1, 4 March 2004.
- United Nations General Assembly Resolution on Rhodesia. *International Legal Materials* 144 (1967).
- United Nations Secretary-General "Guidance Note on the United Nations Approach to Transitional Justice"(2010) Available at: <www.un.org/ruleoflaw/files/TJ_Guidance_Note_March_2010FINAL.

- United Nations Security Council Resolution 1325 (2000) on Women and Peace and Security, S/Res/1325/2000.
- United Nations Security Council Resolution Imposing Mandatory Sanctions on Trade with Rhodesia. *International Legal Materials* 14 (1967).
- United Nations Security Council Resolution of Implementation of Agreements for Independent Zimbabwe, S/Res/463/1980, 2 February 1980.
- United Nations Security Council Resolutions on Assistance to Mozambique during Its Application of Sanctions against Southern Rhodesia 15 *International Legal Materials* 718 (1976).
- United Nations Security Council Resolutions on Sanctions against Southern Rhodesia 15 *International Legal Materials* 720 (1976).
- United States: Executive Order on Trade with Rhodesia. *International Legal Materials 100 (1967).*
- Van Boven T (1993) (Special Rapporteur of the United Nations), 'Study concerning the right to restitution, compensation and rehabilitation for victims of gross violations of human rights and fundamental freedoms' U.N. Doc. E/CN. 4/Sub.2/1993/8, 2 July 1993, 7.
- Van Boven T (1996), 'Revised set of basic principles and guidelines on the right to reparation for victims of gross violations of human rights and humanitarian law', U.N. Doc. E/CN.4/Sub.2/1996/17, 24 May 1996.
- Vienna Declaration and Programme of Action, A/CONF.157/23, adopted 12 July 1993.
- Weller M (2005), 'Towards a General Comment on Self-Determination and Autonomy', E/CN.4/Sub. 2/AC.5/2005/WP.5.
- Zambia State Party Report to Committee on CRC, U.N. Doc. CRC/C/11/Add.25 19/11/2002.

Index

For Product Safety Concerns and Information please contact our EU representative GPSR@taylorandfrancis.com
Taylor & Francis Verlag GmbH, Kaufingerstraße 24, 80331 München, Germany

www.ingramcontent.com/pod-product-compliance
Ingram Content Group UK Ltd.
Pitfield, Milton Keynes, MK11 3LW, UK
UKHW011002180926
475701UK00004B/526

* 9 7 8 0 3 6 7 7 2 8 4 3 4 *